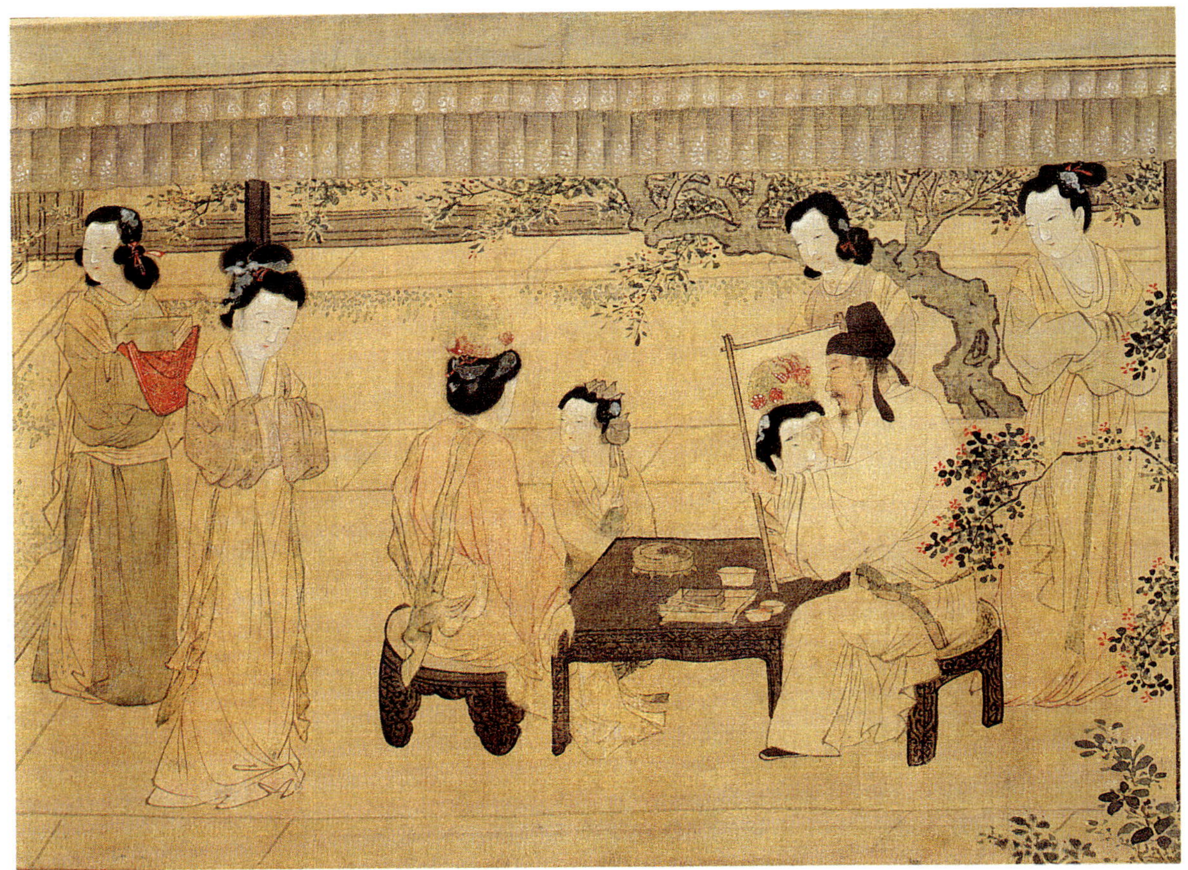

Tu Chin, "Ladies in a Garden."
Section of a handscroll, ink and colors on silk, ht. 30.5 cm. Shanghai Museum.

Li Shih-ta, "The Elegant Gathering in the West Garden."
Section of handscroll, ink and colors on paper, ht. 25.8 cm. Suchou Museum. From slide, see *Chung-kuo mei-shu ch'üan-chi* 8, plate 65.

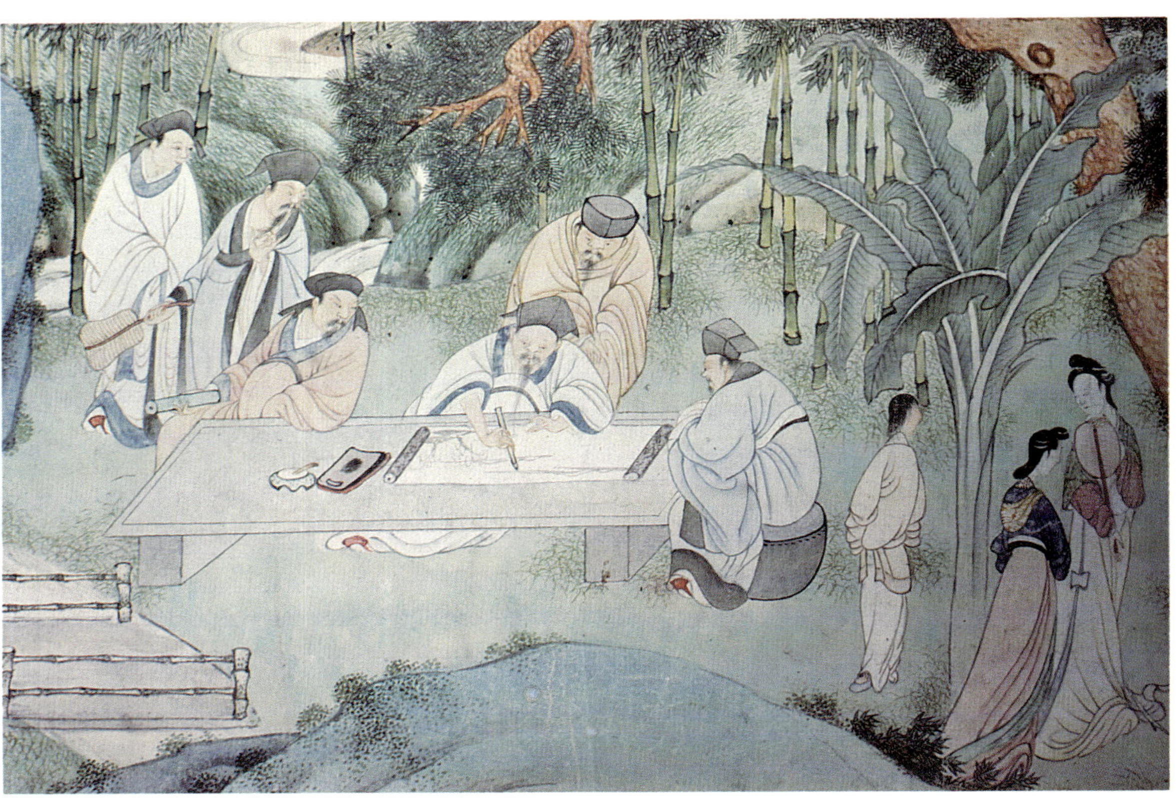

The Painter's Practice

•

HOW ARTISTS LIVED AND WORKED IN TRADITIONAL CHINA

Bampton Lectures in America
Delivered at Columbia University

Bampton Lectures in America

•

Arnold J. Toynbee, The Prospects of Western Civilization, 1940

Paul R. Hawley, *New Discoveries in Medicine: Their Effect on the Public Health,* 1950

Charles H. Dodd, *Gospel and Law: The Relation of Faith and Ethics in Early Christianity,* 1951

Lewis Mumford, *Art and Technics,* 1952

James B. Conant, *Modern Science and Modern Man,* 1952

Alan Gregg, *Challenges to Contemporary Medicine,* 1956

John Baillie, *The Idea of Revelation in Recent Thought,* 1956

Lionello Venturi, *Four Steps Toward Modern Art: Giorgione, Caravaggio, Manet, Cezanne,* 1956

Joel Henry Hildebrand, *Science in the Making,* 1957

Brock Chisholm, *Prescription for Survival,* 1957

Eric Lionel Mascall, *The Importance of Being Human: Some Aspects of the Christian Doctrine of Man,* 1958

Sir Anthony Frederick Blunt, *The Art of William Blake,* 1959

William Barry Wood, *From Miasmas to Molecules,* 1961

Paul Tillich, *Christianity and the Encounter of the World Religions,* 1963

Northrop Frye, *A Natural Perspective: The Development of Shakespearean Comedy and Romance,* 1965

Fred Hoyle, *Man in the Universe,* 1966

Robert H. Felix, *Mental Illness: Progress and Prospects,* 1967

Alasdair MacIntyre and Paul Ricoeur, *The Religious Significance of Atheism,* 1969

Sir John Summerson, *Victorian Architecture: Four Studies in Evaluation,* 1970

Jacob Bronowski, *Magic, Science, and Civilization,* 1975

David Rosand, ed., *Titian: His World and His Legacy,* 1982

Anthony Kenny, *Faith and Reason,* 1983

Zellig Harris, *Language and Information,* 1988

The Painter's Practice

James Cahill

HOW ARTISTS LIVED AND WORKED IN TRADITIONAL CHINA

Columbia University Press

New York

Columbia University Press
New York Chichester, West Sussex

Library of Congress Cataloging-in-Publication Data
Cahill, James, 1926–
The painter's practice : how artists lived and worked in traditional China / James Cahill.
p. cm. — (Bampton lectures in America no. 29)
Includes bibliographical references and index.
ISBN 0-231-08180-4
1. Painting, Chinese—Ming-Ch'ing dynasties, 1368 –1912. 2. Painters—China—Social conditions. 3. Painters—China—Economic conditions. 4. Art patronage—China—History. I. Title II. Series
ND1043.5.C35 1994 93-8790
305.9'75'0951—dc20 CIP

∞

Casebound editions of Columbia University Press books are printed on permanent and durable acid-free paper.

Printed in the United States of America
c 10 9 8 7 6 5 4 3 2
p 10 9 8 7 6 5 4 3 2 1

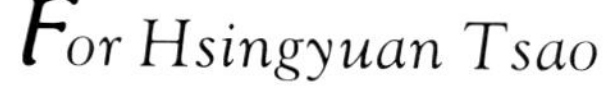
For Hsingyuan Tsao

Contents

Preface
ix

ONE Adjusting Our Image of the Chinese Artist
1

TWO The Painter's Livelihood
32

THREE The Painter's Studio
71

FOUR The Painter's Hand
113

Notes
149

Bibliography (Works in English)
169

Illustrations
177

Index
181

Preface

The four lectures that are the basis for the chapters of this book were delivered at Columbia University as the Bampton Lectures in October 1991. The texts, now freed from the time constraints of the lecture form, have been considerably expanded, but their basic form and arguments remain unchanged. The first chapter is a somewhat contentious introduction that attempts to provide a methodological justification for the whole project; the second and third present collections of data, in part anecdotal, arranged and discussed by topics. The fourth is still another attempt to formulate the great transformation that Chinese painting underwent from its early to its late period, and deals with issues that will not be new to readers of the recent literature in that field, including my own writings. But it is my hope that setting these in different relationships, building new arguments around them, and introducing a few new factors have led to conclusions unlike those toward which previous treatments of these same large themes have tended.

My having introduced at a few points, chiefly in endnotes, some Western art parallels to the artists' practices in China was not done with any intention of presenting this book as a comparative study; I have no such ambition. The parallels are intended only to make the Chinese cases seem less strange, and to suggest how the courses of two artistic traditions can take surprisingly similar twists and turns, usually in response to correspondingly similar sets of circumstances in their societies.

I hope that the book appears at a propitious time for a study of this kind. Specialists in Chinese art who are disinclined toward socioeconomic approaches, and who may be encouraged by recent methodological shifts away from those concerns in Western art studies, are already pronouncing such investigations as old hat, when in fact for the Chinese painting field they are still in their infancy. Documentary studies in the sinological tradition, stylistic studies on the German model, artist-oriented accounts, have been published in great numbers over several decades, and dominate heavily the Western-language literature. Writing aimed at deeper interpretations of individual works, on the other hand, and at defining the contexts of their creation, has appeared in significant quantity only quite recently. The papers presented at Chu-tsing Li's 1980 workshop on "Artists and Patrons," now available in a published book (see Bibliography), offered an innovative beginning that deserves to be followed. Other recent writings that offer useful methodological models will be credited in endnotes. No one will be more aware than myself of the shortcomings of the present book; my hope is that it can offer a kind of sketch-map for explorations of this little-explored terrain, a base from which more detailed investigations can take off, besides providing a stimulus for discussion and, no doubt, argument.

In the fall of 1989 at the University of California, Berkeley, I gave a graduate seminar with the same title as this book, a seminar in which fourteen people participated, five as registered students and nine as auditors and active participants. It was my good fortune to have among the auditors five very knowledgeable Chinese specialists who were in Berkeley for all or part of the period of the seminar; they all made important contributions, both in our discussions and in contributing written references to published or unpublished materials known to them. They were: Mr. Shan Guolin and Mr. Zhu Xuchu of the Shanghai Museum; Mr. Shan Guoqiang of the Palace Museum, Beijing; Mr. Cai Xingyi, formerly of the Chung-kuo I-shu Yen-chiu-yuan or Academy of Chinese Arts, Beijing; and Professor Pan Yaochang of the Art History Department, Che-chiang Academy of Fine Arts, Hangchou. Student participants were: Paola Dematte, Hsingyuan Tsao, Jason C. Wang, Ying Yang, and Susan Young; and, as auditors, Heping Liu, Christopher Reed, and Weikuen Tang. I have used especially two of the seminar papers, those by Jason Wang, "The Communication Between the Scholar Painter and His Client," and Paola Dematte, "The Use of Go-Betweens in Chinese Painting Transactions," but have also drawn occasionally on others. These and the contributions by the Chinese participants will be acknowledged in endnotes. The students were assigned categories of writings to scan for useful clues and references, and turned up a great many. All the material thus generated was introduced and discussed by topic in the seminar, and later entered, again by topic, into a computer database, which I have used in preparing these lectures.

A small caveat, or apology: the references supplied by the Chinese participants were in many cases incomplete by Western standards, following traditional Chinese practice in copying out the texts (in copies that I preserve, and can in principle make available to colleagues interested in following them up) but citing only titles of books, some of them multivolume, without supplying bibliographical information or chapter and page references. I have attempted, with the help of research assistants, to fill out most of these citations, but a few will still lack the information we are accustomed to finding in Western-language endnotes. Moreover, some of the references are to manuscript letters and other unpublished materials in Chinese museums and libraries; for these we can only accept on faith, for now, the texts and summaries of them that the Chinese participants have provided. References to Chinese writings in this book are so numerous that it seemed pointless to repeat them all in what would have been a very long Chinese-language bibliography; I have tried to provide enough information in the endnotes to enable researchers to locate most of the passages.

Several colleagues have read these chapters in earlier forms. I am especially grateful for extensive and valuable suggestions from Jerome Silbergeld and Craig Clunas. Two graduate students in U.C. Berkeley's History Department, Janet Theiss and Andrea Goldman, both well trained in dealing with Chinese-language materials, worked to track down Chinese sources, fill out information, and check translations; I am grateful to both of them for their expert help. Weikuen Tang and Barbara Norgard were skillful in turning the mass of undigested data into a usable database, and I owe them my gratitude for that. Shannon Rowan, a graduate student in our Art History program, did a capable job of editing the endnotes and bibliography to bring them into consistency and make them conform with Columbia University Press guidelines.

Robert Boni, photographer for the departments of History and Practice of Art at Berkeley, made the photographs for many of the illustrations, in many cases under conditions that photographers understandably dislike, such as copying from mediocre reproductions. I have failed to acknowledge Boni's great assistance of this kind in previous books, and do so now with special gratitude. The Committee on Research and the Center for Chinese Studies at the University of California, Berkeley, supplied research assistant and other funding that enabled me to complete this project, and they, too, have my gratitude.

The hospitality of Professor Peter Awn and others of the Bampton Lecture Committee at Columbia University made my stay there pleasant and rewarding, as their efficient arrangements made the lectures go smoothly. Throughout the preparation of the lectures and this book, my wife Hsingyuan Tsao gave support and assistance in more ways than I can name, and I dedicate this book to her.

The Painter's Practice

•

HOW ARTISTS LIVED AND WORKED IN TRADITIONAL CHINA

ONE

Adjusting Our Image of the Chinese Artist

The Western vision of China has undergone striking changes in recent years; perhaps these changes can be summed up by saying that China has lost much of its mystique. Successive versions of China in the West over the centuries, despite ever-increasing knowledge, have all tended to have a somewhat idealized character: a land of philosophers and enlightened rule for eighteenth-century Europeans; a land of spirituality and mystery, often more than a little sinister, for the popular view from the late nineteenth through much of the twentieth century; the egalitarian, morally dedicated society that many of us wanted to believe in for the early decades of the P.R.C. While none of these has been totally discredited, none can be easily accepted as a whole today, and no new idealized version has been created to succeed them.[1] Perhaps watching the awfulness of T'ien-an-men and the repressive torpor of China since then has only pushed further a process long underway in the crumbling of unreal foreign visions of China.

These visions were not merely Western fantasies; they were always based in some part on a more or less uncritical acceptance of particular Chinese accounts of themselves. Chinese versions of their own culture and society make up another, far richer set of special visions, another mystique, created over the centuries principally by their literati-elite, the scholars and writers on whom we mostly rely for our understanding. Those of us in various fields of Chinese studies have not always taken sufficient account of how heavily our sinological formulations have depended on them. These, too, are tending to yield before efforts, carried out by scholars both Chinese and foreign, to uncover important facets of Chinese civilization that lie concealed behind the constructed versions

For instance, in Frederic Wakeman's massive study of the Ming-Ch'ing transition, *The Great Enterprise,* the Manchus conquerors are seen as a far more positive force in bringing stability and effective rule to China than they could possibly have been in any traditional Chinese account, which necessarily pitted civilized and moral Chinese against more or less uncouth barbarians and defined loyalism in simplistic ways. Social historians today are looking at segments of society and subcultures that were largely ignored by traditional Chinese writers; literary historians are doing the same for popular and vernacular literature, insofar as they can recover it. Historians of religion are altering long-transmitted ideas about the relative insignificance of Buddhism and Taoism in the later centuries of China's history, and so forth. Long-standing myths of China's cultural insularity and self-sufficiency,[2] and of the virtues of elegant amateurism both in practical affairs and in the arts, are similarly losing their hold on us. It is not a matter of bursting balloons; no disrespect is entailed in looking for a more real-world China behind the partial or deceptive visions. It certainly is not a matter of launching some subtly "orientalist," demeaning assault on traditional Chinese formulations and values. It is an attempt, rather, to give more attention to those "voiceless" segments of Chinese society (the majority, by far, in sheer numbers) whose views and experiences are unrepresented or distorted in the literati accounts. At least in intent, it is a matter of removing a mask to find an equally admirable, perhaps even more likable, real person underneath.

The creation of the myth of China in writings by the Chinese literati-elite was itself a great cultural achievement, comparable to the creation of the myth of romantic love and chivalry in late medieval Europe, or that of man as a rational being in the European Enlightenment. We can admire it without continuing to believe it; we are increasingly unwilling elsewhere to accept as simple truth the self-enhancing structures that intellectual elites build as history, and there is no reason why China should be an exception. For China, it was the Confucian literati who wrote the texts in which the myth was formulated and propagated.

Looking beyond these texts can be difficult, obliging us typically to turn to unofficial sources such as letters, informal jottings, local records (as in Jonathan Spence's *The Death of Woman Wang*) and other little-tapped materials. And it obliges us also to dissociate ourselves sometimes from traditional Chinese positions, a process that can bring about friction with some of our Chinese colleagues, and foreign ones as well, since it can be seen as undermining the sacrosanct. But it nonetheless needs to be done. Susanne Rudolph, in her 1987 presidential address to the Association for Asian Studies, spoke of how in China "the scholar-official controlled the means of historical production," being "in a position to delete by dynastic history those who could not be deleted in social reality," and she added: "The virtue of imposing external categories into the indigenous account is precisely that they raise questions that the indigenous accounts would like to let sleep."[3]

My argument here will be that the "indigenous accounts" of Chinese painting by traditional literati writers created just that kind of myth around their subjects, pushing into the shadow matters that others would consider to be of legitimate concern, but which they "would like to let sleep"; and that both Chinese and foreign scholars are only beginning to look into this shadowed area. Some of the most interesting recent scholarship in our field has explored ways in which doing this, sidestepping the myth, changes our readings of Chinese paintings, especially our inferences about the circumstances of their creation and what the artists intended, and about the meanings and functions the paintings originally had. These essays will continue in that direction and will attempt to bring together information from diverse sources about the "unmentionables" of Chinese painting, questions of how Chinese painters made their livings and practiced their art. We will begin with a brief consideration of the late seventeenth-century master Cheng Min, an artist of the Anhui School, as an illustrative case that will help to define the conditions of our search.

The Case of Cheng Min

A landscape album leaf in a Hong Kong private collection can serve to represent him (figure 1.1). Like others of the Anhui masters of this period, Cheng Min painted landscapes, mostly unpeopled and unembellished by enlivening detail, in a manner that relies heavily on line-drawing, or sketching of contours in dry brushwork, to render the forms. More or less overt references to the Yuan period master Ni Tsan are common in his works, as they are in other Anhui School paintings.

Since Ni Tsan is the paradigm of the cultivated amateur in Chinese painting, and his style is the very emblem of Confucian high-mindedness, this painting would alone set up expectations about the artist's status and the basis on which he worked in anyone familiar with the signification of styles in Chinese painting; and those expectations would appear

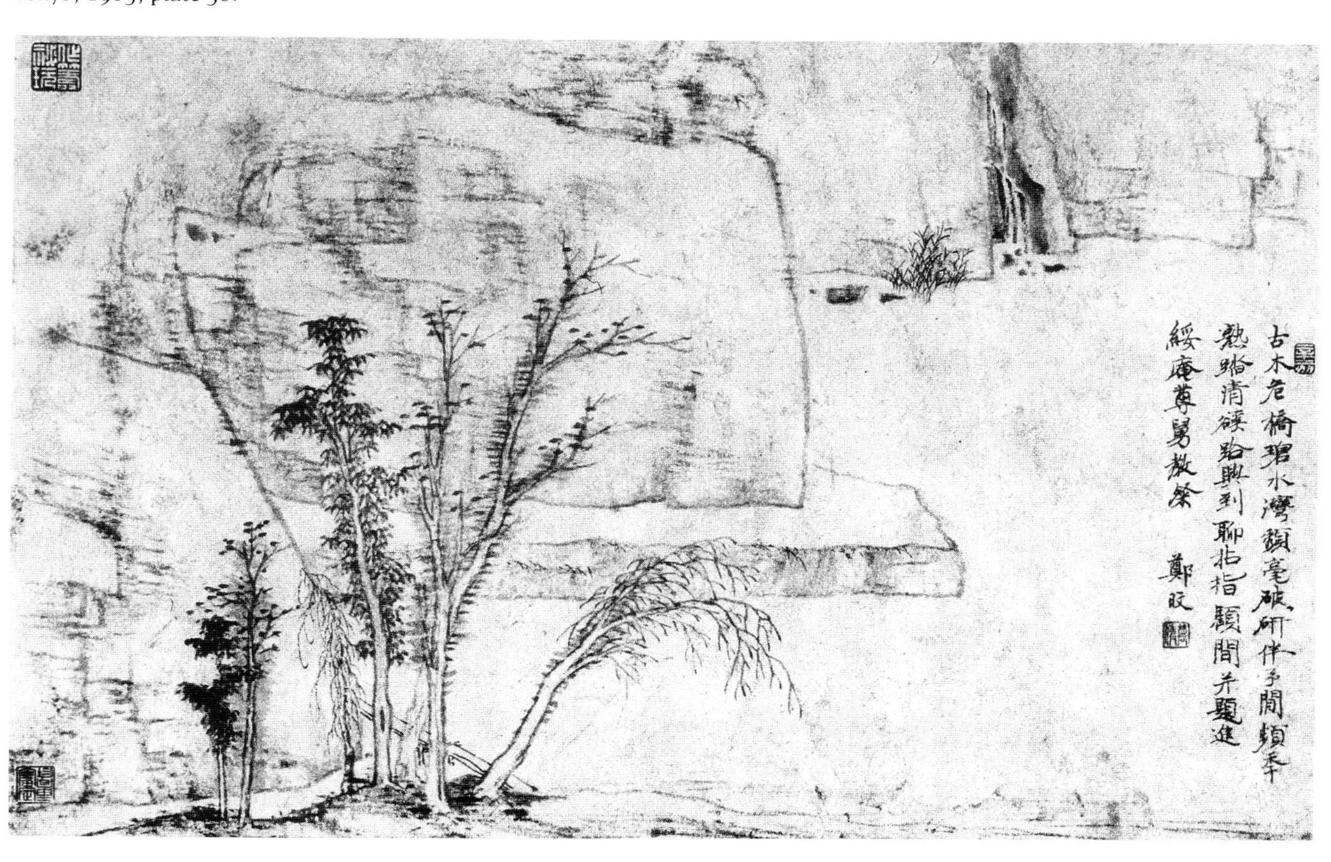

1.1. Cheng Min, "Old Trees by a Bridge." Small hanging scroll, ink on paper, 25.5 × 40.5 cm. Collection of Liu Chun-liang (Low Chuck Tiew), Hong Kong. From *Hsü-pai-chai ts'ang shu-hua hsüan,* Tokyo, 1983, plate 38.

to be confirmed in what we read about Cheng Min. His contemporary T'ang Yen-sheng, who frequently inscribed works by artists of the time, writes this about him:

The master immerses himself in old books, not caring whether it is cold or hot, living tranquilly, uttering few words, magnanimous in disposition, his mind fixed on distant goals [that is, unconcerned with day-to-day affairs]. All difficult questions in the classics and histories he can resolve. He is an accomplished seal-carver, using the pre-Ch'in and Han [scripts] as models. His painting style is lofty and antique, completely following the *ch'i-yün sheng-tung* ("engendering movement through spirit consonance") mode of expression. Accordingly, he can rival the Yüan masters. In the most refined of his works, whether feelings of sadness and melancholy or complaint and anger, if these were not aroused by his great talents then they must come from his own experience.[4]

The image of the artist presented here is a familiar one: a person of deep cultural refinement, he lives quietly, caring nothing for worldly matters, engaged in scholarly pursuits, doing paintings or calligraphy as an avocation, to express his emotions—and, to follow through with the usual implications of scholar-amateur status, presumably giving them to his friends, expecting no recompense other than occasional gifts and favors in return.

This image has not always been accepted uncritically—suspicions have been expressed, especially in recent years, that it must often mask some more down-to-earth reality. But art historians have tended to repeat it and allow it to underlie their writings and their understanding of the paintings without giving it much thought. Even the most skeptical have seldom argued for any really radical mismatch between image and reality.

At a symposium on Anhui School painting held in China in 1984, Huang Yung-ch'üan presented a paper on the newly discovered diary of Cheng Min, quoting some passages from it that record his activity as painter and calligrapher. Here are a few excerpts:

[1672] tenth month, fifth day: I did three fan paintings for Fu-wen.

Seventeenth day: cloudy. Yen-ch'ing and K'uan-chung "moistened my brush" [gave me money for painting] and I added bamboo and rock for them [to some previously done painting?]

Eleventh month, eighth day: I went into town and wrote a fan for Yen-ch'ing . . . Keng-yü summoned me, and I added to [retouched?] a painting by T'ang Yin for him. . .

[1673] sixth month, third day . . . Mu-ch'ien ordered a painting for Hsü Erh-ming, and I used the money for food.

[1674] second month, sixth day: cloudy. After supper I visited Tzu-yen, and entrusted him with three paintings to sell for me.

Sixth month, sixth day: I visited Hsüeh-hai, where the owner of the I-kuan [an inn?] . . . summoned me to do a painting for him.

[1676] first month, sixth day: rainy. Ssu-jo visited me to order a painting, bringing payment [lit. "moisture," as above.]

Ninth month, eighteenth day: for my "elder brother" Yin-nan I did a painting on satin. Also did five fans for . . . [names].

Twelfth month, fourth day: This line [of poetry] came to me: "To get through the year, I need the money from selling paintings."

Twenty-ninth day. Snow has been falling for the whole month. Fortunately, I have managed to get through my New Year's obligations with the small income from my paintings. I sit recalling that there are a great many really poor people now, and wish that I had a spacious, myriad-roomed house [to entertain them in]—an empty thought.

Other entries record his carving seals for clients in return for grain or presents, and borrowing money from one of them to buy food.[5]

In the cases of most artists, we have no such detailed information about the actual conditions of their daily lives, and even if we had it, the disparity between conventional image and what we might call adjusted image would not always be so great as with Cheng Min. But as

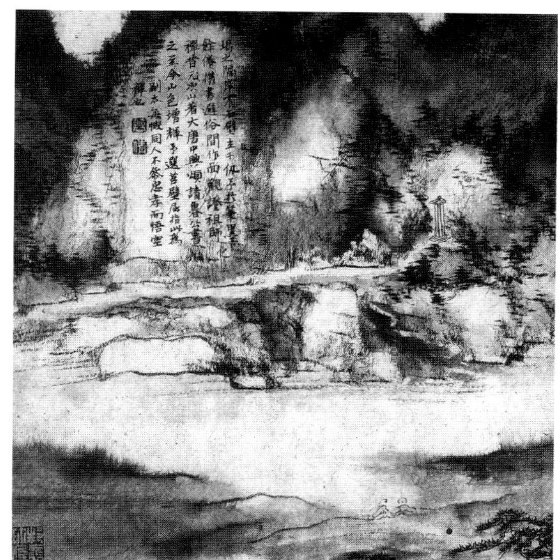

1.2. Cheng Min, "Viewing a Waterfall," from *A Record of Travels in Hsi-lo.* Dated 1673. Leaf from an album of twelve, ink on paper, 21.3 × 20 cm. Shanghai Museum.

more evidence is uncovered about the circumstances in which Chinese paintings were created, how they were acquired by clients and collectors, and how the artist was rewarded, as well as about other practical details of the painter's occupation, the degree to which standard accounts of Chinese artists are idealized and untrue to their realities is increasingly apparent.

Uncovering this evidence is not easy. Chinese writers, old and modern, with very few exceptions, scrupulously avoid discussing such matters, feeling that even to acknowledge them as serious concerns of the artist would demean that artist. Economic factors are thus excluded from accounts of artists, like sex from Victorian novels, by people who were familiar enough with them in their everyday lives but felt it improper to allude to them in their books. Information about these matters must be recovered from scattered sources outside the formal belleletristic literature—letters, diaries, jottings, untypically revealing inscriptions. This is exactly the kind of information that I and my students and the Chinese participants attempted to assemble in my 1989 seminar described in the Preface.

The Amateurization of Painting

Along with a new, badly overdue recognition of how this distortion of the conditions under which the artists worked has affected our understanding of Chinese painting, it is worthwhile to consider how it came about. At the root of the problem was the insistence, at least among educated Chinese, on distinguishing amateurism from professionalism within virtually any respectable practice, and resolutely preferring the former.[6] The argument behind this "amateur ideal" was that the cultivated mind of the amateur practitioner would make the right decisions intuitively, or on the basis of Confucian "right principles," on a level above expertise, free also from base motives of material gain. This attitude prevailed even when professional skills and expertise would presumably have brought real benefits. Nathan Sivin, for instance, writing about the practice of medicine in China, assures us that "In the minds of the educated elite, not only did the [technically trained] imperial physicians hold no special position, but their names were anonymous. The only doctors whose names were likely to be on everyone's tongue were gifted and brilliant amateurs from the top of the scholar-official class. What brought them fame as physicians was their social status, not vice versa."[7] If we can imagine ourselves choosing to have our ailments treated by talented amateurs who made their names elsewhere than in the practice of medicine, we will be that much closer to understanding the Chinese literati bias toward amateurism in the arts.

The exaltation of amateur art-making was also a late move in the centuries-long campaign to legitimize painting as an upper-class cultural pursuit, not just an artisan's craft—an effort that is paralleled, of course, in the history of Western art and art theorizing, although nothing that quite corresponds to the Chinese preference for amateurism is to be found there. Making painting into a proper leisure-time occupation for cultured men allowed it to lay stronger claims to intellectual content and to elicit suitably cultivated responses. In such a painting as Chao Meng-fu's "Orchids, Bamboo, and Rocks" (figure 1.3), for instance, one was expected to admire the brushwork and forms as reflecting qualities of the mind of this eminent man. The idea of the high-minded and hence superior artist arose in conjunction with an increasing practice of painting by aristocrat-artists, scholar-official artists, people whose status not only freed them from the

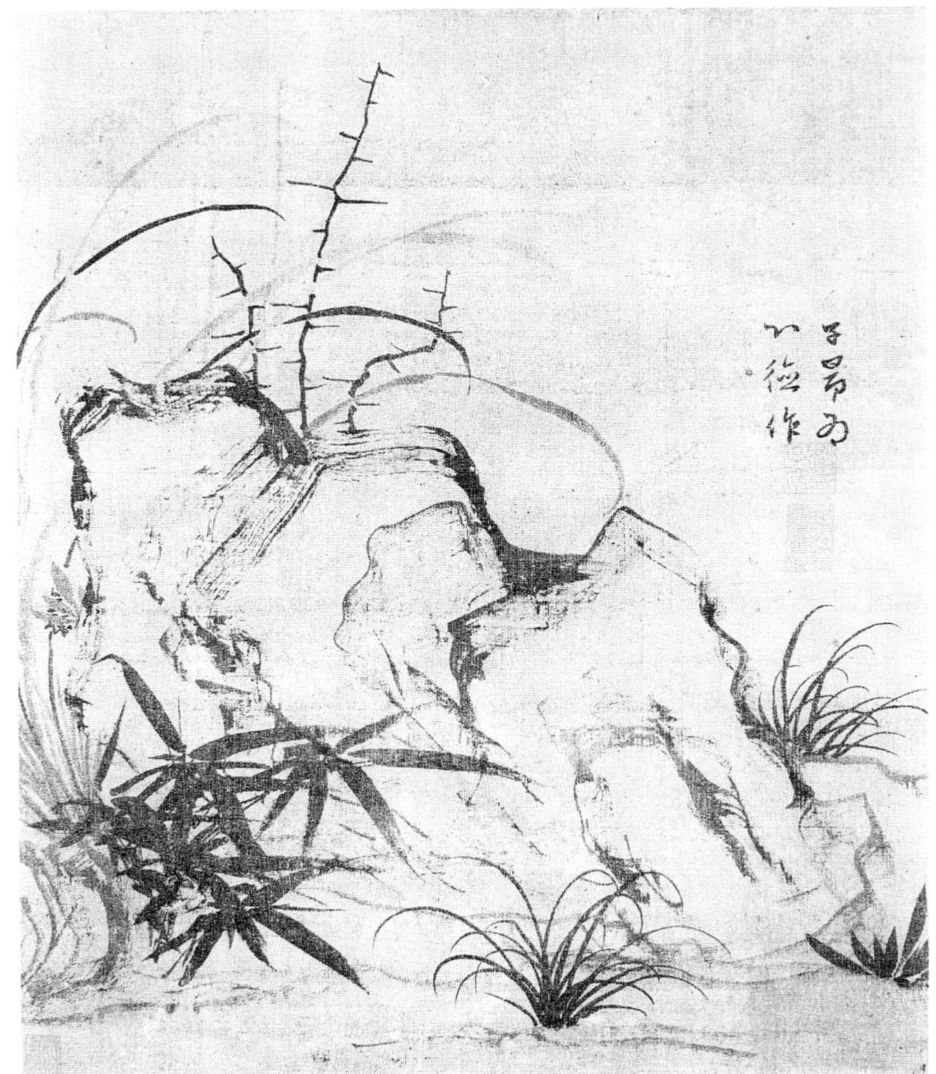

1.3. Chao Meng-fu, "Orchids, Bamboo, and Rocks." Small hanging scroll, ink on silk, 44.6 × 33.5 cm. Shanghai Museum.

necessity of benefiting economically from their painting but set powerful social strictures against their doing so. To praise the materially disinterested basis on which these people produced paintings, then, and the relative artistic independence that they consequently enjoyed, was in itself a natural move, with some validity.

The problem arose when a set of powerful conventions for writing in praise of artists and their works, originating principally in early appreciations of the scholar-amateur painters and in recorded statements by those painters themselves, spread beyond the categories to which they properly applied—the truly avocational artists and their works—to encompass virtually the whole of Chinese painting. At the root of the problem was the mismatch between admiration for outstanding artists who were committed, more-or-less full-time practitioners and the failure of the traditional Chinese social order to accord honored places to people in that position.

In the rhetoric of post-Sung (late thirteenth century and after) painting theory, the positive terms available for evaluating the achievements of artists were mostly those applicable to the amateurs; no truly equivalent ways of praising the professional masters were developed. Intensifying the problem was the increasing practice of painting on an income-earning basis, from the mid-Ming (fifteenth-sixteenth century) on, by learned and cultured people, as rising levels of affluence and education created a much larger pool of men qualified for bureaucratic service (the Chinese scholar's traditional occupation) than the bureaucracy could absorb, and many of them were forced to turn to other ways, including painting, of putting their learning and talents to use in earning their livelihoods. Artists in this situation required and received absolution, so to speak, from the sins of professionalism, just as their audiences needed constant reassurance that the painters they admired and supported were free of those sins. Attitudes and criteria for evaluation that pertained properly to the amateur painters, then, came to be applied more broadly to artists of other kinds, until a situation is reached in which a writer scarcely could praise a painter, even an unambiguously professional one, without making some effort to accommodate him, however forcedly and misleadingly, to the amateur ideal.

And praise is what writings on artists usually had to be: most of the literature on which we depend for our understanding of them takes the form of encomia of one kind or another: tributes to the painter included in inscriptions on his paintings, posthumously written tomb biographies, entries in books made up of "biographical" accounts of artists, and so forth.

Anne Burkus, in her study of the late Ming master Ch'en Hung-shou, discusses the eulogistic nature of Chinese "biographies," as distinct from "what has come to be defined as biography in the West, the developmental charting of a life," and argues that their essential character was commemorative, deriving in form from family cult records. The writers of "biographical" notices on Ch'en Hung-shou, she points out, prefer to ignore his frequent references to himself as a "painting master"—that is, a professional artist. "The story of Ch'en Hung-shou selling his paintings," she writes, "would have intruded upon the pattern of the uninhibited and iconoclastic artist who paints only upon inspiration."[8]

What we have to deal with, then, is the forced accommodation of artists' lives and circumstances to preexisting types, and the expunging of whatever actualities fail to fit these types. Anyone working in the field of Chinese painting can produce numerous examples from memory. They include cases in which an artist who may in fact have been a hard-working master for whom painting was his principal occupation is described as one who only dabbled in the art, and painted out of purely inner motivations. The eleventh-century writer Kuo Johsü considered Li Ch'eng, the great landscapist active a century earlier, to have been productive enough that a collector of Kuo's time could be credited with owning over ninety of his winter landscapes.[9] By the thirteenth century Chao Hsi-ku, a proponent of the new literati or scholar-amateur painting doctrines, wrote of Li Ch'eng, along with Fan K'uan, to whom the characterization is even less appropriate, as "scholar officials who, when they were inspired, would leave behind a few brushstrokes." (Let us take a moment to call to mind the great "Travelers Among Streams and Mountains" by Fan K'uan, and ponder how well it accords with the idea of a painter who "leaves behind a few brushstrokes" when inspiration strikes him.)

After scholar-amateur painting rose to greater prominence in the Yuan period, it became even more difficult to praise artists of other kinds except by misrepresenting their situations. A highly placed contemporary of Tai Chin's named Wang Chih describes that great fifteenth-century master as one who "takes pleasure in poetry and calligraphy as a means to pursue the Way, and splashes ink with a brush in order to delight his heart."[10] The late Ming literati painter and critic Tung Ch'i-ch'ang describes his contemporary Wu Pin, an excellent and prolific specialist in both figures and landscapes (figure 1.4), as a lay Buddhist who "painted in his leisure time."[11] And there are many other cases of this kind.

To be sure, a kind of propriety is at work here, which in itself deserves respect. Wang Chih and Tung Ch'i-ch'ang meant to praise Tai Chin and Wu Pin, according to the writing conventions of their time. But they also exemplify a kind of high-minded fastidiousness that surely had its negative effects. One wonders how the artists, who were meanwhile no doubt hard at work fulfilling commissions in the practice of their livelihoods, can have responded to this well-intentioned but quite misdirected kind of "praise," which could be seen as tacitly

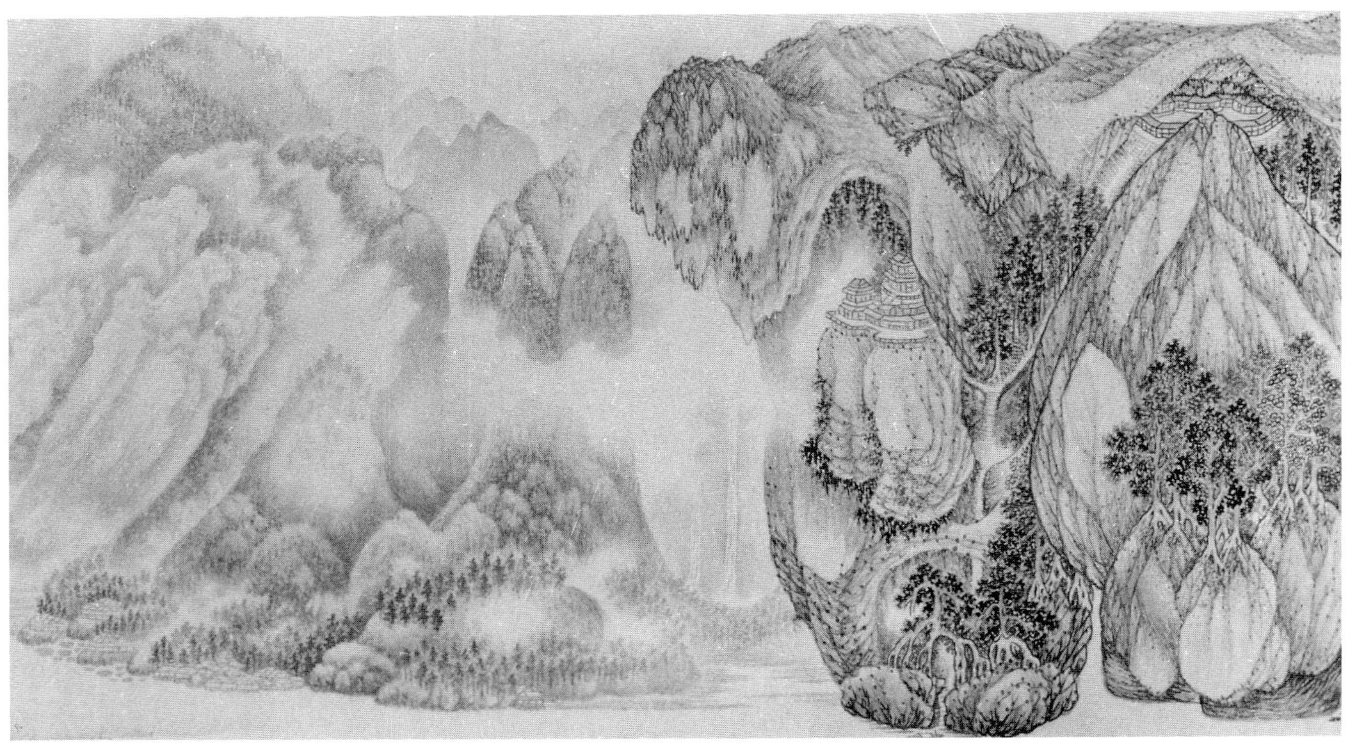

1.4. Wu Pin, "The Road to Shang-yin." Dated 1626, dedicated to Mi Wan-chung. Section of a handscroll, ink and colors on paper, ht. 32.1 cm. Shanghai Museum.

maligning their real situations by implying that these were somehow dishonorable, and so could not be reported truthfully. Treating the realities of their lives as unmentionable, that is, must have had the effect of making them seem also somehow sordid.

Even more numerous are cases, like the one of Cheng Min with which we began, in which the standard accounts are contradicted by other, presumably more reliable evidence. The late Ming figure master Ts'ui Tzu-chung is regularly presented in the standard biographies as one who painted to express his lofty ideals and scorned potential buyers of his paintings; but from letters and other evidence we know that in fact he depended on sales of his paintings for his meager livelihood.[12] The most frequently-quoted biography of the late seventeenth-century Individualist master Pa-ta Shan-jen tells us this about him:

> He often used to pass his time at a Buddhist temple outside the town. When the novices there jokingly asked him for a picture and actually tugged at his sleeves or his belt, he did not resist, nor did he refuse when some scholar friend offered him a gift for a picture. But if highly placed people offered him a whole barrel costing many gold pieces, they got nothing. If they brought painting silk with them, he would take it without hesitation but then would say: "I shall make stockings of it!" For this reason the highly placed people were accustomed to approach the poor scholars, mountain monks, or butchers and inn-keepers when they wanted calligraphies or pictures by Shan-jen, and to buy from them.[13]

Preserved letters from Pa-ta Shan-jen, however, reveal him accepting commissions, using go-betweens, receiving money and gifts for his works, worrying about finishing them on time—engaged, that is, in the same practices that Cheng Min writes about, practices that will be explored later.[14] And, as is known from a colophon to the Pa-ta album in the Ho Yao-kuang collection, the Nanking collector Huang Yen-lü had no trouble getting an excellent album from the artist. He sent a sum of money ("all the money at my disposal," he writes) and twelve sheets of paper through one of Pa-ta's patrons, who acted as his agent in getting commissions for him. After a year he received his album, with which he was very pleased, remarking in his colophon that Pa-ta would never have given him the kind of rough and hasty sketches he did to repay gifts from the Kiangsi salt merchants.[15] (A sketchily painted panel from a screen done in 1692, figure 1.5, can probably be taken as representing the kind of painting that Huang Yen-lü hoped he would not get.) Again, these are two images of the artist that cannot easily be brought together—that seem, in fact, incompatible.

The "amateurization" of artists in Chinese writings, or at least most of those who were considered to merit approval at all, is part of a larger complex of interdependent ideas and attitudes, all aimed at dematerializing the art, removing from it all taint of vulgarity, commercialism, functionalism, philistine response. They include: an all-but-exclusive emphasis on art as personal expression, and a concomitant de-emphasizing of most other factors that motivated its production, including, much of the time, those that in fact had brought the work into being and constituted the basis for its reception in its original context. In connoisseurship, a focus on determining authorship and authenticity, on appreciating the painter's hand (which will be the subject of the final chapter), and a diversion of attention from the subject of the work and its meanings, its value as a somehow significant image. And in criticism, a preoccupation with brushwork and other aspects of style, both the artist's individual style and his uses of older styles, or references to them.

These attitudes are interdependent, one more or less leading to the others. The connoisseur's concentration on authenticity, for instance, allowed the viewer to read the picture as the personal expression of a particular master, and to appreciate his personal character and feeling as manifested in his painting. It

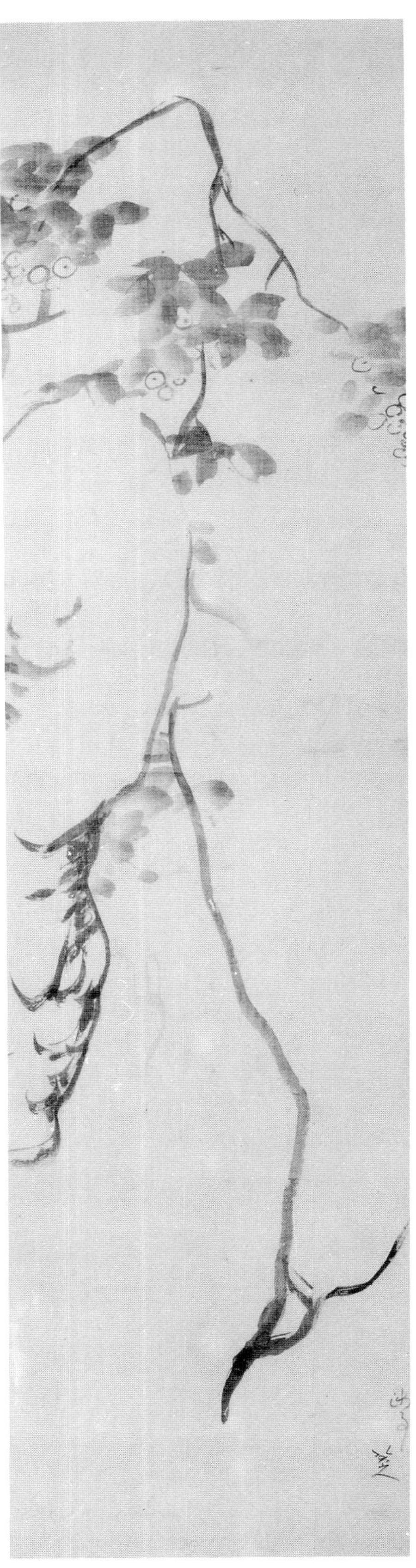

allowed the viewer also to ignore, as the prevailing critical theory said he should, the technical prowess of the artist, his representational skills, the decorative values of the work, whatever narrative or symbolic or other human-interest content it might have—the qualities that had originally allowed it, in a great many cases, to function in some social situation of its time. All qualities of the work other than the disinterestedly aesthetic, all motivations other than those of personal expression, tended to be relegated to the lower levels of response, the philistine, the *su* or banal.

Indoctrinated constantly with this ideology, Chinese collectors and painting enthusiasts of the later centuries appreciated paintings, and wrote about them, in ways often quite divorced from the original contexts of the works. This aestheticization and decontextualizing of the Chinese painting tradition makes it difficult, much of the time, for us now to recover the meanings and functions that the paintings originally had. In attempting to do so, then, I am not undermining some universal "Chinese" readings of the works, but trying to free them from later misreadings, or extremely partial readings, and to uncover something of their original character.[16]

I was myself, for my sins, one of the pioneer foreign exponents of the literati-amateur painting ideal as a key to understanding certain kinds of Chinese painting. Now, forty years later, I return to the same set of problems, but from a very different perspective, arguing instead that what seems remarkable now is the degree to which this ideal has been permitted to pervade our own interpretations of Chinese painting. In our culture, while we have had our versions of the amateur ideal, it is generally true that no special stigma is attached to pro-

1.5. Chu Ta (Pa-ta Shan-jen, 1626–1705), "Flowers Growing on a Cliff."
Dated 1692. One of four panels from screen, ink on silk, each 161.8 × 42.4 cm. Shanghai Museum.

fessionalism in art—if a painter holds an exhibition and sells all the paintings in it, we see this as cause for congratulation, not disdain—although it is also true that studies that make production for profit a major factor in interpreting the artist's works, such as Svetlana Alpers' recent book on Rembrandt (see Bibliography), can still call forth angry responses from those who contend that the element of artistic genius has been slighted in the process.

With studies of the social and economic contexts of artistic production so prominent in other areas of art-historical writing, it is all the more strange that those of us in the Chinese painting field have seemed not only disinclined to recognize the inherited biases that impede our own investigations of this aspect of the subject, but are even prone to share the traditional Chinese squeamishness about discussing it. We have written, too often, as though we were defending the artists we admire by downplaying the artists' engagement in the somehow shameful business of profiting from their art. We have written as though we had forgotten, for the moment, what in fact everybody knows: that in the real world of making art, outside the romantic and literati myths, a creative act motivated in some part by economic need and partly shaped by external demands is no more likely to produce bad art than one carried out in a condition of relative freedom from such outer dictates. (If we don't know this, we can quickly find it out by going, say, from an exhibition of works by the leading Sung academy masters to another made up of works by Tung Ch'i-ch'ang and his scholar-amateur contemporaries, and seeing which is richer in great and moving and satisfying pictures.)

The outcome of our reluctance to violate the Chinese literati taboos has been, I think, a badly unbalanced view of the subject. And it is only balance that I mean to advocate here, not some heavy emphasis on the social and economic factors behind artistic production (although these essays will of course concentrate on those, since they are my subject). Without undervaluing the self-revelatory capacity of art one can play it against other, more earthbound and socially conditioned functions, and try to understand how the one impinged on the other. Without slipping into a reductive approach, one can aim at a more clear-eyed recognition of the true situation, sometimes the predicament, of the artist behind the work, the kind of recognition I will attempt to arrive at in these pages.

The Effects of the Later Practice of Connoisseurship

In searching for the roots of the phenomenon I am trying to define we find ourselves confronting, as so often, the figure of Tung Ch'i-ch'ang—certainly not as the originator of this set of attitudes, but as an especially influential exponent of them. With all the recent outpouring of scholarship on the achievements of this great early seventeenth-century painter and theorist, one area of his activity may still warrant more looking into: his advising of collectors, especially some of the newly rich collectors of Sungchiang, Huichou in Southern Anhui, Yangchou, and other places where wealth was concentrated in this period. Collecting art, especially the kinds associated with the gentry and literati class, was one of the ways the Hui-chou and other merchant families elevated their status in society. Many of them, relatively new to the game, needed advice on what were the right kinds of art objects to collect and, once they had made their acquisitions, on whether they had bought wisely.[17] The argument has even been made that a sharp increase in the collecting of art is what *produces* art historians,[18] and it is true that the two phenomena appear more or less together in China, in the context of an unprecedented rise in the number of people who could afford to indulge in art collecting and connoisseurship.

Tung Ch'i-ch'ang and others who served in this capacity were, in effect, the art historians of their time, and old-style Chinese art historians today are in important ways their descendants. Their basic act, and what Tung Ch'i-ch'ang must have done supremely well, was (and is) to stand in front of a painting and pronounce with an authoritative air on its authenticity, along with naming the stylistic tradition or old master's style that the artist was following. Connoisseurship on an ideal level represents an individual exercise of taste, a way for aesthetes to exercise their discrimination and for collectors to pursue the highest quality in their holdings. But on a more practical level, as men like Tung Ch'i-ch'ang performed it for others less knowledgeable, it could be a way of reassuring buyers that they had got what they paid for (an assurance that could, especially when inscribed on the work, raise its value substantially),[19] or to warn them to be more careful next time.

And this latter kind of connoisseurship necessarily focused less on quality than on age and authenticity, the assignment of a name to the painting that would validate its importance and value. Those who performed it could identify, from their visual memories, the individual styles of a great many major and minor masters, and match these against the work at hand, providing an account of its stylistic antecedents and sometimes, in an unattributed or misattributed work, even of its authorship. They were inclined, as traditional Chinese connoisseurs are today, to assume that good paintings must be by famous artists; excellent works by followers thus ended up with attributions to the masters, often reinforced by interpolated signatures of the major artists replacing the original signatures of the minor ones, which were cut off. We frequently disagree with Tung Ch'i-ch'ang's attributions and judgments as they are recorded in his many inscriptions on extant paintings—for example, his acceptance of the "Wintry Trees by a Lake" (figure 1.6) not only as a genuine work by Tung Yüan but, if we take his inscription above the painting at face value, as "the number one Tung Yüan under heaven." But we respect his judgments as on the whole astute for an age when no photographs or reproductions were available to allow the kind of close comparative studies one can make today.[20] This Chinese tradition of connoisseurship and scholarship was an honorable one, and we are all very much in its debt. But perhaps it is time to recognize some of its negative effects, for present-day scholarship, along with the positive.

And the negative effects have been, I now believe, serious ones, exactly those outlined earlier: the decontextualizing of a great deal of Chinese painting, the divorcement of much of it from its original meanings and purposes, the distortion of its very character, too often, to make it fit a more or less inapplicable set of ideals.[21] The Chinese connoisseurs' bases for evaluating paintings and painters—judgments of authenticity, the hand of the individual master, expressive brushwork, rightness of stylistic lineage, the inherent superiority of the amateur tradition and of paintings of a nonfunctional character, intended to evoke purely aesthetic responses—these were so widely accepted that artists and paintings that did not conform were pressed into doing so, or else were rejected. Large areas of Chinese painting were pronounced to be "not suitable for refined enjoyment" by critics, and so have had poor chances of survival. A well-recognized example is Ch'an or Zen painting (figure 1.7) which, were it not for the happy circumstance of its appreciation and preservation in Japan, where many great examples survive, would be virtually lost to us. We now recognize as masterpieces works that in their time and afterward were dismissed by Chinese critics for their coarse brushwork and unelevating subjects.

To be sure, one must beware of making "the Chinese literati" or "Chinese critics" into monolithic entities with uniform sets of opinions and biases, as the above discussions may seem to do. There were always some doubters and iconoclasts, ready to undermine the orthodox opinions, and a few of their enter-

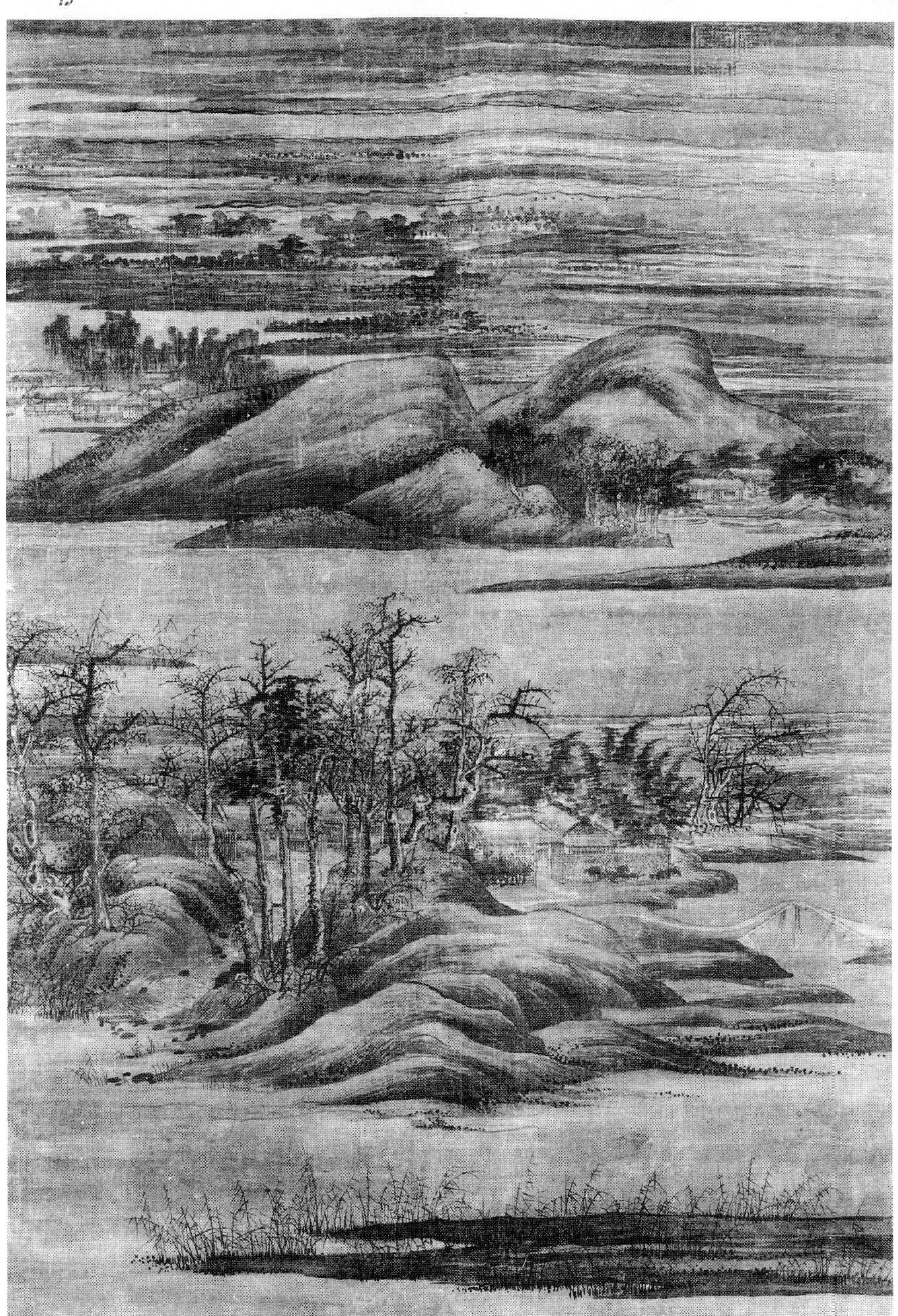

1.6. Attributed to Tung Yüan (d. 962), "Wintry Grove and Layered Banks." Hanging scroll, ink and light colors on silk, 181.5 × 116.5 cm. Kurokawa Institute of Ancient Cultures, Nishinomiya. Inscription by Tung Ch'i-ch'ang (1555–1636).

tainingly sarcastic commentaries will be quoted in later chapters. And arguments went on always between writers on painting who express divergent beliefs and preferences. Granting this, it remains true that an unhealthy degree of uniformity on certain basic assumptions seems to have obtained in the later centuries, and to have affected both the evaluation and the practice of painting in ways I am attempting to outline here.

The effects of this set of attitudes on the production of living artists were as severe and constricting as they were on the collecting of old paintings. The pressures must have been both external and, for painters who were themselves persuaded, internal, disinclining them from practicing styles and kinds of painting that had come to be regarded as less than respectable. But the conformity, again, was not universal. I have written about the predicament of painters in the later centuries who chose to pursue, against the current, basically representational ways of painting, relatively free of cultured allusions to the past and all the distancing devices that signified a high-minded detachment from the subject, and about the difficulty these artists had in being taken seriously by critics and collectors.[22] Our admiration for the "harmonizing" mode of traditional Chinese culture should not distract us from a recognition of its damaging effect on those who were tuned in to different harmonies and resisted being absorbed into the great all-embracing one.

The literati, then, for the most part "controlled the media," and their pro-amateur bias is hard to escape in the texts. In trying to imagine how the professional masters of the Ming-Ch'ing period (who may in fact comprise most of the best painters) can have felt about the constant denigration and distortion of their achievements, there is (as one might expect) little evidence in writings by any of them from which to reconstruct their responses. Even though they were mostly literate, they did not belong to the class of literati whose writings were likely to be preserved and published; only a few isolated statements survive from such masters as Li Shih-ta and Sung Hsü, reported in books by others.[23] We long to have a Chinese counterpart to the English artist and novelist Wyndham Lewis' *The Apes of God,* that brilliantly vitriolic attack on upper-class amateurism in the arts and the confusion of critical values it can lead to. But, here as elsewhere in traditional Chinese society, there was no orga-

1.7. Wen Jih-kuan (late Sung period, 13th cent.), "Grapes."
Horizontal painting, ink on paper, 31.2 × 83 cm.
Ching Yuan Chai collection, Berkeley.

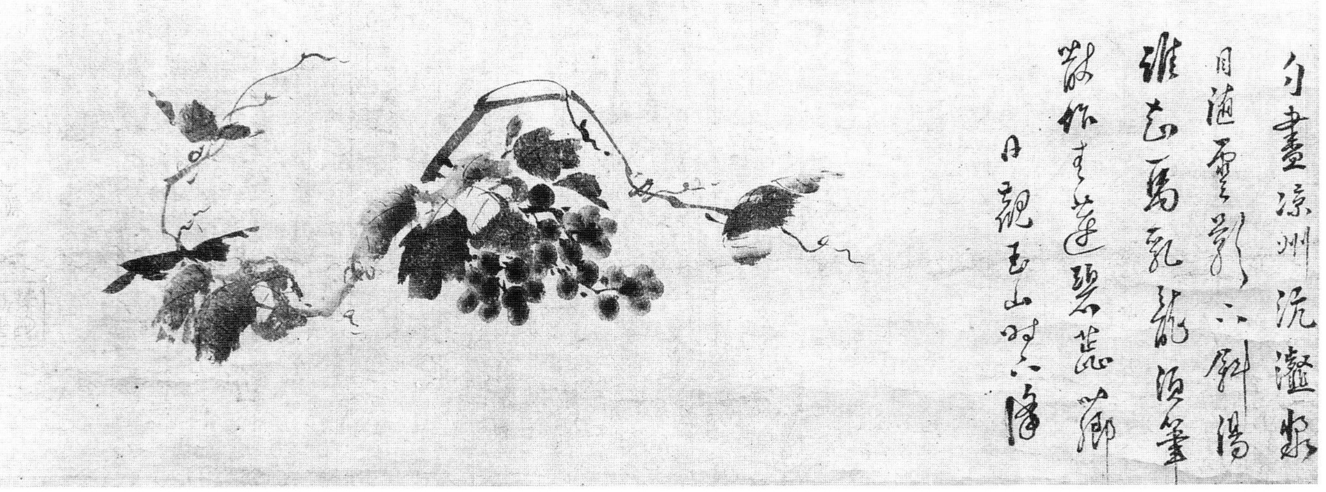

nized voice of opposition, no countervailing force to the gentry-literati dominance. (An essay by Ch'en Hung-shou, whose remarkable self-portrait we see in figure 1.8, is an exception, an isolated instance of a professional artist criticizing the amateurs. But even he, we must note, goes on to criticize his fellow professionals just as severely.)[24]

My purpose, however, is not so much to advocate a reassessment of the professional painters' tradition in China as to suggest that we do these artists no service when we perpetuate the well-meant Chinese myths in which they are made respectable by being transformed into disinterested amateurs. Nor is it useful to adopt the Chinese genteel distaste for the down-to-earth economic realities of the painter's practice, as we have tended to do, motivated not so much by attitudes prevalent within our own culture as by an uncritical acceptance of what one social historian lists among the "enduring characteristics of late imperial China," an "orthodoxy that to a greater or lesser extent viewed commerce with suspicion and disdain."[25] Apart from the desirability of giving as complete and balanced an account of my subject as I can, I find these realities to be thoroughly absorbing in themselves. The varied and often roundabout ways in which some seeker after a painting conveyed his wishes to the artist; the equally diverse ways in which the artist was rewarded if he complied (and of course he did not always comply); the dilemma of the artist who accepts too many commissions and must deal with impatient clients while trying to step up his rate of production—these prove to be engrossing and enlightening, as I hope to show later. This chapter will conclude by offering a preliminary answer to the question raised by any inquiry of this kind: does all this

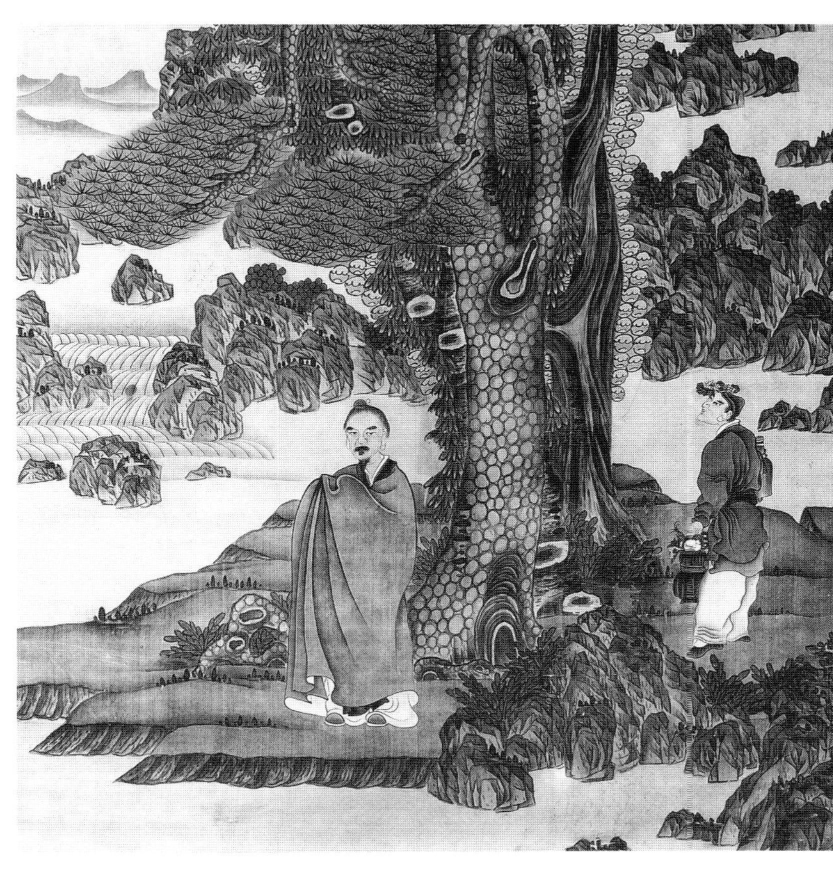

1.8. Ch'en Hung-shou, "A Tall Pine and Taoist Immortal (Self-Portrait in a Landscape)." Dated 1635. Hanging scroll, ink and colors on silk, 202.1 × 97.8 cm. National Palace Museum, Taiwan, Republic of China.

really affect our appreciation of the works of art themselves? I will argue, using a few examples from recent studies by myself and others, that it does, profoundly, and in the direction of enrichment. Understanding the context of their creation, that is, and some of the factors behind it, or adopting different hypotheses about it, can change the grounds on which we interpret and appraise the paintings themselves, and deepen our readings of them.

Rereading the Paintings: Occasional Works

An example is a series of small paintings mounted in a handscroll, one of two found in 1982 in a late fifteenth-century tomb at Huai-an in southern Jiangsu province.[26] From inscribed dedications it is clear that the paintings were done by a number of artists for an official named Cheng Chün. The artists include several noted masters who were active in the imperial academy or in court circles, such as Ma Shih (figure 1.9), along with minor and unknown painters. The paintings are all simple and sketchy in character; in the cases of those by the academy masters, this sketchiness contrasts sharply with the technical finish of the large, elaborate works that are usually taken as representative of their output. This difference has been interpreted, following the orthodox Chinese way of reading quick and spontaneous kinds of painting, as proving that the academy masters also worked in the *hsieh-i* mode (literally "sketching the idea"), a kind of painting typically used by the scholar-amateur artists for what were taken to be direct, untrammeled expressions of feeling.

I have argued elsewhere for seeing the paintings, not as amateurlike self-expression, but as examples of the kind of simple, quickly produced pictures, more or less conventional in character, that were dashed off in large numbers by artists of all kinds for small gifts, to repay lesser obligations or to win the favor of a minor official, as Cheng Chün was. Seen in this way, the Huai-an tomb series takes on great interest as representing the kind of collection that such a Ming official might bring together as he moved about between the capital and the provinces in his official capacity, a collection of a kind that is nowhere else preserved intact. Such an interpretation also en-

1.9. Ma Shih. "Watching Geese on an Autumn River."
Short handscroll, ink on paper, 19.5 × 42.2 cm. From *Huai-an Ming-mu ch'u-t'u shu-hua* (Peking, 1988), plate 7.

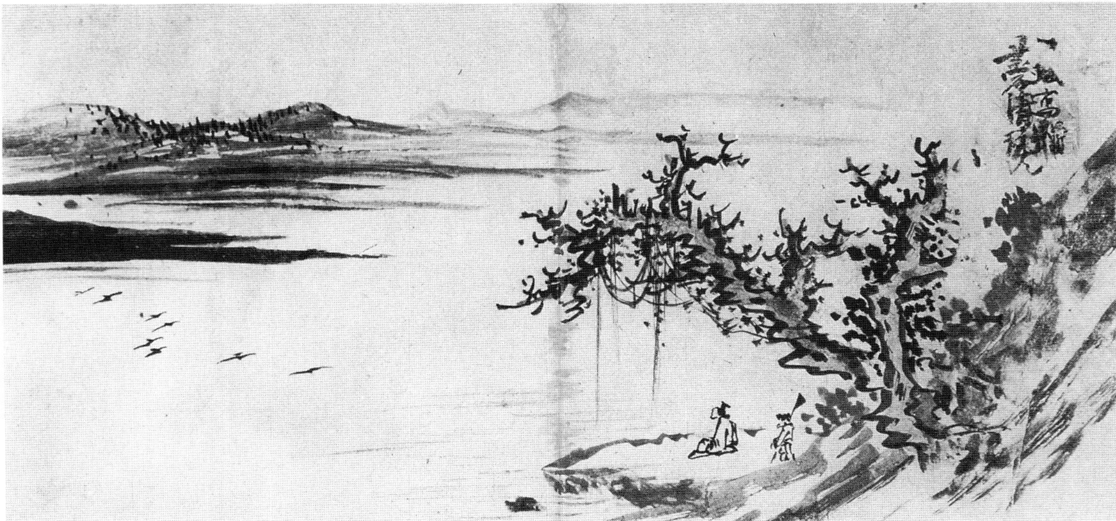

courages us to look for, and I believe to find, political implications in the subjects of the paintings.

Small, functional paintings of this kind, seen more properly as cursory than as cursive, must have been produced copiously by many if not most Chinese artists (as they are today) in response to a diversity of demands and circumstances. Few have been preserved, presumably because their value was considered to be ephemeral; collectors chose works of greater substance to treasure and transmit, works in which the artists had invested more time and creative thought. When they survive at all, it is usually by some special happenstance, as with the Huai-an tomb paintings, or through preservation in Japan. Simple and conventional farewell pictures presented to Japanese monks on their departure from Ming dynasty China, for instance, have been transmitted to the present day in Japanese temples, and serve to fill out our knowledge of this interesting if minor genre.[27] An example by the early sixteenth-century academy master Wang E can serve to represent them (figure 1.10); its conventional, ready-made character is apparent when it is put beside another by Wu Wei, who was also active in the imperial academy about a generation earlier (figure 1.11).

Recognizing that even the best artists produced quantities of quick, more or less perfunctory pictures in addition to their serious works enables us to differentiate correspondingly within the artist's oeuvre, as contempor-

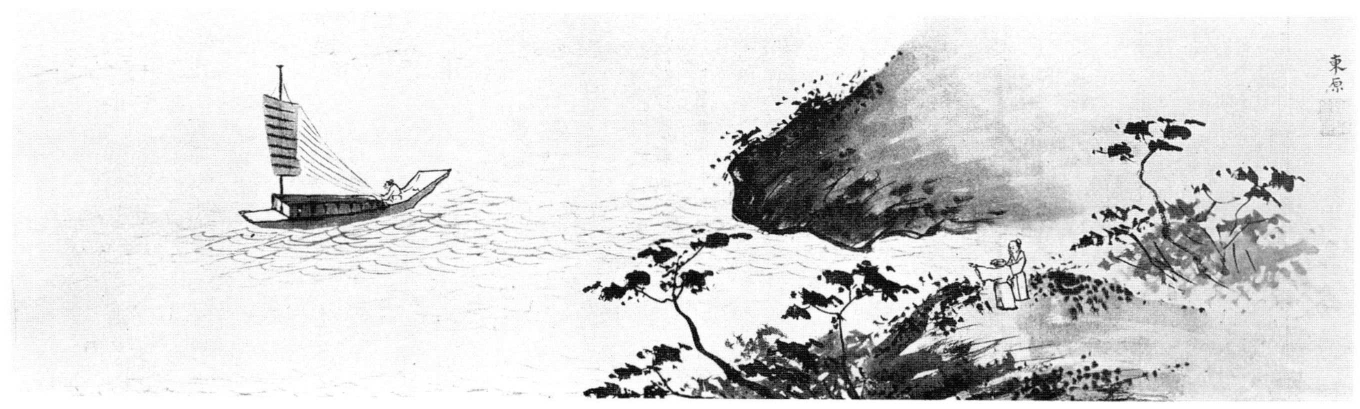

1.10. Wang E, "Farewell to Sasaki Nagaharu." Handscroll, ink on paper, ht. 29.7 cm. K. Wada collection, Osaka. From *Bijutsu kenkyū*, no. 221 (March 1962).

1.11. Wu Wei (1459–1508), "Farewell at Lung-chiang." Handscroll, ink on paper, 32 × 128.5 cm. Shantung Provincial Museum. From *I-yüan to-ying*, no. 12 (1981), p. 4.

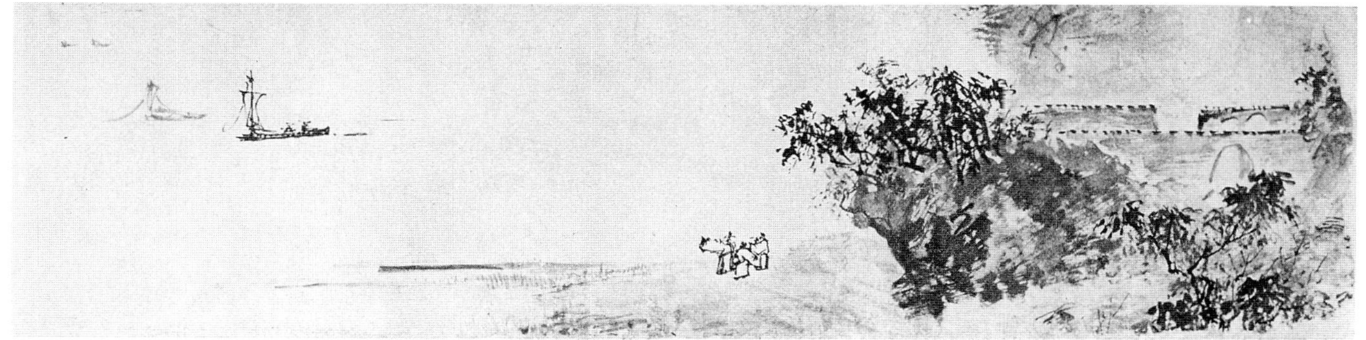

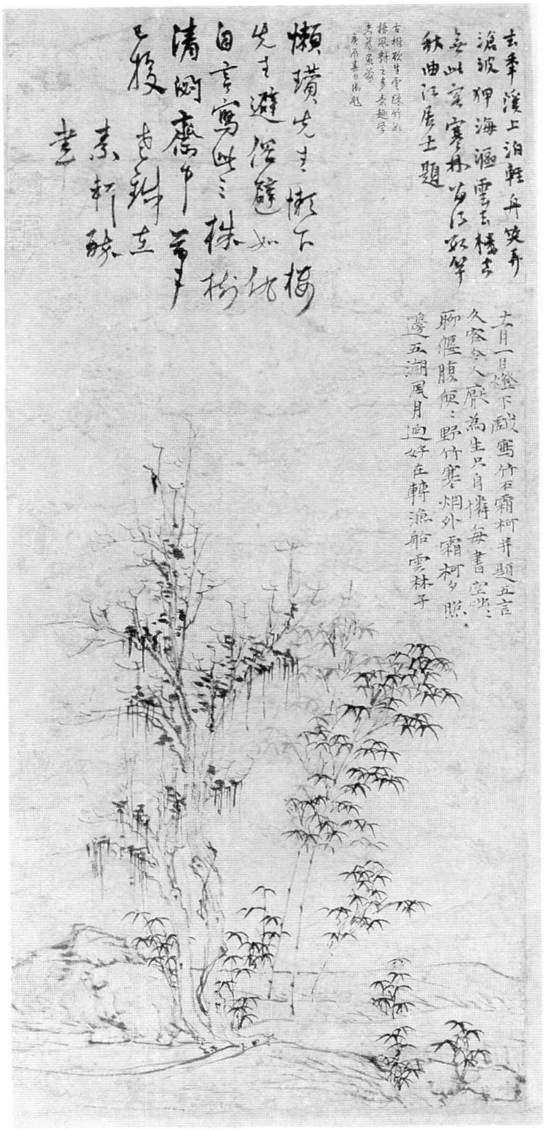

1.12. Ni Tsan, "Bamboo, Rock, and Frosty Trees."
Hanging scroll, ink on paper, 73.8 × 34.7 cm.
Shanghai Museum.

aries of the artists surely did. The inscription quoted earlier by Huang Yen-lü on the album by Pa-ta Shan-jen, expressing his pleasure with the album and remarking that Pa-ta would never give him the kind of hastily dashed-off pictures he made to repay gifts from the salt merchants of his home province, is revealing in this regard. So is a statement by the Yüan writer Hsia Wen-yen that Ni Tsan in his late years painted "in a sketchy and simple way to repay obligations. Thus [his works] seem to have come from two different hands."[28] Pa-ta and Ni Tsan were such prestigious masters, and the tolerance among their audiences for sketchy and amateurish execution so advanced, that one is inclined always to give positive readings to these qualities in their paintings, adopting the literati-amateur rhetoric to argue that ordinary value judgments are inapplicable to works of this kind. Perhaps, with adjusted understanding of the factors behind this sketchiness, one can have the courage to say sometimes: This may well be a genuine product of the hand of Ni Tsan, but it is nonetheless a graceless scrawl (figure 1.12).

Some works that are now dismissed as fakes, on the other hand, might be rehabilitated and accorded a measure of respectability if we recognize them as studio works, done in part by the master, in part under his direction by assistants. Evidence for this practice is scanty, to be sure; a few examples by the late Ming figure master Ch'en Hung-shou and his disciples will be introduced in a later chapter. Inscriptions on these are exceptional in recording the participation of several hands—such collaborations usually go unacknowledged in inscriptions on the individual works, although they are not infrequently attested to in writings about artists. Here, too, investigating the conditions under which the work was produced will affect our appraisal of it.

This is no less true of some aesthetically high-level works, such as the famous series of scenes from the life of T'ao Yüan-ming that Ch'en Hung-shou painted in 1650 (figure 1.13). Knowing that the picture was done for his important patron Chou Liang-kung, who was then holding an official post under the new Manchu regime and, since T'ao Yüan-ming was the great exemplar for the practice of retiring from official service, that it may well have been meant by the artist to urge this course of action on Chou (who failed to take the advice, and suffered by consequence), surely enriches our experience of the work. So does the information that it was one of a series of paintings that Ch'en executed, or at least began, during a ten-day binge with Chou Liang-kung and others on the West Lake at Hangchou, and that the coloring was done (one hopes afterward) by his son. Building a structure of circumstance and meaning around the work will carry us beyond the simple divisions of an artist's oeuvre into earlier and later, genuine and spurious, to which we used to be largely limited.

An important part of the painter's practice in China was the production of pictures of particular subjects, belonging to types or genres, to fulfill needs on certain social occasions. Determining what these needs and occasions were is not always easy, for the reason suggested earlier, the Chinese writers' distaste for the functional aspects of art. But recent studies have begun to identify the special imagery of some of these types, and future research will clarify many more. Recognizing them allows us to judge, in addition to the independent aesthetic merits of the work, the artist's success in conveying the desired message in pictorial form, or in inventing original plays on established types.

Birthday pictures often featured symbols of longevity, such as pines and cranes (figure 1.14), although other subjects were also com-

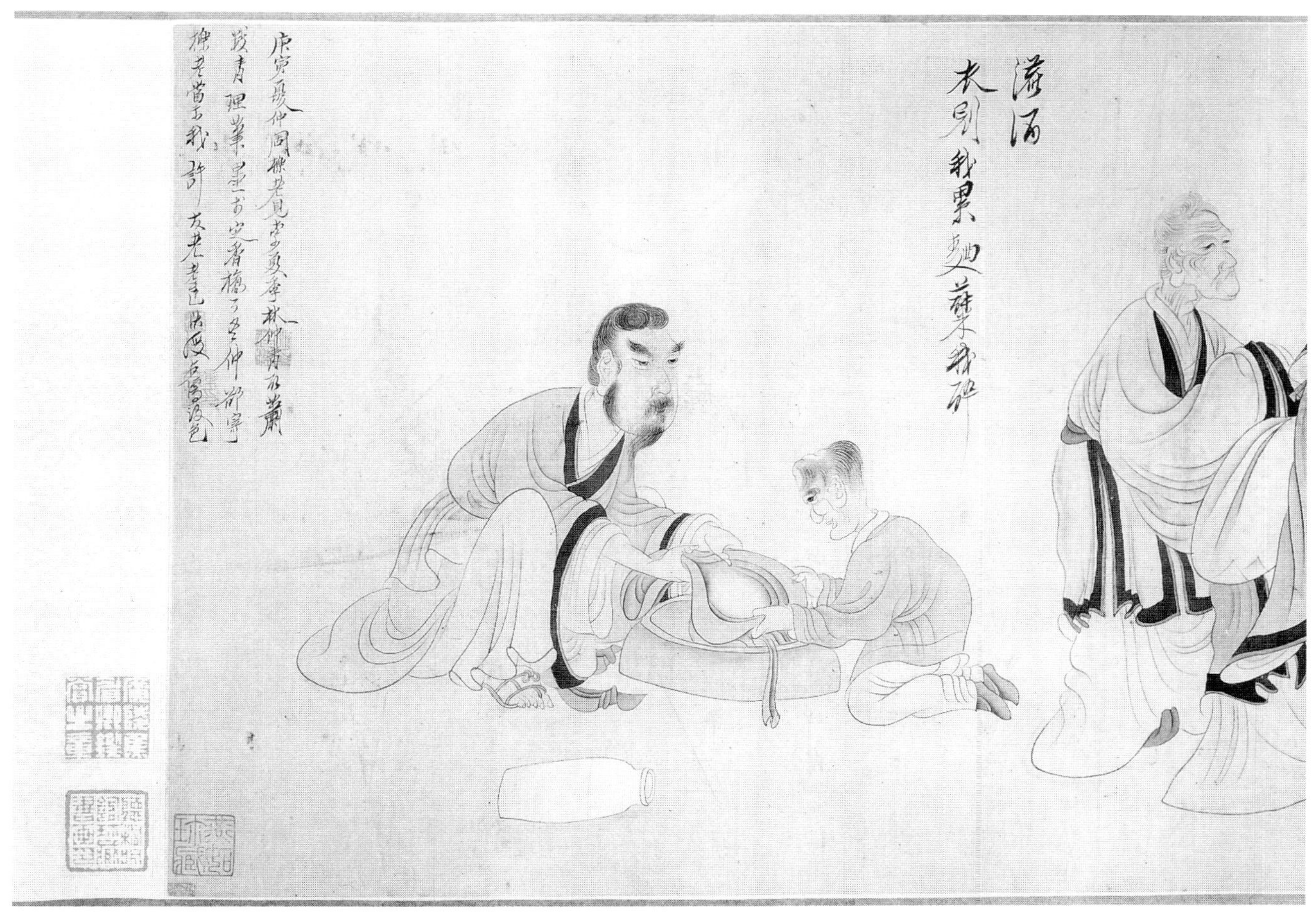

1.13. Ch'en Hung-shou. "Scenes from the Life of T'ao Yüan-ming."
Dated 1650. Section of a handscroll, ink and light colors on silk, ht. 31.4 cm. Honolulu Academy of Arts (1912.1).

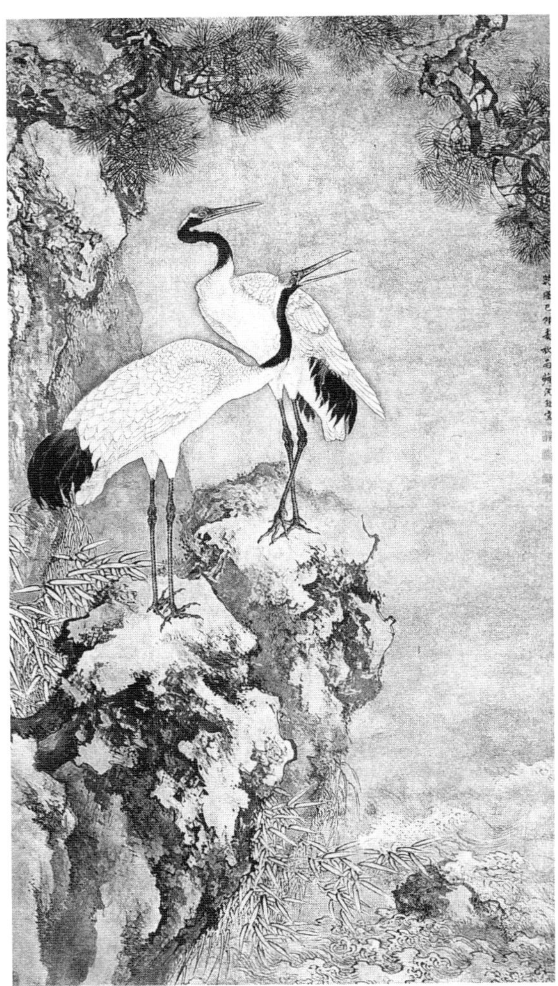

1.14 (left). Shen Ch'üan, "Pines and Cranes." Dated 1759. Hanging scroll, ink and colors on silk, 170 × 91 cm. Collection of Chu Huai-min. From *I-yüan to-ying* 23 (January 1984), p. 47.

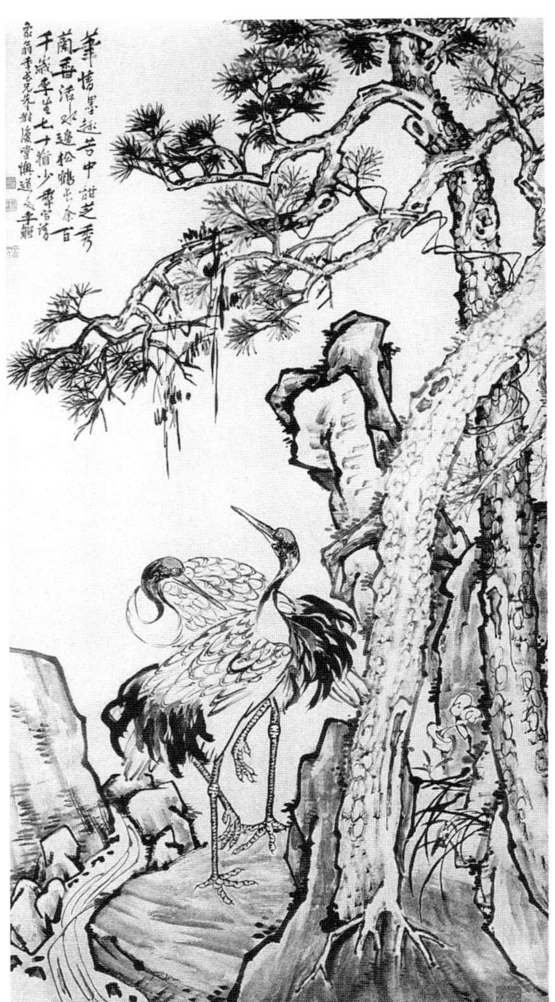

1.14 (right). Li Shan, "Cranes and Pines, for the Seventieth Birthday of Huang-weng." Hanging scroll, ink and colors on paper, 181 × 94.5 cm. Kuang-tung Provincial Museum. From *Kuang-tung sheng po-wu-kuan ts'ang-hua chi* (Canton, 1986), plate 201.

mon.[29] Wedding pictures commonly included pairs of mandarin ducks, emblems of marital harmony, sometimes with other paired birds and auspicious imagery (figure 1.15). Paintings intended to felicitate someone's retirement from an official post might depict the person dwelling in seclusion above the cares of the world, or might represent some bucolic scene to stand for his long-awaited return to the rural delights of his home village;[30] or it might, as we will see later, portray the paradigm of retirees, the poet T'ao Yüan-ming. Paintings might also congratulate someone embarking on a profession: Ch'en Hung-shou painted, for a man who had decided to become a herbalist, pictures of the legendary emperors Huang-ti, to whom the "Classic of Internal Medicine" was ascribed, and Shen-nung, who is credited with the invention of agriculture but who was also a god of medicine.[31] New Year's pictures presented certain auspicious subjects, or portrayed a New Year's gathering with friends

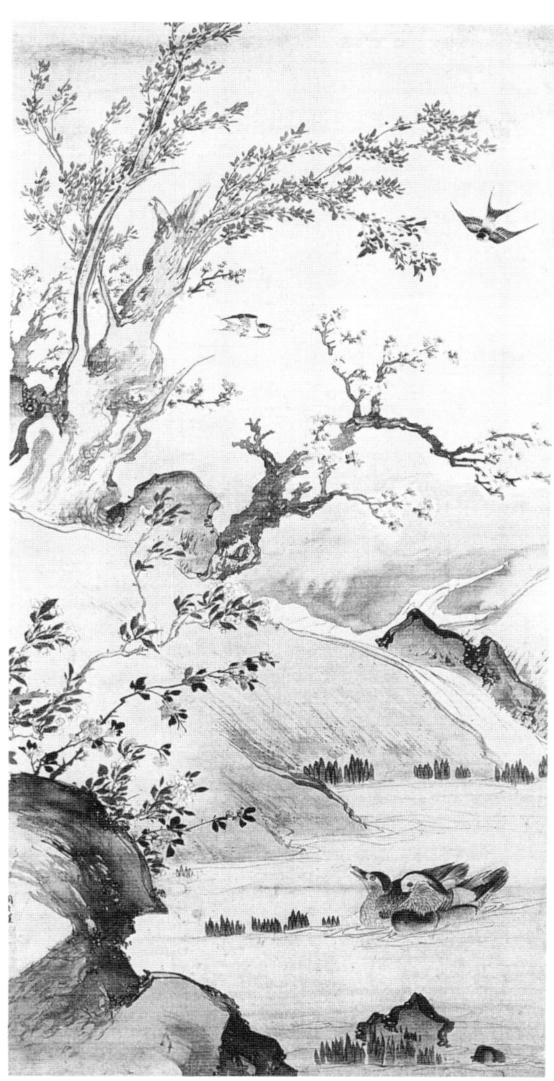

1.15 (left). Chou Chih-mien (active early 17th cent.), "Paired Swallows and Mandarin Ducks." Hanging scroll, ink and colors on silk, 186.5 × 91 cm. Palace Museum, Beijing.

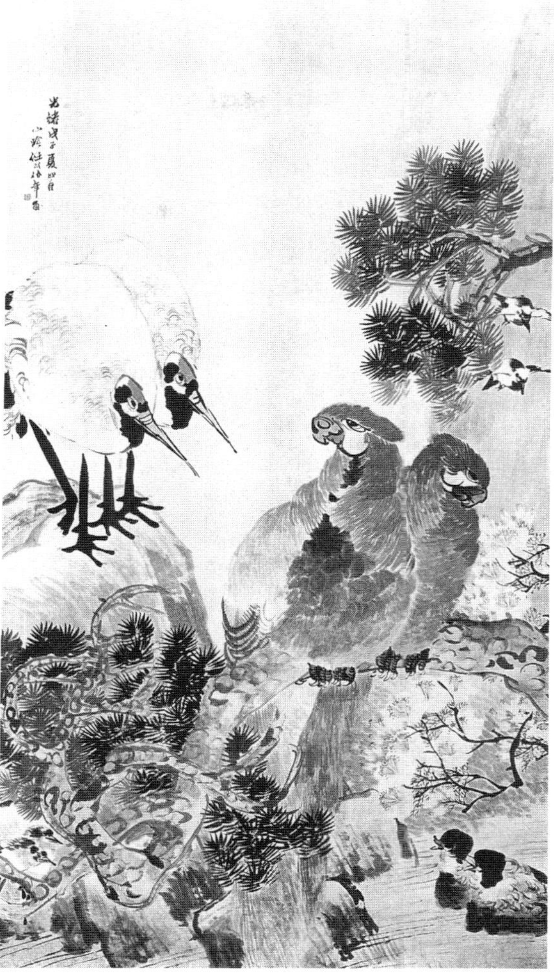

1.15 (right). Jen I (1840–1896), "Pairs of Birds with Pine Tree." Dated 1888. Hanging scroll, ink and colors on paper, 177.8 × 95.3 cm. Former collection of Alice Boney, New York

gathered in a house and, typically, children setting off firecrackers in the yard outside.[32]

Subjects such as bamboo, orchids, and plum, the favorites of the scholar-amateur artist, might seem too general in their symbolism to be suited to occasions of this kind. They are ordinarily read as expressions through symbolic forms and expressive brushwork of the elevated Confucian attitudes of the artist, his personal character, his freedom from commercial constraints, and so forth. The paintings of Cheng Hsieh (better known as Cheng P'an-ch'iao) seem to invite this kind of reading. Cheng was one of the most prolific and popular artists of the Yangchou School in the mid-eighteenth century, an artist whose poems, calligraphy, and paintings are taken to be expressions of his romantic personality. Cheng's paintings (figure 1.16) nearly always represent the same symbolic subjects: bamboo, orchids,

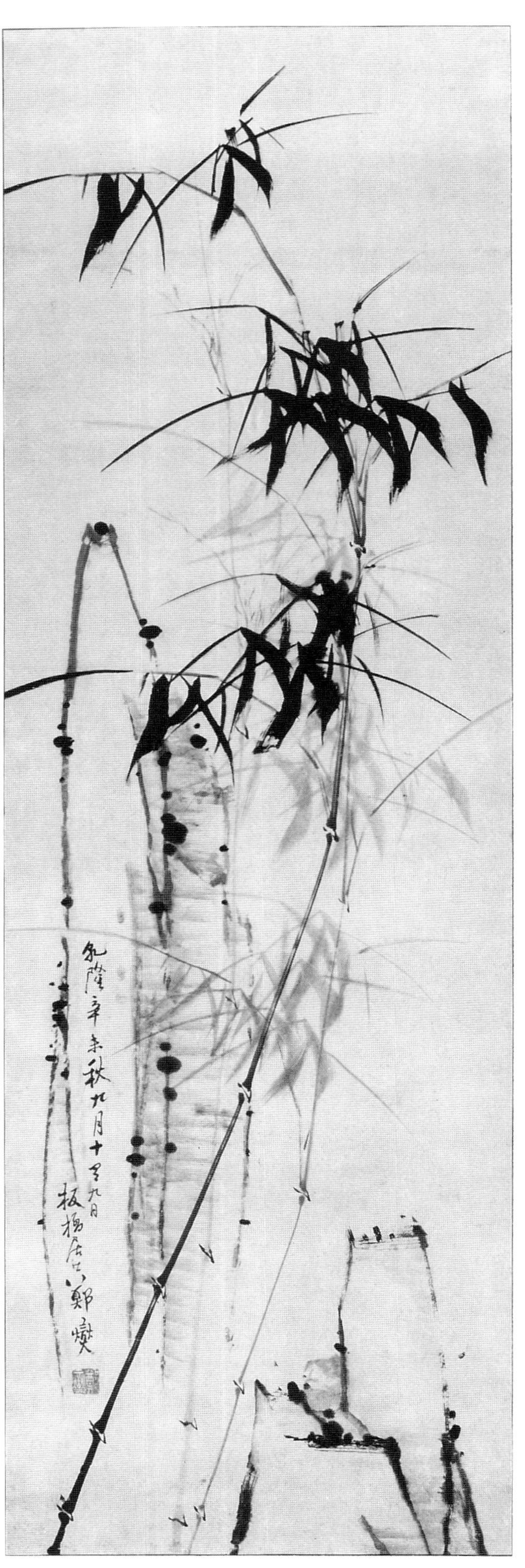

and rocks. Most of them were done in his later years, when he was living in Yangchou after retiring from a bureaucratic career.

Both in subject and in style, then, Cheng Hsieh's paintings appear to typify the scholar-amateur mode. And so they do, in the sense that literati culture and the values of cultivated amateurism had come to be commodified in eighteenth-century Yangchou. Like the landscapes of the Anhui master Cheng Min with which I began, Cheng's bamboo and orchid pictures gained in commercial value by presenting themselves as amateur expressions. It is well known that Cheng posted a price-list for his works, in the belief that selling them openly to anyone who brought the asking-price was more honorable than attaching oneself to a rich patron and painting at his bidding.[33] Cheng-chi Hsü, using the price-list and others of Cheng's writings as evidence, has argued that much of Cheng's painting was intended for an economically middle-level audience, made up in large part of people whom the artist did not know, and that this character of his clientele affected the nature of his output: where the more common practice earlier had been to produce one-of-a-kind pictures for particular patrons and recipients, Cheng and other Yangchou masters of the period paint more prolifically, often somewhat repetitively, in styles that allow quick production.[34] Seeing them in this light certainly alters our reading of the so-called *hsieh-i* manner, which, as noted earlier in connection with the Huai-an tomb paintings, is ordinarily read purely as a mode of self-expression.

Cheng-chi Hsü also explored the ways in which Cheng Hsieh was able, through ingenious manipulation of his highly restricted repertory of subjects, to suit it to a wide range of

1.16. Cheng Hsieh (1693–1765), "Bamboo Growing by Rocks."
Dated 1751. Hanging scroll, ink on paper. Former collection of Alice Boney, New York.

situations. For instance, when he retired from his official post, he presented a painting of bamboo to the people of his district, indicating in an inscription that the slender stalk represented the fishing rod symbolizing the reclusive life he intended to lead. Bamboo could also stand for longevity, and so serve for birthday paintings. The vigorous growth of the plant made a picture of it (properly inscribed) suitable to congratulate someone on the birth of a son. The orchid had long been established as a metaphor for the talented and virtuous man; blossoming in the wild, it stood for unrecognized talent; growing in pots, it could represent capable scholars who had been drawn into service. So pictures of orchids, suitably inscribed, could carry a diversity of messages to members of the Confucian bureaucracy, and could be used as presents to them, either from the artist himself or from his clients. Cheng even used a painting of a profusion of orchid plants to congratulate a woman on her thirtieth birthday and to wish her many children.

The blossoming plum stood for purity, because of its whiteness and fragility; it also stood for rejuvenation, since it puts forth flowers after surviving the cold winter. Chin Nung, another painter active in Yangchou in the mid-eighteenth century, used the image of blossoming plum branches, as his friend Cheng Hsieh used bamboo and orchids, for a variety of meanings. One such painting by him, dated 1759, is in the Freer Gallery of Art (figure 1.17). We have tended to read the conventional meaning into the image and pay little attention to the inscription. But when we *do* read it, we learn that Chin did the painting to congratulate a friend who had acquired a love-

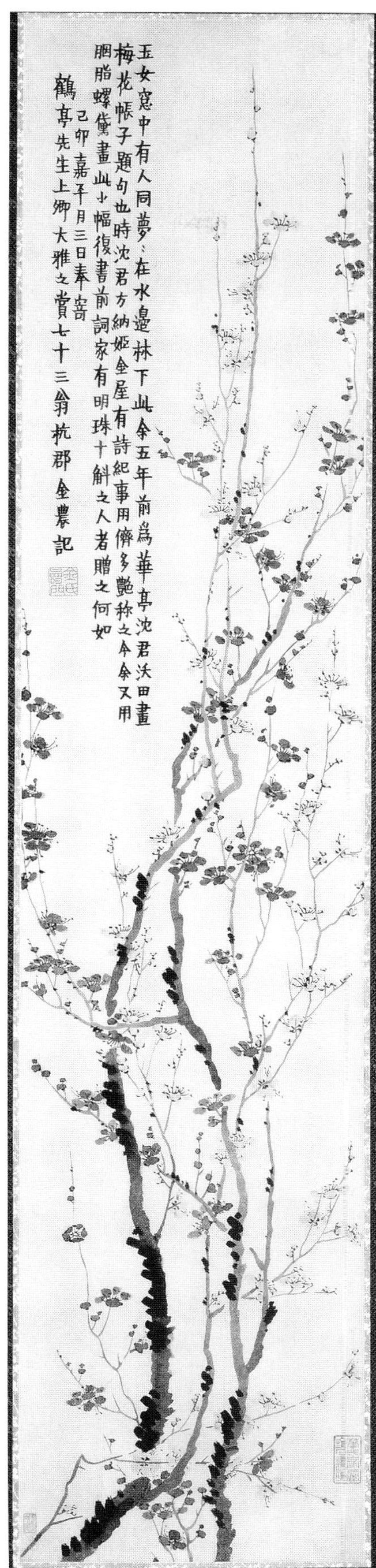

1.17. Chin Nung (1687—after 1764), "Branches of Blossoming Plum." Hanging scroll, ink and color on paper, 130.3 × 28.5 cm. Freer Gallery of Art, Washington, D.C. (65.10).

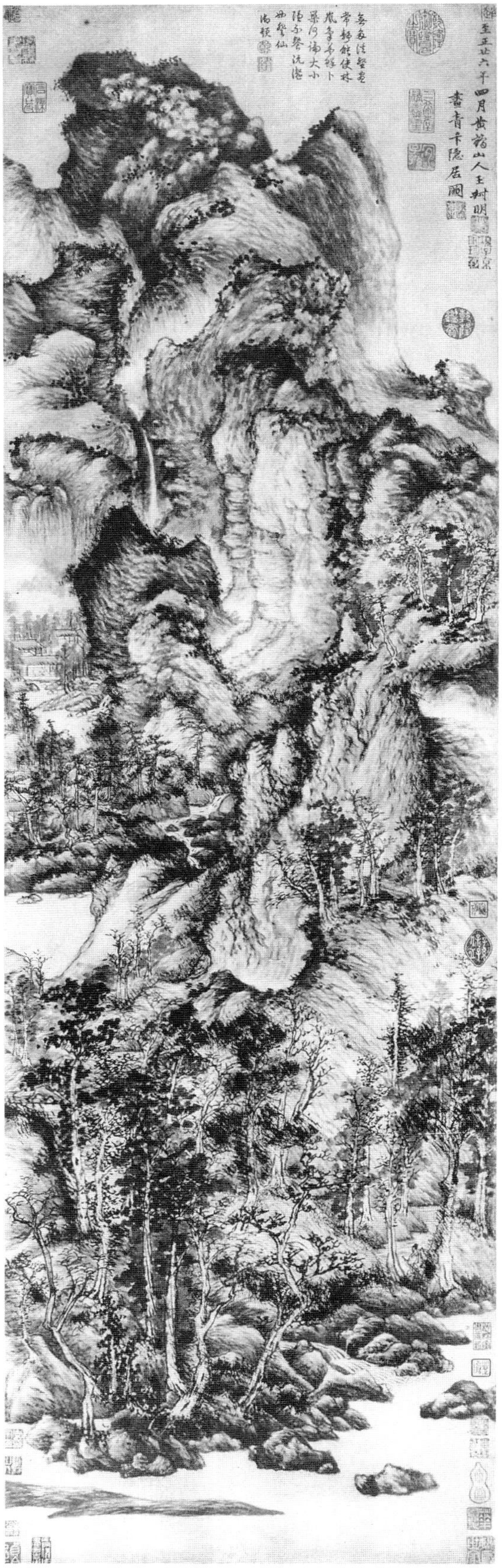

ly new concubine, likening the red color of the blossoms to her rouged cheeks, but also calling up the more conventional associations of the subject to felicitate his friend's continuing virility.[35]

Rereading the Paintings: Landscapes and Handscrolls

Landscape is another subject that may seem ill-suited to being charged with special meanings and produced for particular occasions, and much of it can indeed be accepted as having had a general, nonfunctional character, in harmony with such statements as Mi Fu's that landscape is "a creation of the mind, and thus intrinsically a superior art"—superior, that is, to pictures of other subjects that could be done simply by copying their appearances.[36] Some significant part of Chinese landscape painting, however, was more specific in its application to everyday situations. I have written elsewhere about the meanings and functions of landscape painting in China, and will recall only a few representative examples here.[37]

Writing about the great "Dwelling in the Ch'ing-pien Mountains" by the late-Yüan artist Wang Meng, painted in 1366 (figure 1.18), I quoted from a 1939 article by my teacher Max Loehr: "The picture seems not so much to describe a passage of mountain scenery as to express a terrible occurrence, an eruptive vision." That was in my 1976 book on Yüan painting; I went on to see this and others of Wang Meng's paintings more specifically as reflecting his "engagement with the agonizing circumstances of the late Yüan and early Ming."[38] Pushing this kind of interpretation one large step (and one generation) beyond Loehr and myself, Richard Vinograd has ar-

1.18. Wang Meng, "Dwelling in the Ch'ing-pien Mountains."
Dated 1366. Hanging scroll, ink on paper, 140.6 × 42.2 cm. Shanghai Museum.

gued convincingly that the picture was probably done for Wang's cousin Chao Lin (it bears a seal that is probably his) and represents the Chao family retreat at Mt. Ch'ing-pien, located north of their home in Wu-hsing, just at the time when this region was being swept over by the armies of two contenders for the imperial throne, one of whom, Chu Yüan-chang, was to found the Ming dynasty two years later.[39] While it is scarcely possible for anyone who has read Vinograd's article to return to the old interpretation in narrow terms of self-expression, that kind of reading is by no means rejected altogether; Vinograd's treatment of the painting does full justice to Wang Meng's individual creative genius. The new awareness of the context of creation, however, opens the way for deeper readings that find in the work Wang Meng's response to the predicament in which he and his relatives found themselves at a particular historical moment. The composition can be recognized as a variant of a type used by Wang and other landscapists to signify the idea of seclusion from the world, with the retreat located in a closed-in section of the picture; but here the sense of security usually conveyed by compositions of this type is powerfully violated in order to invest the composition with the special meaning that Wang means to express.

We saw earlier a few conventional examples of farewell paintings. A much finer one is by the Ming master Wen Cheng-ming (figure 1.19).[40] From the inscription we learn that when in 1555 Wen Cheng-ming's old tutor Te-fou, after living with the family for fifty years, was about to leave, Wen chose this painting, done some time earlier, for presentation to him as a farewell gift. It was not painted, that is, to serve that function, but was made to do so by the artist. The question then becomes: why was this picture seen as suitable for the occasion? And the answer must be that it conforms generally to a composition type that we know from numerous other examples of farewell paintings, works done specifically for that purpose. The composition offers a gradual, articulated passage from a clearly defined foreground (here occupied by mossy trees, which could be read as standing for age and integrity) into a dim distance; it can thus be taken as embodying in pictorial form the idea of the recipient's journey to some faraway place, and the loneliness of those who remain behind. Wen Cheng-ming may well have had such a use in mind when he painted it and gave it this expressive structure. If we say that "form follows function" in such works, our colleagues, especially architectural historians, will wince; it is not a formulation with much currency today. It nevertheless has a limited truth for a significant segment of Chinese painting, for which purely stylistic readings are thus inadequate.

"Taoist Temple in the Mountains" (figure 1.20), a painting that was included in the great Chinese Art Treasures exhibition of 1960 as a work of the tenth-century landscapist Tung Yüan, bears an inscription attributing it to that master written by the late Ming calligrapher Wang To (1592–1652), who, like his contemporary Tung Ch'i-ch'ang, performed the role of connoisseur and adviser to collectors; his inscriptions are found on many old paintings.[41] Dismissed as obviously later than the time of Tung Yüan by modern scholars, the painting has received little attention. The few who have written about it, from Wang To to myself, have been concerned with authorship, dating, and style. I suggested on stylistic grounds that it is by an early Ming follower of the Yüan landscapist Kao K'o-kung,[42] but have not until recently given serious consideration to the subject and the implications of the inscribed title, "A Grotto-Heaven and Palace in the Mountains."

When examined more closely (figure 1.21), it reveals a Taoist configuration known also in other paintings: a grotto through which one passes to reach a realm of immortals; a paradise beyond, sheltered from the outside world. The tall pine trees, palace buildings, rich green and blue colors, and heavy clouds all belong to the iconography of this type. The sheer size and technical proficiency of the work suggests a court artist, and we can place it provisionally as representing the kind of painting done by early Ming masters of the court academy for certain occasions, to carry political messages, in this case probably the familiar one of *ch'ao-yin* or "reclusion in court," or, as Peihua Lee puts it at the end of a study of this painting, "the ideal of constantly longing for escape from the pressure of official service."[43]

Chinese paintings in handscroll form are frequently followed by series of colophons, prose and poetic inscriptions written by contemporaries of the artist. On the question of how such a composite work came into being, we art historians were once inclined, when we thought about the matter at all, to suppose that the painting was done spontaneously by the artist as a gift for the recipient, and to consider the colophons as appendages to the painting, imagining that they were done at some social gathering of the participants, or that the owner of the work would invite a succession of literary men who visited him to inscribe their appreciations of it. Recent studies have suggested a quite different pattern, in which someone would organize the whole project systematically to produce a collaborative

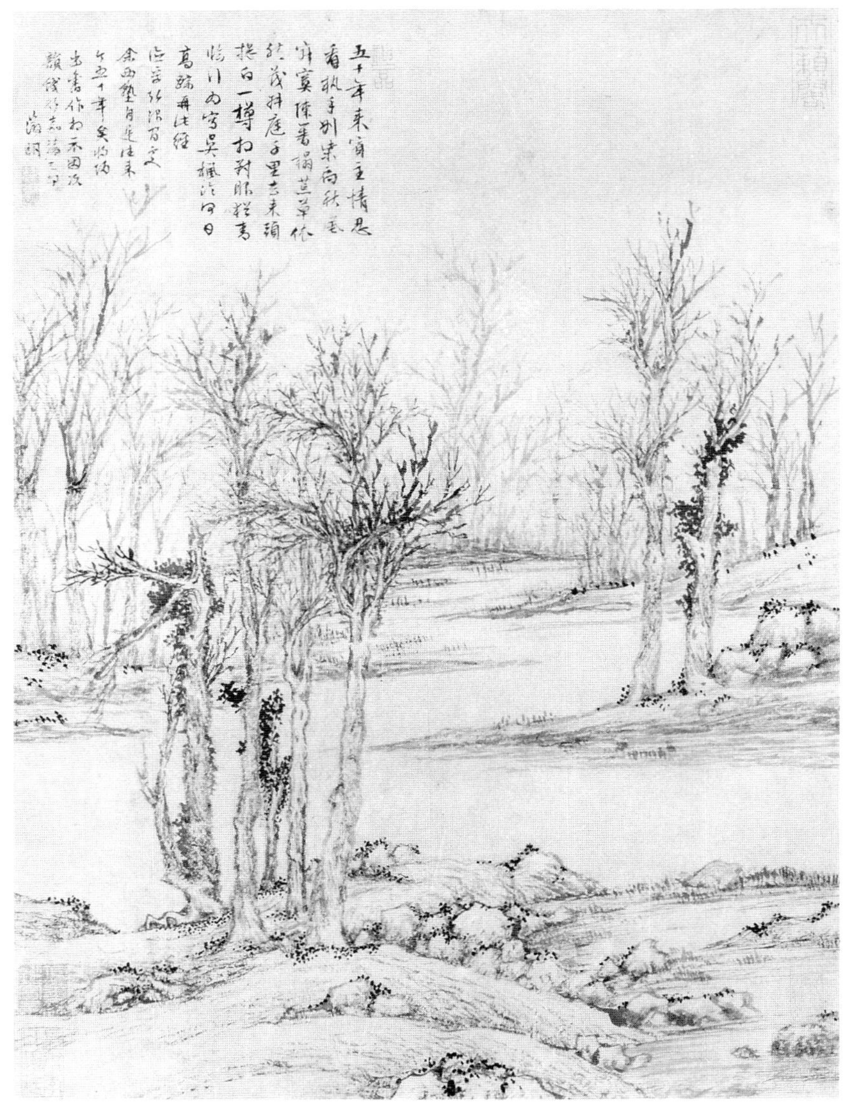

1.19. Wen Cheng-ming (1470–1559), "Farewell to Te-fou." Dated 1555. Hanging scroll, ink on paper, 54.1 × 41.3 cm. Shanghai Museum.

work for presentation to someone else, recruiting painter, calligrapher, and poets, and no doubt rewarding them for their contributions. David Sensabaugh's study of the paintings of the late Yüan litterateur Ku Te-hui's Jade Mountain Retreat, in which artists and calligraphers were enlisted by Ku himself as patron to produce collaborative works that were "kept in the hall or studio with which they were associated," was an important step toward a truer understanding of how these paintings came into existence; Sensabaugh cites other Yüan-period works of the same type to support his argument.[44]

A slightly earlier example is a series of illustrations to the "Returning Home" ode of T'ao Yüan-ming by the early fourteenth-century artist Ho Ch'eng, who was active in the Mongol court (figure 1.22); it was done to accompany a work of calligraphy, a copy of the ode that had been written in 1309. Chao Meng-fu and other court officials of the time added colophons. While there is no clear indication in the inscriptions of the kind of occasion for which it was made, a recorded inscription on another scroll of this subject from the same period and the same court circle is more informative. It reads, in part:

> The gentleman-official P'i of Ch'ing-chiang administered Nan-en with benevolent government. One day he left [this post] of his own will and returned home to live out his old age. Wang Shih-ch'u of Li-ling admires his noble integrity and, with a painting of T'ao Ch'ien's "Returning Home," has asked scholars and gentlemen of the inner court to compose poetry [to accompany it] which would then be given him.[45]

We know from other evidence that paintings of this theme, celebrating the poet's decision to leave official service and return home to live as a gentleman-farmer, were commonly presented on the occasion of an official's retirement.[46]

A substantial part of Ming landscape painting, especially that of the Wu School or Suchou masters of the middle Ming, is made up of what Anne Clapp calls "commemorative paintings,"[47] memorializing events such as birthdays and retirements, depicting someone's retreat or villa by the river, or portraying the person in some characterizing action or setting. Again, both Chinese and Western studies of these scrolls have mostly been written on the assumption that they were produced spontaneously at informal gatherings: the artist and a group of calligraphers and poets come together at a party, perhaps, and someone says, "Hey, gang, let's make a handscroll to express our exhilaration!" or whatever the Ming equivalent would be. But the regular patterns to be observed in the make-up of these scrolls, and the recurrence of the same group of colophonists and poets in one scroll after another, already cast doubt on this supposed pattern of impromptu creation.[48] Anne Clapp's recent study of a series of such scrolls for which T'ang Yin produced the paintings dispels it altogether. She writes:

> The memorial scrolls made by T'ang Yin were commissioned works, the commission being given by a patron with himself as subject and recipient of the work, or for presentation to another person, who would then of course be the subject. In either case it is evident that the patron planned the program of the scroll and coordinated the pictorial and literary components himself.[49]

And:

> It is clear from the content and phraseology of the prefaces [prose essays preceding the series of poems] that these scrolls were not intended for the private enjoyment of the recipient alone but were aimed at a larger audience of the literati class.[50]

And:

> Even this preliminary discussion will have made it apparent that few of these long handscrolls can have been executed on the inspiration of the moment, as conventional accounts of literati aesthetics would have us believe.[51]

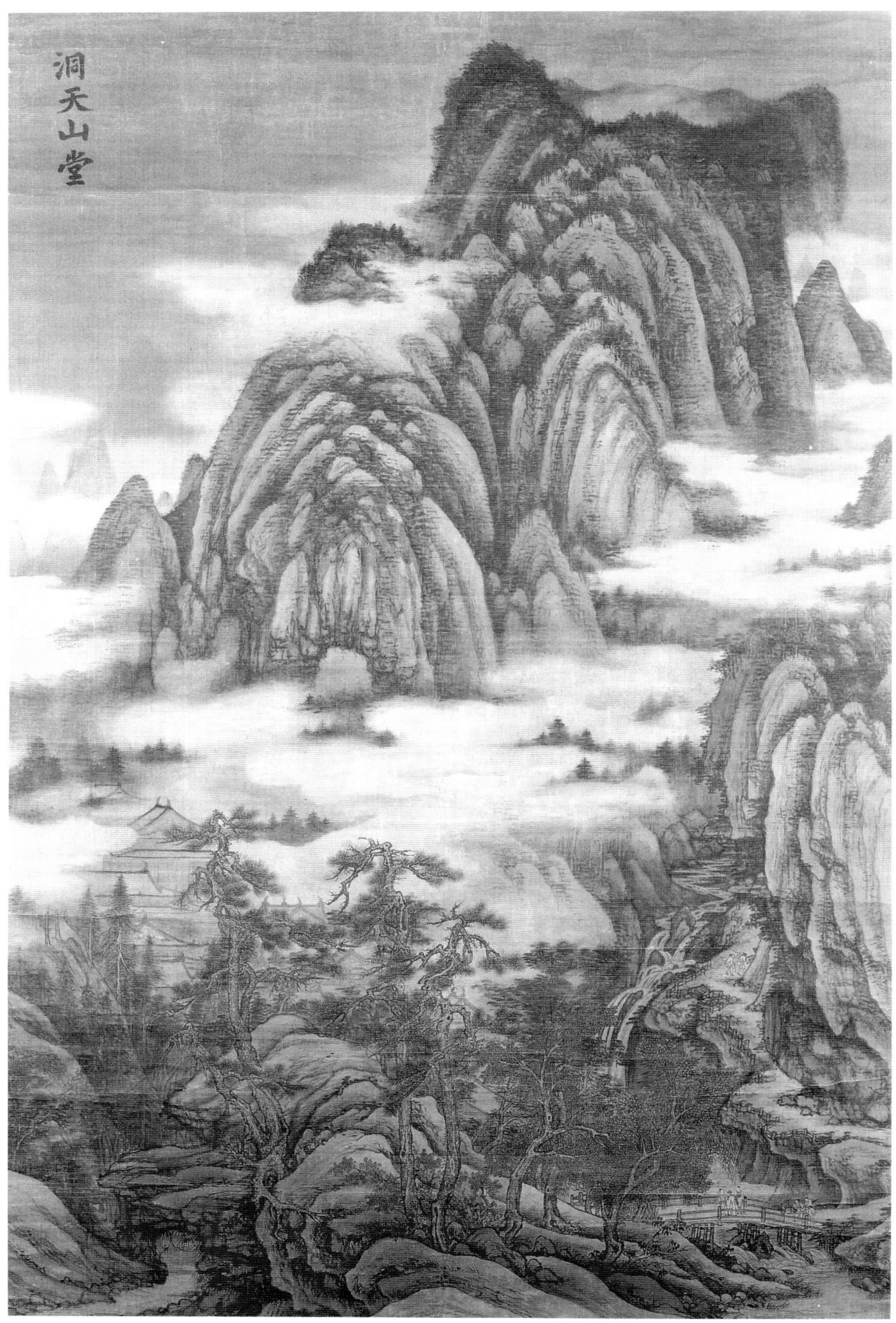

1.20. Anonymous late Yüan or early Ming dynasty (old attribution to Tung Yüan), "A Taoist Temple in the Mountains." Hanging scroll, ink and colors on silk, 183.2 × 121.2 cm. National Palace Museum, Taipei, Republic of China.

A good example discussed by Clapp (figure 1.23) is a scroll painted by T'ang Yin around 1496 to celebrate the opening of a studio called the Yeh-t'ing or "Rustic Pavilion" built on his estate by a young man named Ch'ien T'ung-ai, the son of a wealthy family in the medical profession.[52] To mark the occasion Ch'ien commissioned T'ang Yin to portray him in his new pavilion, then went to the famous statesman Wu K'uan to ask him for a preface. Wu K'uan obliged, concluding his essay by noting that all the famous writers of the day composed poems in honor of Ch'ien and his pavilion. T'ang Yin's painting presents him seated in it with brush and inkstone. This much is conventional; more particular is the boy servant approaching the pavilion with a hoe over his shoulder carrying a basket of herbs and fungi. Clapp writes: "The artist introduces these, possibly on the patron's instructions, as an al-

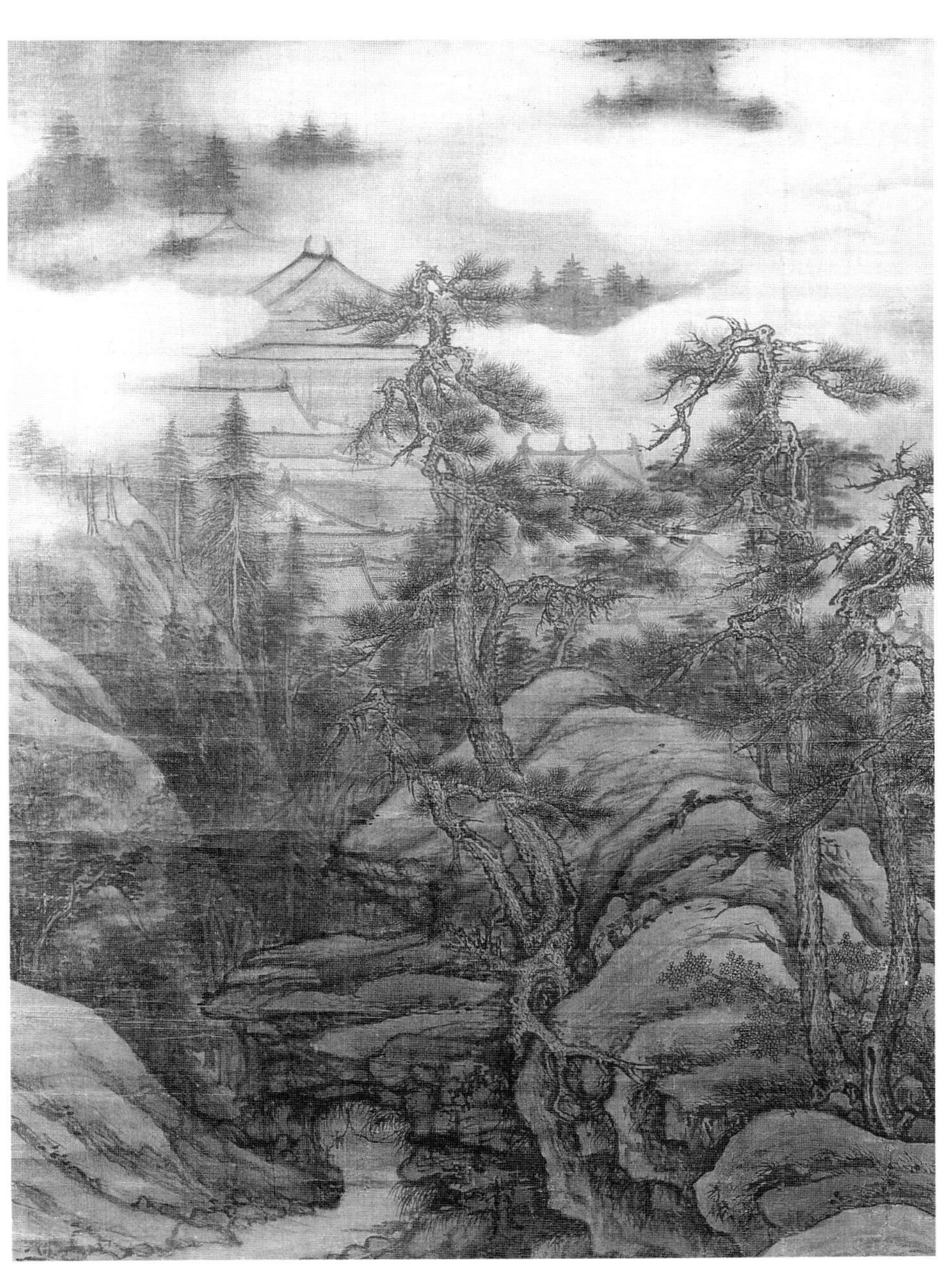

1.21. Detail from the same painting.

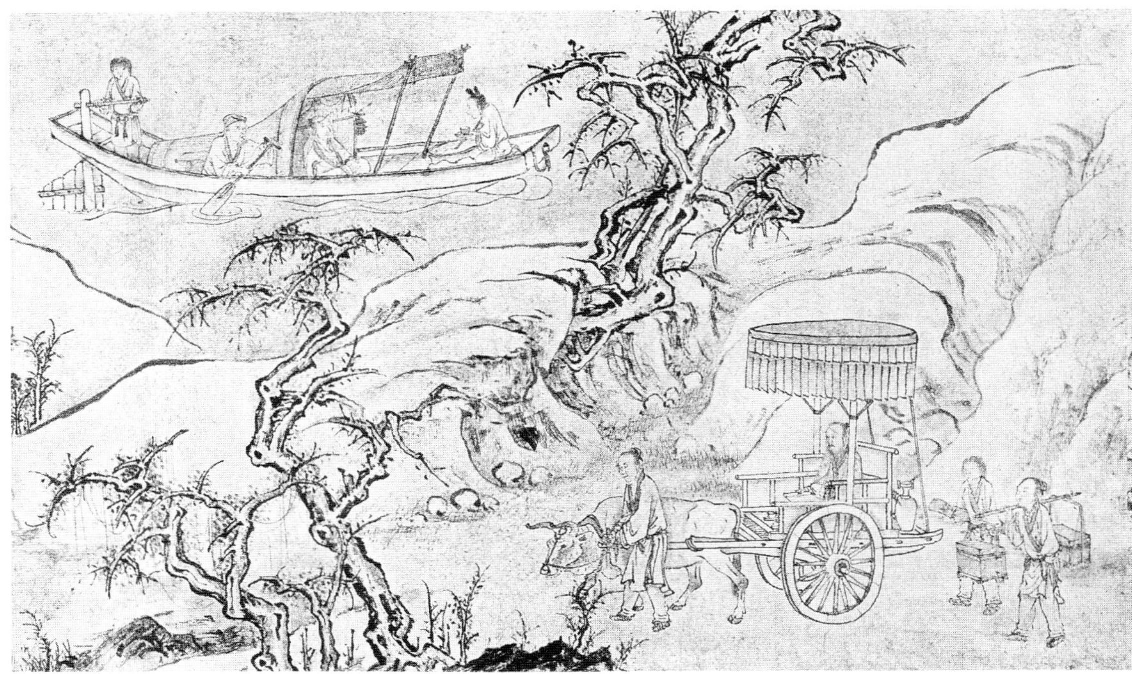

1.22. Ho Ch'eng, "Illustrations to T'ao Yüan-ming's 'Homecoming' Ode.
Early 14th cent. (accompanying inscription dated 1309). Handscroll, ink on paper, ht. 41 cm. Chi-lin Provincial Museum, Ch'ang-ch'un.

1.23. T'ang Yin (1470–1535), "Auspicious Clouds Over Yeh-t'ing (Wilderness Pavilion)."
Section of a handscroll, ink and colors on paper, 26.4 × 123.3 cm. Collection of Marie-Helene and Guy Weill, New York.

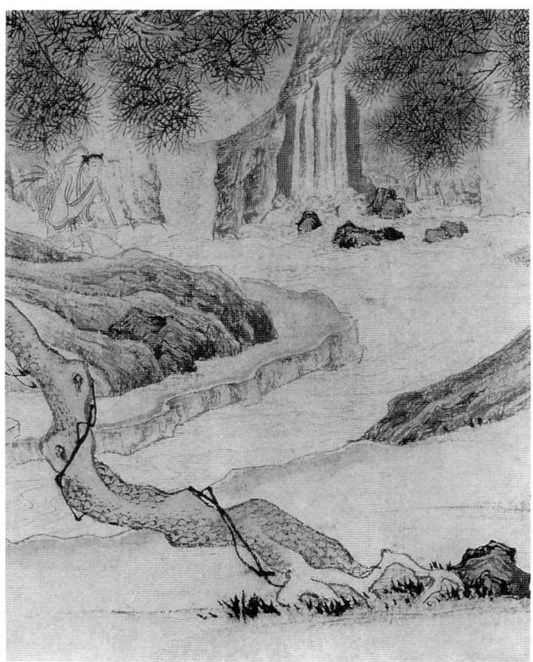

lusion to the Ch'ien family's reputation for medical skill. Their presence implies that [Ch'ien] T'ung-ai, then about twenty, had already acquired some expertise in medicine and wanted the painting to announce the fact."

Clapp discusses other cases in which the scrolls could be used as "promotional documents," for instance to advertise the skills of a *ch'in* player. In treating the style and imagery of the paintings, she takes into consideration their efficacy in conveying these messages as one factor behind the artist's choices, along with factors of inner-directed aesthetic preference, for accounts of the paintings that are in this respect fuller and better balanced than those we have usually been given in the past.

More examples will be introduced in subsequent chapters. Studies such as these alter our readings and interpretations of the paintings, which are affected by the knowledge and expectations we bring to the experience. Ernst Gombrich, writing of the necessity of determining the genre to which a work belongs before interpreting it, gives the example of an audience attending a tragedy in the mistaken belief that it is a parody, and laughing when they should be awe-stricken.[53] Art historians have made many mistakes of this kind in the past in their readings of Chinese paintings, and their interpretations have gone wrong accordingly. Some of their qualitative appraisals of the paintings may also be changed as we now read them in better-understood contexts.

Overall, we will not find our admiration for the Chinese artists diminished, but we will find new ways to admire and praise them—not as people who scrupulously lived up to, or even tried to live up to,the ideal code and constraints that the literati writers were forever urging on them, but as people who, working under what were often difficult conditions, subject to the pressures I have described, managed to keep their levels of originality and achievement as high as they did, producing impressive bodies of excellent work and sometimes masterpieces. Most of them, moreover, did this while managing through their painting to earn their livings, precarious as these often were, or at least to supplement their incomes and benefit significantly their material circumstances, in ways they could not be entirely open in acknowledging. The next chapter will explore some of these ways.

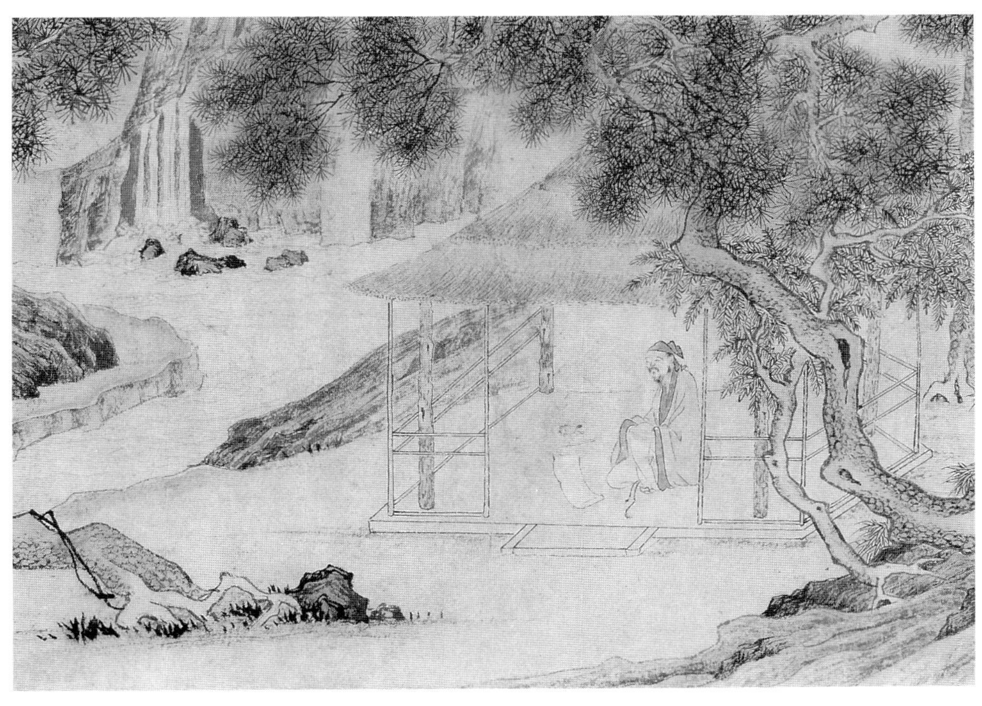

TWO

The Painter's Livelihood

There are a few inescapable conditions for our investigation that should be acknowledged at the outset. The evidence we have for all the topics to be treated is scattered and anecdotal; I have tried, with only partial success, to avoid letting these essays take on the same character. But to argue general practice from individual cases raises other dangers: how far can one extrapolate from a series of records of separate events? There is no other way, however, to explore these or other practices that the Chinese writers never wrote about in any extended way. And we can be sure, at least, that however we interpret it, the scattered data on artists amassed through this kind of search will be truer to their real situations than the conventional "biographies," which were always subject to the taboos and distortions described in the opening essay.[1] We should try also to distinguish apocryphal anecdotes, which belong to the myth I am attempting to cut through, from accounts that seem more acceptable as revealing the real situation of the artists and their clients. How can one make such distinctions? There is no easy answer, usually no way either to verify the stories or prove them false; all that can be said is that the apocryphal, idealizing anecdotes are more likely to occur in the artists' "biographies" and other encomia, the more reliable data in informal writings such as letters, casual jottings, and certain kinds of inscriptions. And even the invented anecdotes can supply information in their minor details, apart from the intended point of the stories.

Also, limitations in both the data and the space allotted here prevent a properly historical structuring of the accounts I will offer. It goes without saying that artists' practices differed from period to period, as well as by region, schools or lineages, social class, and other conditions. All these factors will be touched on, but cannot be exhaustively taken into account, in this exploratory study. One must make a beginning; I hope only to lay down provisional patterns that can be tested as more cases come to light. It should be understood, however, that since (for reasons to be suggested later) most of the available information comes from the late period of Chinese painting, the sixteenth century and after, the patterns and hypotheses should be taken as applying principally to that late period.

A final condition is that while the records may concern particular paintings, these are often identified only loosely, and in any case are mostly not the same paintings that have survived and are known to us. My illustrations, then, will mostly present other works by the same artists, or other depictions of the same subjects, serving only as aids to visualizing how the painting in question may have looked. I will try to indicate as I go the kinds of relevance the paintings reproduced might have to my discussions; sometimes the connection will be tenuous. Since I usually will not, for these reasons, be discussing the paintings themselves in any depth, and mostly not at all, the essays will of course be open to the charge of attending insufficiently to the works themselves—to being the kind of patronage study that, as Norman Bryson puts it, "will read anything rather than read the painting."[2] I hope that memories of my excruciatingly prolonged readings of particular Chinese paintings on other public occasions will serve to soften this charge, and I would point out also that it is precisely the paucity of studies like this one that hampers us from finding traces of the circumstances of patronage in the paintings themselves, as Bryson would have us do. Centuries of effective inhibition have ensured that we mostly do not know what the signs are, much less how to read them.

The Uses of Paintings

We can begin with a basic question: under what kinds of circumstances would a Chinese family, or a Chinese individual, want to acquire a painting? It could be simply for decorative hanging in the house, or for private enjoyment, or to impress visitors with the host's wealth and taste (figure 2.1). Paintings were needed in well-appointed households for auspicious or apotropaic functions, bringing blessings or warding off baleful forces—pictures of the demon-subduer Chung K'uei are good examples of the latter. A late Ming text written around 1615–20, the *Chang-wu chih* (a title which, according to James Watt, can be rendered either as "On Superfluous Things" or as "On the Things of This World")[3] contains a lengthy guide to the appropriate subjects for scrolls to be hung during successive months of the year and on particular holidays.[4]

There is no earlier list of this kind, and the reason why will serve to introduce a recurring subtheme in these essays: the profound changes in the character of Chinese society beginning from the late Ming, the later sixteenth and early seventeenth century.[5] The rising affluence brought about by a burgeoning mercantile economy was spawning in this period a large number of new collectors who needed the kind of advice the *Chang-wu chih* provides, and writers and publishers were meeting the demand with a larger output than ever before of catalogs of works of art, compendia for collectors, guides to connoisseurship and good taste. Rules for elegant and ceremonial living that had traditionally been transmitted orally and by example within a restricted number of gentry families were thus opened to a wide reading public of people with enough money and leisure to pursue this way of life. The author of *Chang-wu chih,* Wen Chen-heng (1585–

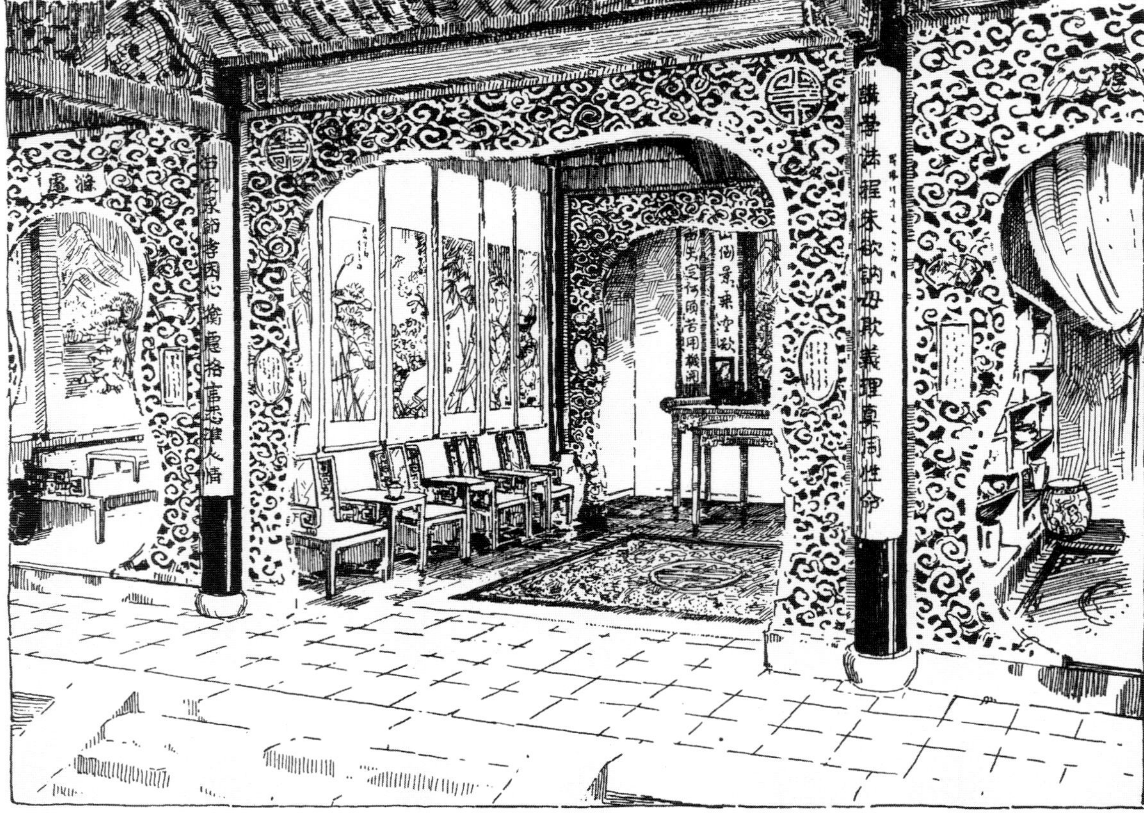

2.1. General View of the Main Hall of a Chinese House. Drawing by Tai Nien-tz'u. From R. H. van Gulik, *Chinese Pictorial Art as Viewed by the Connoisseur,* fig. 3.

1645), himself a minor painter, was great-grandson of the great sixteenth-century artist Wen Cheng-ming and scion of a clan whose members, besides being gentry landowners and officeholders (Wen Cheng-ming briefly held a post in the Han-lin Academy; Wen Chen-heng's elder brother Chen-meng was Grand Secretary for an even briefer period) had served through several generations as aesthetic arbiters and advisers for artistic transactions.[6] Wen Chen-heng was thus perfectly qualified to provide instruction for those less favored in their upbringing and family backgrounds.

Part of the demand for paintings, then, was from individuals and families that needed a supply of them, old or new, for this kind of use. The collectors' guides advise that paintings should be changed regularly, not left hanging for long periods, so that one would not get tired of them and the scrolls would not suffer from overexposure to dust and drying.[7] Paintings of appropriate subjects could also be commissioned or requested for hanging and presentation on special occasions—birthdays, weddings, retirements, and the like. A twelve-scroll series done in 1652 by Lan Ying and a portrait specialist named Ch'en Yu-yin for hanging at someone's birthday party (figure 2.2), showing the man surrounded by Taoist fairies and longevity symbols, is an example that seems perhaps overadapted to the occasion; one wonders how often the series would have been hung afterward.

Most welcome of all from the artist's standpoint, however, was the collector who simply admired his work and wanted an example of it, whatever the subject, for no special purpose other than to arouse aesthetic pleasure. Paintings acquired on this basis were appreciated, just as old paintings were, primarily for their artistic qualities. The artist who supplied functional pictures on demand was clearly at the low end of the social scale, while the one whose paintings were sought after as works of art tended to be (but was not always) at the upper end. And the means by which the paintings were asked for, obtained, and paid for varied accordingly. The low end was ordinarily occupied by professional masters, the upper end by amateurs or pseudo-amateurs, along with professional artists who had won enough acclaim and popularity to enjoy this status and this degree of artistic independence.

Such was the underlying, simple pattern, which I will now go on to muddy up, since artists and their clients, as always, followed no set rules and interacted in more complicated and interesting ways than these. One should, nevertheless, keep the pattern in the background as an ideal construct, like the professional-amateur distinction itself, off which the particular instances were played, and without which they cannot be fully understood.

Obtaining a Painting I: Commissions and Letters

Obtaining a painting that one needed for some occasion from a professional master was relatively simple: one placed the order, received

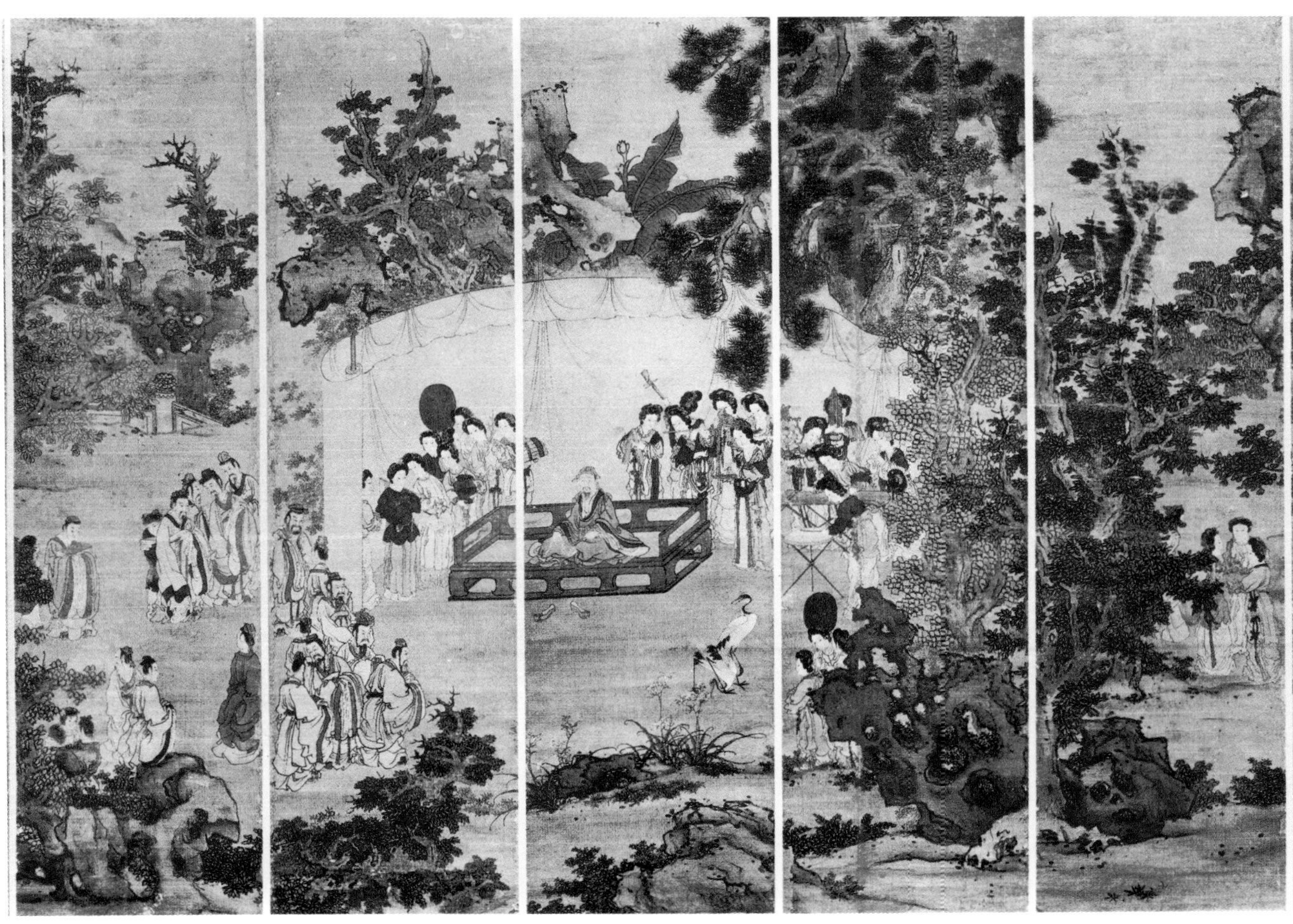

2.2. Lan Ying and Ch'en Yü-yin, "A Gentleman Celebrating His Birthday." Dated 1652. Screen consisting of twelve hanging scrolls, ink and colors on silk, each 187 × 51.5 cm. From Christie's auction catalog, New York, June 23, 1983, no. 687.

2.3. Ch'iu Ying, "Divine Realm at the Peach-Blossom Spring."
Hanging scroll, ink and colors on silk, 175 × 66.7 cm. Tientsin City Museum. From *Chung-kuo mei-shu ch'üan-chi* 7, plate 63.

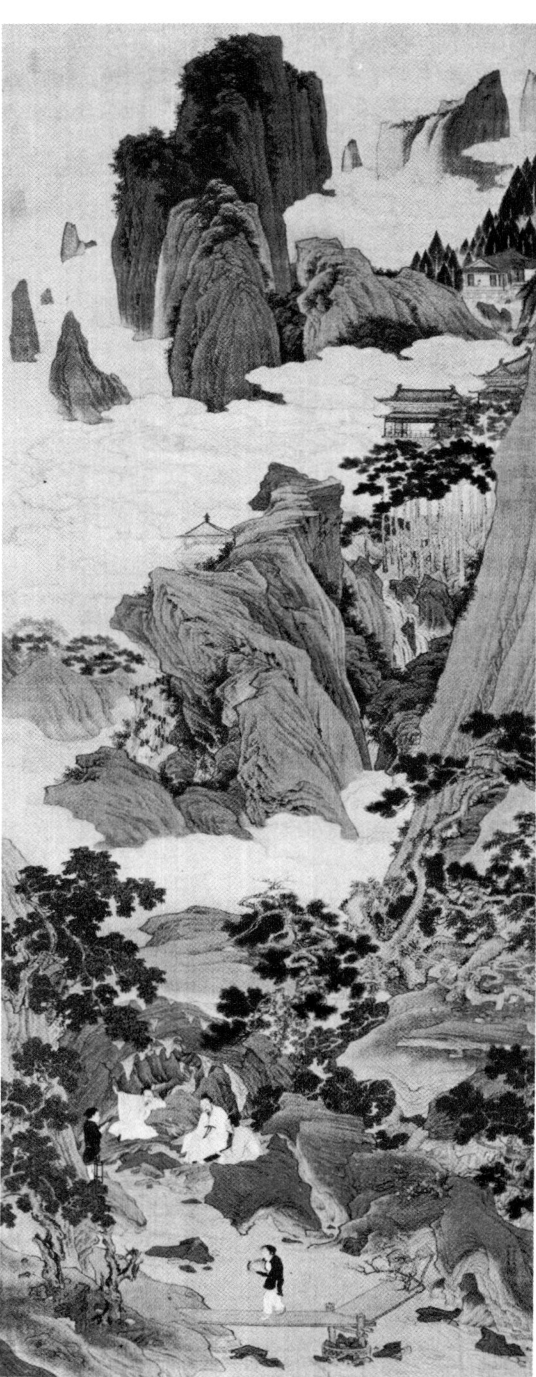

the painting, made payment. A preserved letter from the Suchou painter Ch'iu Ying (ca. 1495–1552) to one of his patrons, an official who held a post in the Han-lin Academy at the imperial court, reveals clearly how it was done.[8] The man had requested a birthday painting, no doubt expecting one of Ch'iu's highly finished works full of auspicious imagery (figure 2.3), and the artist responded. After an obsequious opening, Ch'iu writes:

> Recently you favored me with an order to make a painting for a birthday celebration. It has been respectfully completed and hereby presented for approval and acceptance. When you place another order, just send a word to me and it will be done and delivered; but please do not place any more orders through Hsi-ch'ih. Although he and I are relatives, we do not get along at all. Kindly keep this in mind. The other two paintings will be delivered soon. Not yet recovered [from an illness], I have written this in too careless a hand. Hoping for your forgiveness, I am
>
> Ying, who bows again, putting this in the envelope, on the sixth day.

Ch'iu adds a postscript: "I heard that in your house many Hsi-hsien pills have been prepared. I want to beg for a few doses. If you have [Hsi-hsien] leaves, please give me some too. Please be sure to have a copy of the Manual on Health printed for me . . . Also, I received the payment in silver from your brother Fang-hu. Please be sure to give him my thanks. . . [Returned are] the remainders of the silk."

Besides recording the simple transaction, the letter touches on several other issues of interest: the use of a go-between; the fact that the patron provided the silk on which the painting was to be done; and the practice of presenting the artist with gifts (the medicine and the Manual of Health that Ch'iu requests) in addition to, or frequently instead of, monetary payment.

Most commonly, in this simple pattern, the seeker after a painting would send someone, usually a servant, to place the order, and again later to receive the painting. In a play by the early Ch'ing writer Li Yü—fictional, but no doubt basically faithful to accepted practice—two government officials send their servants with request letters to Tung Ch'i-ch'ang.[9] The first asks for a birthday poem and a preface to a book; the servant delivers the letter, makes the request orally, and says that another messenger will come in a few days to pick up the finished writings. The second servant comes to ask for a painting and a calligraphy fan, presenting the letter from his master and saying he will wait while Tung does them. Tung, deeply upset, complains to his friend Ch'en Chi-ju, not so much about doing the painting and calligraphy under pressure as over having to write a reply to the official's letter. No mention is made of payment, which in Tung's case, since he himself held official rank and was thus far above Ch'iu Ying in social level, would probably have been in the form of gifts, or some extended transaction involving mutual obligations, instead of in money.

There are many other instances of servants bearing commissions, payment, and paintings back and forth. An anecdote concerning the late nineteenth-century Shanghai master Jen Po-nien relates the plight of a servant whom two of Jen's friends, visiting the artist, discover weeping on his doorstep: since the painter will not finish a long-promised and paid-for picture and give it to him, the servant is afraid to return to his master, who will think he has stolen the money. The two men escort the servant inside and force Jen to complete the picture while they wait.[10]

In another case, one of the patrons of the early Ch'ing landscapist Kung Hsien, a man named Liang I-chang, sent a servant with a letter to the artist apologizing that he himself was too busy to come to visit, much as he wanted to do so, but that the servant would wait and bring the painting back. Liang added in his letter that he would like a composition "dense as if there is no sky, empty as if there were no ground."[11] I will turn later to the question of how far the recipient could properly stipulate the subject and style of the picture; in this case, Liang's request sounds more like an expression of appreciation for Kung Hsien's own stylistic preferences, and an acquiescence to them (figure 2.4).

Another would-be patron of Kung Hsien, a man named Hu Ts'ung-chung, wrote a letter to the artist saying that he had heard that the painter intended to spend the summer in seclusion. Since he intended to request a painting from him, he wrote, he would send a servant-boy to live in the same neighborhood and keep the artist supplied with basic necessities such as rice and salt. And he himself would come by from time to time to visit. Would this be all right? The artist's response is not preserved; one may hope that the determined Mr. Hu got his painting.[12]

Requests to artists for paintings, then, were commonly sent in the form of letters. Many of this kind are included in the various printed collections of letters by Ming and Ch'ing writers, and some actual examples have survived. Moreover, Anne Burkus has recently called our attention to the existence of letter-writing manuals that contain, among other types, models for letters to artists.[13] Examples of these manuals date from as early as the T'ang dynasty, but they become especially popular from the seventeenth century, when, as noted earlier, a demand for such instructional books was created by the sharp increase in the number of well-to-do participants in cultural pursuits of all kinds. The manuals, again as one might expect, advise the use of a deferential tone in writing to artists, perhaps in the belief that anyone who needed to consult such a manual would be especially well-advised to adopt a posture of modesty. Original, preserved letters from clients and patrons tend to be more direct. A model letter quoted by Burkus begins (in her rendering):

> On the paper, smoky clouds; at the tip of the brush, watery rocks. What is this thing? You, sir, are able to make clever contest with the work of Heaven

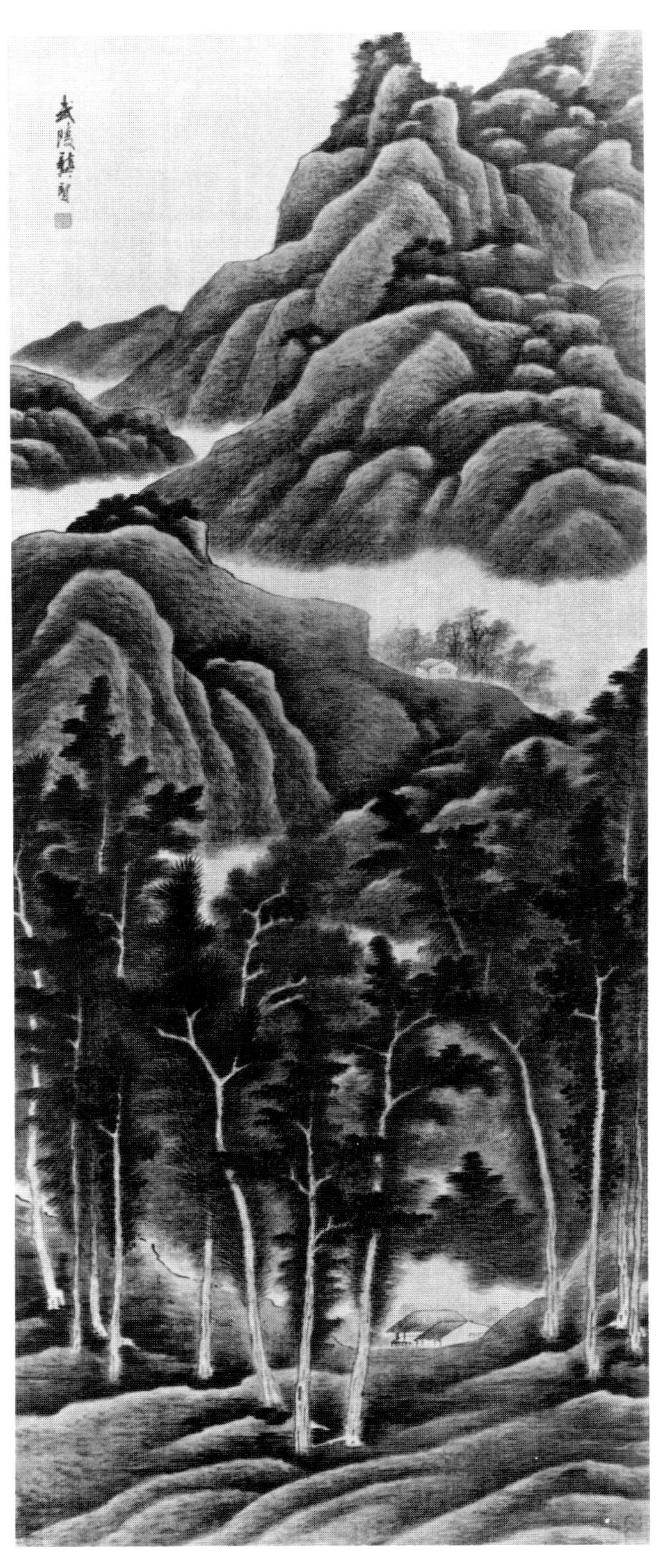

2.4. Kung Hsien (1618–1689), "Summer Mountains After Rain." Hanging scroll, ink on silk, 141.9 × 57.6 cm. Nanking Museum. From *Nan-ching po-wu-yüan ts'ang-hua,* Shanghai, 1981, plate 20.

. . . I beg that you bestow upon me several pictures from your flourishing wet brush to hang in my central room. Thus the three tributaries of the Xiang River, the Five Marchmounts, the stone chambers of Mounts Heng and Lu, may be seen without emerging from out my door.[14]

Another manual from the early nineteenth century, similar in purpose, suggests the following opening:

Your brush is so flourishing that you can compete with Ching [Hao] and Kuan [T'ung]; it is so shining that you can succeed [such great artists of antiquity as] Ku [K'ai-chih] and Lu [T'an-wei]. The smoky clouds splashed on the paper are so wonderful that it is as if spring had come—what you achieve can be compared to the work of Creation.[15]

Once the painter had been won over by such flattery, presumably, one could go on to make one's request, in suitably oblique language. The editors advise, however, that one's desires for particular subjects and styles should be stated only in a very general way, so as not to offend the painter by cramping his artistic independence.

Obtaining a Painting II: Go-Betweens and Agents

When, for whatever reason, clients did not want to approach artists directly, or even by letter, go-betweens were employed. The *chung-jen or chung-chien jen,* literally the "person between," was a fixture in all kinds of social and economic exchanges in China, facilitating transactions, carrying proposals and responses back and forth. The go-between could serve as middleman and guarantor, responsible for payment being made; the seller need not even know the identity of the principal, unless he failed to receive payment.[16] The go-between might be a relative of one of the parties, or simply someone trusted by both; for transactions involving works of art, he was frequently an expert who could advise also on price and, for antiques, on authenticity. Artists sometimes augmented their income by acting in this capacity when asked, turning to profit their special intimacy with paintings, collectors, and the market. Wen Cheng-ming's son Wen Chia (1501–1583) is one who did this, as his father himself had done on occasion. The late Ming writer Chan Ching-feng tells us that in his time such go-betweens received 10 percent of the sale price, including their fee for appraisal.[17]

Go-betweens employed to approach literati amateur or quasi-amateur artists for their paintings had an additional function. In these cases, the transactions were thought of as social, not economic exchanges; when the artist was a person of some status, one should properly obtain a painting from him as an item in some exchange of favors and obligations, or in return for gifts, not by commission and promise of cash payment. Such nonmonetary transactions took place, however, within the great Chinese institution of *kuan-hsi* networks, webs of relationships *(kuan-hsi)* based in principle on *jen-ch'ing* or human feeling, and on reciprocity, rather than on considerations of material gain; and one could not have such a relationship with a stranger. When the client lacked direct access to the painter, then, he would utilize a go-between to intercede for him, someone who had the necessary *kuan-hsi,* often one of the artist's relatives or close associates.[18] A few examples will illustrate the types of situations in which go-betweens were used.

The litterateur and playwright K'ung Shang-jen, a prominent patron of artists in early Ch'ing Nanking, met the great Individualist painter Shih-t'ao at a party in 1689 and afterward wrote to his friend the poet Cho Erh-kan, who had been master of ceremonies at this gathering: "[Shih-t'ao's] poetry and paintings are like the man himself. We met briefly at the poetry gathering, but I was unable to express my hopes. When we parted, he presented me with a beautiful painted fan which I showed to my friends . . . I wanted to request an album of paintings from him that I might look at when composing poetry. but I feared making such a direct request and hope you might convey it for me."[19] Go-betweens of this type acted on behalf of the client in approaching the artist.

Another type of go-between, who might more properly be called the artist's agent, handled his commissions and promoted the sale of his works. People serving in this capacity could be motivated by friendship, or by disinterested admiration for the artist, or by expectation of commissions, or any combination of these. The case of a collector who ordered and received an album of landscapes from the early Ch'ing Individualist master Chu Ta or Pa-ta Shan-jen through his agent was introduced in the first essay. The agent, Ch'eng Ching-e, was the father of the artist Ch'eng Cheng-k'uei, who later claimed that his father had "discovered" Pa-ta Shan-jen and persuaded others of the value of his paintings.[20]

The sixteenth-century calligrapher P'eng Nien served as this kind of agent for the painter Ch'ien Ku in obtaining an important commission. He writes to the painter: "I am sending you a blank silk album. Hu-liang [a man named Chang Hsien-i] engaged me to ask you for an album of pictures of [scenes on the route to] Mt. Pai-yüeh [in southern Anhui] so that he can send it to the River Official Ho. I hope that within a day or two I can assemble a few woodblock-cutters to work on it. Master Ho has a great understanding of literature and will certainly appreciate your ingenious art. I beg you with all sincerity to finish your pictures in one or two days."[21] An extant album by Ch'ien Ku, "Pictorial Record of a Journey from T'ai-ts'ang to Yangchou" (figure 2.5), can no doubt be taken as an approximation of what Hu-liang expected.

Behind P'eng Nien's terse communication

2.5. Ch'ien Ku, "Pictorial Record of a Journey from T'ai-ts'ang to Yangchou."
Leaf from an album of 32 leaves, ink and light colors on paper, each 28.5 × 39.1 cm. National Palace Museum, Taipei, Republic of China.

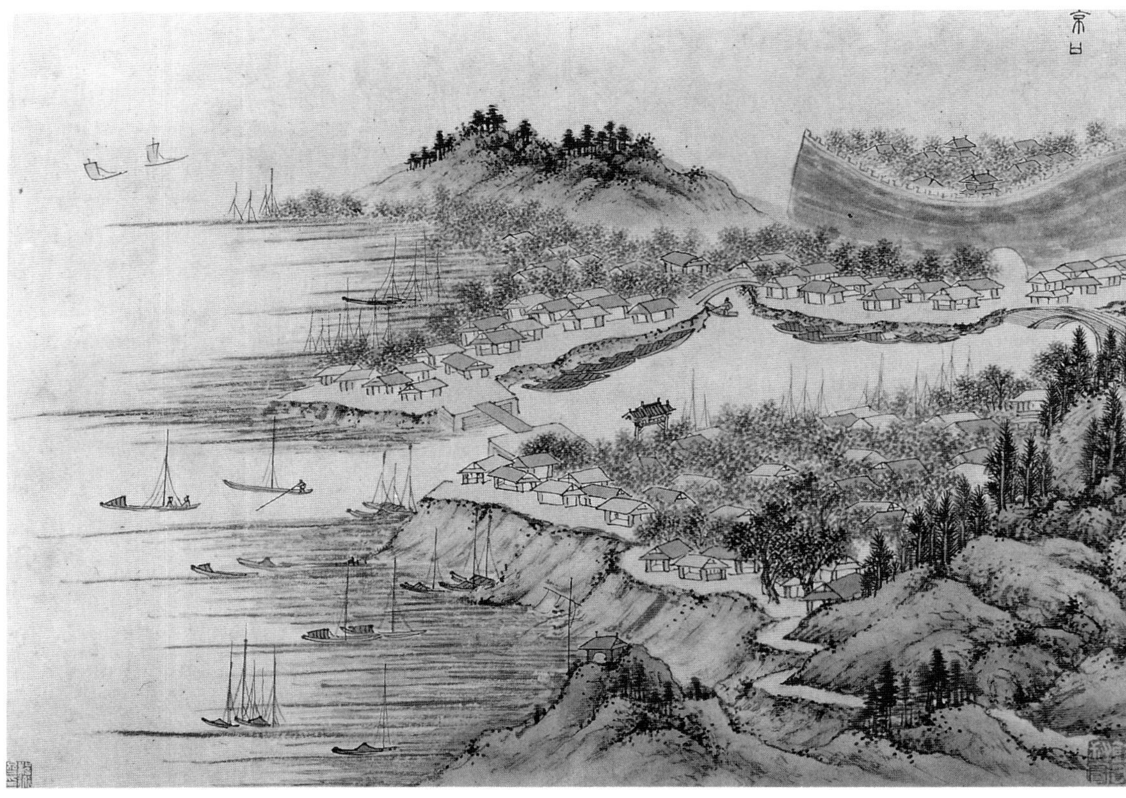

we can imagine a set of circumstances like those that produced the "Landscapes of T'ai-p'ing County" by Hsiao Yün-ts'ung in 1647–48.[22] Some local official is leaving a post where he has served for some years; his friends commission, or the official himself commissions, a series of pictures of notable scenes in the region he has administered, as remembrances, and these are reproduced by woodblock for dissemination among his friends, to honor his period of service.[23]

A case of an artist insisting on using a go-between to avoid engaging too directly in a transaction with the recipient is that of Wang Fu (1362–1416), an artist whose status was somewhat ambiguous in that he held minor posts at the imperial court in Nanking but was also active there as a painter.[24]

> One day, [after] retiring from court, Mu Sheng, the Duke of Ch'ien-ning, came running after him [Wang Fu], shouting his name. Fu made no answer. A colleague said to him, "That is the Duke of Ch'ien-ning." Fu replied, "I heard him, but he only wants a painting from me." Sheng [then] came up to him and determinedly asked for a painting. Fu only nodded. After several years, Sheng wrote a letter to inquire if Fu had started to paint. Whereupon he [Wang Fu] remarked, "I cannot just give my painting to the Duke of Ch'ien [-ning]; the Duke's guest is P'ing Chung-wei, my friend. It is through my friend that it [the painting] will come. When the Duke of Ch'ien [-ning] begs [P'ing for the work], only then will it be possible [for the Duke to have it]."[25]

Shan Guolin argues that the use of go-betweens in the earlier centuries, up to the eighteenth, was more likely to be a matter of friendship, while from the Ch'ien-lung era (1735–95) on it was more institutionalized and openly commercial. The literati painters in this late period, he maintains, because they were in greater need of selling their works for their livelihoods, had closer relations with agents and dealers, and also accorded them more respect than before. In support of the last point he cites a letter from P'an Kung-shou (1741–1794) to a family member asking him to turn over some birthday paintings for sale to a certain dealer in brushes and ink named Lin Hao-sheng, and adding that when Lin comes he should be treated politely.[26]

However, as we have seen in a number of examples, the more commercialized employment of agentlike go-betweens was not unknown in the earlier centuries; and even in the late period it could still be motivated by friendship, or by admiration for the artist. The early nineteenth-century figure master Fei Tan-hsü, a specialist in pictures of beautiful women who also occasionally did portraits (figure 2.6), began his career selling paintings from a stall on the Ch'eng-huang Hill in Hangchou. T'ang I-fen, a well-established landscape painter and official, happened by, admired his paintings, and decided to help him. T'ang introduced Fei to a newly rich man who wanted to associate with artists and scholars, telling him that Fei would become famous in the future. The man took Fei into his home and paid him a salary; he also introduced Fei to his friends, and gave him the opportunity to study his collection of old paintings. Fei's reputation rose rapidly.[27]

Jen Hsiung (1820–1857), an artist still little-known outside China but one of the brilliantly versatile masters of recent Chinese painting, had his career launched in a similar way. A noted litterateur of the time named Yao Hsieh found him selling paintings on the streetside and took him into his household as an artist-in-residence.[28] Jen Hsiung's major project for Yao Hsieh to repay his hospitality was a series of albums illustrating lines from Yao's poems; a number of these albums survive (figure 2.7). On one occasion, the story goes, Yao Hsieh held a banquet at which playing cards designed by Jen Hsiung were used for the drinking games. After the guests had admired them, Yao called in the artist and introduced him. Everybody ordered paintings.[29]

Quite a few letters between artists and their agents are preserved and, like the passages from Cheng Min's diary quoted earlier, help to

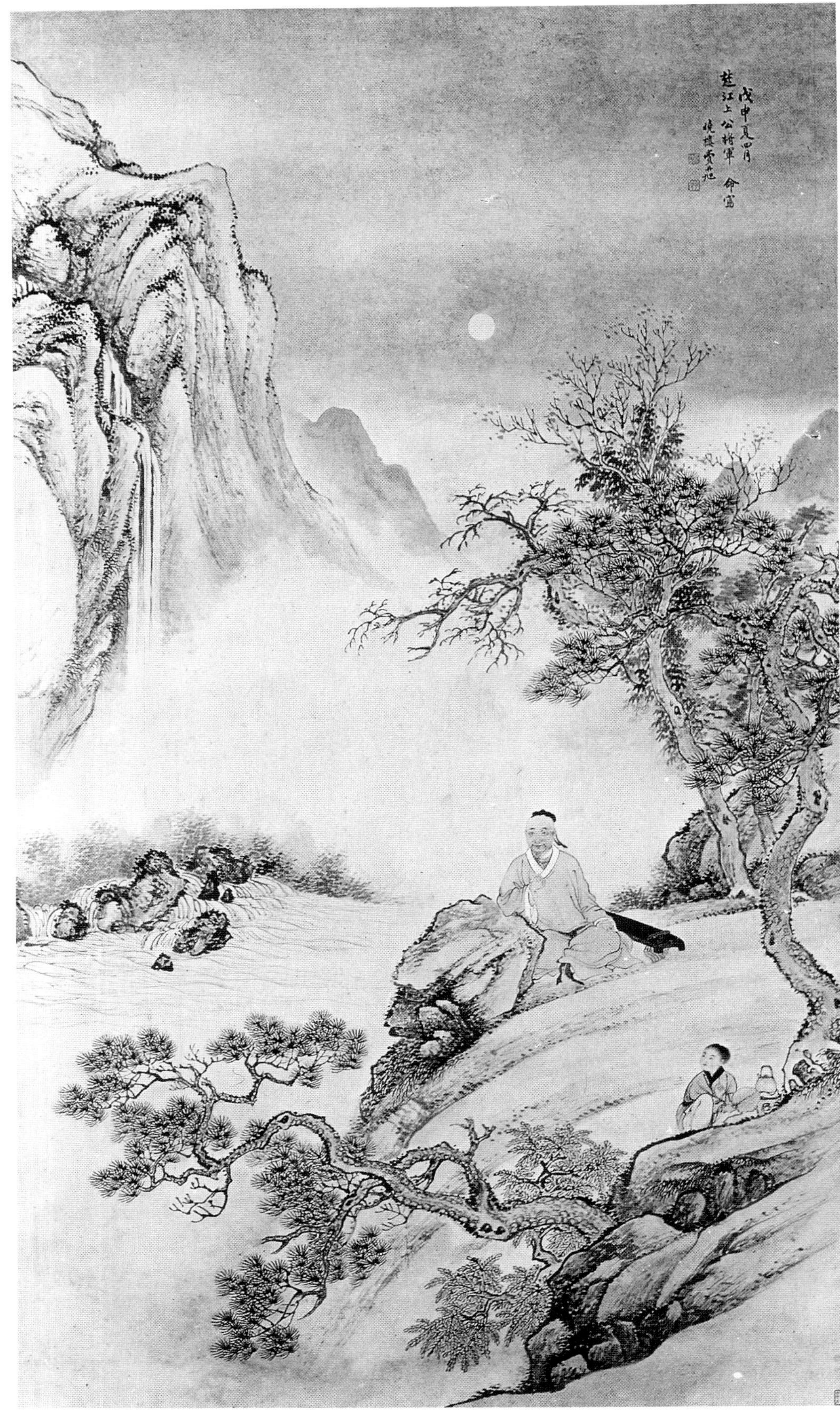

2.6. Fei Tan-hsü, "Portrait of General Ch'u-chiang by Moonlight." Dated 1848. Hanging scroll, ink and colors on paper, 174 × 97 cm. Kuang-tung Provincial Museum. From *Kuang-tung sheng po-wu-kuan ts'ang-hua chi* (Canton, 1986), plate 201.

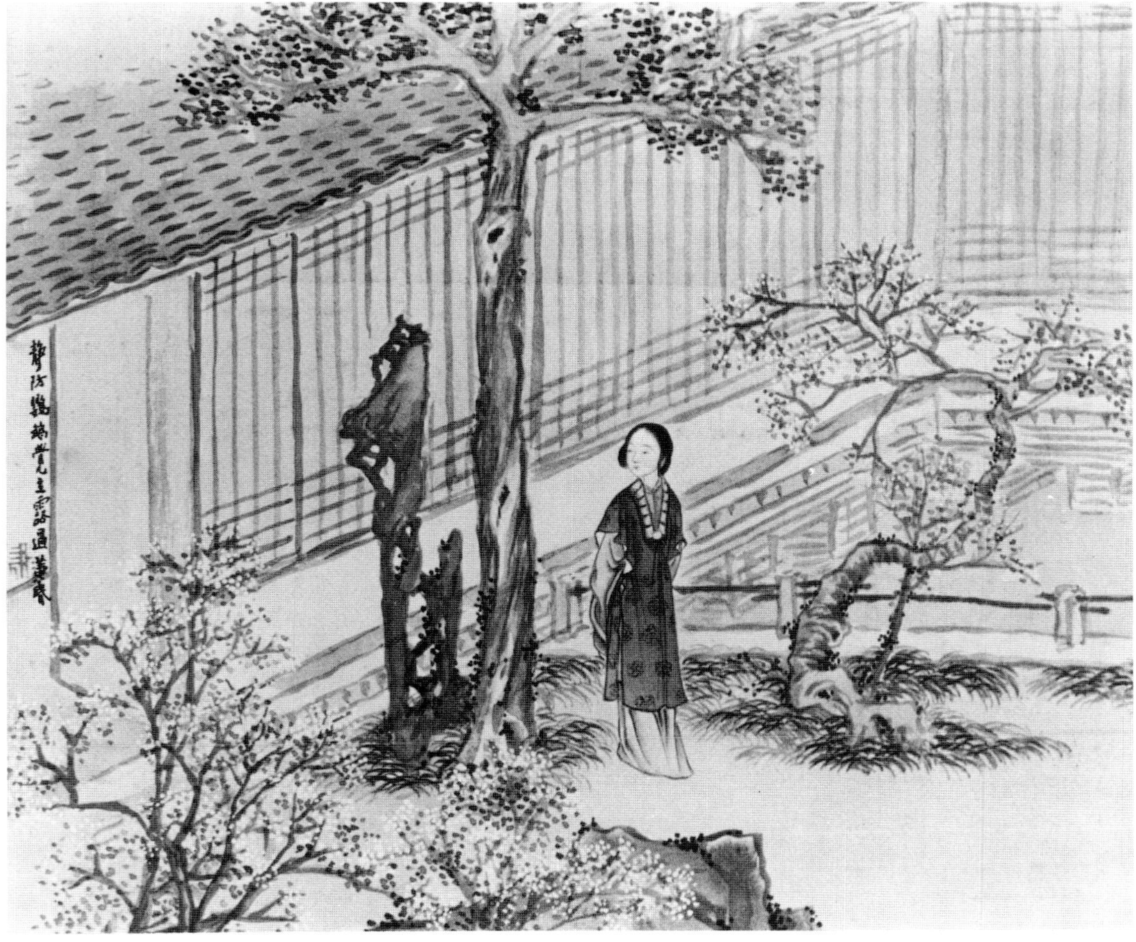

2.7. Jen Hsiung, "Lady in Garden."
Leaf from series of albums, 120 leaves illustrating poems by Yao Hsieh. Ink and colors on paper, each leaf 27.3 × 32.5 cm. Palace Museum, Peking. From *Jen Hsiung Yao Hsieh shih-i t'u-ts'e* (Shanghai, n.d.).

round out the economic realities of the artists' lives. In one of these Hua Yen, a versatile master active in the mid-eighteenth century, writes to a dealer named Huo T'ing complaining about the amount he received from the sale of his paintings; Huo had sent him only 60 percent of the agreed-on amount, and Hua wants the other 40 percent.[30] In another letter to his agent Chang Ssu-chiao, Hua writes: "The 'Pines and Cranes' picture I gave you was painted with great effort, because I am old. I hope you will consider this and ask for more money than the amount established before."[31] A number of pines-and-cranes paintings by Hua Yen are extant (figure 2.8). A certain Chang Yü-chang wrote in a letter to the Orthodox School master Wang Hui, for whom he seems to have acted as a kind of agent, urging him to finish a number of paintings for which the clients had already paid; in another letter he writes that he has acquired ten of Wang's paintings from a third party, and now sends them to Wang to be inscribed, presumably for sale to others.[32]

From the styles used by the late eighteenth–early nineteenth century landscapist Hsi Kang (figure 2.9), which typically follow such models as Ni Tsan, Huang Kung-wang, and the Orthodox masters of the early Ch'ing, we might assume him to have been a pure-minded, leisure-time artist unconcerned with considerations of gain; these styles were still closely associated with the literati-amateurs. But Hsi's preserved letters reveal him working hard to sell his paintings, sometimes through more than one agent at a time. A letter to a certain Ch'ieh-shan, evidently a patron who acted as his agent, reveals that Hsi delivered paintings to him on a regular basis; Ch'ieh-shan would arrange to transfer them to other customers.[33] In a letter to one Nien-lü, another of his agents, Hsi reports on his progress in coping with commissions at hand, complains that he needs more time if he is to keep the quality of his works high, and writes about commissions he had accepted through still another agent.[34] In another letter, accompanying a group of fan paintings and albums turned over to one Hsi Li-t'ien (probably a relative) for sale, Hsi Kang discusses the purchase of painting materials and complains about being pressed by debtors.[35] Like Cheng Min in chapter 1, Hsi Kang was responding to a demand for pictures expressive of a state of pure leisure and freedom from worldly entanglements that had little resemblance to his own personal circumstances.

There was nothing new in this. Chinese

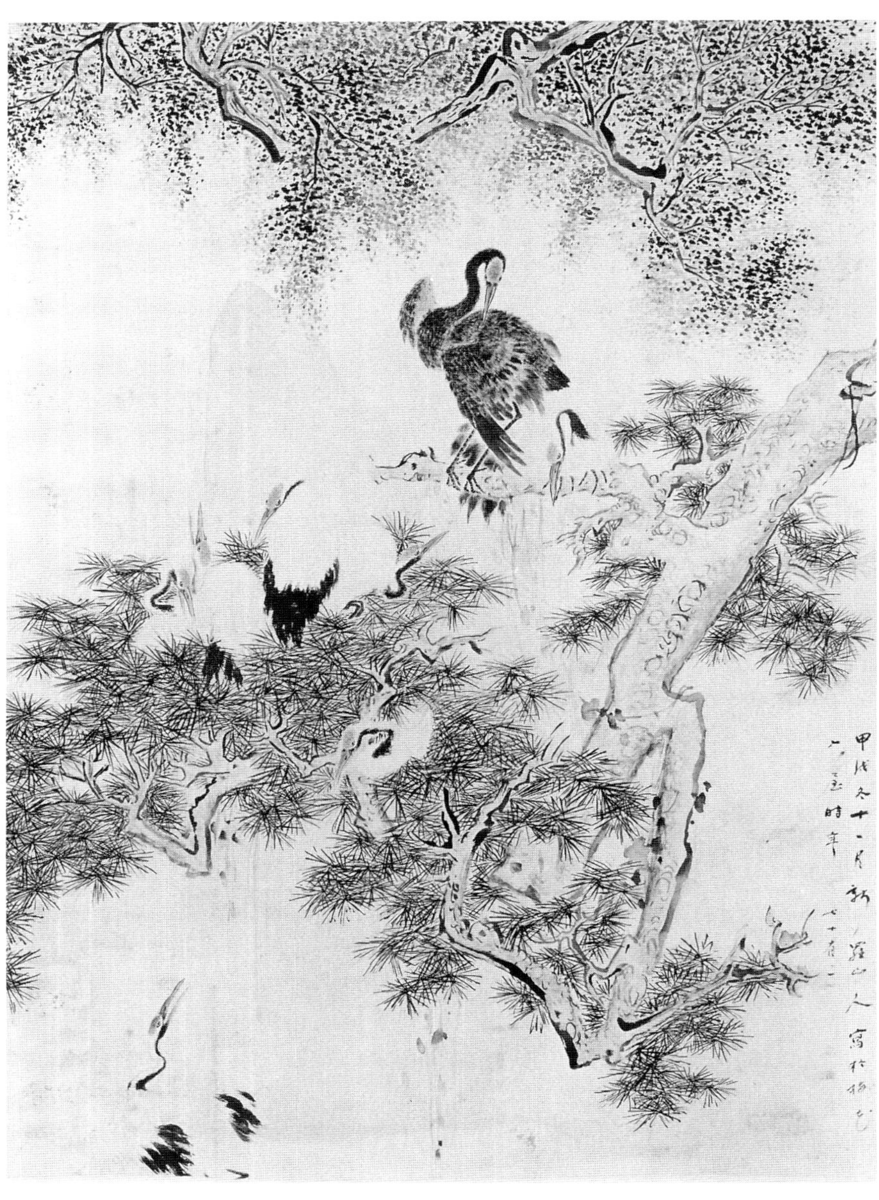

2.8. Hua Yen, "Cranes in Pines." Dated 1754. Hanging scroll, ink and colors on silk, 192.5 × 136 cm. Former collection of Victoria Contag.

landscapists for centuries had produced paintings that signified certain social values more of less independently of their own situations. But such cases should caution us once more against what has been a persistent tendency in studies of Chinese painting, inspired by the practice of the Chinese connoisseurs themselves: reading the works as though they were simple expressions of the artists' true situation and inner life. One would probably do better to approach most traditional Chinese cultural expressions, even those that offer themselves as revelations of individual feeling, with the assumption that they present an invented persona for the writer or artist, and represent ideals that bear only problematic relationships to the everyday realities of their authors.[36]

It is apparent from these cases and others to be introduced later that paintings were obtained from artists for a variety of purposes by a variety of intermediaries: go-betweens, agents, friends concerned with the painter's welfare, outright dealers, as well as collectors who might intend to use them as gifts to others—the great seventhth-century patron Chou Liang-kung used paintings by artists of his circle in this way. We have been accustomed to taking as typical the simple kind of transaction in which artist paints the picture and someone else receives or acquires it from him directly. But while this simple transfer of the art work was common enough, the more complex three-person transaction was common also, perhaps even more so in the late period.

Obtaining a Painting III: Markets and Studios

Painters also had the option of selling their works openly in the market (figure 2.10), but it was an option they took only when others were

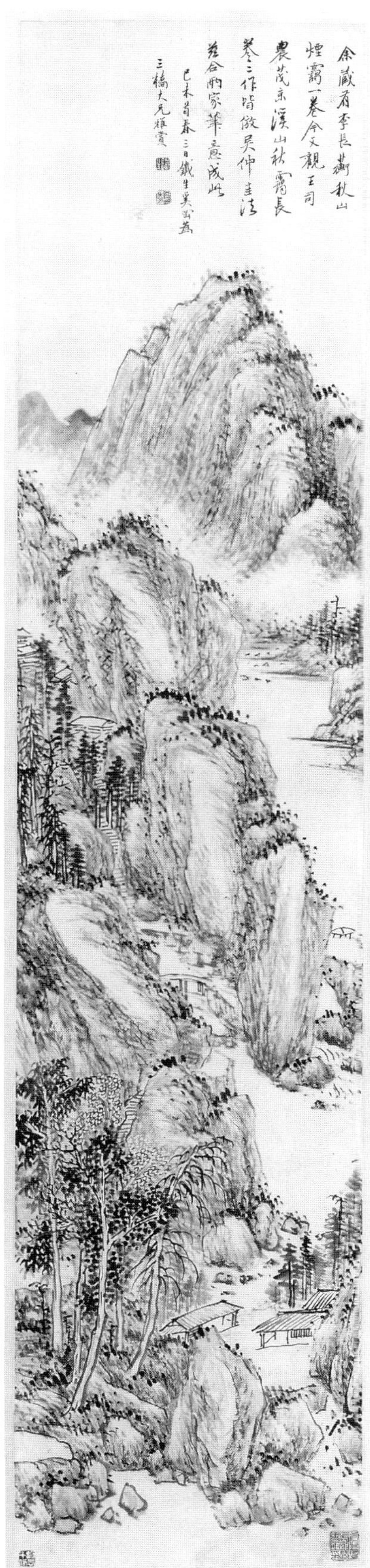

2.9. Hsi Kang, "Mist and Haze in Autumn Mountains."
Dated 1799. Hanging scroll, ink on paper, 130.2 × 31.4 cm. Honolulu Academy of Arts (5516.1), Gift of Mr. and Mrs. Mitchell Hutchinson.

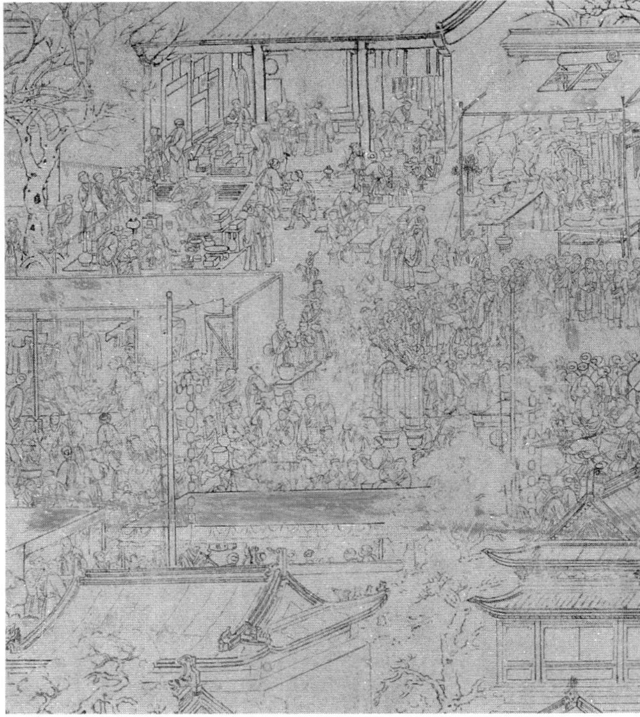

2.10. Anonymous, Ch'ing period (18th cent.?), "Painting and Antiques Store," from New Year's Lantern Market.
Section of a *fen-pen* (draft sketch) handscroll, ink on paper, Ht. 29 cm. Shanghai Museum.

closed to them, since it was considered degrading, putting them on the level of street-vendors. We have heard about Jen Hsiung spreading out his paintings on the streetside, and Fei Tan-hsü displaying his in a stall; both artists were rescued from these lowly conditions by patrons. A late Ming critic, blaming the decline of painting in Suchou on its commercialization, writes caustically that artists there "smear and daub on a mountain, a stream, a plant, a tree, then hang it in the marketplace to trade it for a peck of rice."[37]

Too little is known about what "hanging it in the marketplace" actually meant, but indications are that a variety of public places served for the display of paintings for sale. An anecdote concerning Chou Hsün, an early Ch'ing specialist in pictures of dragons in clouds (figure 2.11), tells that he once hung one of his works in the Yellow Crane Tower near Wuhan with the very high price tag of 100 taels of silver on it. When at last someone appeared who was willing to buy it at that price, Chou gave him the painting as a gift—he had only wanted, he explained, to find someone who admired his painting enough to pay that much for it.[38]

From the early periods there are some records of markets where old paintings and other antiques were sold, fairs held in Buddhist temples, and shops in certain quarters of cities (figure 2.12).[39] Chan Ching-feng, writing in the late sixteenth century, tells of the buying and selling of paintings at the Lantern Market in his city, probably She-hsien,[40] and the dealer Wu Ch'i-ch'en, in his *Shu-hua chi* (ca. 1677), relates that in his hometown in Hui-chou antiquities were sold at the Dragon Palace Temple during the eighth and ninth lunar months.[41] An amusing poem titled "Bogus Antiques" by Shao Ch'ang-heng (1637–1704) describes the rows of antique stores at the Ch'ang-men city gate in Suchou, where mostly fake paintings were sold: "The good artists do not create their own works" any more, says Shao, but "copy and take pride in their close-likenesses" to the styles of the old masters, that is, in their forgeries.[42]

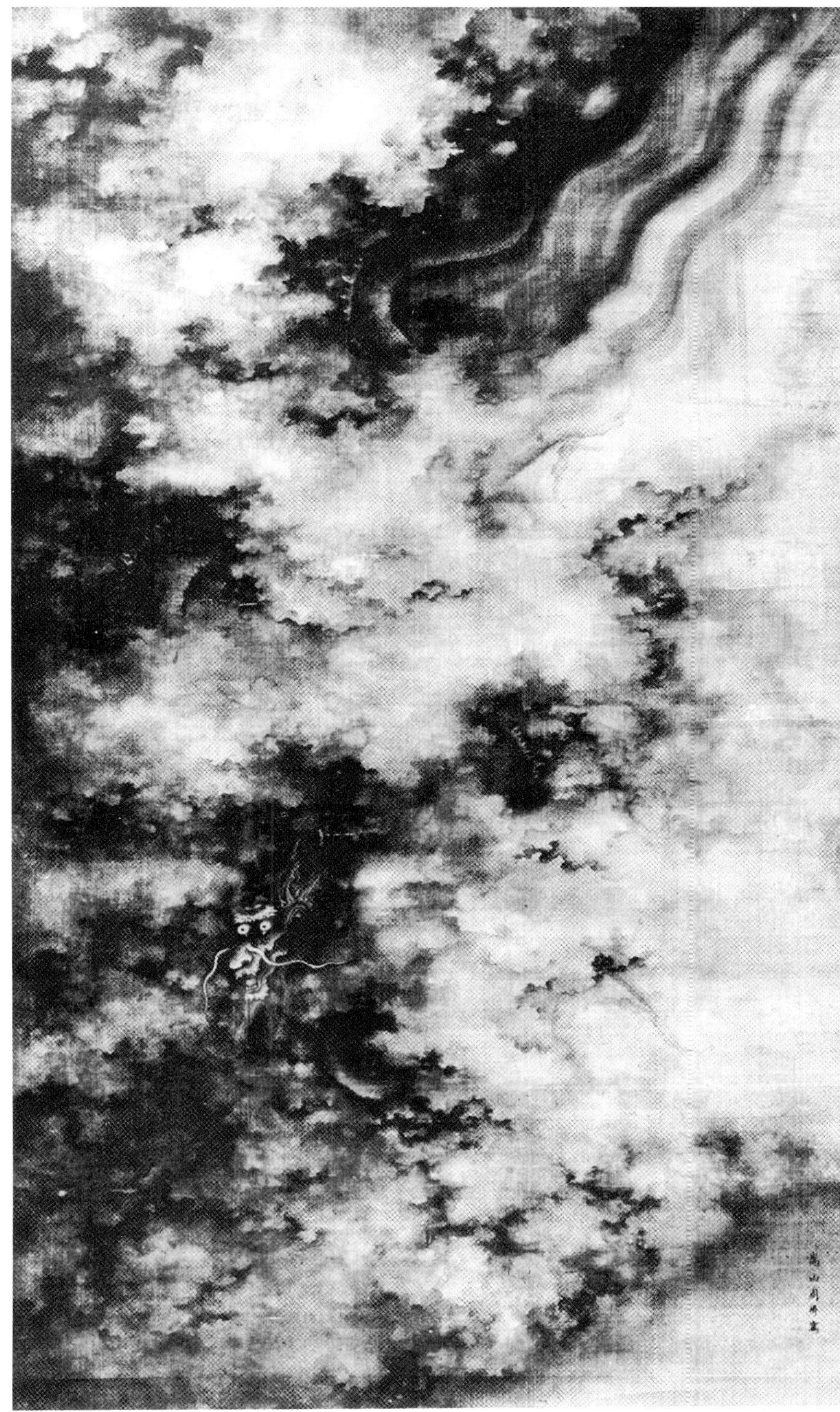

2.11. Chou Hsün, "Dragon in Clouds." Hanging scroll, ink on silk, 131.5 × 74.6 cm. Ch'ing-tao City Museum. From *Chung-kuo mei-shu ch'üan-chi* 7, plate 42.

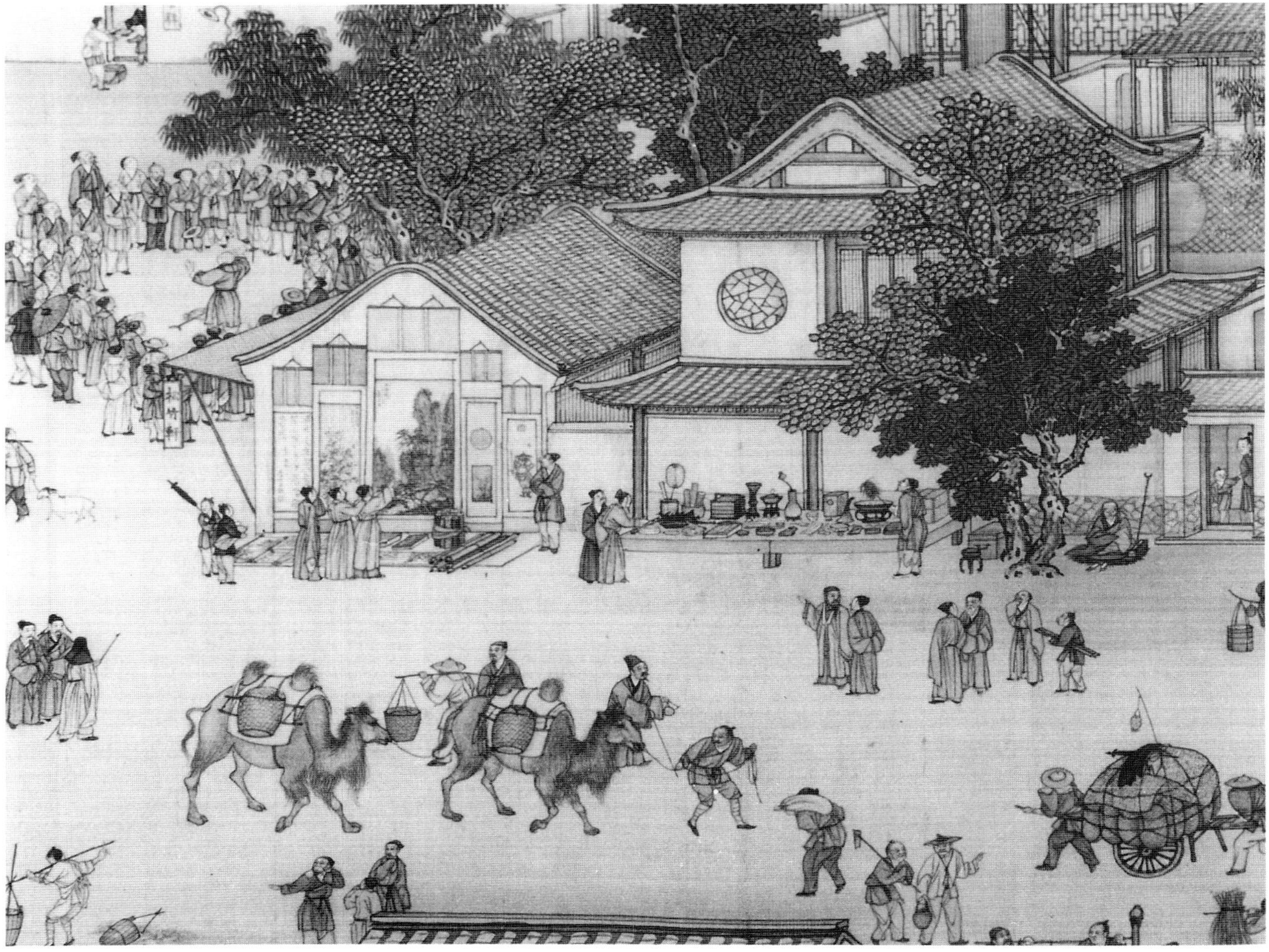

2.12. "Painting and Antique Markets." Detail from Ch'en Mei et al., *Ch'ing-ming shang-ho t'u* (Spring Festival on the River). Dated 1735. Handscroll, ink and colors on silk, ht. 35.6 cm. National Palace Museum, Taipei, Taiwan.

From the middle Ch'ing, temple fairs at the Pao-kuo Ssu in Beijing were outlets for the sale of paintings, forerunners of the antique and book shops of the famous Liu-li-ch'ang district.[43] Paintings changed hands also in pawnshops, and were hung for sale in tea-houses, such as the famous one in the Yü Garden at the City God's Temple in Shanghai. In the late period, at least, they could be bought at fan shops, mounters' shops, and brush-and-paper shops, where one could also see, along with old paintings, price lists and sample works of local contemporary artists and place orders for paintings by them.[44] One would purchase a piece of painting paper (or silk, or an album) of a certain size—the size in part determined the price—on which would be written (small, in a corner, or on the back) one's requirements for the subject, and one's name for identification and use in the dedication. This would then be delivered to the artist, who would execute the work and deposit it at the shop, where the buyer would receive it.

Also in recent times, and especially in Shanghai, there were artists' clubs or associations where the members would work together and where the paintings were sold, with part of the purchase price going to the club for expenses, including painting materials.[45] Similar organizations, but less commercialized, must have existed earlier: a late Ming miscellany tells of a club for poets and painters in Nanking where the members would collaborate, the poets composing poems and the painters illustrating them. Whether these were sold by the club is not reported.[46]

One pattern by which a painting could be obtained from a literatus-artist was simply to visit his studio or residence, if one had the proper entree, and ask him for one. A poem by K'ung Shang-jen tells of visiting the seventeenth-century painter Cha Shih-piao in this way and finding him with "loose, thinning hair under a cap, carelessly worn,/ Like the pots of wistful grass which he planted himself./ A monk was invited to remain and was not begrudged a meal./ Anyone requesting a painting should come bringing his overnight things."[47]

Not all artists were so hospitable; some would rebuff seekers after their paintings indignantly, especially if they were strangers and their approach was somehow gauche. Artists commonly kept stocks of finished paintings for visitors to see, in addition to accepting, under the right conditions, requests or commissions for new ones. Anne Clapp, writing about the economic situation of T'ang Yin, concludes from the nature of his output and the written evidence that he "produced minor works for the general market, chiefly fans, which were not ordered but kept in stock for the casual buyer."[48]

Artists who did not sell their paintings for money, as T'ang Yin acknowledges doing,[49] but used them for political and other gifts, might similarly keep a stock of "unbespoke" paintings for visitors to see and sometimes take away. The early Ch'ing landscapist Ch'eng Cheng-k'uei began his series of "Imaginary Journeys Among Rivers and Mountains" scrolls (figure 2.13) in 1649, intending to paint a hundred of them; later he extended his objective to five hundred, and may have finished over three hundred.[50] He did these, he tells us in an inscription on the earliest one extant, to assuage

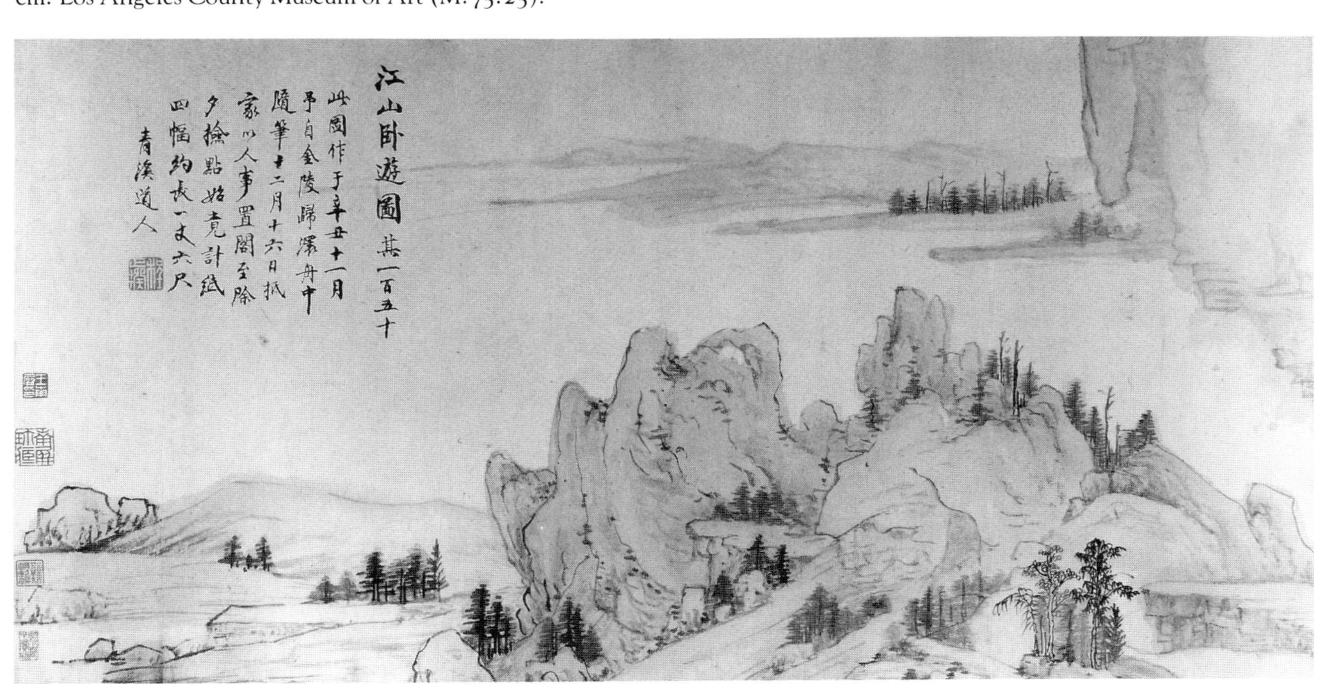

2.13. Ch'eng Cheng-k'uei, "Imaginary Travels Among Streams and Mountains."
Dated 1661 (no. 150 in series). Section of a handscroll, ink and light colors on paper, ht. 35.9 cm. Los Angeles County Museum of Art (M.75.25).

the "hardships" of those who, like himself, were serving in the capital: no natural landscape to enjoy, no calligraphy or paintings to appreciate.[51] By 1651 he had finished more than thirty, but all except one, as he writes in another inscription, had been "taken away" by "acquisitive people"—a euphemism that we should probably understand to mean that they were given as gifts to fellow officials. In his inscription on one of the later scrolls he admits that someone had charged him with doing these to "flatter people," i.e., to gain favor with those who could further his career. No, he protests, he only did them in his leisure time, after he had finished work, to amuse himself, and never showed them to anyone.[52] (How, then, one would like to ask him, did so many "acquisitive people" manage to carry them off?)

I have suggested, in a recent essay, that more or less the same pattern was followed by Tung Ch'i-ch'ang, whom Ch'eng Cheng-k'uei had known briefly during his first period of service in the capital from 1631.[53] Quite a few of Tung's paintings are inscribed twice by the artist. His "Drawing Water in the Morning," inscribed by him in 1607 and again in 1611, is an example (figure 2.14). The first inscription may supply a title and date, but seldom a dedication; the later inscription sometimes dedicates the painting to some particular recipient, or refers to the owner of the work at the time when the artist reencounters it. Moreover, these doubly inscribed works tend to be hanging scrolls of a rather impersonal character, generally less innovative and interesting than the paintings Tung did for close friends on particular occasions, which bear more particularized, intimate inscriptions.

What all this suggests is that Tung painted the lesser works as his time permitted with no recipient in mind, and kept a number of them in his studio; when some visitor came, perhaps with an introduction, he would show them as a matter of hospitality; if the visitor expressed admiration for one and indicated a desire to own it, Tung might give it to him, sometimes adding an inscription. But of course the recipient was expected to make some recompense, or feel himself obligated to Tung and discharge the obligation later. It is clear also that Tung used his paintings as political gifts to other officials. In a preface written early in his career he denies having ever done this, as Ch'eng Cheng-k'uei was to disclaim the practice later;[54] but even if Tung's denial was true when he made it, he certainly relaxed his principles afterward.

Paying for a Painting I: Cash Payments and Prices

The ways of paying for a painting in China were as diverse as the ways of requesting one, and similarly tend to correlate with the positions of the artist and the client on a socioeconomic scale. Ch'iu Ying could be paid in money, Tung Ch'i-ch'ang ordinarily could not. Dire hardship softened the rules, but even under those conditions artists of social standing tried to avoid baldly commercial transactions. The commonly used alternatives were payment in goods—in which case the transaction could seem to take the form of a free exchange of gifts, untainted by commercialism—and exchanges of favors and services, according to the pattern of *kuan-hsi,* reciprocal relationships.[55]

Enough cases are recorded of direct cash payments to artists, or of artists committing themselves to paint by accepting money, to dissuade us from thinking of this as an uncommon occurrence. From the early Sung there is, for instance, the case of an official who gave 500 taels of silver to the flower painter Chao Ch'ang (see figure 2.15, an early painting ascribed to him) "as a birthday gift" and later received from him several paintings.[56] And from the late Northern Sung, the information that I Yüan-chi, a specialist in pictures of gibbons and deer, was given an initial payment of two hundred thousand (cash?) for materials when

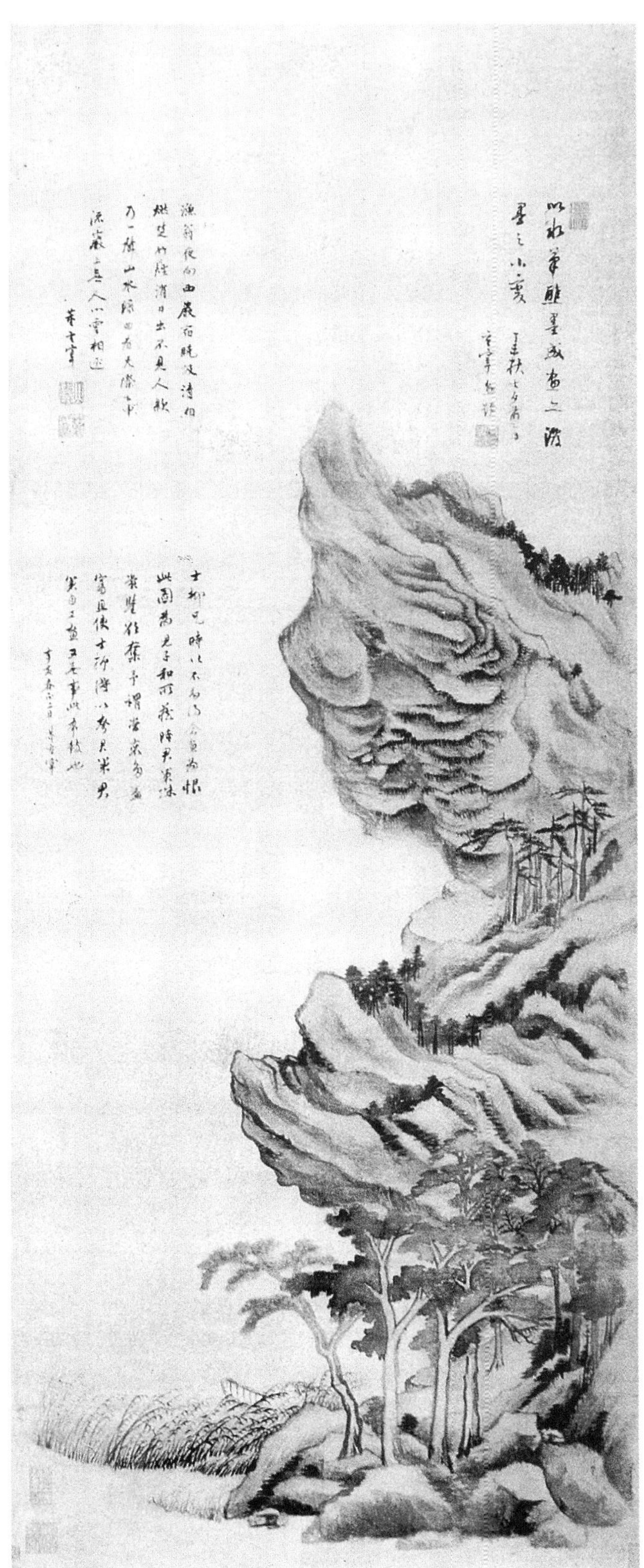

2.14. Tung Ch'i-ch'ang, "Drawing Water in the Morning." Inscriptions by the artist dated 1607 and 1611. Hanging scroll, ink and colors on silk, 117 × 46 cm. Palace Museum, Peking. From *Tung Ch'i-ch'ang hua-chi* (Shanghai, 1989), plate 10.

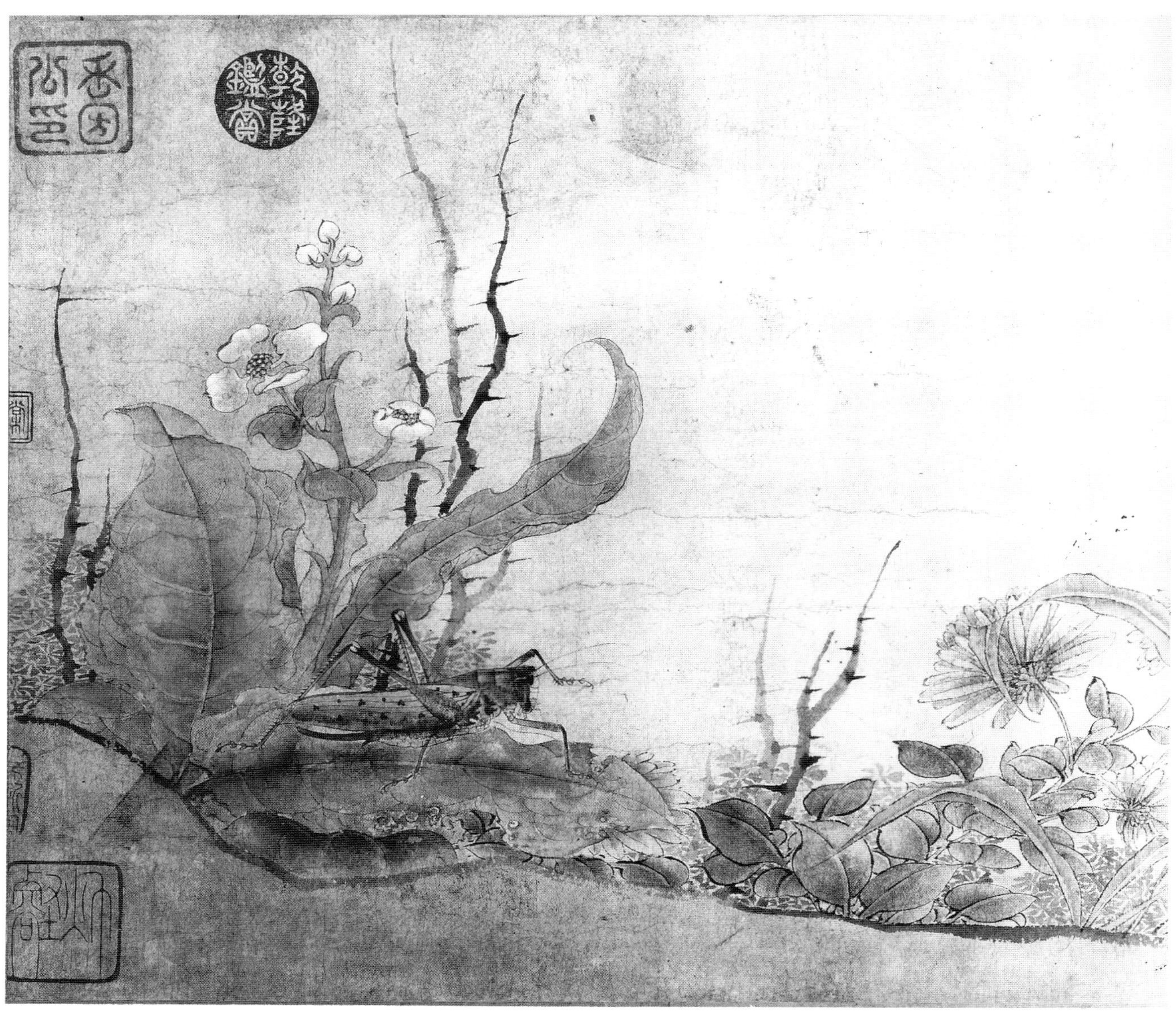

2.15. Anonymous, Sung period (old attribution to Chao Ch'ang), "Plants and Butterflies."
Section of handscroll, ink and colors on paper, ht. 27.7 cm. Palace Museum, Peking.

he received the imperial commission to paint "One Hundred Apes" for a palace corridor.[57] For the Ming period, we learn that a patron named Chou Feng-lai (1523–1555) paid Ch'iu Ying the huge sum of 100 ounces of silver to paint a 50-foot-long handscroll representing two Han-period imperial hunting parks, a project that occupied the artist over several years. Chou intended the work as a present for his mother's eightieth birthday.[58] Around the same time but at the other end of the price scale we find Wen Chia accepting from the collector Hsiang Yüan-pien five hsing (a half-ounce) of silver and a fruit cake for painting four fans.[59]

For the early Ch'ing we can recall an account of how Huang Yen-lü sent a sizable sum of money to Chu Ta's agent and in due course received his album of landscapes. A letter from Kung Hsien to the poet Wang Chi asks for money to pay a debt to a publisher, offering a painting and a poem in return.[60] The eighteenth-century Yangchou master Chin Nung writes, facetiously but revealingly, that the amount he receives for one of his bamboo paintings (figure 2.16) is a hundred times the price he paid for the bamboo plant.[61] Even so, he had to paint prolifically (or have his paintings done by others, a practice I will consider in the final essay) to make a comfortable living. A letter from him to a go-between complains about a delay in payment for an album of paintings he had sent. Chin writes: "Right now, I need the money badly" and asks that the go-between lend him some, to be deducted later from the payment for the album.[62] It was normal for a cash payment, or at least part of it, to be given the artist in advance: after the nineteenth-century painter Hsü-ku died, his friends found many paper-wrapped packets of money in his studio, representing commissions he had accepted but had not been able to complete.[63]

There are, to be sure, stories about artists who sold their paintings only when they needed to buy food, or who exchanged them for food. One of these tells of the sixteenth-century Suchou master Chü Chieh: "When he earned a bit of money with his brush, he would invite his friends in for feasting and drinking; when he ran out of food, he would get up early and do a picture of a lonely pine tree and far-off hills and send a boy out to trade it for some rice."[64] Another such story concerns the early Ch'ing landscapist Lu Wei, about whom we are told:

> The place he lived was south of the Chao-kuo Temple. People who wanted to obtain one of his paintings would climb to the viewing tower of the temple and look over to his house, to see if any cooking smoke was rising from it. If noon passed and no smoke could be seen [an indication that he had no food to cook] they would take rice or silver to trade [for a painting.] If it didn't happen this way, they couldn't get one at all. People therefore regarded him as a simpleton [or eccentric, *ch'ih*].[65]

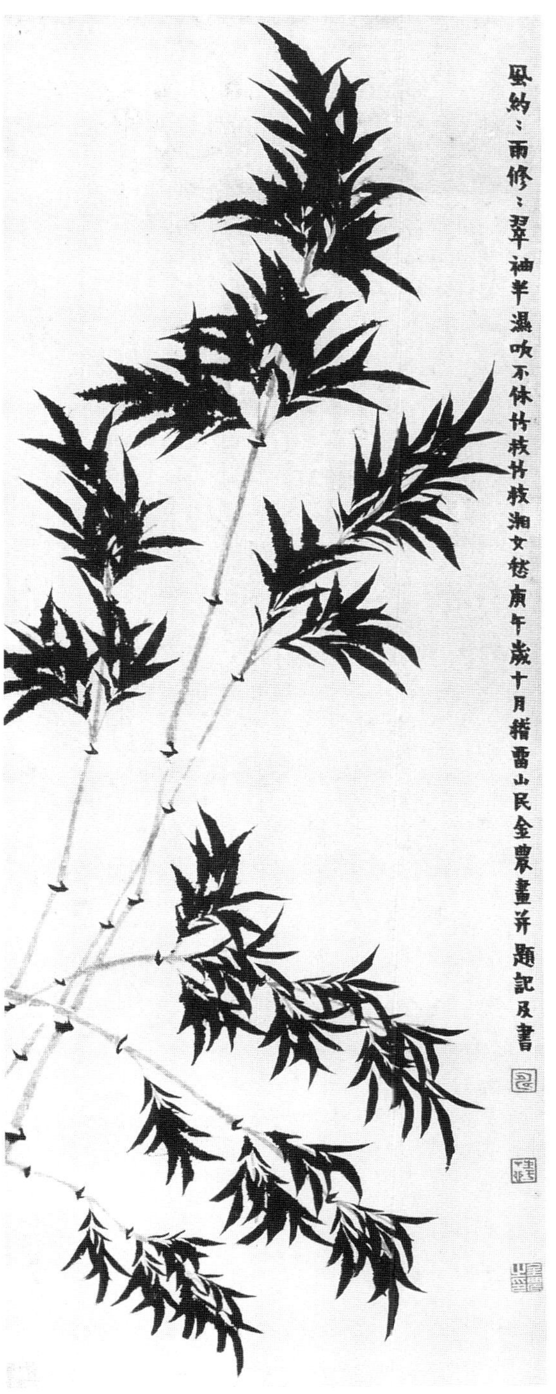

2.16. Chin Nung (1687—after 1764), "Stalks of Bamboo."
Dated 1750. Hanging scroll, ink on paper, 99.2 × 36.8 cm. Sakamoto Goro collection, Kyoto.

Some of Lu Wei's extant paintings (figure 2.17) bear out this judgment, appearing eccentric in their early Ch'ing context, although to foreign eyes their (probably Western-inspired) illusionism makes them curiously unexotic.

Stories of this kind about impoverished artists are always slightly suspect, since they might be invented to praise the painter's integrity in not pandering to the marketplace; but they seem also to have reflected unpleasant reality much of the time. We should not imagine that most artists, even when they were willing and able to sell their works, lived comfortably on their painting; few could command prices that allowed that. Most of them who had no other regular income were in the precarious situation of Cheng Min, struggling to make ends meet. Kung Hsien and many others are known to have lived on the edge of poverty through most of their lives, even when, like Kung Hsien, they were excellent painters and kept up a prolific output. A story about the great early Ch'ing patron Chou Liang-kung is instructive: while he was in jail he was forced to sell paintings from his collection to raise money; his antique paintings he was able to sell, but those by his artist-friends, who included some of the leading masters of his time, did not bring high enough prices, so he kept them.[66]

Even so, as Hongnam Kim's analysis makes clear, a hard-working professional painter could earn more than a teacher of the scholar class. She quotes a remark by a poor scholar in the early eighteenth-century novel *The Scholars* saying "In good times, with a slight gift for painting, I would have no need to worry about each bowl of rice."[67] And she notes the case of Wei Chih-huang, a minor painter from Nanking who, according to Kung Hsien, earned enough from his painting to support a household of forty people.[68] (Curiously, no painting by Wei Chih-huang to be seen today indicates enough artistic talent to allow him to support even himself; his 1604 handscroll in the Shanghai Museum, figure 2.18, represents his highest level of achievement, with others mostly far below.)

Some research has been done on the prices of Chinese paintings at different periods,[69] but that complex question cannot be pursued at length here. For the later centuries, when openly commercial transactions were more common and more accepted, the evidence is fuller. The price-list for his paintings that the mid-eighteenth-century Yangchou master Cheng Hsieh posted on his door, giving prices for large, medium, and small pictures, is well known.[70] Less known is that another retired official, the landscapist Chang Hsün, active in the early decades of the Ch'ing (figure 2.19), had done the same thing in order to support his family upon his return home after the Manchu conquest,[71] or that Chang Hsiu, who took his *chin-shih* in 1643 but later made his living by painting, attached price tags to his paintings stipulating "the proper price for a fan" or "the proper price for a hanging scroll."[72] Or that the great Individualist master Shih-t'ao also supplied prices openly for his paintings in a communication with one of his patrons, specifying that while an ordinary twelve-panel screen painted by him was twenty-four taels, he asked fifty taels for one with a continuous composition (figure 2.20) because it required more time and work.[73] A certain Hu Chen writes in a letter to a client that he has deliberately set his price-list high to discourage people who want his paintings; he is troubled, he writes, by the large amount the client has offered, presumably misled by this inflated price-list.[74] Examples of price-lists by more recent artists such as Jen Po-nien and Wu Ch'ang-shih are still preserved.[75]

From the Ming dynasty on, it was reportedly a common practice for the professional master to have a price-list in his studio to show his clients; it was called a *jun-li* or "rules for moistening [the brush]."[76] The earliest recorded may well be the one made up for the Ming loyalist Wan Shou-ch'i (1603–1652) by one of his friends, giving price ranges for his calligraphy,

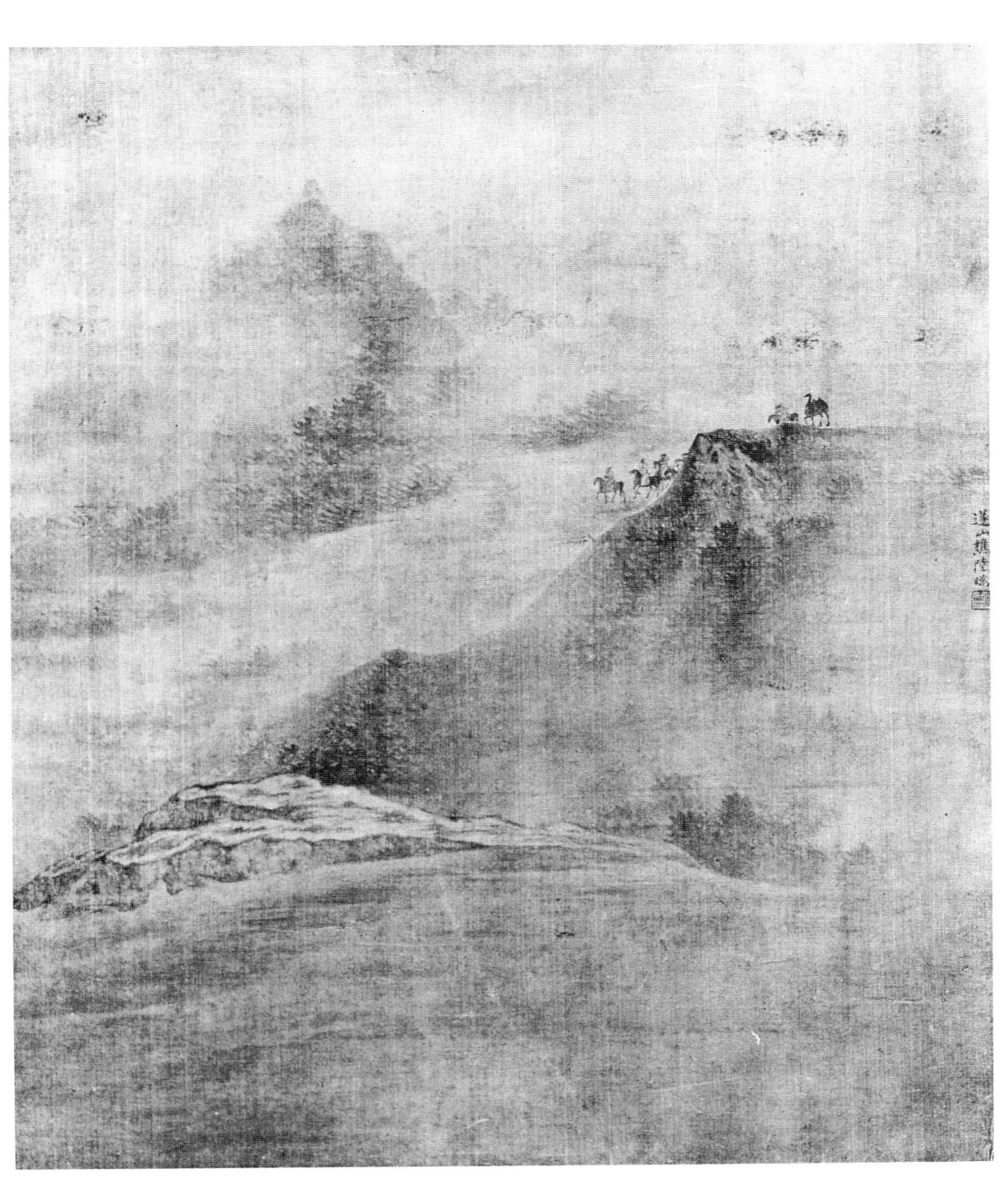

2.17. Lu Wei (d. 1716). "Travelers on a High Plateau." Hanging scroll, ink and colors on silk, 61.2 × 50.4 cm. Nanking Museum. From *Nan-ching po-wu-yüan ts'ang-hua chi* (Nanking, 1966), 2:81.

paintings (figure 2.21), and seal carving. A well-educated and politically active man who had been pushed into poverty by the Manchu invasion, Wan sold his works in his late years to support himself and his family. The price-list reads:

> Calligraphy in small-standard *(hsiao-k'ai)* script: three taels, down to three cents (ch'ien); middle-sized cursive: five taels, down to three cents; large-character calligraphy, five taels, down to five cents. Paintings: Figures, five taels down to one tael; I don't paint [figure] fans. Large landscapes, five taels down to one tael; small pictures and landscape fans, three taels, down to five cents. Seal-carving: stone, five cents; bronze, one tael five cents; jade, two taels.[77]

In more recent times, price-lists might be accompanied by notes specifying conditions under which artists could refuse commissions: when they are given unreasonable deadlines; when they are asked to work on paper or silk of poor quality; or when (as calligraphers) they are asked to copy someone else's inferior calligraphy, or to write flattering sentiments in couplets for birthday presentation, or inscriptions for someone they do not know.[78]

There are other implications to artists publishing price-lists, which again can only be touched on here; in the case of Cheng Hsieh, these have been explored in an article by Cheng-chi Hsü, and also in writings of my own.[79] For the artists to respond so directly to demands of the market and offer their works openly to a broader clientele encouraged, I have argued, a more repetitive and prolific mode of production. Cheng Hsieh, in an inscription written in 1748, states that his in-

2.18. Wei Chih-huang, "A Thousand Cliffs Contend in Splendor."
Dated 1604. Section of a handscroll, ink and colors on paper, ht. 32.5 cm. Shanghai Museum. From *Chung-kuo mei-shu ch'üan-chi* 8, plate 85.

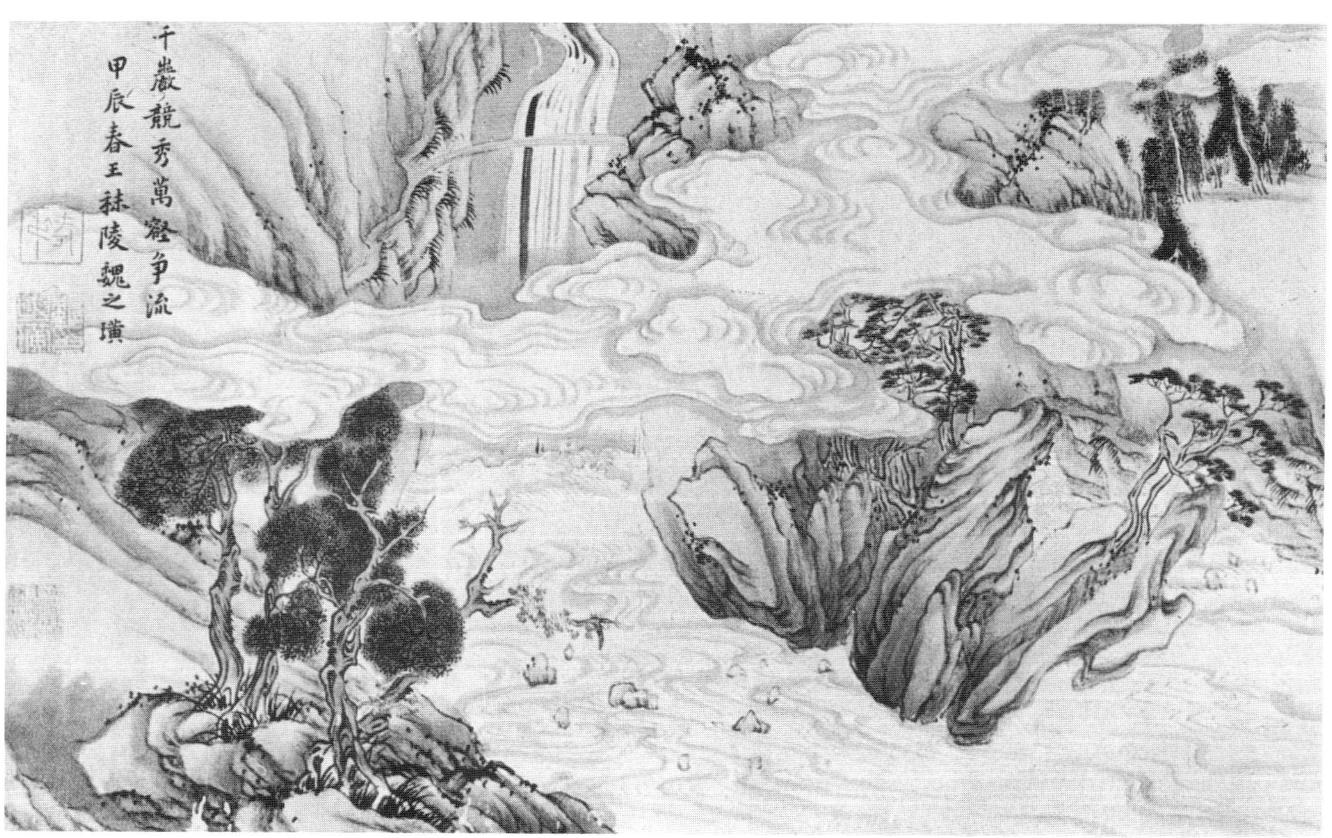

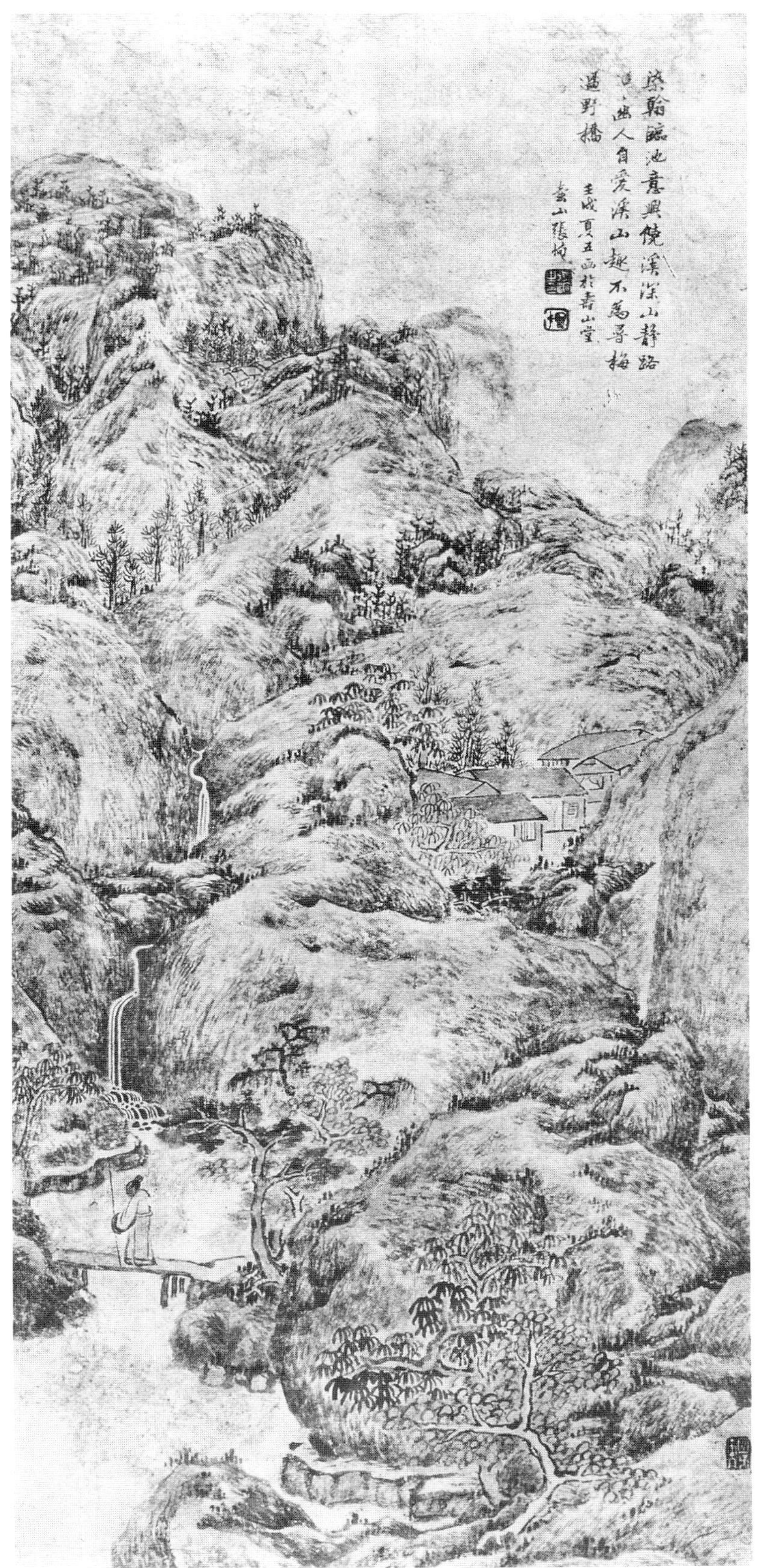

2.19. Chang Hsün, "Landscape." Dated 1682. Hanging scroll, 86 × 40.6 cm. Former Yutani Collection. From Naito Konan, ed., *Shinchô shogafu* (Osaka, 1916), plate 32.

come from sales of paintings and calligraphy was around a thousand taels of silver in a good year. (By way of comparison: a second-rank official at this time received as his basic annual salary 256 taels, a third-rank official such as the superintendent in charge of salt transport 130 taels, a country magistrate's basic salary was below 100 taels; these amounts were augmented after the Yung-cheng period when officials were given special pensions to "nourish incorruptibility." And of course those in official positions could derive other income, from bribes and other sources, so that a magistrate's annual income might be around one thousand a year, roughly the same as Cheng Hsieh's, or much more.)[80]

But since the price Cheng gives in his price-list for a medium-size hanging scroll is only four taels, he would have to produce and sell 250 of these, or about two every three days on average, to make up the annual thousand taels. Such a consideration helps us to understand the nature of the Yangchou masters' paintings, their prolific production, and why Chin Nung, and probably others as well, resorted to using ghostpainters.

Artists of higher status, for whom painting was not their main livelihood, were usually, at least until the late period, less open in responding to the market and in stating their expectations of reward. (This is why the posting of a price-list by Cheng Hsieh, who had recently held a post as a prefect, was considered worthy of note at all.) But with most artists, whatever their status, the refusal to accept money for paintings was probably less a matter of firm principle than a stance adopted for some circumstances, relaxed for others. Typically, for upper-level artists, they would accept money (if at all) from merchants and others outside their social circle, but refuse it from friends or those they especially respected; for these, exchanges of gifts and favors were the proper pattern. The late sixteenth-century scholar Wang Shih-chen tells us that his contemporary Ch'ien Ku took money from ordinary people who came to him requesting paint-

2.20. Shih-t'ao (1642–1708), "Bamboo, Orchids, Plantain, Pine, and Other Plants by a River."
Section of a 12-fold screen, ink on paper, each panel 195 × 49.5 cm. National Palace Museum, Taipei.

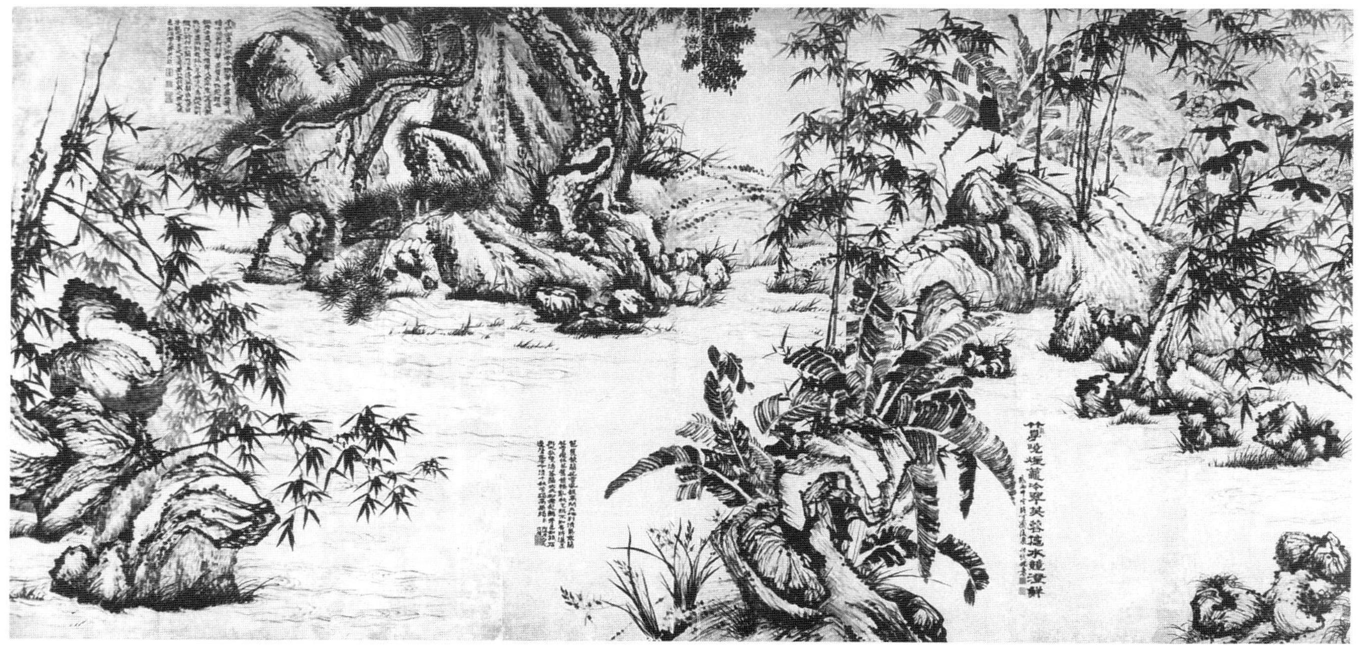

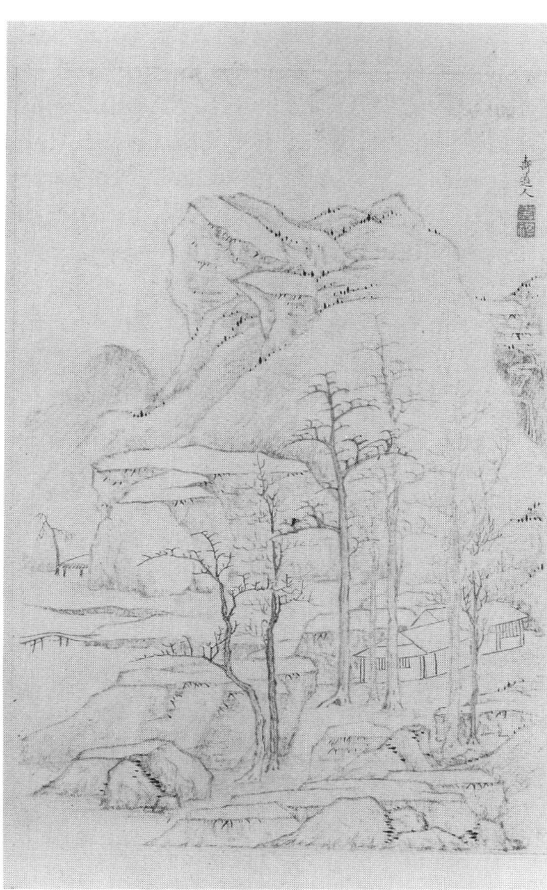

2.21. Wan Shou-ch'i (1603–1652), "Landscape."
Dated 1650. Leaf from an album of eighteen leaves of paintings and calligraphy, ink on paper, 25.8 × 17 cm. Princeton Art Museum (68–206).

ings, but painted an album for Wang himself to reciprocate Wang's invitation to travel with him.[81] Ch'ien's willingness to accept cash payments is corroborated by a preserved letter to him from a certain Ling Kan-ch'u, who appears to have acted as his agent, commissioning him in a straightforward way to paint twenty album leaves, two hanging scrolls, and one framed painting, and naming the price he is sending, an amount in silver for which Shan Guolin calculates the buying power as equivalent to 18 t'an or 1,620 kilograms of rice, along with two catties of tea. The letter states that the two hanging scrolls are for a man named Wang Chün, and that the subjects are to be a Kuan-yin painted in ink and an illustration to the "Dirge of Autumn" by Ou-yang Hsiu. The letter is also of interest in that Ling Kan-ch'u, at the end of it, suggests openly that he himself should be rewarded for acting as go-between. His health is bad, he writes, his friend has died, and also his brother. "Comfort me by giving me some paintings in the styles of the old masters, Ching [Hao] and Kuan [T'ung], Ma [Yüan] and Hsia [Kuei]."[82] Presumably, works in these styles were especially salable or highly valued among Ch'ien Ku's productions.

Paying for a Painting II: Gifts, Services, and Favors

The practice of giving an artist a gift instead of a cash payment for his work belongs in principle, as noted earlier, within the larger *kuan-hsi* system, but was in fact more serious than a simple social exchange of gifts, closer to a quasi-commercial barter transaction. Gifts that the artist might accept in return for a painting or in anticipation of one could be virtually anything he needed or wanted, beginning with the materials and tools of his art: rolls of paper[83] or silk[84], brushes, ink sticks[85] seals [86]. There are numerous instances of people sending these to the painter in hope of obtaining one of his works. Other common gifts, judging from recorded cases, were antiques such as old jades, bronzes, and ceramics, old paintings and calligraphy, or *fa-t'ieh,* rubbings of stone-cut calligraphy inscriptions,[87] all of which the artist could then, if he chose, sell through a dealer to raise cash. Painters could request or accept medicine, as we saw Ch'iu Ying doing in the letter quoted above, or medical treatment for themselves or a relative.[88] Wen Cheng-ming, on one occasion, asked in return for his painting only that the recipient get for him, from a certain official, some medicine for his eyes;[89] on another occasion, he did a fan painting in return for a doctor's prescription to relieve his wife's pain.[90]

An inscription by Ch'en Hung-shou on one

of his extant handscroll paintings, representing a bird on bamboo with flowers and a butterfly (figure 2.22), recounts a complex, ongoing transaction with a patron named Mou-chai. Ch'en acquires a painting by Wen Cheng-ming, which Mou-chai admires, and Ch'en presents it to him. Later, when a friend's son becomes ill, Ch'en borrows one tael of silver from Mou-chai, presumably for medicine. But afterward he feels uneasy over whether he is still in Mou-chai's debt, and sends him an album leaf painted in the "boneless" manner. Still later, he has to borrow another tael from Mou-chai to buy rice for his friend, and in the end paints this scroll for him, recording the entire affair in his inscription.

Exchanges of this kind could continue indefinitely, each party in the exchange fine-tuned to the weighting of the balance at any particular moment, with the artist escaping throughout the stigma of selling his paintings. Ch'en Hung-shou's paintings were surely worth far more, on average, than one tael of silver; he must have accepted that amount as a symbolic gift, like Wen Cheng-ming's acceptance of eye medicine, leaving the recipient still obligated to him, with the surety that the indebtedness would be paid off somehow in the future.

Gifts of food to artists were common—"exchanging one's paintings for rice" was not merely a metaphor. Cheng Hsieh's brush could be "moistened" by a dinner of his favorite dish, dog meat.[91] We read of a nineteenth-century painter named Wu Tai-ch'iu who sold his paintings directly in his early years, but later, when he was better established, could exchange them for anything he needed. He took his lunches at a local restaurant, feeling that the time it would take him to cook for himself could more profitably be spent painting. The exchange rate was one album leaf for each lunch. One day he said to the cook, "Your meals are getting worse every day," to which the cook retorted, "So are your paintings."[92]

The common perception that artists are big drinkers probably accounts for the frequency of references to painters who worked in exchange for wine. The Yüan-period master Kuo Pi records in his diary being offered gifts of food and wine often as inducements to paint.[93] The nonconformist Ming master Hsü Wei (figure 2.23) relates, in an inscription at the end of one of his scrolls depicting flowers and plants in splashy ink-monochrome, that he painted it for a nephew who brought him eight pints of good wine, a hundred crabs, and a leg of lamb; after consuming most of these the painter was truly inspired, with "thunder running through his fingers."[94]

Painting in gratitude for wine, and with one's brush heavily "moistened" from drinking

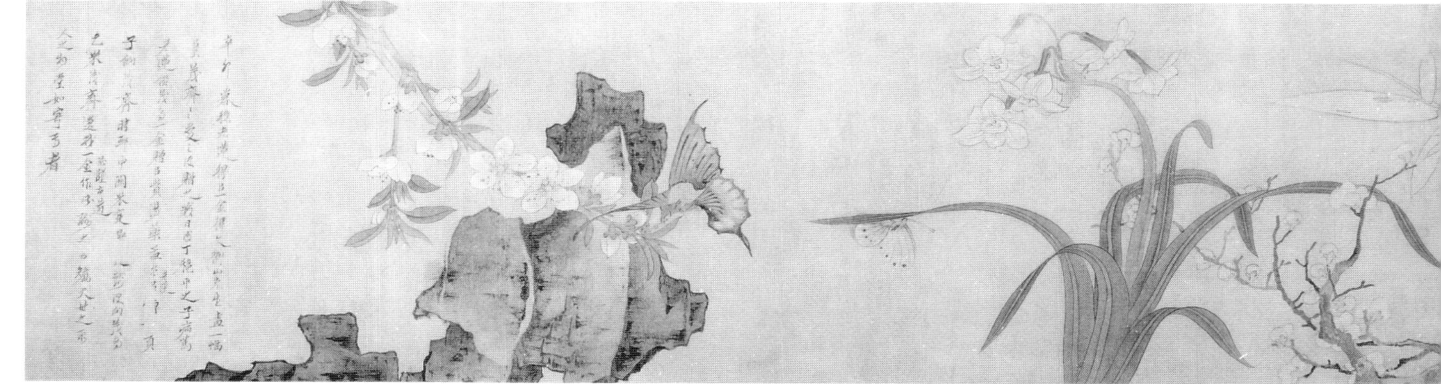

2.22. Ch'en Hung-shou, "Spring Breeze and Butterflies."
Dated 1651. Handscroll, ink and colors on silk, 24.6 × 150.9 cm. Shanghai Museum.

it, was a time-honored practice: the great eighth-century figure painter Wu Tao-tzu had once done wall paintings for a Buddhist temple after the abbot had set out a hundred gallons of wine in the temple gateway to tempt him.[95] I Chün-tso was skilled as poet, calligrapher, and painter; one of his friends, to facilitate his exchange transactions, printed for him a "Declaration of Exchanges for Wine" outlining the three types of wine he would accept for, respectively, a scroll painting with poetic inscription, a couplet, or a scroll of calligraphy.[96]

Gifts to artists could cater to their special tastes and appetites—Kao Feng-han asks in a letter for chrysanthemums and *kuei hua* (sweet-smelling osmanthus) in return for a painting,[97] while the nineteenth-century master Feng Ch'iu-ho could be induced by gifts of sugar.[98] The presents or favors could be thoroughly mundane: we read of painters who received, for their works, a room to live in,[99] or cement to fix their houses.[100] The author of *Ku-tung so-shih,* a collection of odds and ends of information on art and antiques, offers cases of Northern Sung literati artists and calligraphers who accepted, as gifts in exchange for their works, antique paintings and calligraphy, paper of renowned quality, and female slaves.[101]

Artists who were noted womanizers were willing to paint, we are told, for anyone who provided them with an attractive courtesan (a provocative variant on the practice of "moistening the brush"); this is said in particular of two great Ming masters, Wu Wei and Ch'en Hung-shou (figure 2.24).[102] Ch'en also painted directly for prostitutes, we read, when they wheedled him at drinking parties; people who wanted his paintings could later get them from the women, who made a lot of money in this way.[103] The eighteenth-century master Huang Shen (figure 2.25), in another story, drinking with a friend, notices a lovely girl in a neighboring beancurd (tou-fu) shop. Having no money to spend on pursuing her, he paints an impressive picture of Taoist immortals and hangs it in a mounting studio, where it is seen by one of Yangchou's rich salt merchants. When the merchant offers him a high price for it, Huang Shen declines to accept the money and reveals his real desire. The merchant buys the girl for Huang in exchange for the painting.[104]

With stories of courtesans and beancurd-shop girls, we are on the borderline between

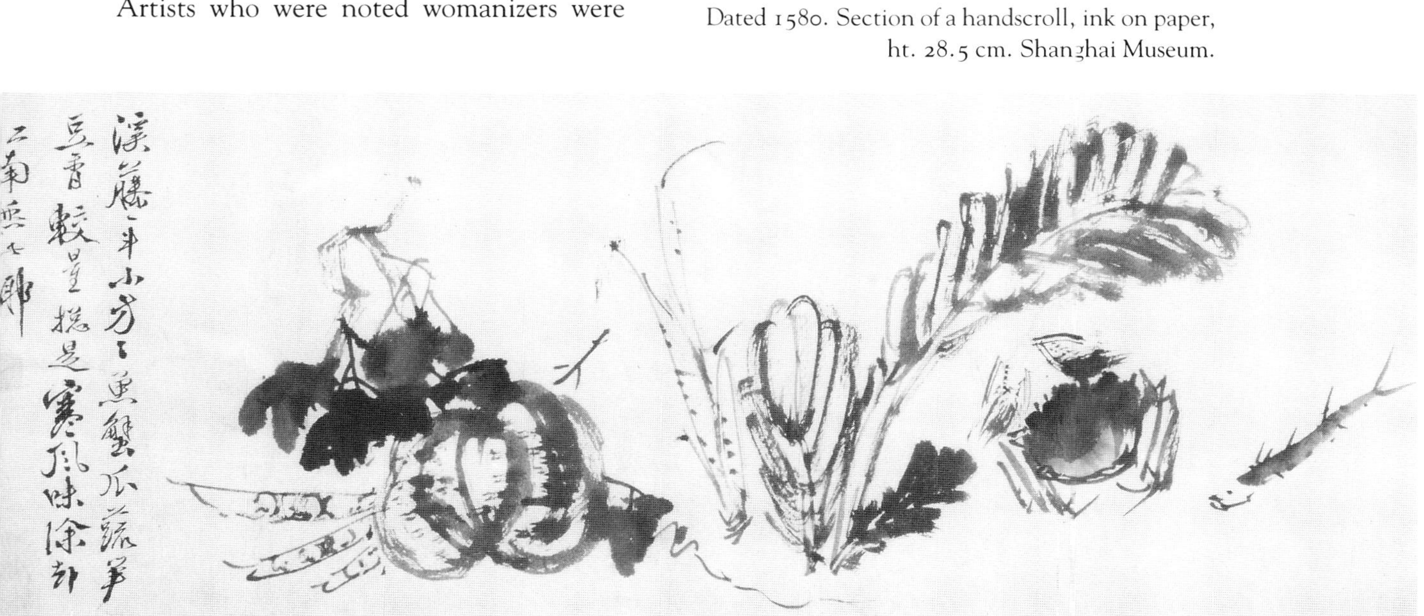

2.23. Hsü Wei, "Crab, Fish, and Vegetables." Dated 1580. Section of a handscroll, ink on paper, ht. 28.5 cm. Shanghai Museum.

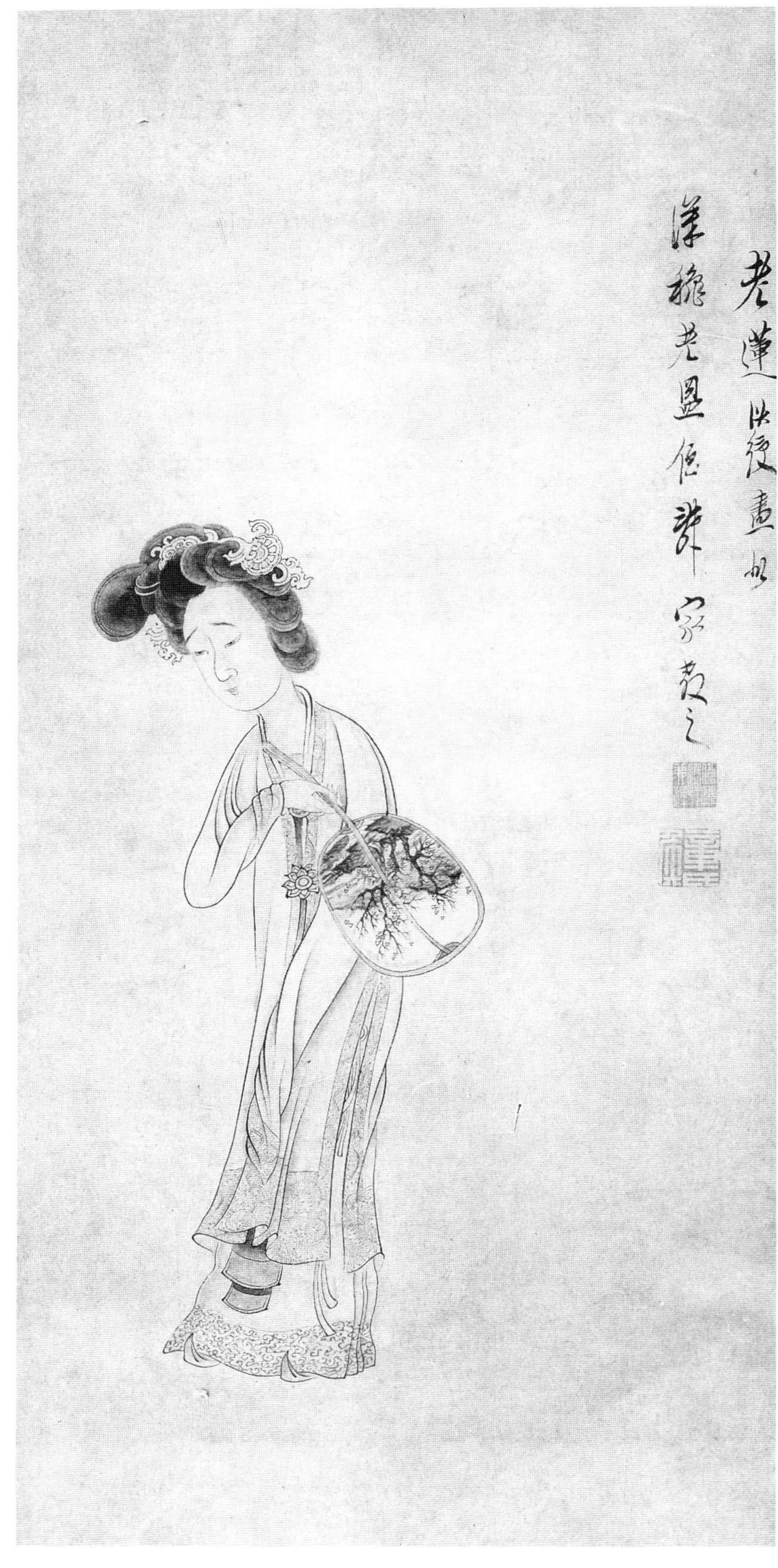

2.24. Ch'en Hung-shou, "Beautiful Lady with Fan."
Hanging scroll, ink and colors on paper. Former collection of J. D. Chen, Hong Kong.

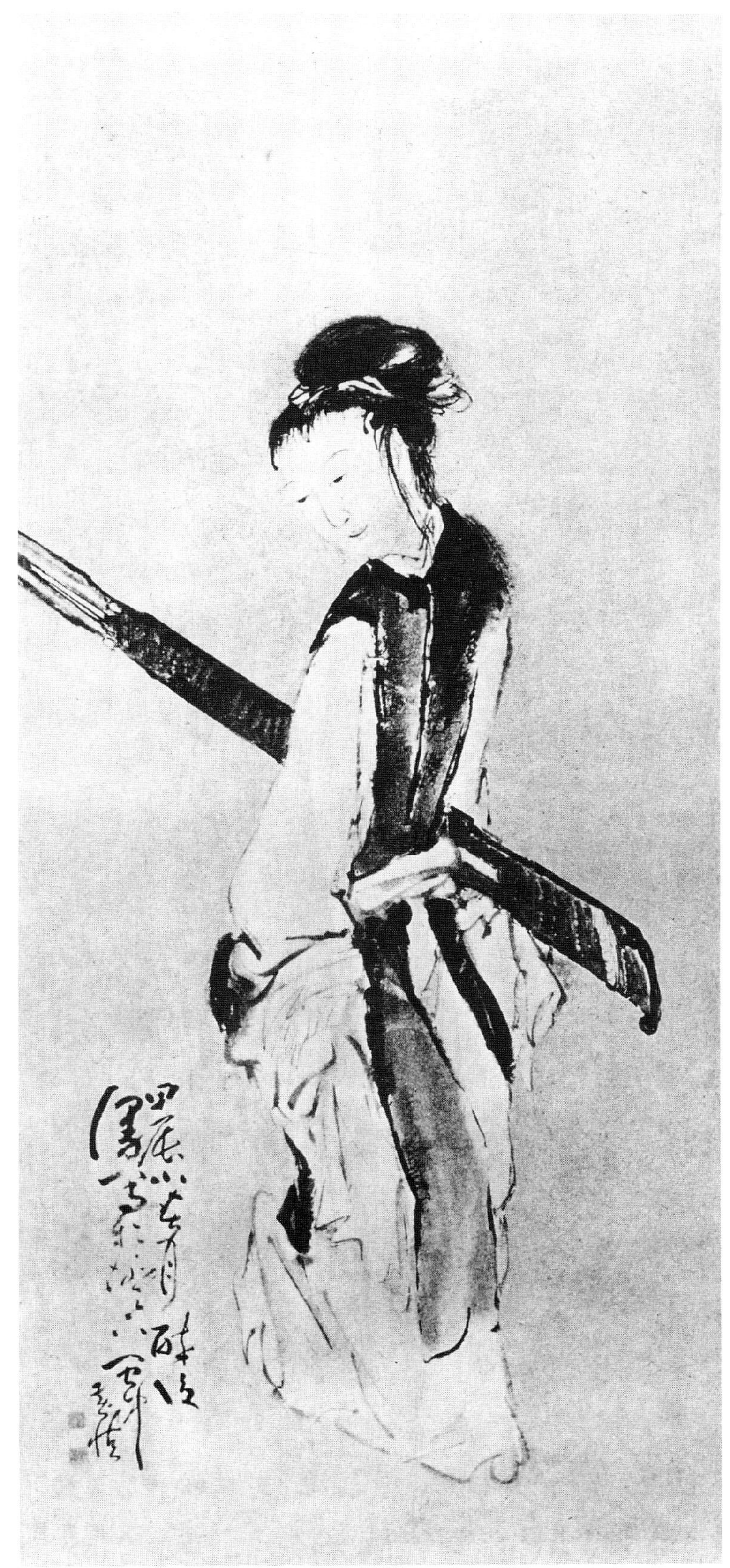

2.25. Huang Shen, "Lady Carrying a Ch'in."
Dated 1754. Hanging scroll, ink on paper. Collection unknown. From *I-yüan to-ying* 8 (March 1980), p. 6.

gifts of goods (as these women were virtually considered to be in Ming-Ch'ing China) and exchanges of favors, the more dignified mode of recompensing an artist for his works. Painters not in immediate need of cash were likely to prefer this latter mode, which placed them in principle on an equal plane with the recipient of the painting—the transaction, that is, could be thought of simply as two friends doing helpful things for each other, each according to his special capacities, without calculating loss and gain. (In fact, if we can judge from present-day practice, the calculation was of a precision and complexity for which the dense Occidental would need a computer to cope.) When the artist had a limited income and bills to pay, on the other hand, favors and friendship were not to the point. Cheng Hsieh adds a note to his price-list spelling this out for his clientele:

> Those who bring gifts and food are certainly not as welcome as those who come with white silver, because what you give is not necessarily what I desire. If you come with hard cash, my heart will be filled with joy so that both paintings and calligraphy will be excellent. Gifts cause nothing but trouble, not to mention deferred payment, which is most unreliable, like bad credit.[105]

Recorded instances in which artists painted to fulfill their side of some social exchange are many. An ideal and often-cited story tells of the T'ang master Wu Tao-tzu being asked by General Pei to make a painting for the funeral ceremony of his deceased wife; Wu refused to do it until the general agreed to perform his famous sword dance. The general danced, and Wu painted.[106] Chao Meng-fu in the early Yüan, while serving as an official in the north under Kublai Khan, wrote to a friend who was an official in his hometown, Wu-hsing, informing him that he was sending his family back to the south so that they could stay with his elderly parents. He asks the friend to look after them, and promises him his "ugly paintings" as gifts.[107] The eccentric painter Shih Chung in the early sixteenth century offered his paintings as his daughter's dowry.[108] His contemporary Shen Chou painted one of his finest works, a long landscape handscroll that took him three years to finish, to repay an obligation incurred when his friend Wu K'uan composed a tomb biography for Shen Chou's father.[109] The litterateur Wang Shih-chen once saw in the studio of the painter Lu Chih a picture of the "Peach Blossom Spring," which he admired and wanted, but dared not ask for; in 1571 he was able to get it in exchange for composing the artist's biography, after Lu had requested this through an intermediary. The two continued to exchange writings and paintings in the years that followed.[110]

Exchanges of a purely aesthetic nature, with no monetary or material benefit on either side, were also common: the artist could send a painting to someone whose musical performance he enjoyed,[111] or, as in many recorded cases, exchange a painting for a poem. People who wanted paintings by the late sixteenth-century Sung-chiang gentry-official artist Ku Cheng-i, for instance, usually got them in return for poems, we are told, since both parties "could not bear to talk about cash transactions."[112] Such fastidious confinement of one's exchanges to the pure aesthetic realm was of course possible only for well-off artists. Cases of this kind are sometimes cited as exemplifying the literati-amateur ideal of free exchanges, untainted by transfers of money or goods. But they were far from being the norm, and the same artists might engage in transactions of a more commercial character on other occasions, under different circumstances and with different recipients.

Artists used paintings to earn the goodwill of government officials, who would sometimes take the initiative in putting pressure on them to get their works. A notable early case is that of the three eighth-century masters Wang Wei, Cheng Ch'ien, and Chang T'ung, who were all imprisoned after the An Lu-shan rebellion for having held offices in the rebel court. The Grand Secretary of the time, Ts'ui Yüan, was an art lover, and interceded successfully in their behalf after they had all done paintings on the walls in his mansion.[113]

It was a regular practice for artists who were themselves government officials to give paintings to other officials as political gifts, in hope of favor, or to repay political obligations; I have mentioned the cases of Ch'eng Cheng-k'uei and Tung Ch'i-ch'ang, and many others could be cited.[114] The early Ch'ing Orthodox master Wang Chien painted four large landscape scrolls for a governor-general who had spared him from a prison term when he was under indictment.[115] The nineteenth-century flower painter and calligrapher Chao Chih-ch'ien expressed his gratitude to someone who had offered his son-in-law an official position by giving him paintings and calligraphy.[116]

I could continue with many more types; the diversity of situations in which these exchanges took place reflects the great flexibility of the *kuan-hsi* system.

Paying for a Painting III: Hospitality—the Artist-in-Residence

For impoverished artists—and, as we noted, those who had yet to make their names and who depended for their livings on their painting were frequently impoverished—the greatest favor might be to have their basic needs supplied, lodging and food, and daily amenities. Receiving someone's hospitality was one of the common ways in which an artist could be rewarded for painting. Again, the types within this large pattern could be arranged at points on a scale of social status.

At the upper end would be the case in which the artist, who might be an affluent amateur, is entertained by someone at a banquet or other social gathering and does a painting spontaneously on the spot, or is an overnight houseguest and agrees freely to do a picture for his host as a bread-and-butter gift; neither situation impinges on his artistic freedom. A surviving handscroll by Shen Chou, recording his journey with friends to Mt. Ling-yin near Hangchou, is an example: Shen's inscription dedicates it to a certain Taoist Hsiang with whom they had stayed overnight there.[117]

Such short-term hospitality could, on the other hand, rescue the artist in times of need: Ni Tsan depended on it in his late years, after he had relinquished his family estate, because of excessive taxes, to lead a wandering life, and Tung Ch'i-ch'ang, after his house had been pillaged and burned by a mob in 1616, lived in this way with sympathetic friends—several of his most impressive paintings date from this period, and may well have been done to repay heavy obligations.

The late Ming figure master Ts'ui Tzu-chung, who spent most of his life in poverty, moved into the Beijing house of a patron named Liu Lü-ting when in 1638 Liu departed to take up an official post; Ts'ui's portrayal of their farewell meeting, done to repay this hospitality and depicting the two of them drinking tea in a garden, is still to be seen (figure 2.26).

The noted official and playwright K'ung Shang-jen wrote to his impoverished friend Kung Hsien thanking him for a "marvelous painting," and inviting the artist to live with him for a time on his boat, intending both to make Kung's life easier and to acquire more of his paintings. "I am going to rise up in the morning and bring my boat around to the Great East Gate," he writes, "and you will be my guest. Since I do not wish to live so far apart from you, let us simply flee together and get away from things."[118]

Such a case seems midway between short-term hospitality, in which the parties are quasi-equals, and the lower end of our hierarchy, the artist-in-residence situation, of which we have already encountered several examples. Here the painter, who is usually a professional master, becomes for some period a member of the patron's household and is expected to produce paintings, often of a time-consuming kind and under the host's direc-

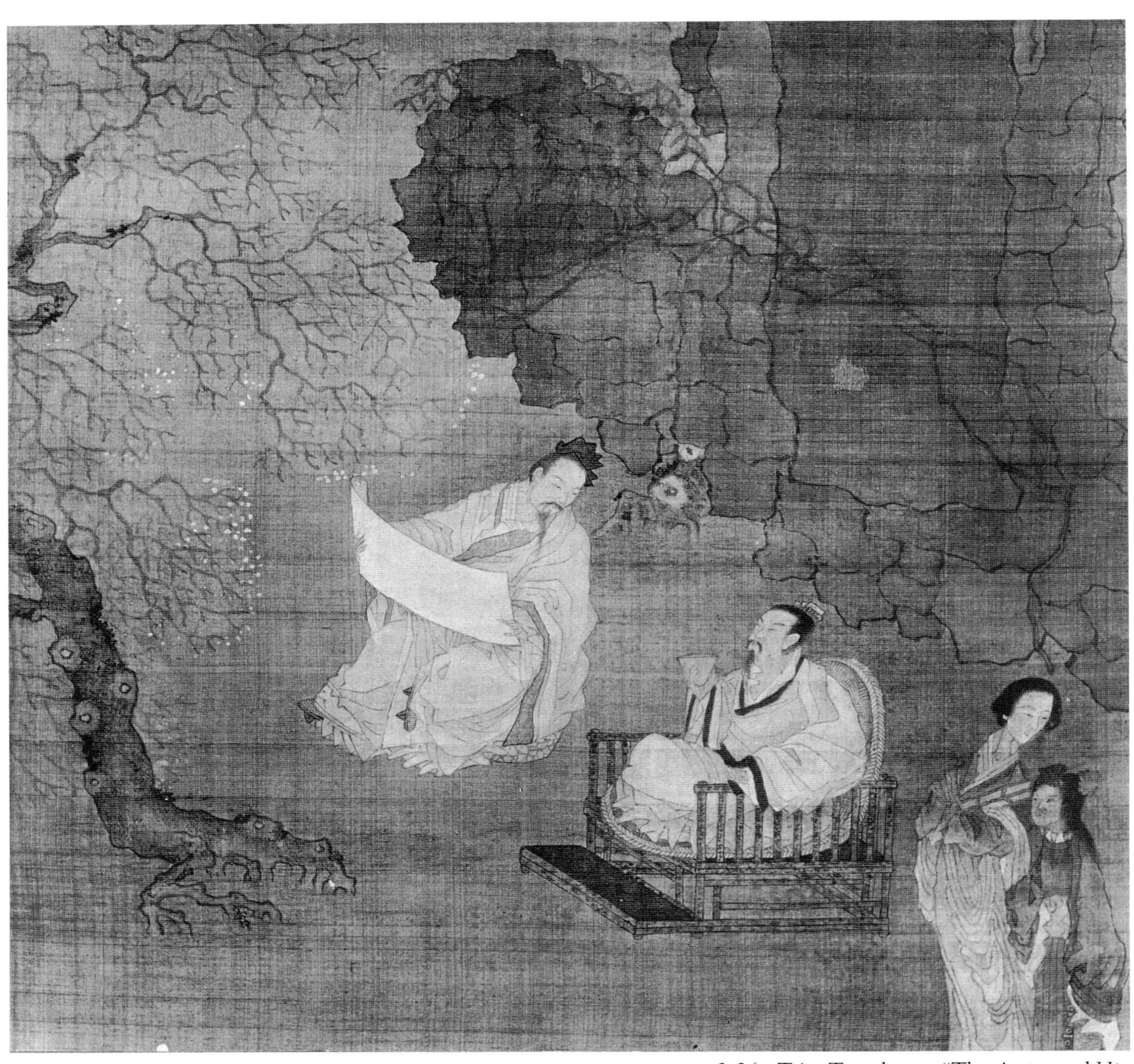

2.26. Ts'ui Tzu-chung, "The Artist and His Host Saying Farewell in a Garden."
Dated 1638. Detail from hanging scroll, ink and colors on silk, 148.8 × 51.4 cm. Collection of Nicholas Cahill, Madison, Wis.

tion. Chinese gentry families might employ a number of live-in artisans and professionals, including tutors, musicians, and entertainers, perhaps a garden designer, as well as writers and painters, all performing their particular services and practicing their arts and crafts.

Accounts of artists spending periods in residence with a patron begin as far back as the early Sung, when a rich imperial relative named Sun Ssu-hao would take artists he admired into his household, and would sometimes present the paintings they produced to the court, to win favor there, or recommend the artist himself to the imperial academy.[119] An early version of the *Sou-shan t'u* or "Clearing the Mountains" theme (see figure 2.27, a late Sung version), painted by one of his house-guest artists, Kao I, is an example; Sun presented it to the emperor.[120]

Kuo Hsi was painter-in-residence for an art-lover named T'ung Shih, along with his contemporary artists I Yüan-chi, Ts'ui Po, and Ts'ui Chüeh.[121] The Ming master Chou Ch'en, when he was forced against his will by the powerful minister Yen Sung to come to Nanking and spend two months painting for him, presumably lived in Yen's household. He was probably put to work copying old paintings in Yen's collection and producing seasonal landscapes for hanging. When Yen's collection was inventoried after his downfall, twenty-two of Chou's paintings were found in it, mostly pictures of these types. Wang Shih-chen writes that "Yen paid him nowhere near the value of the paintings, and Chou went home crushed."[122]

Ch'iu Ying spent periods of time as painter-in-residence with several patrons, the most important of whom was the great collector Hsiang Yüan-pien, with whom he stayed for several years late in his life, around 1550.[123] T'ang Yin spent ten days in 1519 at the home of a rich young collector named Hua Yün, working on an album of illustrations to a thirteenth-century text titled "Long Days in the Quiet Mountains.[124] On other occasions he spent fifty days at the house of a rich collector copying an album of old paintings,[125] and stayed three times with a friend named P'u-an doing 120 leaves illustrating poems by Po Chü-i, finishing the project in 1515, and receiving Shang dynasty antique bronze vessels and some valuable silk as his payment, in addition to the hospitality.[126] A leaf from this album, or a copy or re-creation of it, is extant (figure 2.28). T'ang Yin's inscription on it recounts these circumstances.

The Orthodox School master Wang Shih-min wrote to one of his sons, in a preserved letter dated 1666, about his former protege Wang Hui, who had been staying with him for about a month, painting so many pictures that the elder Wang wonders how he will pay him. This case, along with that of Chou Ch'en, indicates that an artist-in-residence expected a cash payment, which could be equivalent to the market value of the paintings he did, in addition to lodging and hospitality.[127]

The great patron Chou Liang-kung, to whose circle Wang Hui was briefly attached after he left Wang Shih-min, seems to have been a kind of one-man artist colony during his years in Nanking, with a number of painters living with him or dependent on him, among them Hu Yü-k'un and Chang Feng.[128] Chang had reportedly turned down an invitation to become artist-in-residence with a high official during his time in Beijing,[129] presumably out of fear that he would not enjoy the same creative independence that Chou Liang-kung offered his artist-friends. Chou was especially fond of albums, intimate works that he could enjoy in his study and carry with him when he traveled (figure 2.29). But albums, too, could have a public character: the eighteenth-century artist Fang Hsün stayed for a long time with a rich woman, the mother of a high-ranking official, and her son, producing a hundred-leaf album of "Scenes of Peace and Prosperity," which she intended for presentation to the Ch'ien-lung emperor, to felicitate him on his benevolent rule.[130]

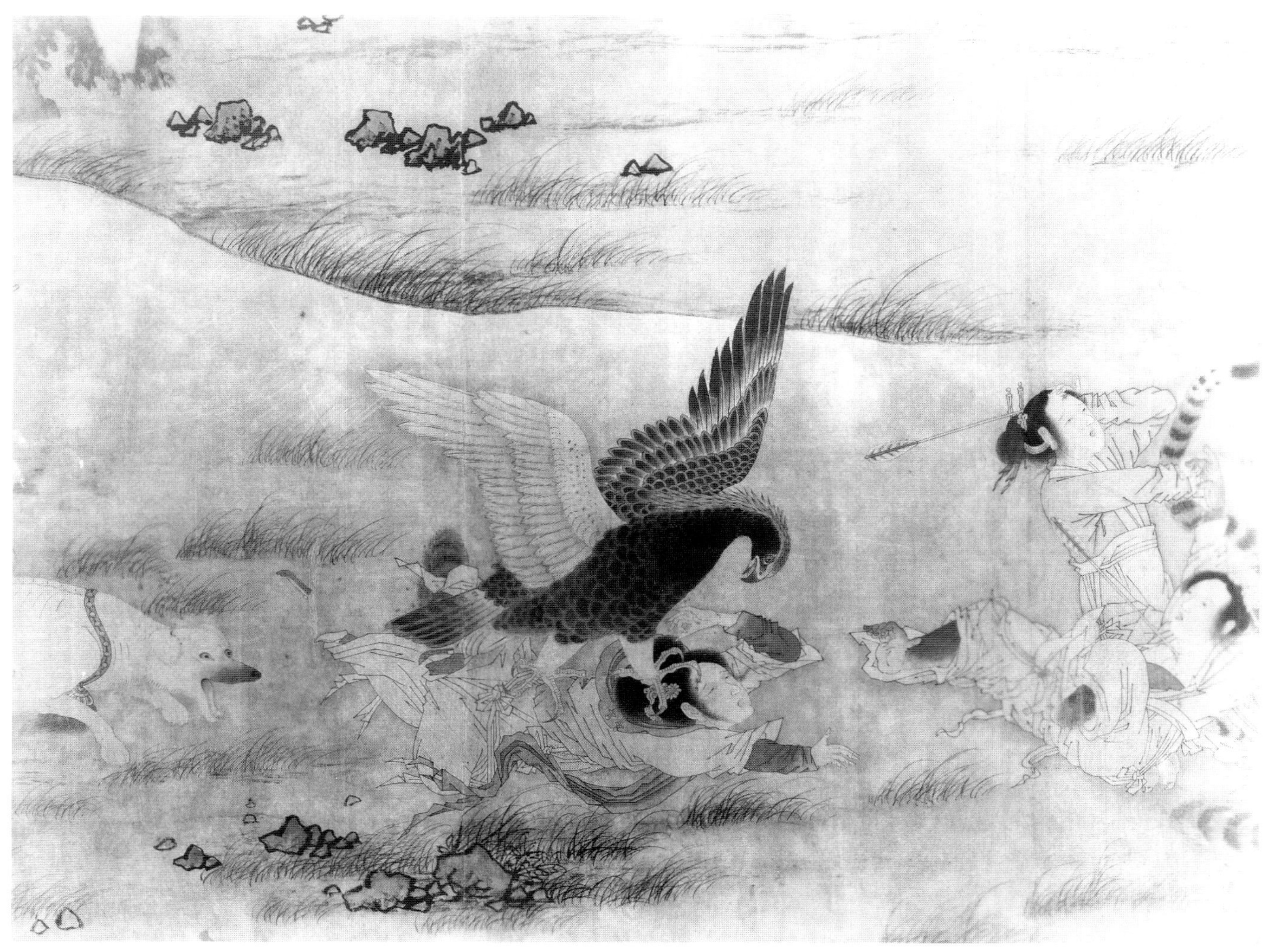

2.27. Anonymous, late Sung or Yüan period (13th–14th cent.), "Clearing the Mountains." Section of a handscroll, ink and colors on silk, Ht. 53.4 cm. Palace Museum, Peking.

The Secretariat, the Academy, Women Painters

A variant of the artist-in-residence situation, especially common in the late Ch'ing period, was for a painter or calligrapher to serve in some powerful official's *mu-fu* or secretariat. These were set up to enlist the services of capable people with a variety of skills. Tseng Kuo-fan (1811–72) and T'ang I-fen (1778–1853), the latter a painter of note himself, were two who employed artists in their *mu-fu*,[131] and Wu Ch'ang-shih served in this way under both Wu Ta-ch'eng (1835–1902)[132] and the Viceroy Tuan-fang (1861–1911).[133] Artists serving in the imperial court academies made up, of course, another type of artists-in-residence, a type I am not considering here, since it has already received a good deal of scholarly attention.[134] One may note, however, that the Empress Dowager Tz'u-hsi broke precedent in bringing talented women calligraphers and painters, along with men, into the court and giving some of them official titles.[135] At least two of them reportedly served Tz'u-hsi as ghostpainters, a practice I will consider in the final essay.[136]

The practice and economic status of women artists in China have only recently begun to be explored—the problem is so interlocked with the larger one of the status of women in traditional China that it cannot easily be summarized.[137] Both courtesans and gentry women could be painters. The latter were frequently the daughters or spouses of artists, and learned the art from family members, or, raised in well-to-do families, learned from tutors just as their brothers did.

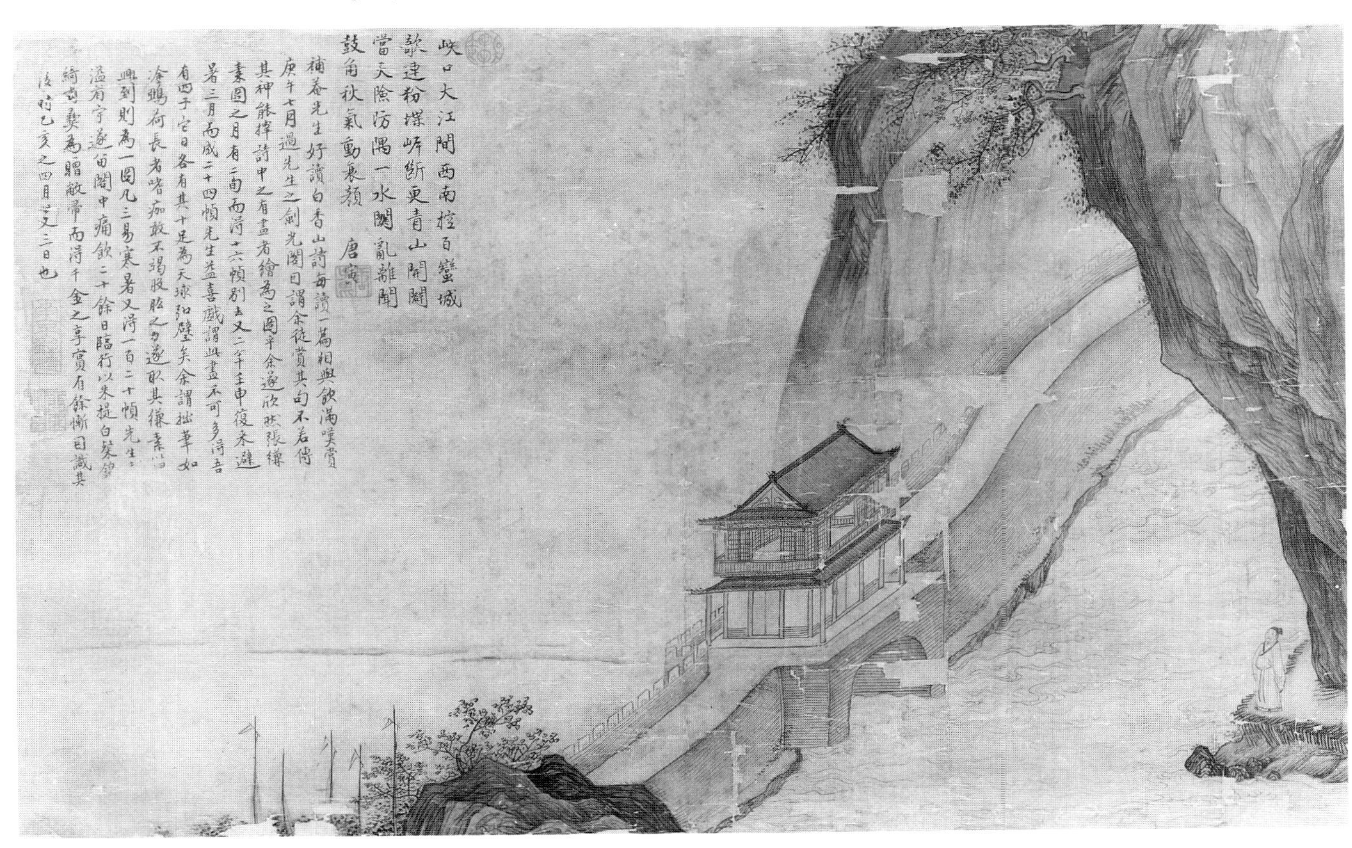

2.28. After T'ang Yin, "Great River at Entrance to Gorge." Leaf from an album, ink and colors on silk, 36.8 × 59.5 cm. Collection of Wan-lo H. C. Weng, Lyme, N.H.

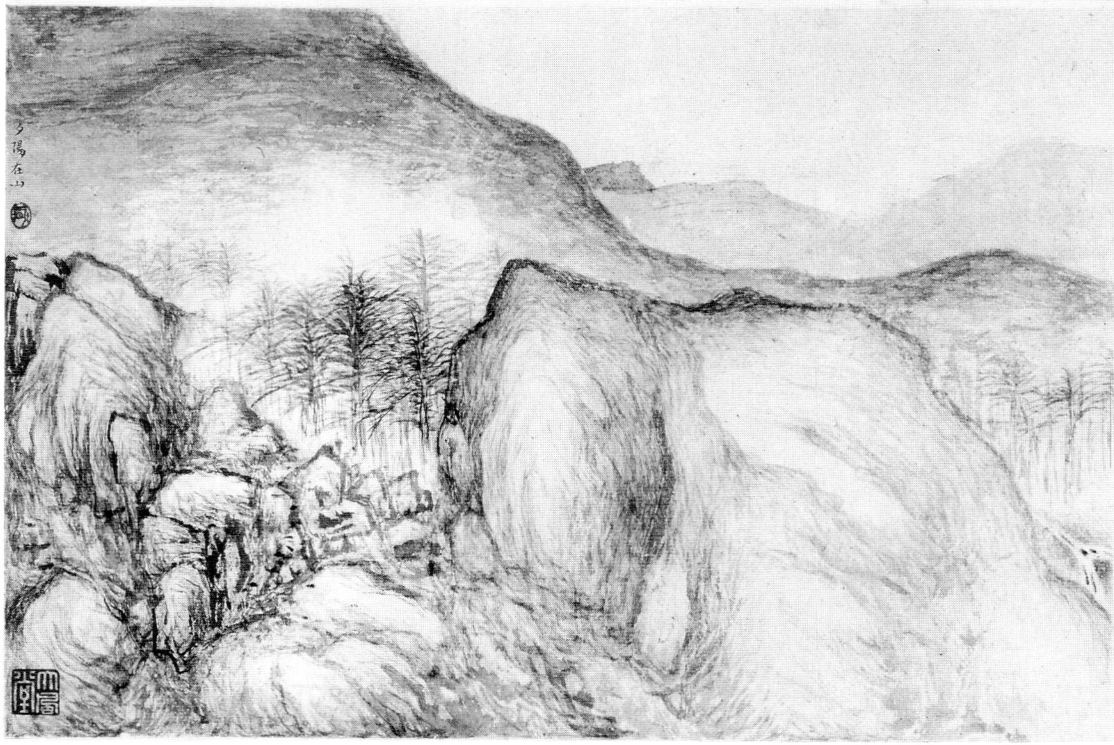

2.29. Chang Feng (active ca. 1636–62), "Landscape."
Dated 1644. Leaf from an album of twelve, ink on paper, 15.4 × 22.9 cm. Metropolitan Museum of Art, New York City (1987.408.2k), Gift of Douglas Dillon, 1987.

A courtesan could use paintings to enhance her personal attractiveness, since cultural accomplishments, if we believe the texts, served better than seductiveness and sexual skills in winning her popularity. She could use them as gifts to her admirers, and to convey more specific messages. A courtesan named Lin Nü-erh is recorded as having used a fan painting of willows to reject a former customer's demand to see her again.[138] A gentry woman artist could use her paintings as gifts in social exchanges, like male literati-amateur artists, or could sell them in times of personal or family hardship, or to supplement family income, or as an honorable way to survive if by circumstance she was forced to live alone.

THREE

The Painter's Studio

The previous chapter outlined and illustrated the kinds of dealings that Chinese artists had with their clients, or patrons or sometimes simply friends who wanted a painting but who were nonetheless expected to do something for the artist in return, and how the client's wishes were conveyed to the painter. It considered how go-betweens and agents were employed, and how the painter was rewarded for his work with money, gifts, or favors. This one will continue with the same themes, but with a shift of emphasis to the artist's working conditions, including studios, use of assistants, the transmission of designs, copying, and other matters of everyday practice. Not to be treated here, since they comprise a large, separate set of topics on which quite a lot of study has already been done, are the materials, tools, and brush techniques of painting.[1]

The accounts given here of situations in which the painting was requested and produced and the artist rewarded have mostly been of the kind in which the transaction went smoothly, and so leave unanswered such important questions as: Under what conditions would the negotiations break down? When and why would the artist refuse to paint? How far could the client stipulate the nature of the painting he wanted?

The Client's Share

I begin with the last question, and with the simple observation that the client's share in dictating the subject, style, and form of the painting he wanted varied, as we might expect, according to his own social position in relation to that of the artist. "Chinese were acutely aware," writes one social historian, "that society was a hierarchical structure within which each person occupied a clearly defined niche. The relationship of one Chinese to another was thus determined by the relative location of their niches."[2] The etiquette by which, especially in the late period, artists were granted some of the privileges proper to social levels above the ones they properly occupied—for instance, welcoming them to gatherings otherwise made up of people of wealth and power, or adopting a deferential tone when writing to them to request a painting—did not fundamentally alter this pattern. A powerful official in early sixteenth-century Suchou might have spoken or written politely to Ch'iu Ying, but he would have expected Ch'iu to follow closely his wishes for the painting he wanted. In inscriptions and other writings of the time we read of someone "summoning the painting-master *(hua shih)*" to do a picture for some occasion, or to portray a garden, or illustrate a text, much as one might call in the carpenter for a needed piece of furniture.

At the other end, the upper end, was the artist who by birth and position was able to treat most of the seekers after his paintings as equals, or even social inferiors, and so could afford to be indignant over the crassness of their demands and the gaucheries of their approaches. The literature is full of such stories, which for obvious reasons were favored, and frequently invented, by the painters and their admirers.

Here, for instance, is Ni Tsan complaining about people who mistook him for an artist of the ordinary type: "Lately when I come to town [presumably Suchou] people asking me to paint often insist that I paint in a certain way and finish at a certain time. They even resort to insults, angry words, or worse. This is not fair. Would anyone blame a eunuch for not growing a beard? What have I done to deserve such trouble?"[3] The Suchou people's demands on Ni Tsan, while they do indeed imply a misunderstanding of his status as a painter, imply also that dictating the nature of the work to the artist and giving him a deadline for its completion were normal practice at that time. But it was not the proper way to deal with Ni Tsan; we can be sure that whatever the wishes of such people, they would get from him (if they got anything at all) only one of his standard, spare river landscapes (figure 3.1), or a bamboo-and-rock picture, painted as he pleased and delivered when he was ready.

In Europe as well, the artist's status affected the question of how far the client could dictate the subject and the speed of completion of the work. Rudolf and Margot Wittkower contrast a contract given to Perugino in 1503, "the terms of which were in the medieval tradition," with the difficulties patrons had in getting paintings from more respected artists such as Leonardo da Vinci or Giovanni Bellini in the same period. The contract given to Perugino stipulated the subject in the most minute particulars, adding that "You are at liberty to omit figures but not to add anything of your own"; it also set the date by which the painting was to be delivered. But when Isabella of Spain wrote in 1501 to an official in Florence asking him to approach Leonardo for a painting, she wrote "If he consents, we would leave the subject and the time to him." Despite these concessions, she never got her picture. And her attempt to get a painting for her *studiolo* from Bellini, again through an intermediary or go-between, was also unsuccessful. The go-between wrote that the artist was willing, but that "the *invenzione* for the composition which, as your Excellency writes, should be suggested by me, will have to be left to his own imagination. He

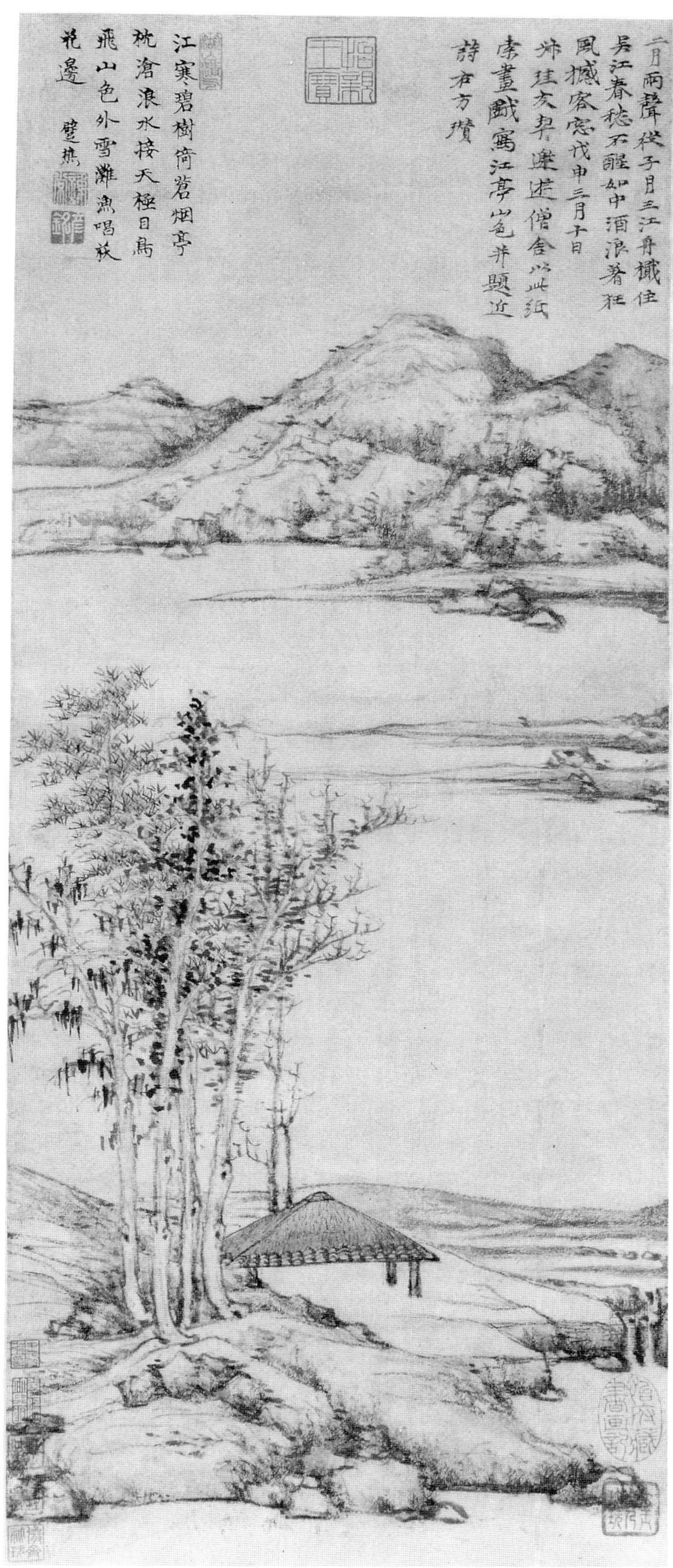

3.1. Ni Tsan, "River Pavilion, Mountain Colors." Dated 1368. Hanging scroll, ink on paper. Asian Art Museum of San Francisco (11989.1), on loan from the Collection of the Tang Family.

dislikes having precise terms imposed on him, preferring, as he says, to let his thought wander in his pictures at pleasure; according to him, they will then satisfy the beholder."[4] Isabella, the Wittkowers write, "could not quite resign herself to the irksome new ways of artists." Later, the idea of the intractable painter came to be more generally accepted. Nevertheless, the institution of educated and prestigious artists who enjoyed, through their status, a large degree of independence from outside demands was never so clearly developed in Europe as in China, where artists of the literati class were more or less unquestioningly accorded the privileges of that class.

The consequences of the literati painting ideal in artist-client relationships was well stated by Anne Clapp in her study of Wen Cheng-ming (figure 3.2). After quoting a close friend of the artist making the claim that "Whenever the rich and titled came seeking his work he was firm and would give nothing; but his poor friends he would help so they might make a good profit"—by selling the paintings Wen gave them, that is—she comments on "the practical results of such a policy and its effect on literati art: the painter and his chosen friends decided on all artistic matters and were the sole arbiters of taste. The recipients of the works took what was given them, so there was no question of a patron dictating themes or styles to the painter."[5] By insulating themselves against economic and other pressures, the claim was, literati artists were able to preserve their creative freedom. But the insulation was imperfect at best, often thin or absent altogether, and the creative freedom was accordingly compromised. Clapp's statement, as she was well aware, is a statement of the ideal, to which actual practice conformed only loosely. It was an ideal that nonetheless pervaded writings and negotiations about paintings. *Ju-mien t'an,* the early Ch'ing letter-writing manual cited by Anne Burkus, advises its user "to indulge in only the most general description of the subject he wished to have painted."[6]

But again, that admonition seems to have been violated frequently. Wen Cheng-ming's disciple Ch'ien Ku, who was like his teacher an educated man and a collector of rare books, and who followed his master's style closely (figure 3.3), is conventionally said to have ignored requests from those who sought his paintings.[7] But we have several records of commissions to him, including the letter in which the client asked for a painting of Kuan-yin in ink and an illustration to Ou-yang Hsiu's "Dirge of Autumn." In another preserved letter, Wang Shih-chen's younger brother Shih-mou orders a painting, again stipulating the subject, and asking the artist to finish the picture expeditiously.[8] I have already mentioned other cases in which the client specifies what he wants to the artist, such as the man who sent his servant to Kung Hsien with a letter asking for a landscape that would be "dense as if there were no sky, empty as if there were no ground." (Perhaps he had seen Kung Hsien's great "Thousand Peaks and Myriad Ravines," now in the Rietberg Museum,[9] and wanted another one like that, as any of us would.) In this case, the artist was left considerable leeway.

The same is true of a client who wrote the Orthodox School landscapist Wang Hui, in a preserved letter, asking for an album of landscapes in old styles and a handscroll in the manner of Huang Kung-wang.[10] With artists who were unambiguously professional, such as portrait specialists, one could be more specific in stating one's desires. In a letter preserved in a collection compiled by Chou Liang-kung, a man writing to the late Ming portraitist Hsieh Pin (see figure 3.4) praises the artist and the portrait he has made—presumably a draft submitted to the sitter for his approval—but goes on to ask the painter to dress him, in the finished portrait, in antique garb, a "brilliant moon" robe and "distant traveling" shoes, and to present him holding a bundle of letters and accompanied by two boys.[11]

Chou Liang-kung himself would probably never have written this way to Ch'en Hung-shou, who as an educated man with a brief period of service in the imperial court occupied a higher social position than did Hsieh Pin. Chou relates in a letter of his own that Ch'en had recently painted a portrait of him in the guise of the fourth-century poet-recluse T'ao Yüan-ming, implying that the decision to portray him this way was the painter's. He comments that Ch'en was not properly a portraitist, but that his work was all the more "strange and wonderful" for this.[12] In 1638 seven of Ch'en Hung-shou's cousins came to him to ask for a birthday painting to present to their mother, his aunt, on her sixtieth birthday. Ch'en accepted the commission, but again it

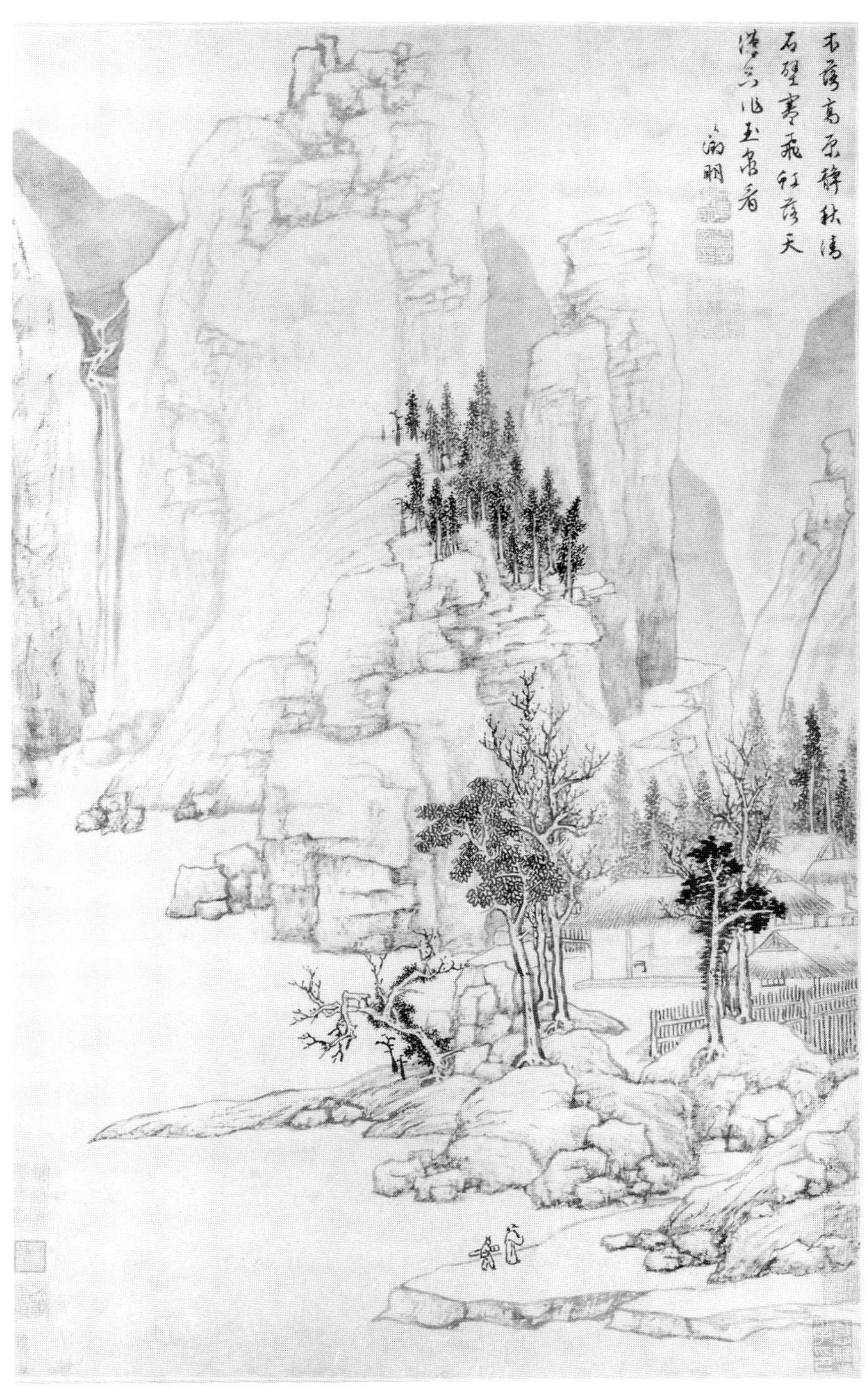

3.2. Wen Cheng-ming, "Stone Cliff and Rainbow," in the manner of Huang Kung-wang.
Hanging scroll, ink on paper, 65.5 × 40.9 cm.
Shanghai Museum.

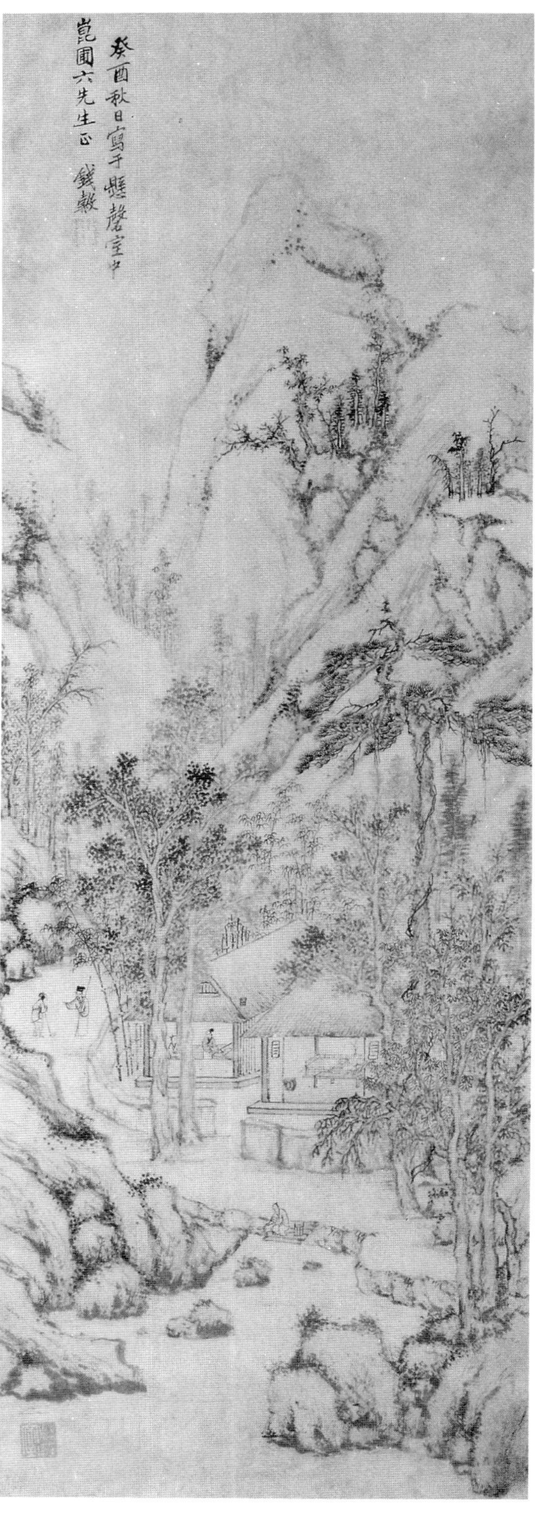

3.3. Ch'ien Ku, "Waiting for a Guest in a Mountain Dwelling."
Dated 1573. Hanging scroll, ink and colors on paper, 86 × 30 cm. Shanghai Museum.

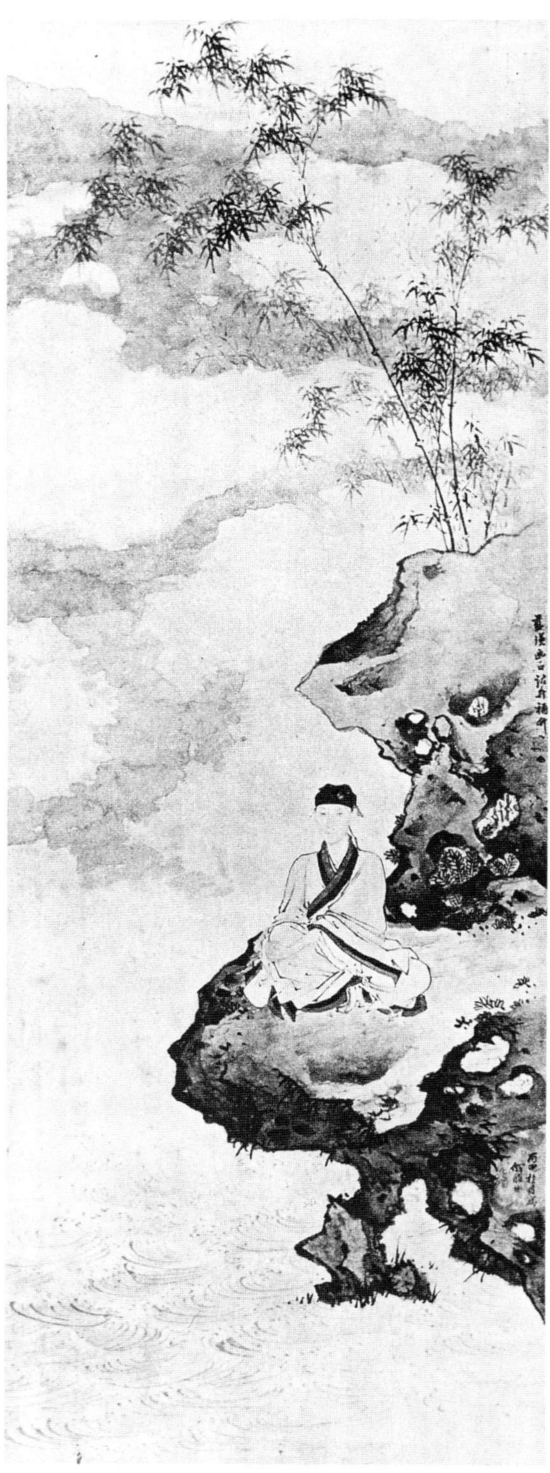

3.4. Hsieh Pin, "Portrait of a Man" (setting painted by Lan Ying and Chu Sheng).
Hanging scroll, ink and colors on silk, 133 × 49 cm. Palace Museum, Peking. From *I-yüan to-ying,* no. 27 (January 1986), p. 15 right.

was he himself who decided to portray the aunt (figure 3.5) in the flattering personage of Lady Hsüan-wen-chün, a learned lady of the fourth century who was invited by the ruler to give lectures on a classical text in which her family had traditionally specialized as scholars.[13]

T'ang Yin (see figure 3.6), inscribing a painting he had done for the birthday of the great minister Wang Ao in 1519 at the request of Wang's eldest son, felicitates Wang as if the painting were a present from himself rather than a commissioned work, and writes of the subject as one he himself had chosen: tall pines, waterfall, and rocks, with a small portrait of Wang Ao inserted by a portrait specialist whom T'ang Yin "engaged" for that purpose. Anne Clapp, in discussing this work, points out that the intimate tone of T'ang's inscription reflects his superior status, above that of the ordinary professional master, and his thirty-year friendship with Wang Ao.[14]

Cases in which the parties involved in the transaction were more or less equals, such as that of Ch'en Hung-shou and his cousins, or in which the patron respected the artist as a cultivated man, as Wang Ao respected T'ang Yin, stand midway on a scale between the domineering client who insists on determining the nature of the painting at one end and the haughty artist who will not be pressured in any way at the other. Under this condition of quasi-equality the artist felt less constrained by demands, but the recipient of the painting also could feel more free to express his wishes. When the great Five Dynasties landscapist Ching Hao exchanged one of his works for a poem by the monk Ta-yü, the poet was allowed to describe what he wanted to have in his painting.[15]

When Kung Hsien asked Wang Hui to paint his garden, he sent a description of it with his request;[16] the same was true when Shih-t'ao asked his distant cousin Pa-ta Shan-jen for a picture of his Ta-ti ts'ao-t'ang or Great Cleansing Hall and its setting. Pa-ta had never seen the place, and Shih-t'ao sent only the tersest of

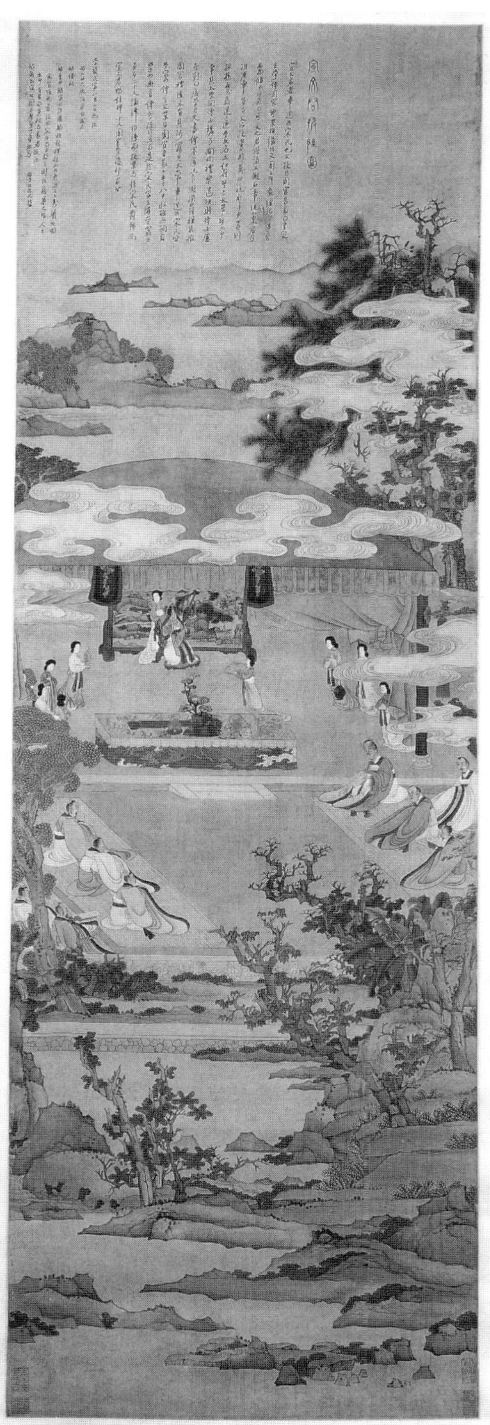

3.5. Ch'en Hung-shou, "Lady Hsüan-wen-chün Giving Instruction on the Classic." Dated 1638. Hanging scroll, ink and colors on silk, 173.7 × 55.6 cm. Cleveland Museum of Art (61.89).

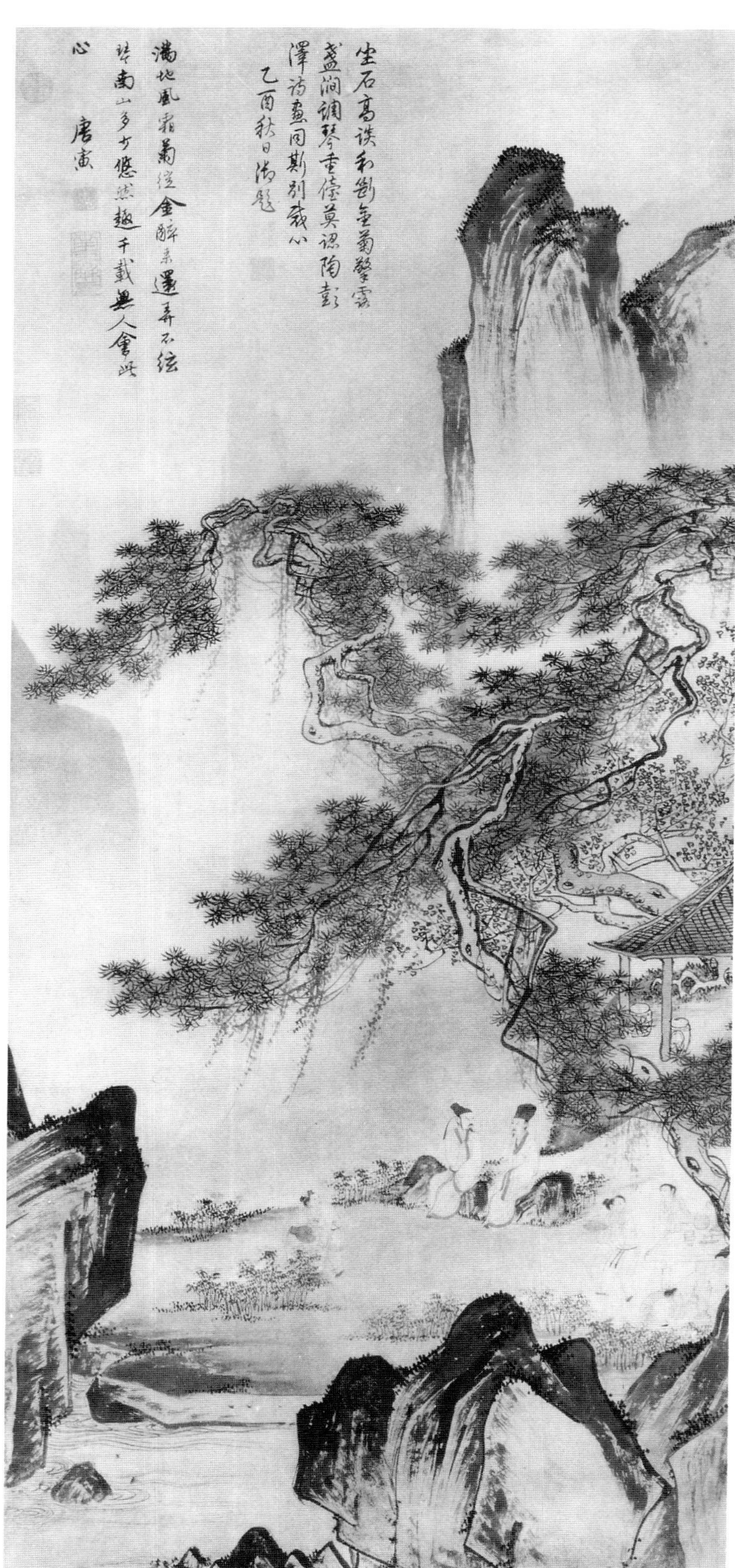

3.6. T'ang Yin, "Enjoying Chrysanthemums by the Eastern Fence."
Hanging scroll, ink and colors on paper, 134 × 62.6 cm. Shanghai Museum.

descriptions: "I would like to beg of you a small hanging scroll three feet tall and one foot wide, [portraying] on a flat bank an old house with a few rooms and a few ancient, useless trees, and in the upper level just an old man, nothing else around. This will represent Ta-ti-tzu [myself] in his Ta-ti-t'ang."[17] The last thing Shih-t'ao wanted was a detailed and visually accurate portrayal of the place. If he *had* wanted that, he would have engaged some local professional such as Yüan Chiang, whose garden pictures are highly informative but far less prestigious (figure 3.7).

What was desirable was to have one's garden or retreat "represented" in the hand and style of a particular respected master. A certain Chi Yung-jen in the early Ch'ing, writing to a monk-painter named Fan-lin, provides a much more detailed description of the picture he wants of his estate in Suchou, which the painter presumably had never seen: "There should be five willows in front of the gate and two paulownia beside the well. Inside a grass-thatched hut surrounded by a bamboo fence, please add a recluse reading with his hair loose on his shoulders."[18] A leaf from an album of garden pictures ascribed to Shen Chou (figure 3.8) gives us some idea of what the finished painting may have looked like.

The best assumption is that such a case was exceptional; what the painter most often had was only some sense of the client's general expectation, conveyed to him verbally or by letter, or simply understood between them. One can suppose that it was usually more like what Michael Baxandall calls a "charge" to the artist, which could be very general, such as

3.7. Yüan Chiang. "The East Garden."
Section of a handscroll, ink and colors on silk, ht. 59.8 cm. Shanghai Museum.

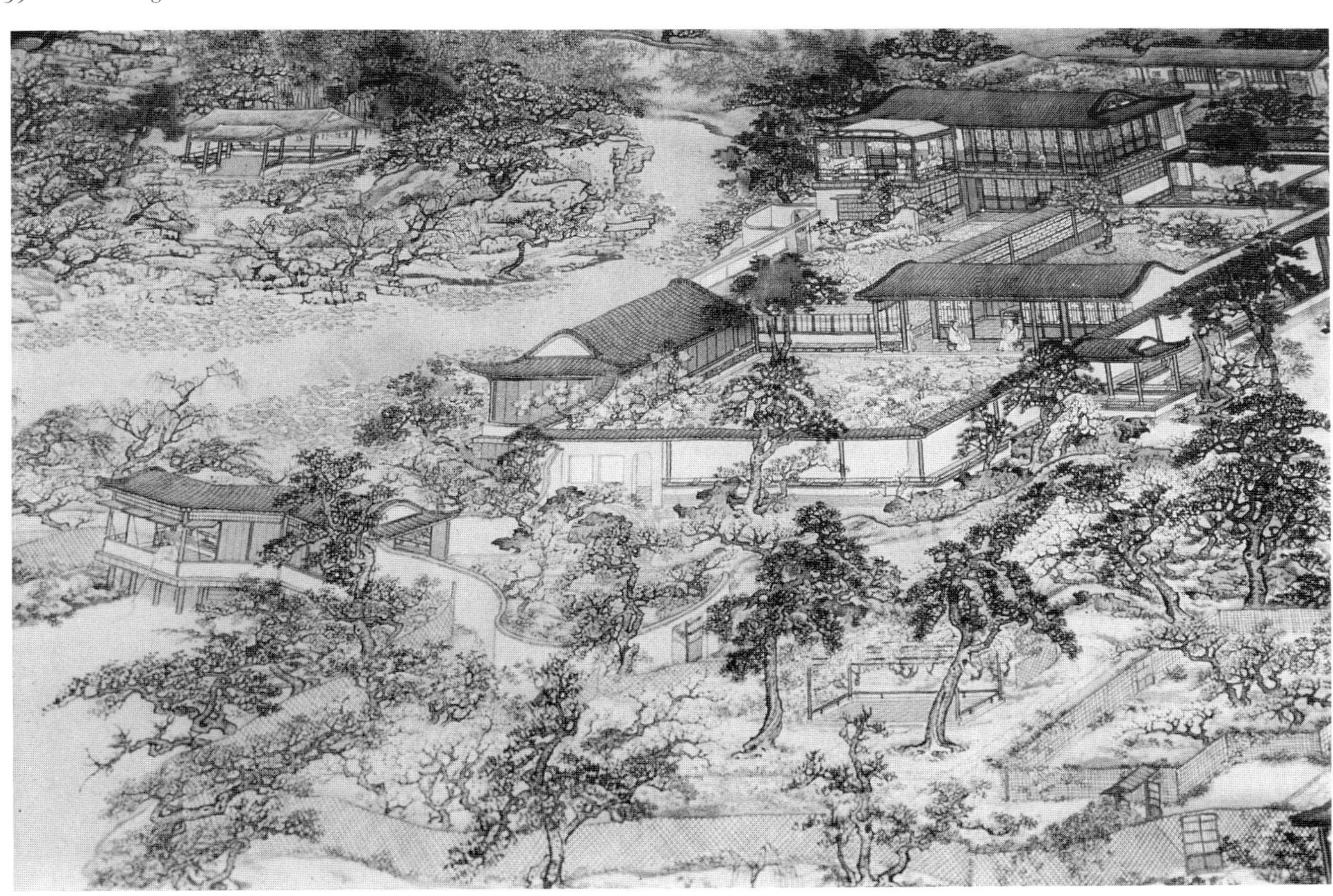

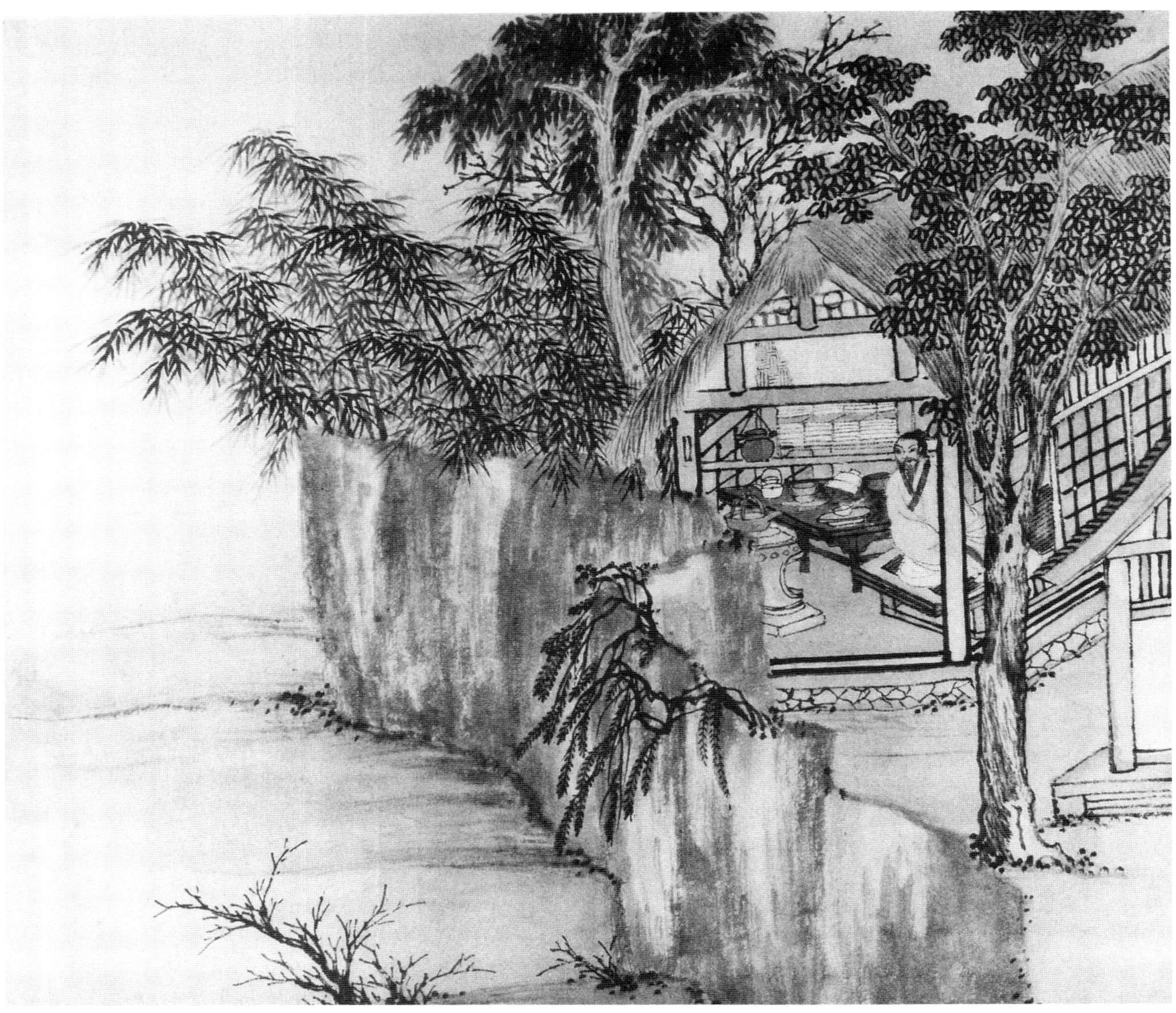

3.8. Attributed to Shen Chou, "The East Garden."
Leaf from an album, ink and colors on paper, ht. 27.7 cm. Suchou Museum. From *Shen Chou Tung-chuang t'u-ts'e* (Nanking, 1966).

"birthday painting, please," than like what he calls a "brief," which would spell out more specifically the client's requirements.[19] Because the expectation tended to be general, it was not so restricting as the literati-painters' high-pitched rhetoric sometimes suggests, and left the artist free to determine the essential artistic character of his work, and to preserve his pride. A letter from an early Ch'ing painter named Chou Ch'i to a client is revealing in this regard: Chou accepts a commission for a birthday picture, and even lets the client dictate the theme, but goes on to claim a special understanding of the man's intention, based on the level of culture he himself has attained:

I have received the vermilion [pigment] you sent, and have used it to add autumn color to one of my paintings—it can be truly said that "the frosty [maple] leaves are redder than the flowers of early spring." [The allusion is to a poem by the T'ang poet Tu Mu.] Thank you. Also, you have ordered a picture of two pines for your friend's birthday, with the appearance of [survival in] wintry cold, standing straight and aloof [to symbolize, that is, the loftiness and integrity of the recipient of the work.] Only I really understand your intention; I am not at all like the common artisan-painters. [He makes a learned allusion to pine trees, and concludes:] I have been reading old books for many years, but end each year in poverty; yet I keep my dignified bearing, without change. How can I be other than the very embodiment of the pine and cedar? I paint pictures for other people, but I really paint for myself, ha ha![20]

No surviving painting by Chou Ch'i is known; we offer as substitute a picture of two pines by Ch'en Hung-shou (figure 3.9).

The Reluctant Artist

To be considered next is the problem of the reluctant artist, and the negotiations that somehow break down. The talk of commissions and agents and payment should not mislead one into thinking that Chinese artists always acceded to requests—many cases are recorded in which they did not. In the standard accounts, artists decline to paint principally when they lack respect for the would-be recipient. The early literature of painting offers many stories of those who refused to work for rich people, or for those who approached them in the wrong way. Although there may well be truth in some of these, we can assume that in large part they belong to the myth of the untrammeled, disinterested painter described in the opening chapter; there is a degree of sameness about them that suggests this. The tenth-century painter Sun Wei, we are told, associated with Buddhist and Taoist monks, but not with rich people, who, even when they offered him huge

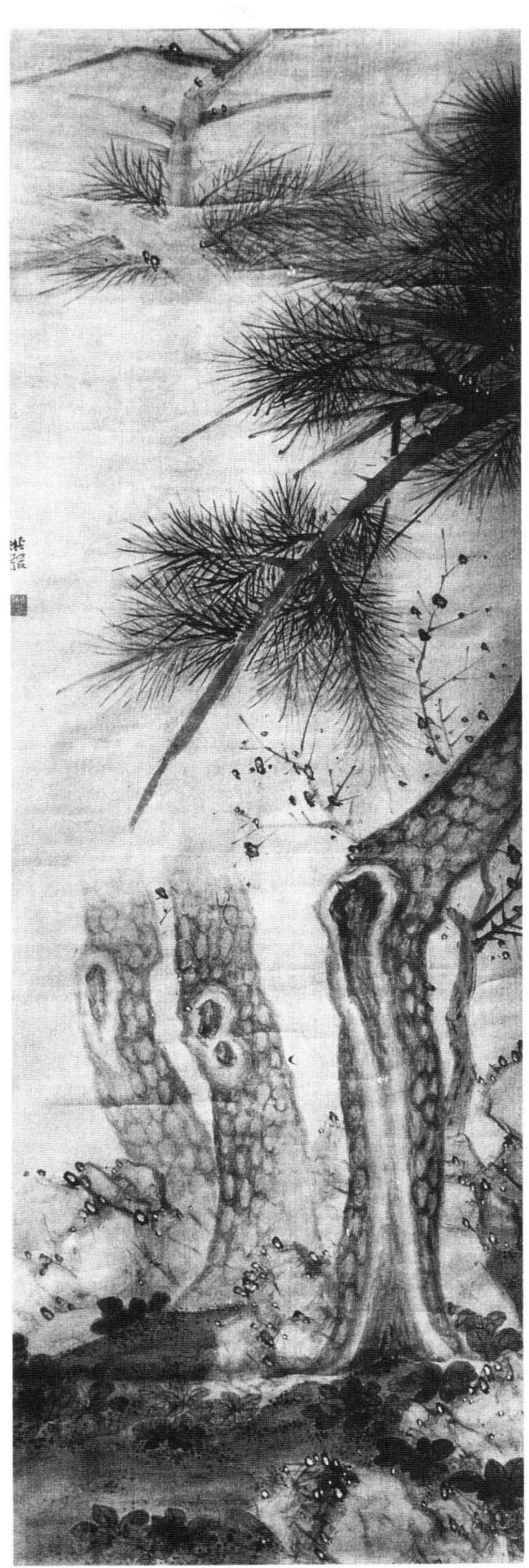

3.9. Ch'en Hung-shou, "Three Pines." Hanging scroll, ink and colors on silk, 154 × 49.5 cm. Kuang-chou City Museum. From *Ch'en Hung-shou tso-p'in chi* (Hangchow, 1990), plate 6.

sums of money, could not get one of his paintings.[21] Among early landscapists, both Li Ch'eng and Kao K'o-ming are said to have refused invitations to paint for the wealthy, in order to preserve their artistic integrity.[22]

The figure master Wu Ts'ung-yüan, active in the early eleventh century, would never let rich people acquire his works. One of them, a business man, importuned him for over ten years, wanting a picture of the Water Moon Kuan-yin. Wu finally agreed, but took three years more to finish the painting, so that when he went to deliver it, the man had died.[23] Of one twelfth-century master, Kan Feng-tzu, we are told that when rich people wanted his paintings he would insult them and refuse to paint for years.[24] Of another named Wei Kuan-ch'a it was said that there was no way to get his paintings at all: using force, proposing to trade goods for them, even offering him official positions, all were of no avail.[25] And so on.

The same kind of story becomes standard for many later artists. A late Ming writer tells of a monk-painter named Ku Ch'ing-p'u, for instance, who painted landscapes in the Mi Fu manner, but did them only for poets and fellow monks, refusing to accept payment for his paintings.[26] It may be recalled that the same was said of the early Ch'ing master Chu Ta, but that paintings by him could in fact be ordered, with suitable payment, through an agent.

Successful painters came to be wary of people who would contrive deceptive "social occasions" with the aim of obtaining works by them. An amusing story is told about how Kuo Chung-shu, a tenth-century master who specialized in detailed architectural painting, dealt with a rich young man, the son of a wine dealer, who invited the artist to a wine-drinking party, set out silk and paper conspicuously, and repeatedly importuned him for a picture. At last Kuo Chung-shu took one of the long horizontal rolls of paper (intended for a handscroll painting), drew at the beginning a boy with his hair in tufts holding onto a reel of kite-string; at the far end, the kite; and connecting them, a thin brushline many yards in length, representing the string. The young man was too dense to see anything unusual in this, and thanked the painter profusely.[27] (A handscroll painting by Hsü Wei, figure 3.10, is an imagined and much truncated reconstruction of Kuo Chung-shu's picture.)

Another story of this kind is told by Chou Liang-kung about his friend Ch'en Hung-shou, in which a man who wants one of Ch'en's works entices the artist onto a boat, pretending that he means to ask his opinion on some old paintings. When his real intentions are revealed, Ch'en scolds the man and removes his cap and clothes, threatening to jump into the water. The man finally gives up

3.10. Hsü Wei, "Boy Flying Kite."
Section of a handscroll, ink on paper, ht. 32.4 cm. Shanghai Museum.

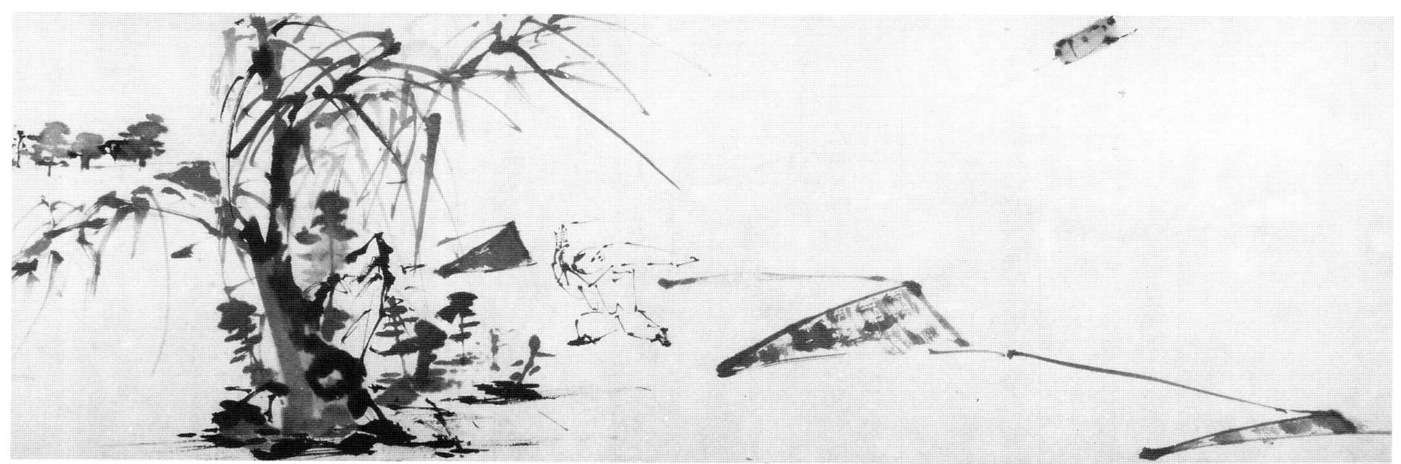

and leaves, but later sends a go-between to request a painting; Ch'en stubbornly refuses.[28]

Chu Ta or Pa-ta Shan-jen, not unexpectedly, is the subject of stories of this kind. In one, he is asked by his host at a party to paint the lotus flowers and pine trees on the host's estate. Pa-ta is inspired and executes the work, with which the host is very pleased. But when one of the guests tries to take advantage of the artist's exhilarated state to get a painting for himself, Pa-ta dashes off a picture of two fighting chickens, behaves strangely, and leaves.[29] As Wang Fangyu sees it, Pa-ta "manipulated his behavior to control social interaction," relying on his reputation for aberrant, "mad" behavior to escape unwelcome importuning. On another occasion he revealed one method, no doubt unfailingly effective, for dealing with a person who invites him to his house in order to get one of his works: "If he were an uneducated military man, I would not be fussy about it. I could simply go there, defecate, and leave."[30]

A typical case of an artist refusing to paint for someone who approached him too directly is that of Wang San-hsi, a minor master active in the later eighteenth century whose position as a respected landscapist doubtless depended largely on his being the nephew of Wang Yüan-ch'i's nephew Wang Yü, and thus, however distantly, in the Orthodox "blood-line" (figure 3.11). A contemporary writes of him:

> Whoever wants a painting from him offers him strings of cash and must write a letter to get it. One day, a person came carrying a large sum of money and knocking on his gate asking for a painting. Wang refused him, saying "Ancient people wrote flatteringly to get a calligrapher's works. [Even] when silk was offered as payment, there had to be a proper ritual of reception. Am I to sell paintings like the crafty people in the marketplace?" The person became angry and left.[31]

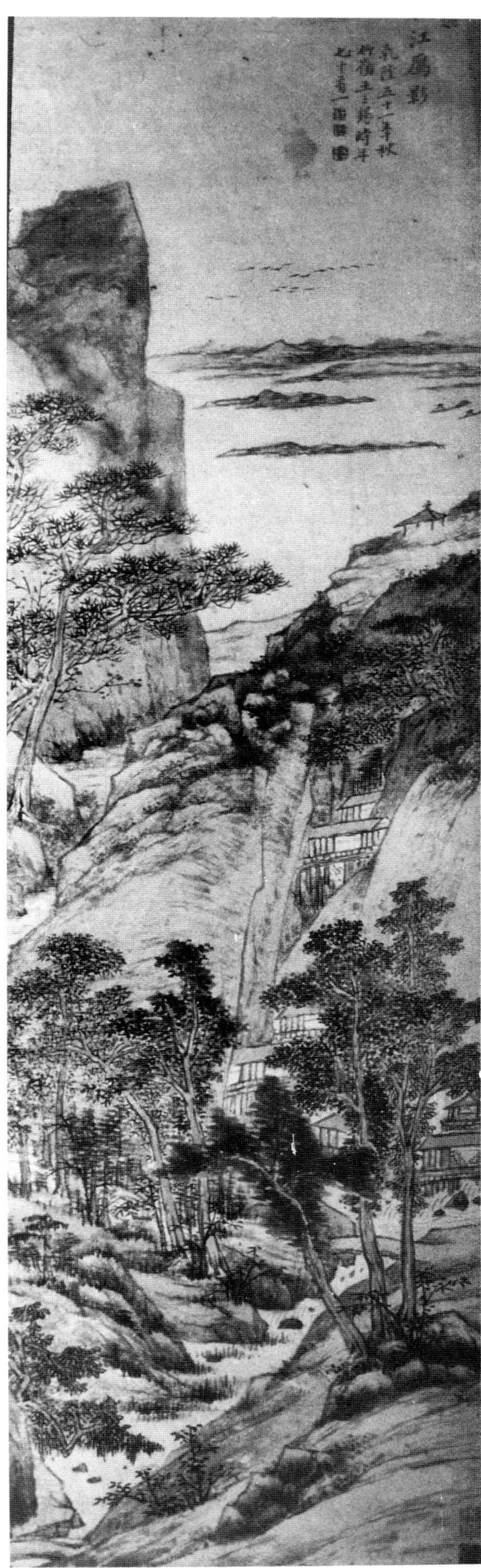

3.11. Wang San-hsi (1720—after 1798), "Autumn Landscape."
Dated 1785. Hanging scroll, ink and light colors on paper; dimensions unknown. Former collection of Chang Yin-chung, Tokyo.

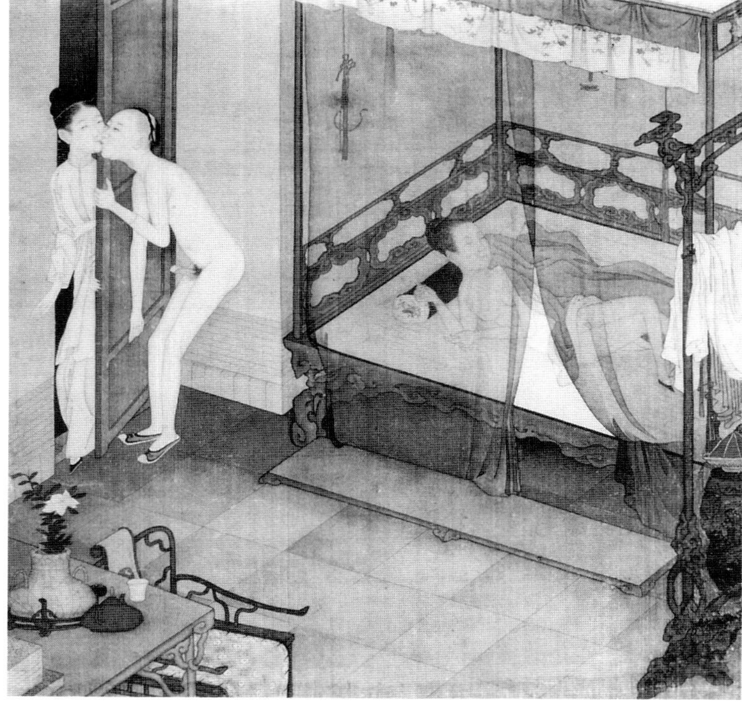

3.12. Leng Mei (active early to mid-18th cent.), "Amorous Couple." Leaf from an erotic album, ink and colors on silk, 29.2 × 28.5 cm. Collection of Sydney L. Moss Ltd., London.

Fang Hsün, active around the same time, was approached by a rich merchant who offered him many strings of cash to do a pornographic painting. Fang refused indignantly, saying "There is no skill worse than tempting evil minds to lust. Although I am poor, I will not do it."[32] Ch'en Hung-shou, by contrast, apparently did paint erotic pictures: the Nanking landscapist Tsou Che writes in a letter that his friends all praise Ch'en's "Scenes of Intimate Play" as wonderful beyond compare, but that he himself finds them offensive.[33] (Unhappily for those of us less prudish, no paintings of this kind by Ch'en Hung-shou seem to have survived. The earliest and best we have appear to be from the eighteenth century; figure 3.12, a leaf from an album by Leng Mei, is a good example.)[34]

An early Ch'ing master named Liu Chiu was angered when a prince, pleased with one of his paintings, compared him to the Ming artist Chang Lu. Since Chang Lu belonged to the critically discredited late phase of the Che School, this could be taken as an insult. Liu took his painting into the next room, saying he hadn't signed it yet, and wrote his given name Chiu (which means wine) hundreds of times all over it. The prince was furious, and threw him out; Liu was happy.[35] Accounts of artists destroying their work are not uncommon. The early Sung writer Liu Tao-ch'un, for instance, tells us of one who painted his pictures in wineshops and used them as collateral against loans; on sobering up, he would repay the loans and destroy the paintings.[36]

Finally, a story about the eccentric figure painter Min Chen, active in the mid-eighteenth century. "Since he is good at portraiture," writes a contemporary,

> People come one after another to request paintings from him [see figure 3.13]. He paints without hesitation for the poor, but asks high prices from the rich. He despises people of high rank, saying "Why should I paint the images of these predators?" The viceroy of [his home province] Hupei heard of Min's reputation and summoned him to paint [his portrait]. Min Chen presented him with a draft *(fu-pen)* in which the form and resonance were complete and the spirit and human feeling skillfully captured. The viceroy was very happy and ordered him to finish the painting quickly.

Min Chen asked for a huge (nearly incredible) amount, 2,000 yi or about 40,000 taels, to "moisten his brush." Chastised for being excessive in his demand, he said "The position of viceroy is a lofty one; if I accept your commission without asking a high price, it means I take the viceroy very lightly and also that I despise my own painting." The viceroy offered 1,000 yi, still a staggering price. Min Chen refused; the viceroy was ready to throw him in jail; and Min Chen had to flee to the capital.[37]

Transactions would break down when the

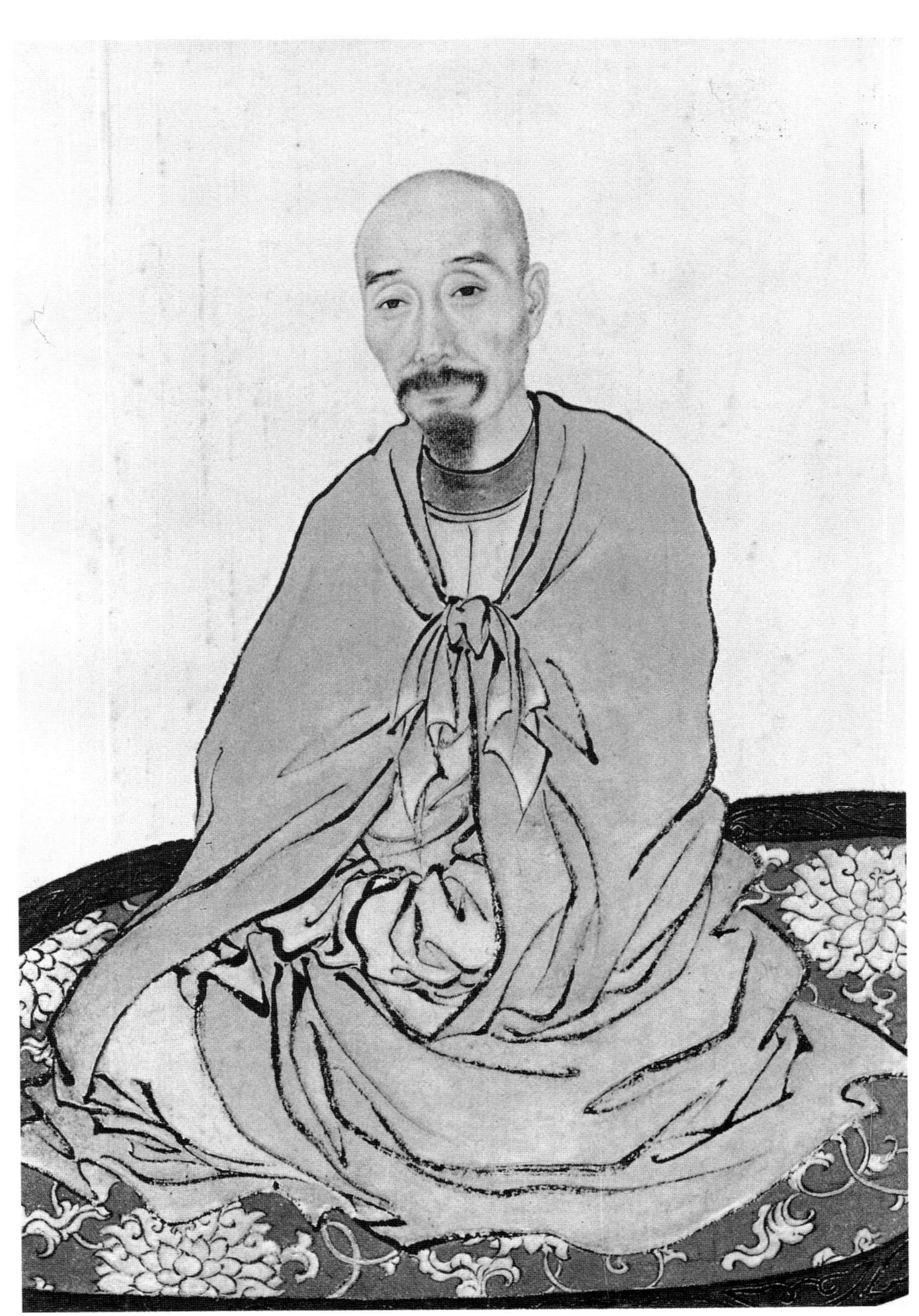

3.13. Min Chen, "Portrait of Pa Wei-tsu."
Detail of a hanging scroll, ink and colors on paper, 103.5 × 31.6 cm. Palace Museum, Peking. From *I-yüan to-ying,* no. 27 (January 1986), back cover.

client failed to make payment,[38] or when the artist accepted payment but then for some reason failed to complete the painting, as in the story about Jen Po-nien recounted earlier. Chou Liang-kung tells us of an artist named Wang Kuo-ch'un who painted in a meticulous style, taking as long as a year to finish a picture. Advised to paint more quickly and sell more, he replied that he would rather be poor than do sloppy work. The trouble was that sometimes the person who had originally requested the painting and paid Wang Kuo-ch'un for it didn't get it in the end, because Wang had already spent the money and had to pawn the picture for more, or sell it to somebody else.[39]

The Dissatisfied Client: Drafts for Approval

Cases in which the client is dissatisfied with the work are more rarely reported, presumably because most of the extant writings are concerned with artists, not patrons, and regularly take the artist's side on any matter. A letter is preserved from one of Ch'en Hung-shou's patrons, Chang Tai, however, in which Chang complains that the paintings he received from the artist were "all unfinished, smeared and rubbed all over the pieces of silk."[40] Presumably he expected examples of Ch'en's fine style, and got his rough style instead (see figure 3.14). We can assume that cases of dissatisfied clients were not uncommon, and that the ways in which they were resolved tended to follow a bipolar pattern: the patron of Ch'iu Ying who did not get what he expected would complain directly to the artist (but was less likely to be disappointed, since Ch'iu would know his wishes and follow them), while the recipient of a work by some highly placed literatus-artist would feel obliged to accept whatever he was given without grumbling, even when he failed to see what was so good about it.

A notable instance of the dissatisfied client that is recorded concerns the famous eighteenth-century Yangchou poet Yüan Mei and the painter Lo P'ing.[41] Lo had apparently contracted to paint the poet's portrait and, like Min Chen in the story related earlier, had done a draft for the sitter's approval, as was the common practice. The draft is still preserved (figure 3.15). Prior approval of the draft would ordinarily minimize the chances of the client's being unhappy with the finished work. However, instead of being delighted with his portrayal like the viceroy in the Min Chen story, Yüan Mei sent the draft-portrait back to Lo P'ing, adding a long inscription in which he explains, employing a facetious tone to soften the message, why he was rejecting it. His family members, he writes, say that it doesn't look like him, and that if they keep it around the house, people will mistake it "for a sketch of the old man who helps with the cooking in the kitchen, or the peddler who comes to the gate with lemonade." Yüan Mei makes the playfully philosophical argument that the picture may well represent himself in a past or future life, as seen by the painter's special vision; but in view of his family's opposition, he is sending it back to the artist so that it can be seen and admired in his studio by their friends.[42] He does not specifically say that what he had received was a draft, but in view of the character and the circumstances of the painting, this seems most likely.

The practice of presenting a draft for the client's approval, as European masters commonly did, before carrying out the finished work is seldom mentioned in the literature of painting; it belonged, presumably, to the category of what everyone knew and no one wrote about. It must, however, have been a normal procedure for the more elaborate, finished kinds of painting, in which more than aesthetic pleasure was at stake and the work was required to serve some particular function. Painters of mural compositions usually did charcoal sketches on the wall before undertaking the painting itself—we know this from negative cases, such as that of the eighth-century figure master Chou Fang, who "astounded his colleagues" by

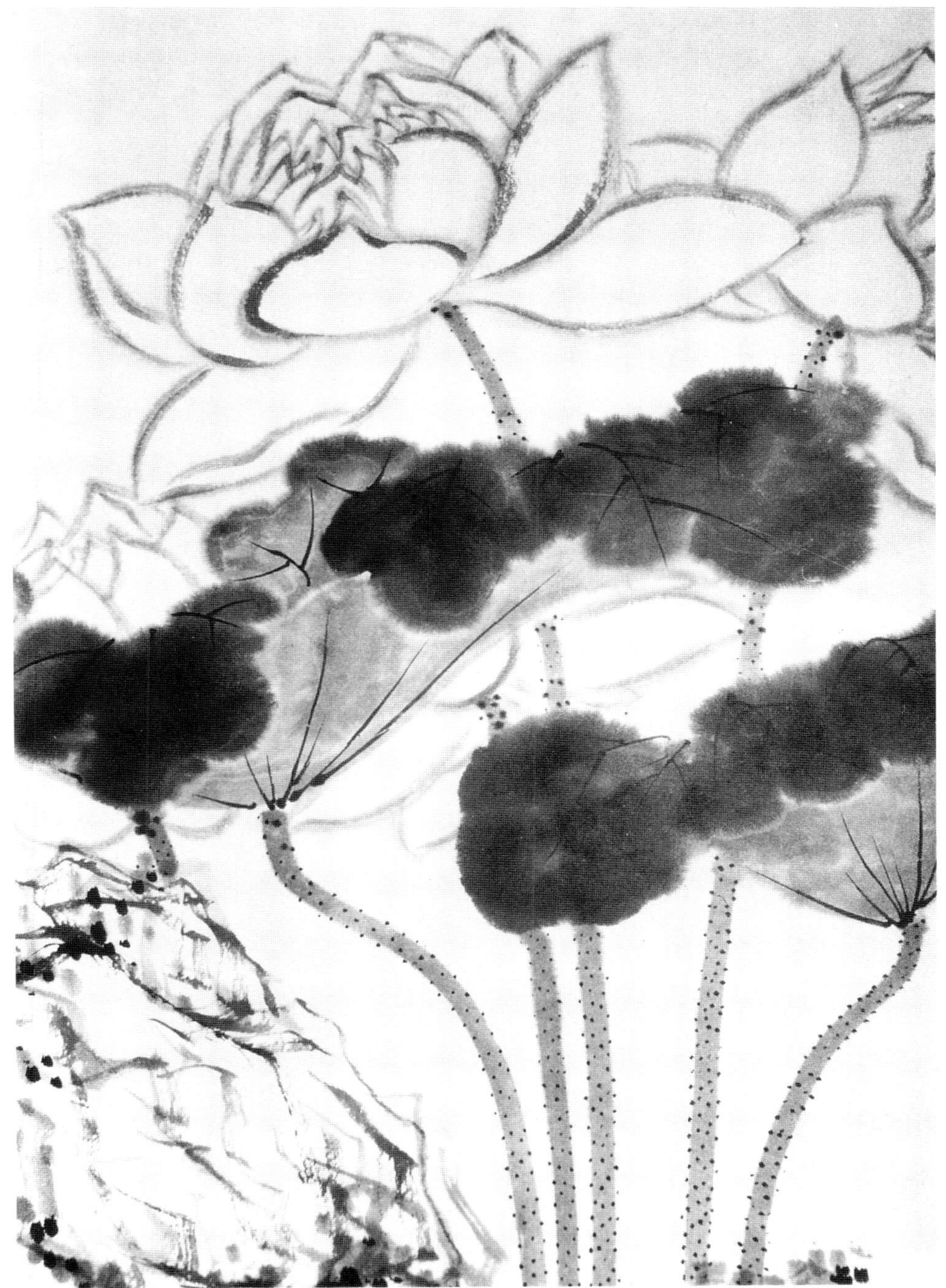

3.14. Ch'en Hung-shou, "Lotus and Rock." Detail from a hanging scroll, ink on paper, 151.4 × 61.9 cm. Shanghai Museum.

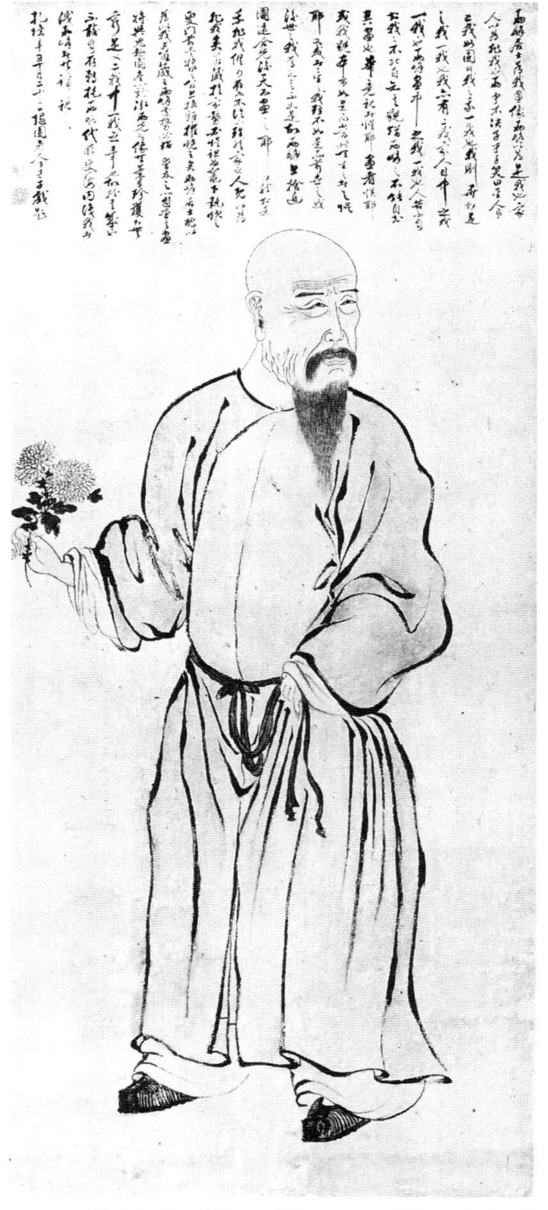

3.15. Lo P'ing, "Portrait of Yüan Mei." Inscription by Yüan Mei dated 1781. Hanging scroll, ink and colors on paper, 158.7 × 66.1 cm. Collection of Professor Shujiro Shimada, Kyoto.

working directly on the wall, without preliminary sketches.[43] Artists serving in the Sung imperial academy, we know, were assigned subjects along with compositional layouts by their supervisors, and made *fen-pen* or drafts that had to be approved before they could proceed.[44] The same practice of making detailed drafts for approval was still followed in the Ch'ing academy,[45] from which some of the drafts survive. The Italian Jesuit artist Giuseppe Castiglione or Lang Shih-ning (1688-1766) was made to follow this practice (already familiar to him from his European training) by the Chinese emperors under whom he worked: the preliminary drawing for his famous "Hundred Horses" scroll of 1728 has recently been discovered (figures 3.16, 3.17).

Fen-pen and Hua-kao

Preliminary drawings for paintings by Chinese artists of later periods can occasionally be found; a number are known, for instance, by the late nineteenth-century Shanghai master Ch'ien Hui-an (figure 3.18). A great many more may lie hidden in private collections or museum storerooms in China, although questions addressed to a few Chinese curators have so far failed to turn them up.[46]

Another kind of sketch was the drawing made from life, transcribing some object or scene for later use in a finished painting. Early texts tell of artists making such sketches from nature: the early Sung flower painter Chao Ch'ang, for instance, would reportedly go into the garden each morning to draw the flowers in their full freshness. Chinese artists were studio painters, however, and the finished work was always done there, even when it was based on sketches.

The Yüan-period landscapist Huang Kung-wang, in his notes on landscape painting written in the mid-fourteenth century, advises the painter to carry a sketching brush in a leather bag when he travels, so that "when you see in some scenic place a tree that is strange and unique, you can copy its appearance then and there as a record."[47] But there are few mentions in the literature of later artists heeding his advice, nor do their paintings, with some notable exceptions, indicate much close study of nature. Huang Kung-wang's younger contemporary Ni Tsan writes in a poem about having sketched from nature in his youth: "When I

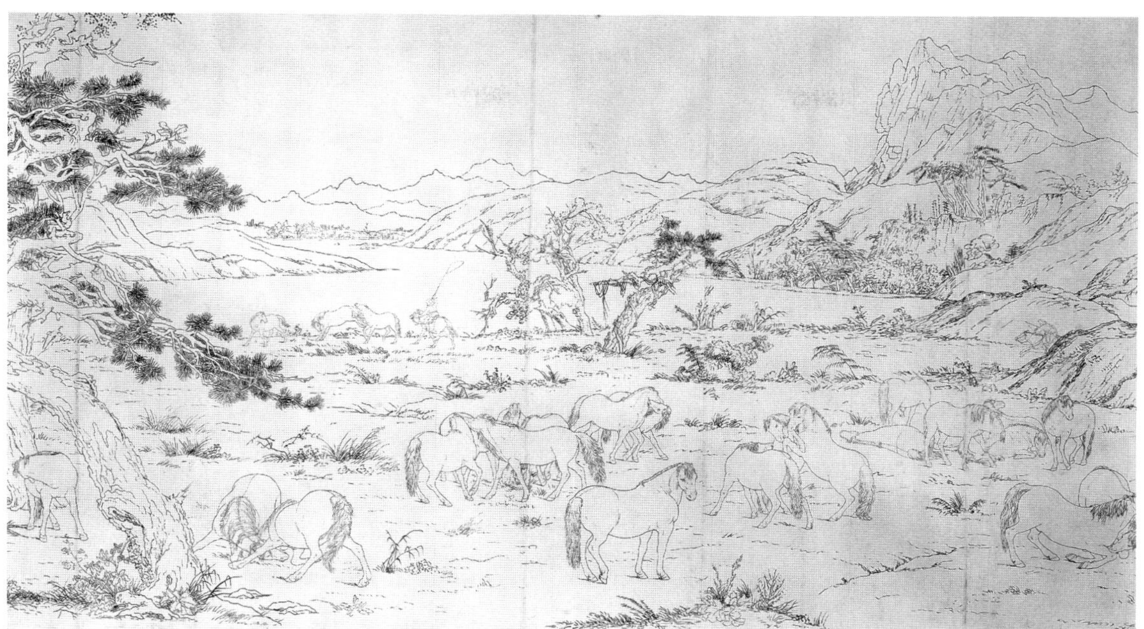

3.16. Lang Shih-ning (Giuseppe Castiglione, 1688–1766), "One Hundred Horses (*fen-pen,* or draft).
Section of a handscroll, ink on paper, ht. 94 cm. Metropolitan Museum of Art, New York City (1991.134), Purchase, Friends of Asian Art Gifts, in honor of Douglas Dillon, 1991.

3.17. Lang Shih-ning (Giuseppe Castiglione, 1688–1766), "One Hundred Horses."
Section of a handscroll, ink and colors on silk, ht. 94.5 cm. National Palace Museum, Taipei, Taiwan.

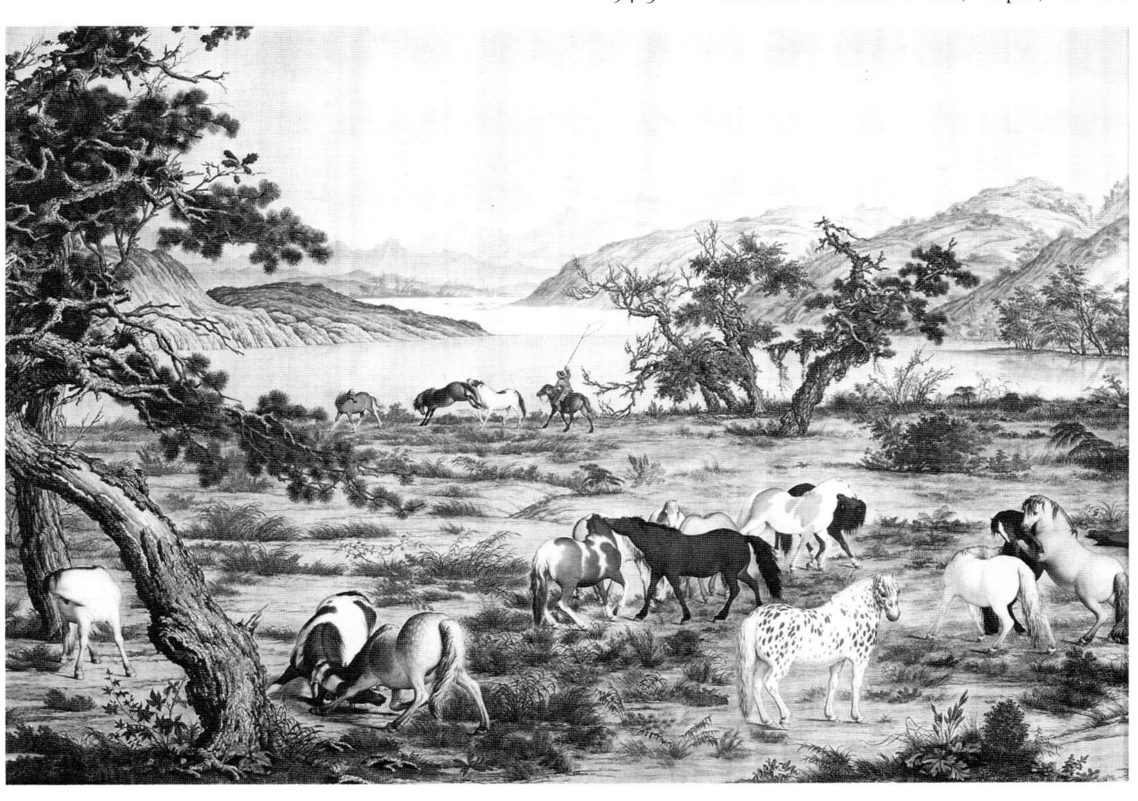

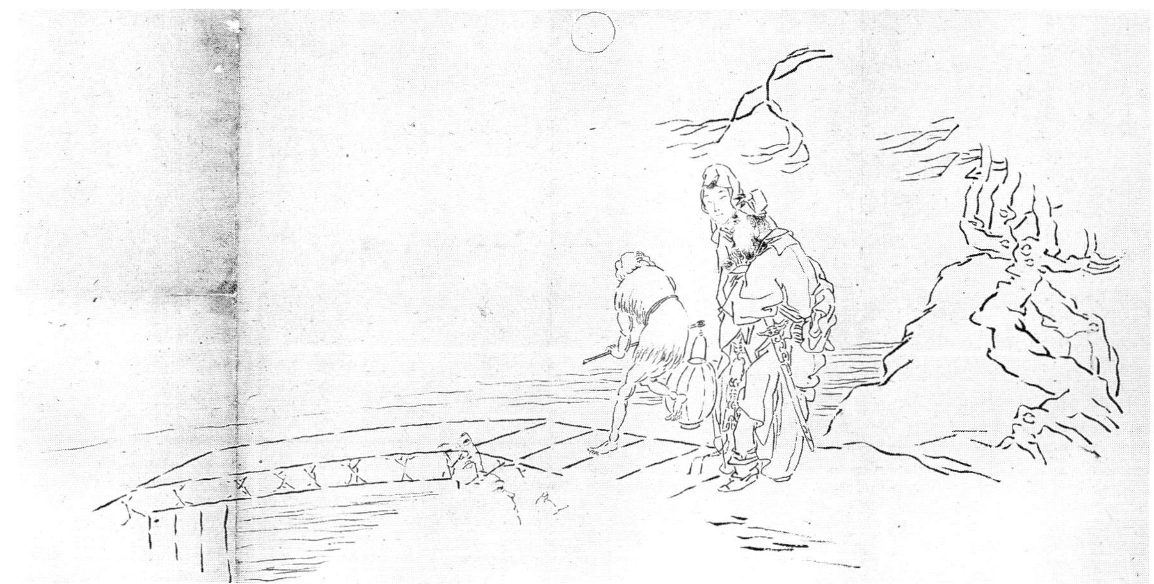

3.18. Ch'ien Hui-an, "The Night Journey of Chung K'uei and His Sister." Fan painting, *fen-pen,* ink on paper. From *Chung K'uei pai-t'u* (Canton, 1990), plate 28.

first learned to use a brush,/ Seeing an object I tried to capture its likeness./ Whenever I traveled, in country or in town,/ I sketched object after object, keeping the sketches in my painting basket."[48] But he writes this from the removed position of someone who has transcended such attachment to objects, someone who could also write "Why should I trouble myself over whether [my painting] resembles something or doesn't?" and "I never seek for formal likeness, because I paint only to amuse myself."[49] The late Ming landscapist Li Jih-hua similarly writes of sketching from nature while on walks, but one would never guess this from his landscapes, which, like most others of the late period, are made up of conventional forms largely learned from other paintings (figure 3.19).[50]

Portraitists were an exception. They would do preliminary drawings of their sitters from life as a basis for the formal portraits, presumably making these as true to life as their methods allowed. The introduction of Western illusionistic techniques in the late Ming period permitted further degrees of lifelikeness—or so we are told by writers of the time, who, happily innocent of more advanced theories of representation that make any image as lifelike as any other, exclaim in wonderment over portraits that looked "like reflections of the models in a mirror" or that would "glare and gaze, knit their brows or smile, in a manner alarmingly like real people"[51] (see figure 3.20.)

In my book on late Ming painting I discussed briefly an album of portraits of eminent men from Chekiang Province, preserved in the Nanking Museum, and reproduced four leaves from it (figure 3.21 is one of them), commenting on the extraordinary realism of the pictures, which seem to present their sitters "warts and all."[52] Further thought and another viewing of the album have convinced me that I and others have missed the truth about them: they were not meant as finished paintings, but are some portraitist's preliminary studies, presumably done from life and (like Lo P'ing's Yüan Mei) uncomfortably penetrating, studies that would probably have served as the basis for tamer, more idealized formal portraits. The fact that they are on coarse paper and bear no encomia—the inscription on one of them has the character of a casual note—supports this conclusion, along with the nature of the paintings.[53] Apart, however, from whether this conclusion is correct or not, we can observe once more that while the paintings themselves remain unaltered when we arrive at a different understanding of their genesis and purpose, we necessarily respond to them differently, and use them differently in any art-historical account we may construct, such as a study of the boundaries of realism in late Ming portraiture.

A third, equally important function of *fen-pen* was to transmit motifs and designs. Just as the artists of the Renaissance drew on classical models for figure types, Chinese painters would incorporate individual figures and groups from earlier paintings into their own, both to ease their task and to lend an air of antique authenticity to their pictures. The sources for these can often be identified in extant paintings. Ch'iu Ying is said to have made copies of all the T'ang-Sung paintings he had access to, for use in his own works,[54] and numerous figure groups and motifs in his paintings can be traced to these antique sources. The common method of preserving and transmitting the designs was through *fen-pen*—this term, introduced above in the sense of "draft," was used also for study-copies. The basic meaning of the word is "powder copy," referring to the pounce method of copying in which pricks are made in the original at many points on the lines that make up the design, and a powder bag is patted onto the surface; the powder goes through the holes onto the paper beneath to make a dotted outline which serves as a guide to the copyist.[55] But the word *fen-pen* was used more broadly to designate other kinds of cop-

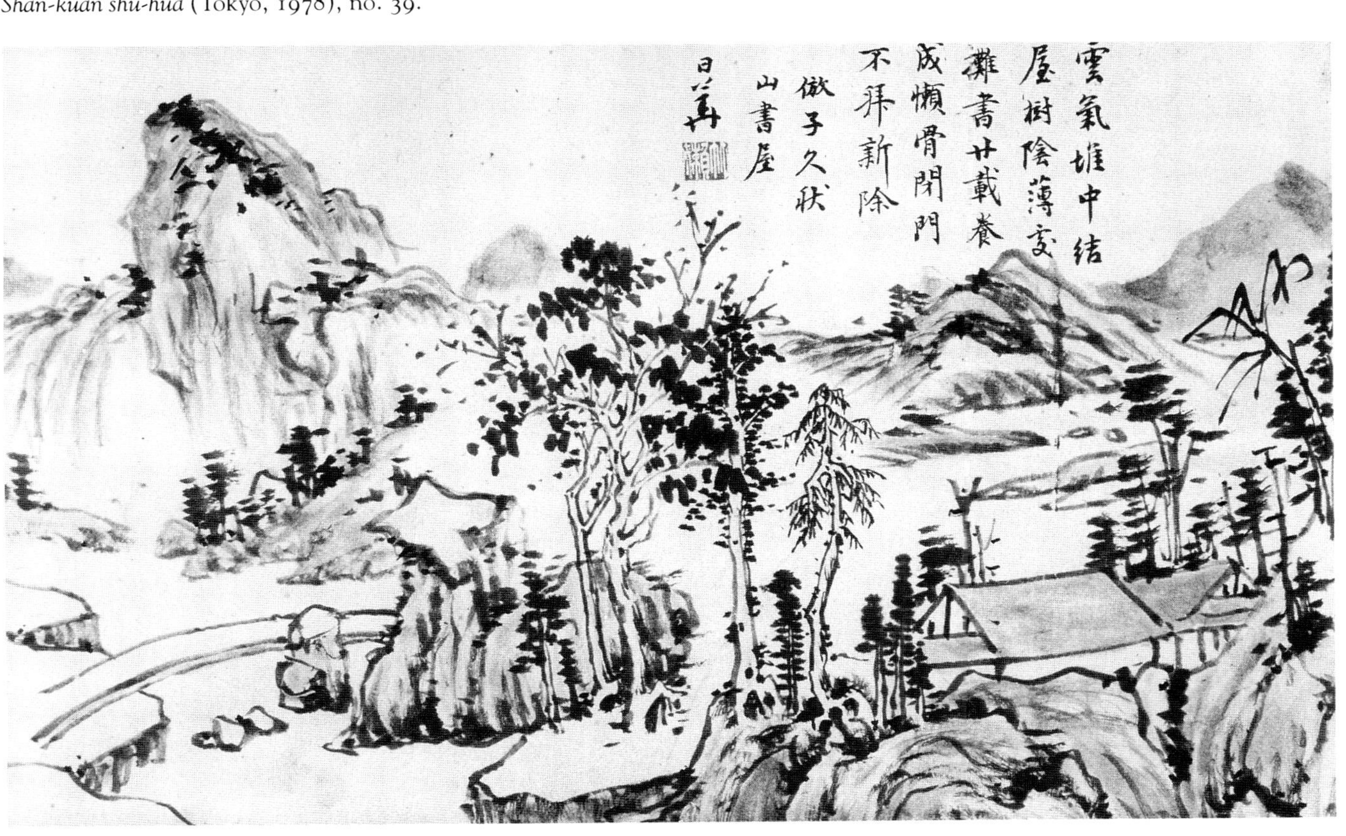

3.19. Li Jih-hua, "Landscape in Huang Kung-wang Manner.

Leaf 7 from an album of 10 leaves, five paintings and five calligraphy, ink on paper, ht. 25.8 cm. Collection of Lin Po-shou, Taipei. From *Lan-ch'ien Shan-kuan shu-hua* (Tokyo, 1978), no. 39.

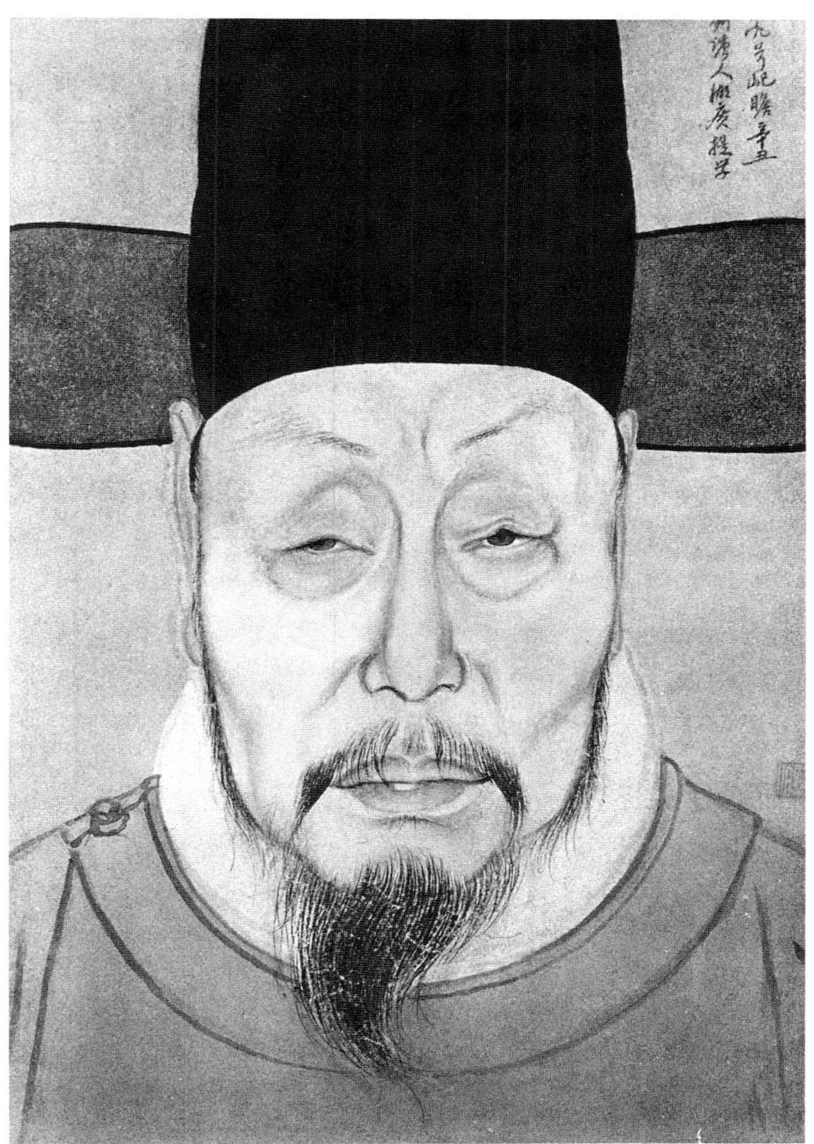

3.21. Anonymous, late Ming period, "Portrait of Ko Yin-liang" Leaf from an album of twelve portraits of men from Chekiang Province, ink and colors on paper, 41.6 × 26.7 cm. Nanking Museum. From *Ming-jen hsiao-hsiang hua* (Shanghai, 1979).

ies, as well as draft-sketches, otherwise known as *hua-kao.* A fourteenth-century writer tells us that examples of these from the Sung period and earlier were prized by collectors "for their rough and unplanned look, a spontaneous quality." Those from the Sung court artists were especially wonderful.[56] Extant early examples are mostly of Buddhist paintings, iconographic sketches of the kind kept in temples (figure 3.22),[57] but a few other works survive that appear to be *fen-pen* in the sense of *hua-kao,* preliminary drawings or cartoons for mural paintings.

An example is the handscroll ascribed to the early Sung figure master Wu Ts'ung-yüan, probably a cartoon for a large-scale painting executed on the walls of some Taoist temple and representing a procession of the Celestial Rulers of Taoism and their attendants (figure 3.23). The majestic sweep and momentum of the composition, the energy generated by the drawing of the figures (echoing probably the style of the great T'ang master Wu Tao-tzu), seem too great for the confines of a handscroll. Wall paintings were also copied full-size: in an early eleventh-century book we read of one

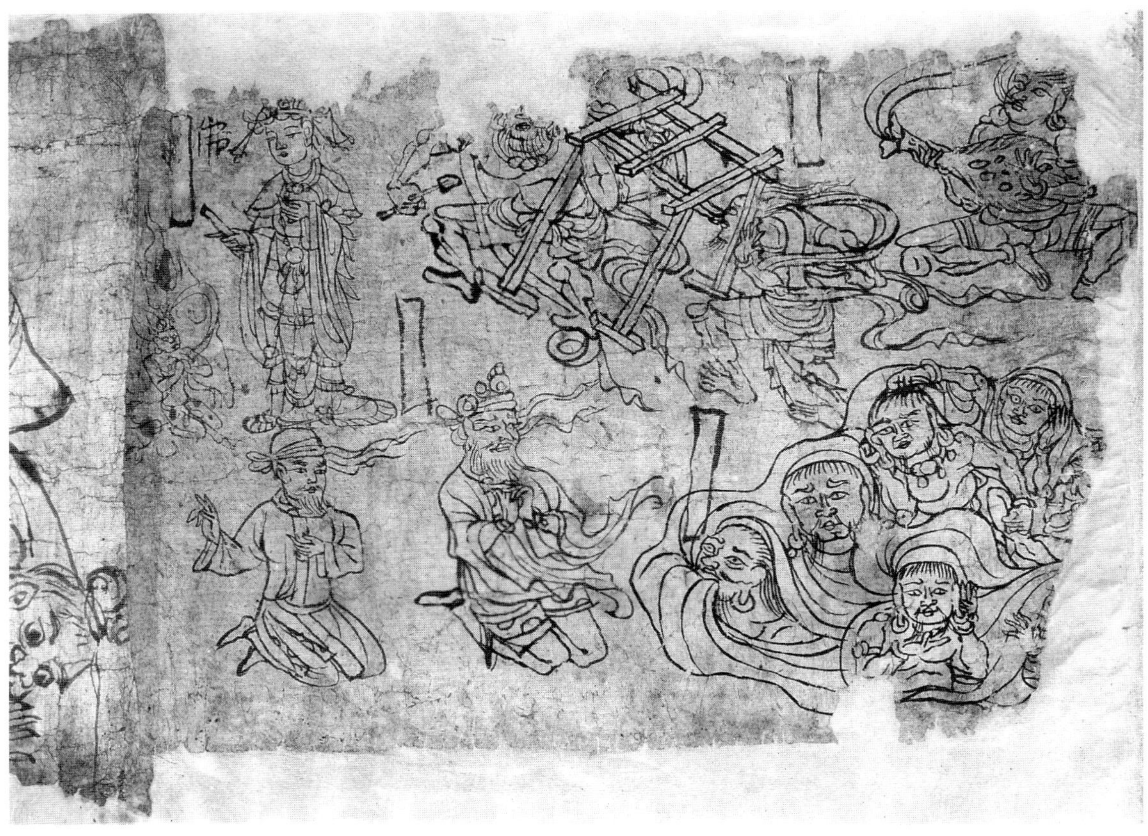

3.22. Anonymous, T'ang period (8th cent.?), Preparatory sketches (*fen-pen* for a Buddhist painting.
Section of a scroll, ink on paper, approx. 30 cm. × 179 cm. Bibliotheque Nationale, Paris. See Jao Tsung-i, *Peintures Monochromes de Dunhuang* (Paris, 1978), vol. 3, plate 17.

artist, Kao Wen-chin, copying the wall paintings of another by using "wax stencils," presumably some kind of translucent paper.[58]

The first recorded usage of the term *fen-pen* is in the well-known account, which appears in the mid-ninth-century *T'ang-ch'ao ming-hua lu,* of how Wu Tao-tzu painted a landscape of the Chia-ling River in Szechwan on a palace wall after returning from a trip to that place. The emperor asks whether the artist has brought back *fen-pen,* and Wu replies that he doesn't need them, the scenery is all in his mind.[59] An album of linear drawings transmitted under the name of Wu Tao-tzu himself, but of later date (thirteenth–fourteenth century?), is made up of three separate series of figure compositions, either preparatory studies for handscroll paintings or *fen-pen* preserving the designs of some earlier works (figure 3.24). The study-copies that Ch'iu Ying and others made from T'ang and Sung paintings must have looked like these.

Through the wisdom of the late Laurence Sickman in acquiring materials in China that were ignored by others, we have an album of forty-six leaves of *fen-pen* studies copying details from old paintings by the early Ch'ing master Ku Chien-lung (1606–1684), with Ku's annotations. The album is apparently the only survivor from a large number of such albums made by Ku over many years.[60] Ku was a conservative painter who served for a time in the Ch'ing court as a portraitist and specialized in imitating old styles; his *fen-pen* albums thus served him, and presumably his students, as repertory books. A few of the details in Ku's album can be matched up with extant paintings

—for instance, a nomadic yurt and a gateway in a pass taken from an early handscroll attributed to the Liao artist Hu Kuei, representing Khitan herdsmen and soldiers pasturing in the northern grasslands (figures 3.25, 3.26).

Drawing from Life vs. Copying Old Models

What is remarkable is that nothing in Ku's album is drawn from nature or life; it appears to be composed entirely of motifs and passages copied from old paintings. The same is true of other so-called sketchbooks by Chinese landscapists, such as the Tung Ch'i-ch'ang album in the Boston Museum of Fine Arts (figure 3.27); they appear to be made up, not of drawings after nature, but of practice sketches of rocks and trees presumably intended for incorporation into paintings.[61] A handscroll by Tung Ch'i-ch'ang of "Sketches of Traditional Tree and Rock Types" in the Palace Museum, Beijing, has the same character, mediating between old paintings and Tung's own, rather than between trees in nature and those in his paintings. We have, in fact, the testimony of his friend Ch'en Chi-ju, in a short note appended to the scroll, that it was made up of Tung Ch'i-ch'ang's "sketches of the trees and rocks by various old masters. Whenever he made a large composition, he copied from these sketches."[62]

Sketchbooks or scrolls of sketches might also take the form of models for teaching pupils, as does an album of tree and rock sketches after Ni Tsan (figure 3.28),[63] or the albums

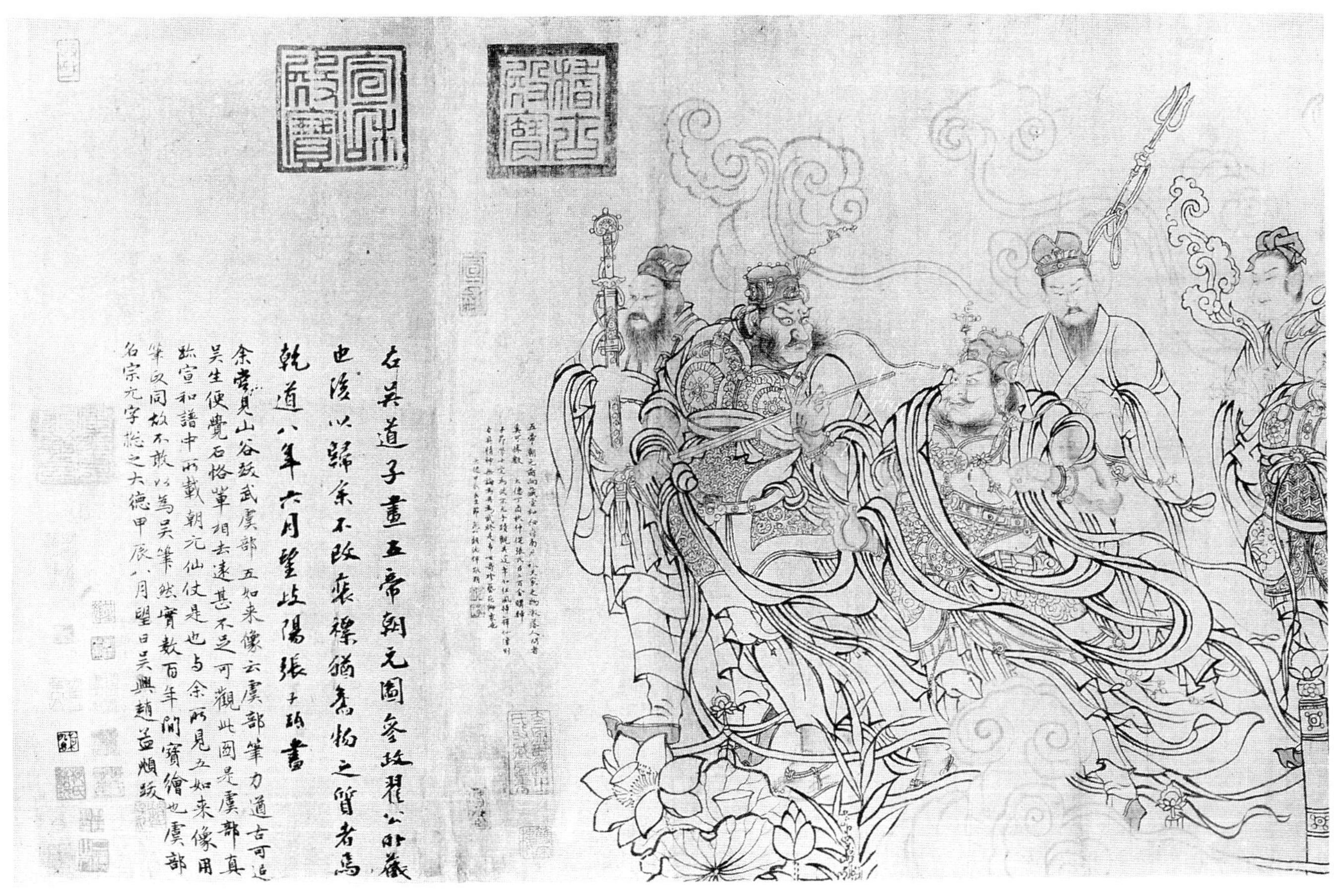

3.23. Attributed to Wu Ts'ung-yüan (d. 1050), "Celestial Rulers of Taoism in Procession." Section of Handscroll, ink on silk, ht. 40.6 cm. Collection of C. C. Wang, New York.

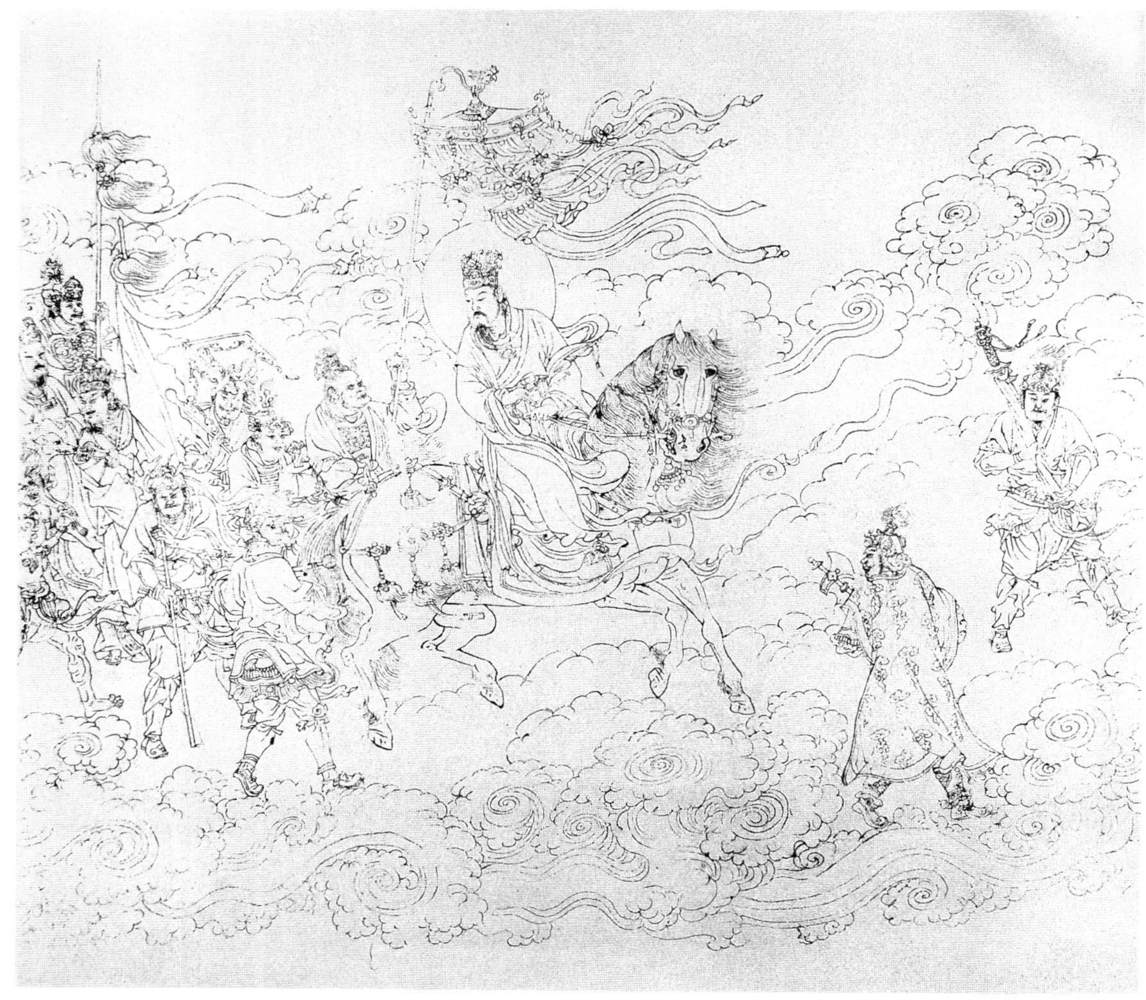

3.24. Anonymous, Sung or Yuan period (old attribution to Wu Tao-tzu), "Taoist Deity in the Clouds."
Leaf from an album of *fen-pen* copies of old paintings, ink on paper. Juncunc collection, Chicago. From *Tao-tzu mo-pao* (Beijing, 1963), plate 4.

and handscrolls of this kind by Kung Hsien.[64] They represent, that is, the intermediate or final products rather than the raw materials for the development of brush conventions that will serve to represent visual forms. While portraitists continued to draw from life, along with academic bird-and-flower painters and others who followed the much-criticized practice of "transcribing appearances," landscapists, even those who were in some sense portraying real places, did so mostly by putting together learned conventional forms into more or less conventional compositions.

The same was true for most later figure painting, which, as Richard Barnhart showed in an important article published twenty years ago,[65] depends more on past traditions than on observation. Chinese figure masters did not, so far as we know, bring in models from the street as Rembrandt did, to pose them in costume and draw them; instead, they would pull out old *fen-pen* from their cabinets and use those. Chou Ch'en's 1516 series of portrayals of beggars and street characters (figure 3.29) might be seen as an exception, but even here it is not clear that they are based on sketches from life

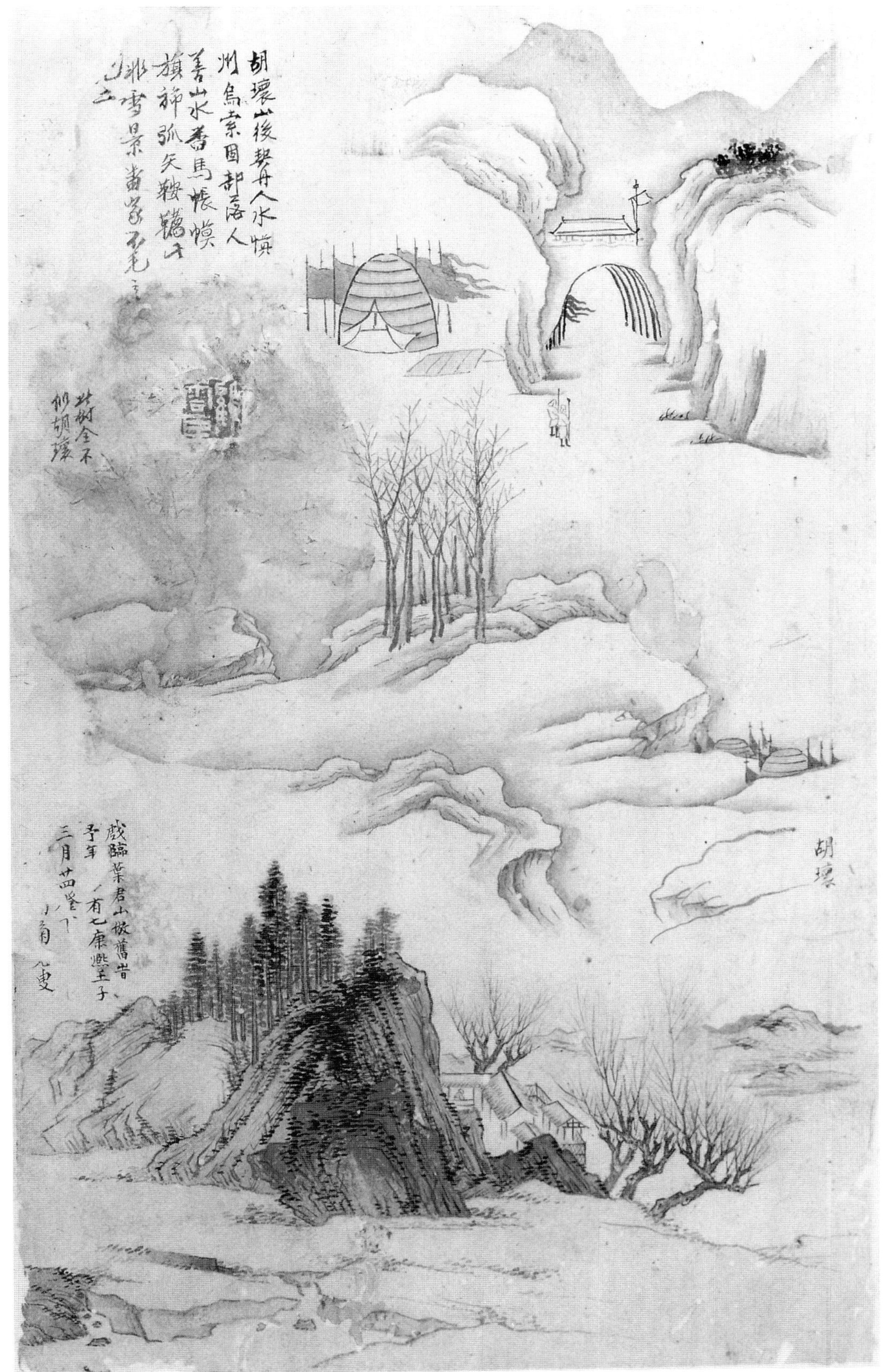

3.25. Ku Chien-lung (1606–1687), "Various Scenes." Leaf from 46-leaf album of sketches *(fen-pen)* after Old Masters. Ink on paper, 30.2 × 18.8 cm. Nelson-Atkins Museum of Art, Kansas City (59–24/14).

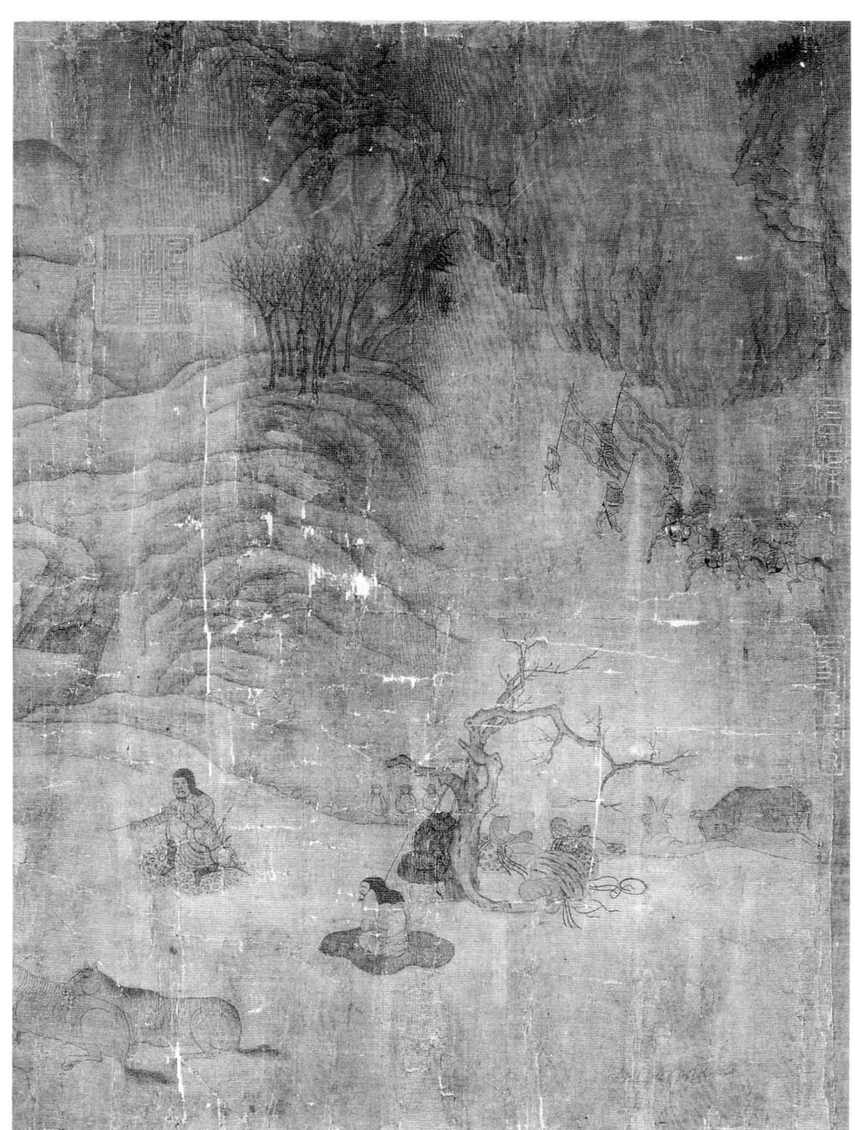

3.26. Attributed to Hu Kuei (10th cent.), "Tartar Horses on a Plain." Section of a handscroll, ink (and slight colors?) on silk. Dimensions unknown. National Palace Museum, Taipei, Republic of China.

(although the paintings themselves persuade us that they must have been); Chou Ch'en writes only that as he was "idling under the window," there came to his mind "all the appearances and manners of the beggars and other street characters whom I often saw in the streets and markets," and that he took up his brush and ink and "put them into pictures in an impromptu way."[66] Depictions of real life were not what the clients wanted, or what the artists, with very few exceptions, produced.

As I have argued in earlier lectures and writings, the development of representational techniques for the visually convincing or "lifelike" rendering of natural objects had reached its height in the tenth and eleventh centuries, and was scarcely continued as a serious concern of artists afterward, in part because of the adverse reaction among powerful theorists and critics in the Northern Sung period.[67] In the early centuries, sketching from nature was the normal practice of the painter, and it was common to say of major artists that they "took nature as their teacher"—Han Kan learned from the horses in the imperial stables, Fan K'uan from the mountains and streams, and so forth.

Sketches of this kind have not in themselves been preserved, but a short handscroll in the Palace Museum, Beijing (figure 3.30), if we believe the inscription, was done by the Szechwan master Huang Ch'üan (903–968) for his son Chü-pao, presenting him with a set of models for painting insects, birds, and other creatures. Huang Ch'üan himself presumably painted them from life (he was famous for *hsieh-sheng,* which implies that); but his having done this copy-book for his son indicates that he understood, as later critics often pretend not to, that a realistic style was hard-won, not a simple matter of looking at something and depicting it the way it looks, and normally needed to be learned, initially at least, from other artists and paintings.

Another preserved early set of models for painters is a handscroll in the Palace Museum, Beijing, called "Anonymous T'ang" but probably later than that in date, representing "A Hundred Horses" (figure 3.31). It cannot be read as a coherent composition (as can, for instance, the "Herding Horses" handscroll by Li Kung-lin in the same collection),[68] and appears to be a studio repertory scroll for horse specialists, presenting the equine subject in multiple aspects: frolicking, neighing, tied to posts, being fed or washed in the river. Early handscrolls sometimes have this taxonomic

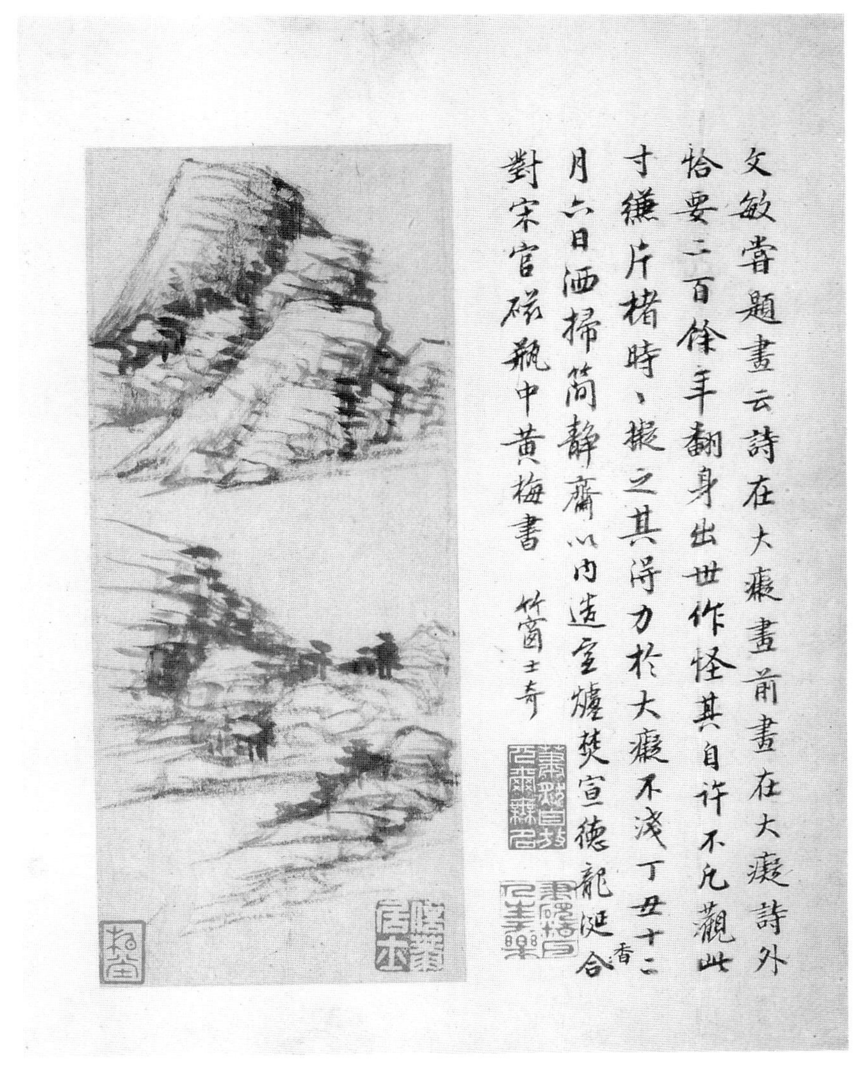

3.27. Tung Ch'i-ch'ang (1555–1636), "Rocks." Leaf from 20-leaf album of ink sketches. Inscription by Kao Shih-ch'i (1645–1703). Ink on paper, 18.1 × 25.6 cm. Museum of Fine Arts, Boston (39.35), Otis Norcross Fund.

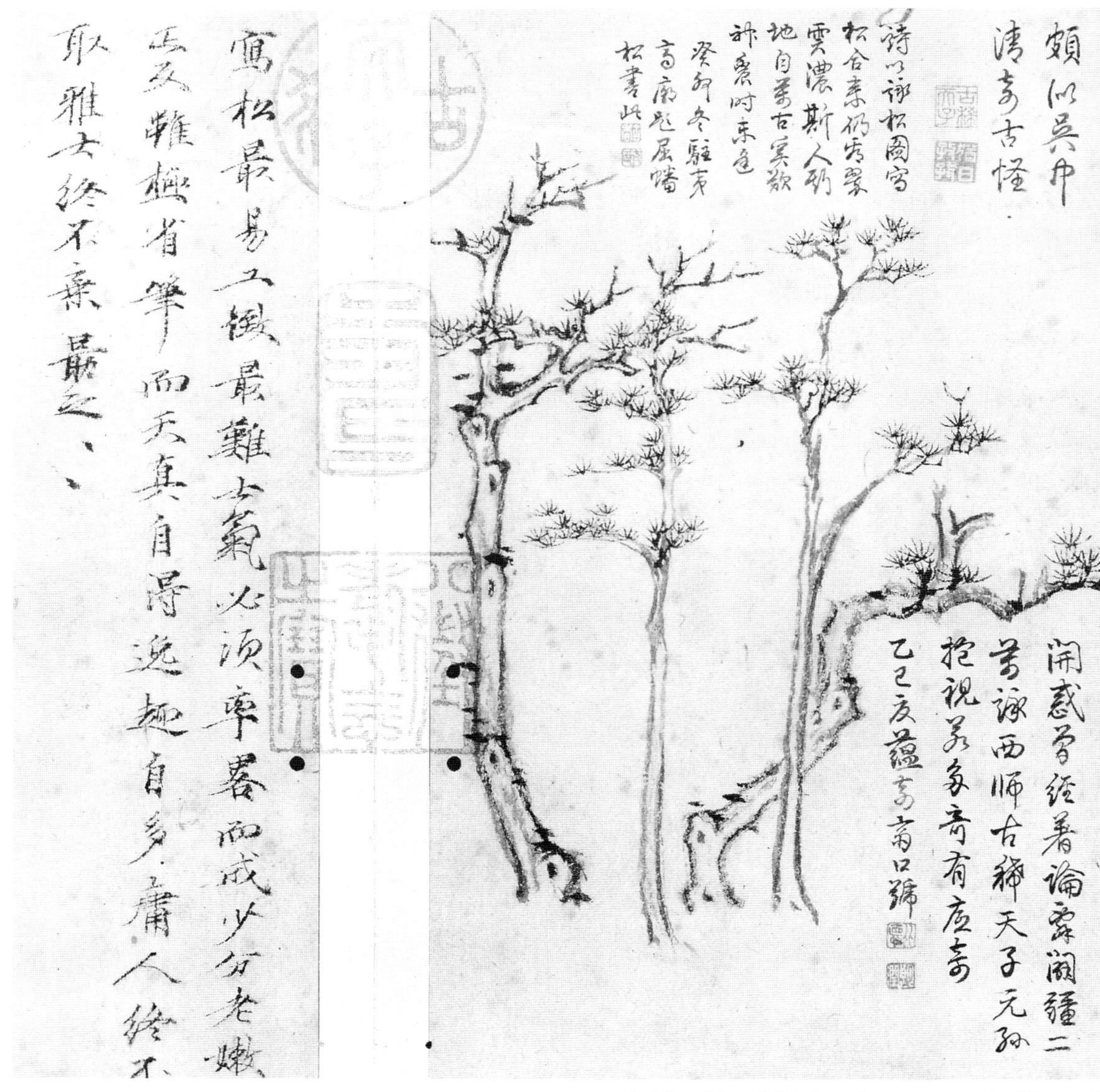

3.28. After Ni Tsan (1301–1374), "Trees." Leaf from an instructional album of ten leaves, ink on paper, each leaf 23.6 × 14.2 cm. National Palace Museum, Taipei, Republic of China.

character—Chao Kan's "Along the River at Early Snowfall," for instance, is a kind of taxonomy of fishermen, their dwellings and their apparatuses for lowering and raising nets.[69] (The nature of Chinese taxonomies, in art and elsewhere, and what lies behind Foucault's funny citation of Borges quoting "a certain Chinese encyclopaedia" at the beginning of *The Order of Things,* would make another essay, but cannot be pursued in this one.)[70]

The well-known *Chieh-tzu-yüan hua-chuan* or "Mustard Seed Garden Manual of Painting," of which the first part on landscape was published in 1679, is essentially a traditional painter's manual or repertory book gone public, taking a form that had served the private uses of masters and their pupils in studios and making it widely available through woodblock printing.[71] Its appearance at this time responds to the phenomenon noted earlier, a huge increase in the number of people with leisure to take up such pursuits as painting and

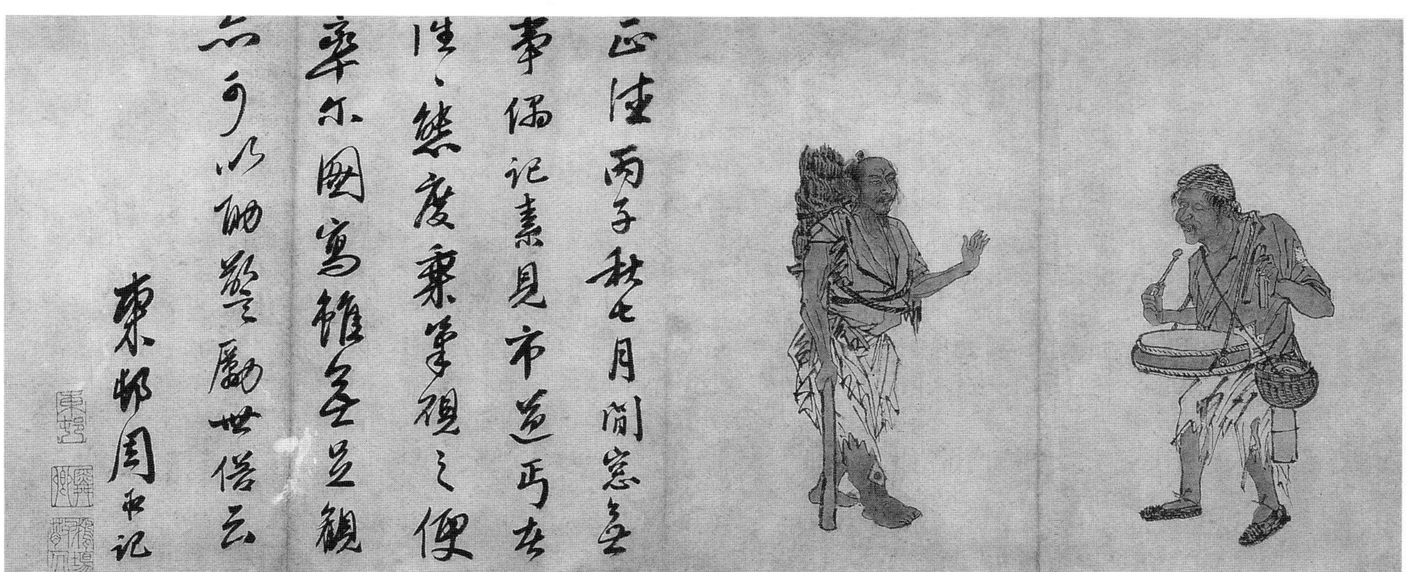

3.29. Chou Ch'en (active ca. 1500–1535), "Beggars and Street Characters."
Dated 1516. Album leaves mounted in handscroll, ink and colors on paper, ht. 31.9 cm. Cleveland Museum of Art (64.94).

3.30. Huang Ch'üan, "Birds and Insects Drawn from Life."
Short handscroll, ink and colors on silk, 41.5 × 70.8 cm. Palace Museum, Peking.

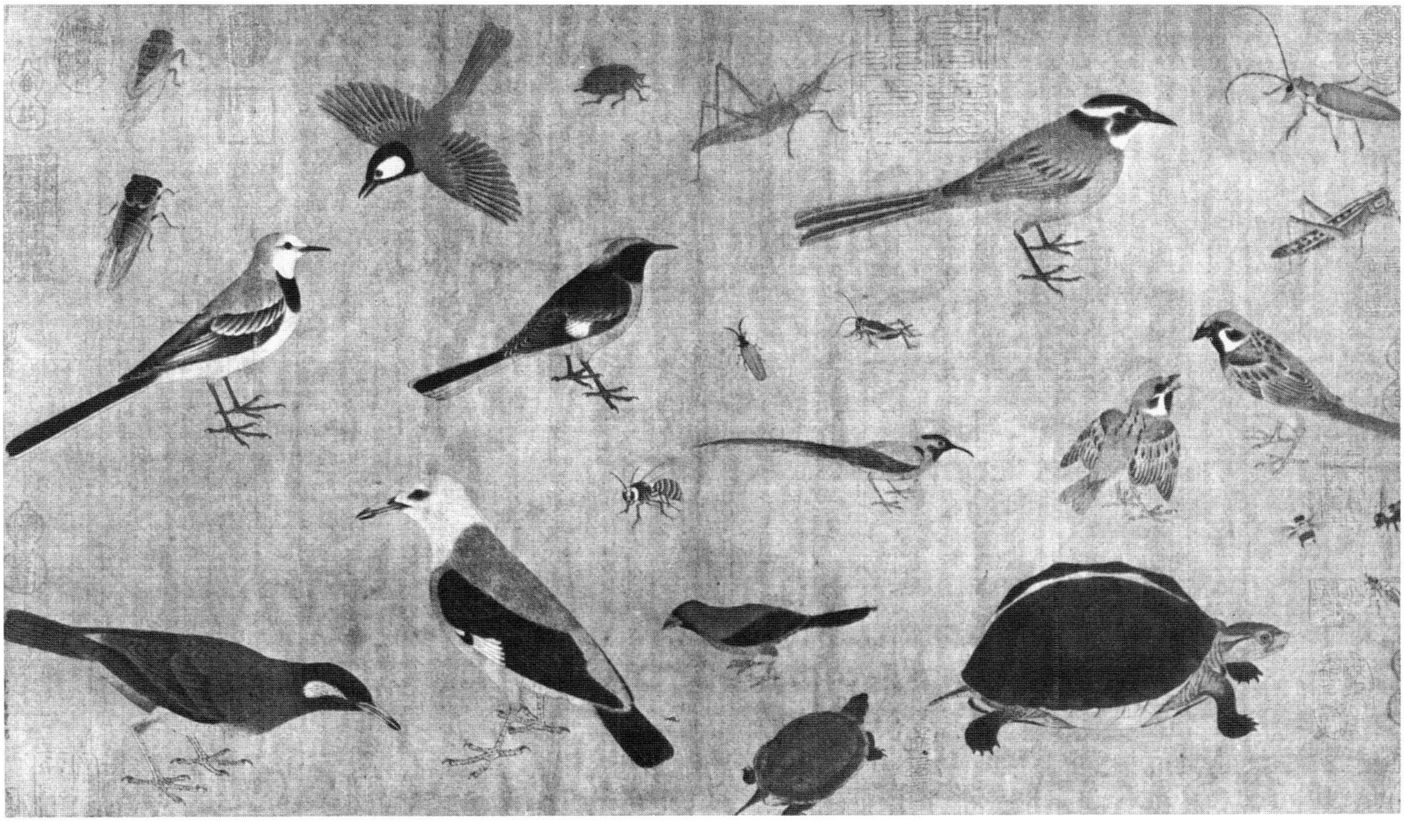

with money to buy these books, along with the paintings that artists using them could produce in greater quantities.

Pictorial prints had been made in China from the ninth century or earlier, but reached a high artistic level only from the middle Ming,[72] and especially in the late Ming and early Ch'ing, with major masters participating in designing them along with anonymous artists, and technical innovations such as multi-block color printing enhancing their quality and popularity. These became another resource for painters who needed figural and other motifs. Ch'en Hung-shou's series of portrayals of the heroes of the *Shui-hu chuan* or "Water Margin" novel, for instance (figure 3.32), produced in the 1630s, could be utilized by an artist of the southern Anhui region named Wang Chia-chen in 1667 for a historical scene (figure 3.33). Wang was primarily a landscapist, and the requirements of a figure composition of this kind, probably done to answer some particular requirement, either his own or a client's, taxed his modest skills. He solved his problem by lifting two of Ch'en Hung-shou's figures and inserting them into his own composition. It depicts another tale of artistic temperament: the fourth-century Tai K'uei confronting the messenger sent by an imperial prince to summon him to perform on the *ch'in.* Tai responds by breaking his *ch'in,* saying "Tai An-tao is no prince's household musician!" Ch'en Hung-shou himself had enlarged his repertory of figure types through the study of a set of stone engravings after figure paintings attributed to the Sung master Li Kung-lin representing the Seventy-Two Disciples of Confucius.[73]

The Artist's Studio

Painters' studios in traditional China, like those in premodern Europe, were mostly organized within the artist's household and employed his family members and servants, along with, if he were successful enough, apprentices and assistants. Each family would have a trademark style or specialty, carried on from one generation to the next. Examples are many: for the Ming period, Wen Cheng-ming and his sons and nephew;[74] Ch'iu Ying, his daughter

3.31. Anonymous, T'ang period or later, "One Hundred Horses."
Section of handscroll, ink and colors on silk, ht. 26.7 cm. Palace Museum, Peking.

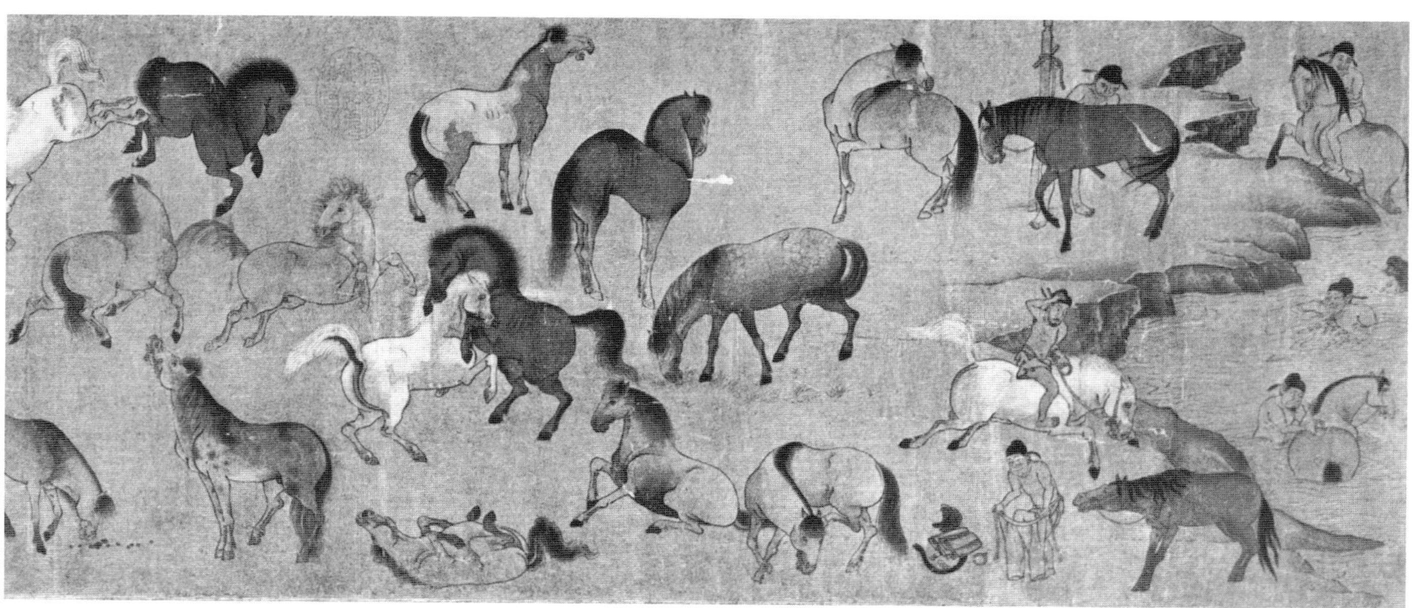

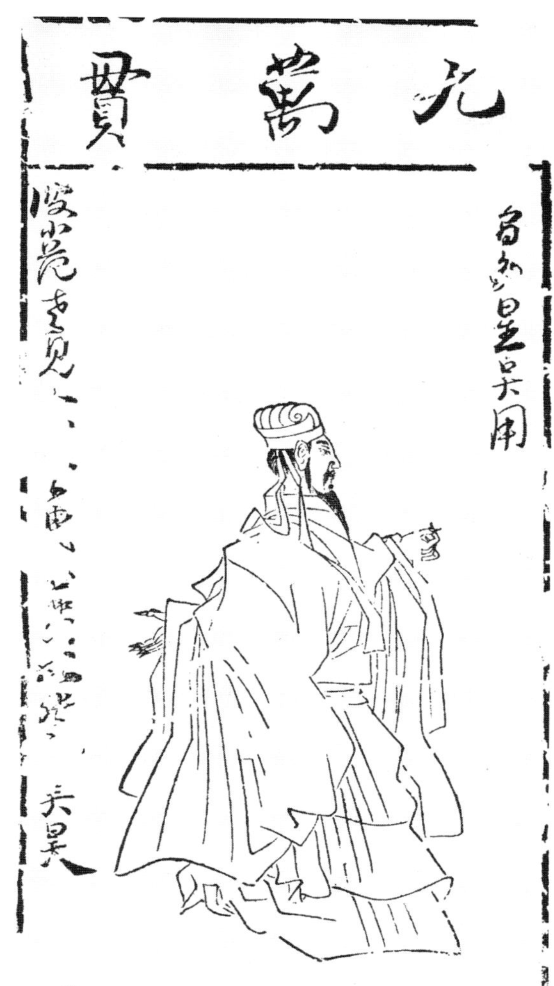

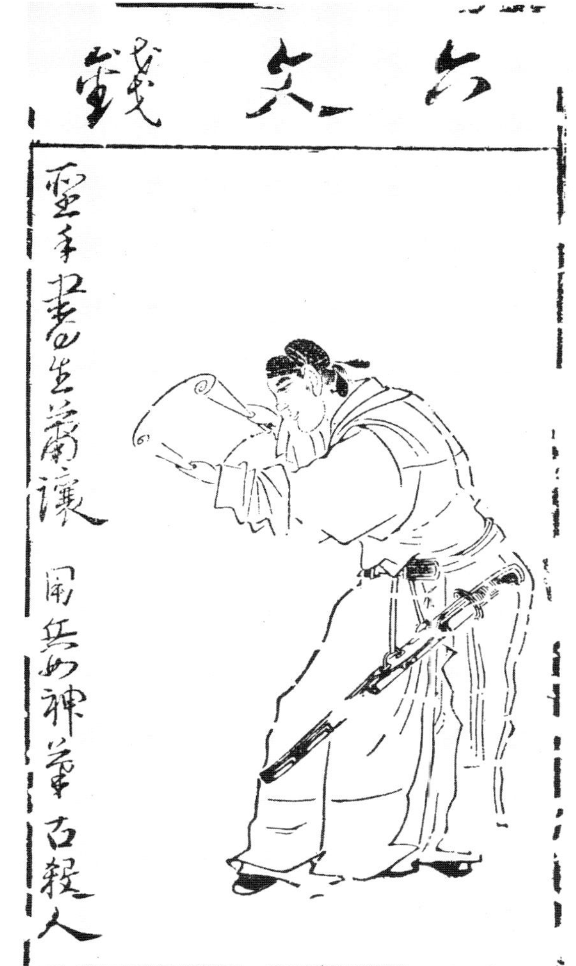

3.32. Ch'en Hung-shou, Two leaves from *Shui-hu yeh-tzu* (Water Margin Playing Cards): Wu Yung, Hsiao Hsiang. Woodblock prints. Undated (1630s). From *Ming Ch'en Hung-shou Shui-hu yeh-tzu* (Shanghai, 1979).

Ch'iu Shih, and his son-in-law Yu Ch'iu; Ch'en Hung-shou and his son Ch'en Tzu (along with his disciple Yen Chan, not a relative), come immediately to mind. The early Ch'ing master Yün Shou-p'ing, while away from home, wrote to his wife (in a letter preserved in the Shanghai Museum) asking her to send his nephew to help him with coloring and otherwise preparing some paintings, presumably works he had promised to a patron.[75] The Ch'ing imperial archive records an oral memorial presented by a courtier to the Ch'ien-lung Emperor in 1735 reading: "The painter *(hua-hua jen)* Leng Mei has a son who is helping him paint. I plan to pay the son the second-grade painter's salary. Is this acceptable? I await your majesty's instruction."[76]

Studio workshops outside the household probably existed also, but it is difficult to find evidence for them before very recent times. Insofar as they existed, they seem to have been organized for lower-level, craftlike production, like the artisans' workshops that were located in the cities and in the suburban areas around them.[77] A workshop regulation dated 1895 describes the operation of a painters' workshop in the Chekiang area organized like a guild, and

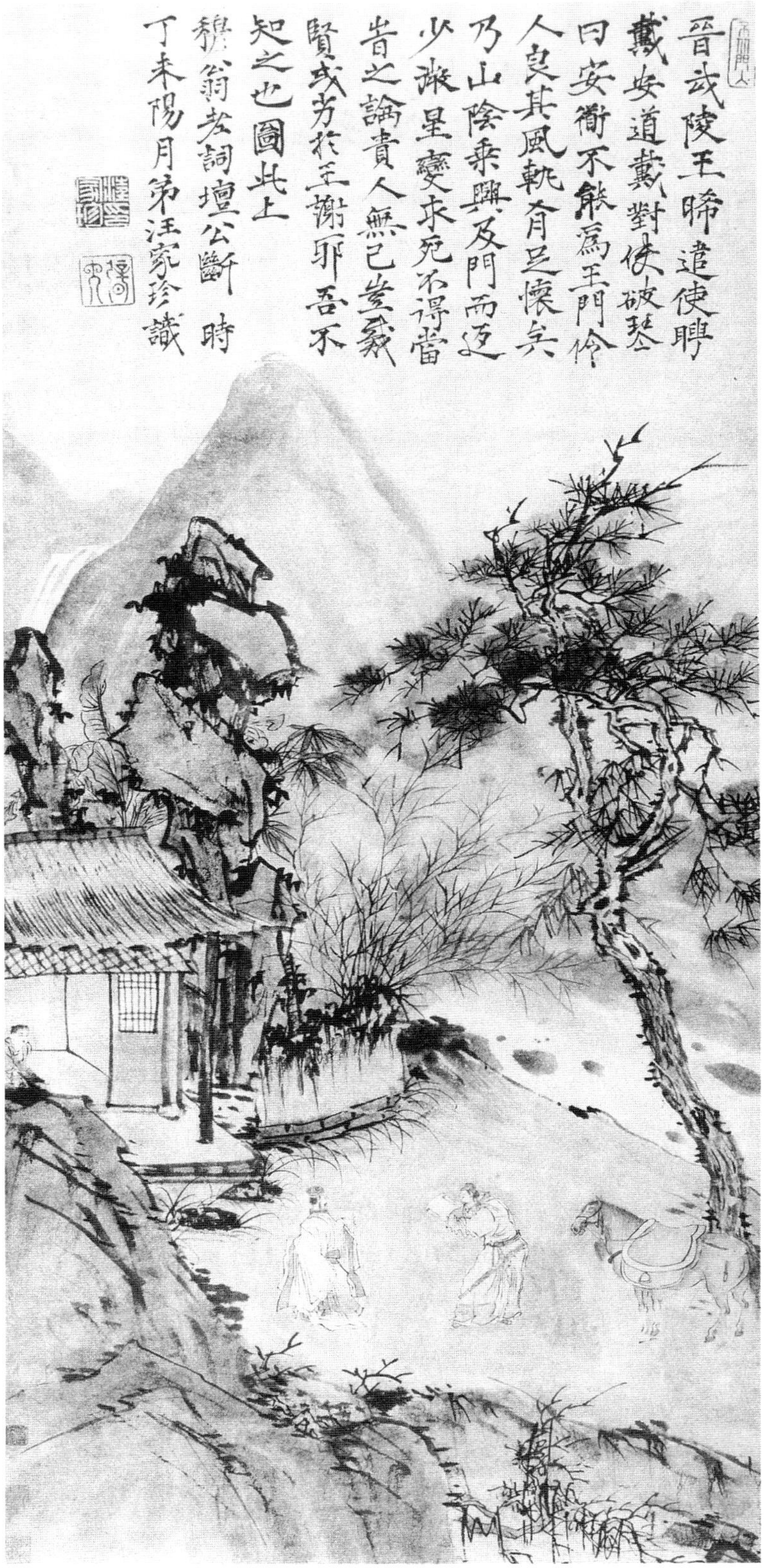

晉武陵王晞遣使聘
戴安道戴對使破琴
曰安道不能為王門伶
人皃其風軌有足懷矣
乃山陰乘興及門而返
少微星變求死不得當
旹之論責人無已豈義
賢哉方於王謝耶吾不
知之也圖此上
穉翁老詞壇公斷 時
丁未陽月弟汪家珍識

provides information on the monthly worshiping ceremony (Wu Tao-tzu served as their patron deity), as well as "the apprenticeship period, the hierarchy, tuition, wages, and the bonus system of the guild."[78] And it is known that by the eighteenth century there were guilds in large cities for skilled workers and craftsmen, probably including those who made Buddhist paintings and sculptures, iconic images of Door Gods, and other functional representations.[79] The organization of artists into workshops appears to have been a function of the increased commercialization of painting from the eighteenth century on, and the need to augment output to meet larger demands. Huang Shen, when he traveled about as an itinerant painter, took with him several of his *men-jen* or disciples, who were themselves painters and who came, like himself, from Fukien. Presumably they helped him in producing the works he was obliged to complete for patrons along the way. Chin Nung's group of servants and disciples seem to have similarly made up a kind of movable workshop, traveling with him and helping him to produce marketable objects such as engraved inkstones and paper lanterns.[80] In his late years, when he turned more to painting for his income, they would serve him sometimes as ghostpainters.

For the organization of the household workshops in which both professional and amateur masters practiced their art we have little evidence, but a humorous essay written by Li Jih-hua in 1629 may give a fair idea of how roles were assigned to maximize the master's productivity, if we assume that the essay is a parody of some real practice and discount a bit Li's facetious exaggerations. He had just retired to his home in Chia-hsing after serving five years in the Ministry of Rites in Peking,[81] and like his

3.33. Wang Chia-chin, "Tai K'uei Receiving the Emissary."
Dated 1667. Hanging scroll and detail from same, ink on paper, 115 × 63 cm. Collection of Liu Jun-liang (Low Chuck Tiew), Hong Kong.

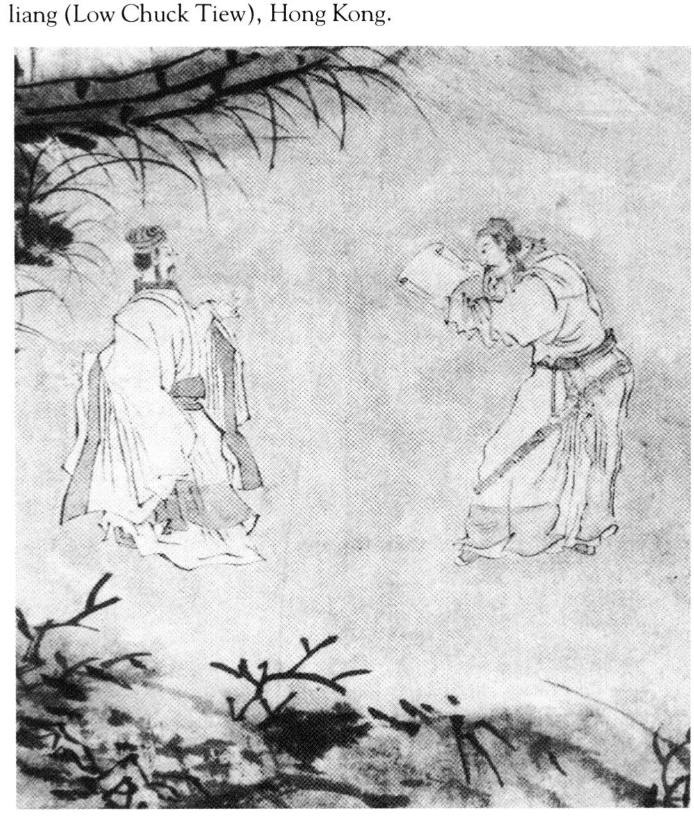

friend Tung Ch'i-ch'ang, found himself harassed by people wanting his calligraphy and paintings (figure 3.34), partly for the status-symbol value they derived from Li's high official rank.

We should remember that it was Li Jih-hua who had attributed the decline of painting in Suchou to the commercialization of its artists.[82] (His expressed disapproval of selling paintings did not deter him from profiting from his own works, presumably because he did so only to supplement his income and because he followed the proper literati conventions in accepting payment.) His essay is probably meant in part to satirize those who were more openly mercenary. He writes:

I have been living in the woods with a lot of leisure time, and my friends keep pouring in to ask for my calligraphy. Therefore, I made a playful regulation for my accountant: "Ink Section of Tai-ti Cave, the single immortal Chu-lan instructs his attendants: The door is open to people who come for calligraphy; it won't be necessary to equivocate. Register all the fans which are accompanied by high payments and first-rate frames as soon as they are brought in for inscriptions. [He orders his accountant to record the date and circumstances of receiving, and specifies the payments to servants who bring them in.] All the fans with registration numbers must belong to people who are literati, gentry, or Buddhist monks and Taoists. The fans which belong to common townspeople and philistines must not be mixed with the first kind. At eight o'clock on each of the days with three, six, or nine, enough ink should be ready for the fan to be inscribed, and then presented [with the fan] for me to write on. If someone asks for small and fine *k'ai* script, they will be charged one tael of silver. . . All fans, after I write them, should be stored carefully, ready for delivery. The date of delivery should be written down clearly. When the requirement is for a scroll or album with a great number of words, the ink grinding fee will be twenty wen; a sign-board gets thirty wen; each single hanging scroll of draft calligraphy gets five wen. Paper that is not of good color and quality

3.34. Li Jih-hua, "Landscape with Houses." Section of handscroll, ink on paper, ht. 21.5 cm. Former collection of Mayuyama Ryusendo, Tokyo. From *Kokka*, no. 791 (February 1958), plate 5.

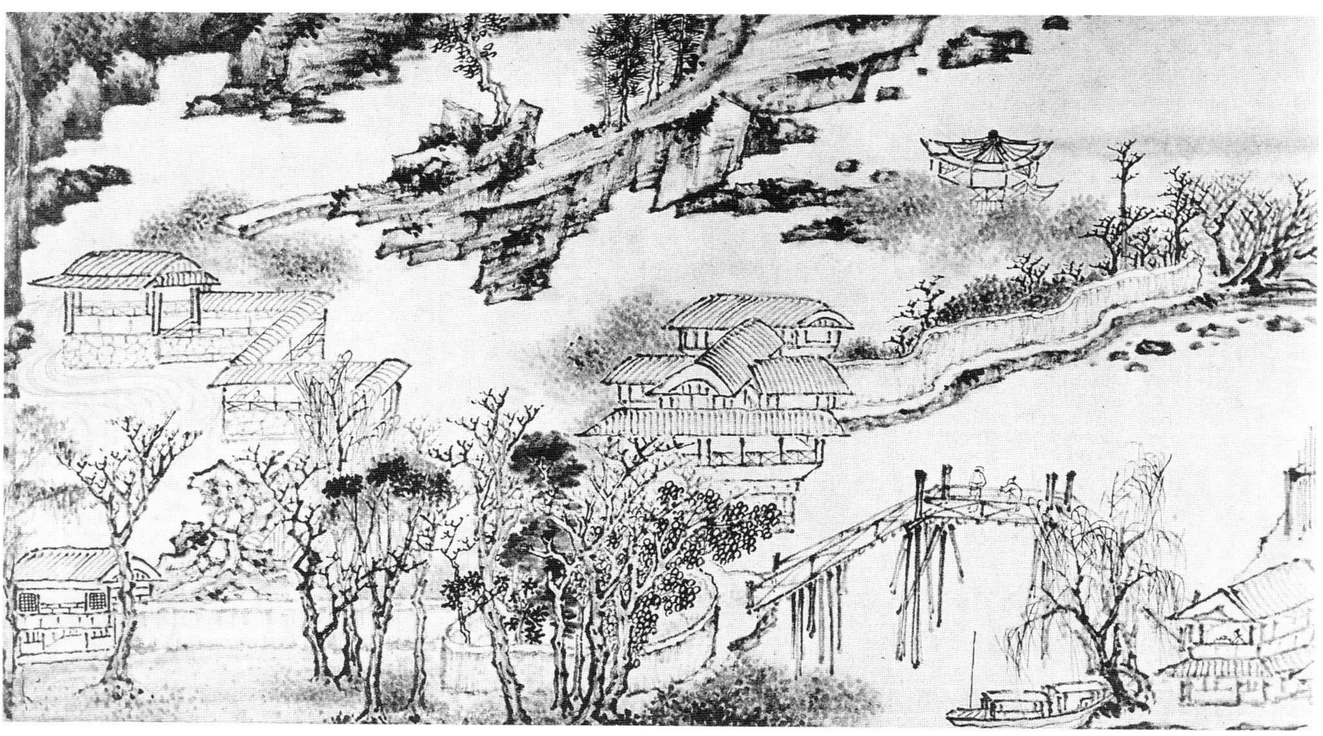

should not be given to me . . . I try to pay you people, and you should not demand unreasonable payment."

Four years later, in 1633, Li Jih-hua wrote that he was tired, and that the signboard (advertising his calligraphy and painting) should be taken down; his servants should take up the hoe and plough to help with the farming, instead of continuing to depend on their master's "ploughing with the brush." Again, the tone is facetious, but the note nonetheless serves as another indication that the 1629 essay should not be dismissed as pure fabrication.[83]

Using Assistants

The theme of the overworked artist who cannot keep up with the demand for his work, takes on too many commissions or obligations, and is pressed by impatient clients is so regularly found in the literature, including reliable sources such as letters between painters and their agents, that it can be accepted as representing a common problem.[84] Painters complain that they are obliged to fritter away their time doing these minor works to the neglect of their major ones. Hsiang Sheng-mo, for instance, in the inscription on his 1626 "Calling for Reclusion" handscroll, writes that he could not work on it because he "had to spend time meeting requests from various people."[85] One relief was to make use of ghostpainters, a practice noted above for Chin Nung that will again be considered in the final chapter. Jen Po-nien, we read, after his paintings had come to be in demand, was under intense pressure to produce more, particularly from his parsimonious wife who served as his manager and allowed him no rest. Jen's addiction to opium and his temperamental laziness diminished his productivity, and "the scrolls which he was obliged to complete piled up mountain-high."[86] Eventually, in his late years, he took to employing his daughter Jen Hsia as his ghostpainter, signing her works as his own.

Another, less deceptive expedient was to employ assistants, whether family members or outsiders, to do some of the time-consuming and less demanding work, such as adding the coloring to the master's ink-drawing, as Yün Shou-p'ing did. The practice was at least as old as the T'ang dynasty, when, according to the ninth-century *Li-tai ming-hua chi,* both the landscapist Wang Wei and the figure master Wu Tao-tzu had their works colored by assistants.[87] Later critics interpret Wu's lack of interest in color as a strength, a reflection of his overriding concern with powerful, representationally effective brush drawing in ink.[88] An artist who concentrated on color and neglected drawing, by contrast, might be criticized, as was the flower painter Chao Ch'ang by Kuo Jo-hsü, who writes that Chao "most often made use of tracings from a cartoon" so that "the spirit of his brush was bald and weak, as he cared only for success in handling colors."[89]

The early Ch'ing finger-painter Kao Ch'i-p'ei (figure 3.35) was one who employed his pupils and friends to color his paintings; his paintings were valued (like Wu Tao-tzu's) for their drawing—in his case, done with his fingers—and Kao reportedly enlisted other artists of the time such as Yüan Chiang and Lu Wei to add colors with a brush to his large paintings. Small works such as albums and fans were done entirely by himself, and were better in quality.[90]

Inscriptions on several of Ch'en Hung-shou's paintings reveal that some part of the work was done by others than the master himself. On his famous "Scenes from the Life of T'ao Yüan-ming" of 1650 (figure 1.13), he adds a note to his signature saying that the coloring was done by his son Ming-ju. On a painting of "Female Immortals in the Palace Museum," Beijing (figure 3.36A), it was his disciple Yen Chan who did the coloring, and probably also the intricate, repeated pattern on the robes.

Other versions of the same composition are to be found in the Palace Museum, Taipei (figure 3.36B) and the Yen-huang Art Museum,

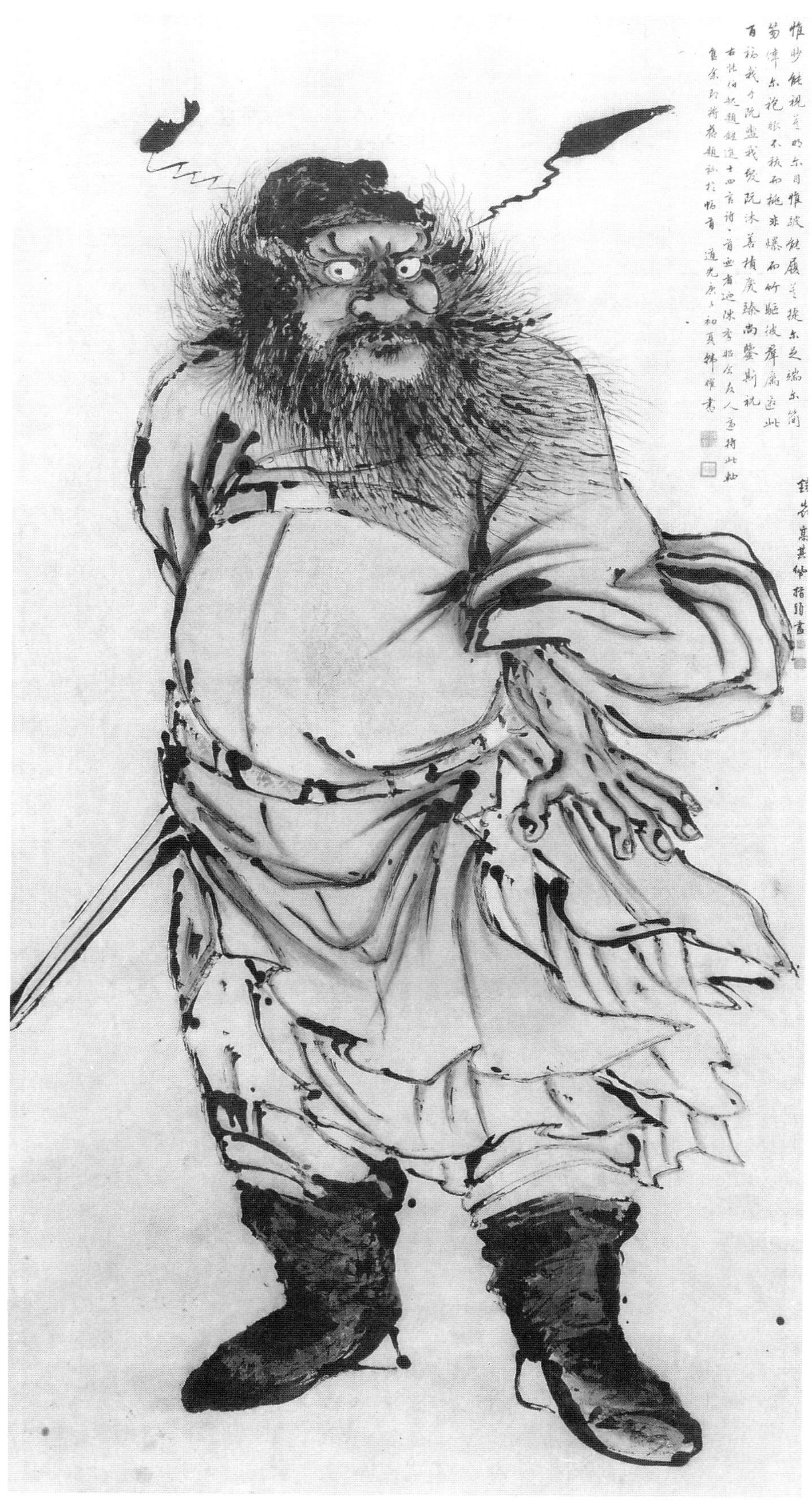

3.35. Kao Ch'i-p'ei, "Chung K'uei" (finger painting). Hanging scroll, ink and colors on paper, 136.5 × 72.6 cm. University Art Museum, Berkeley (1967.24).

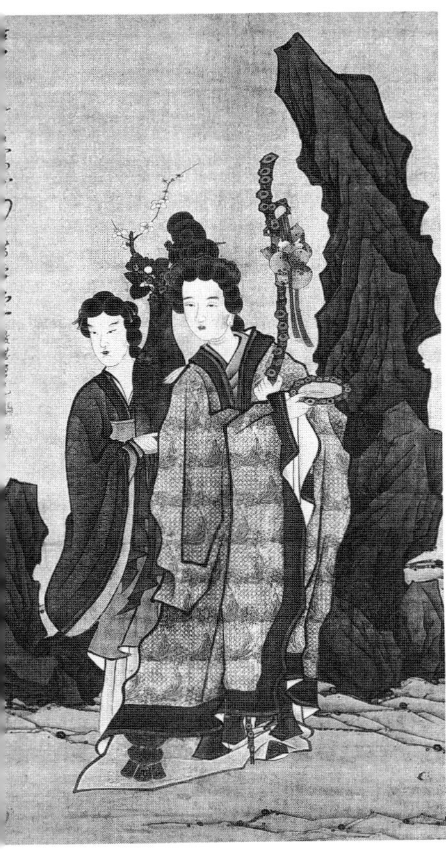

6 (left). Ch'en Hung-shou and Yen an, "Female Immortals."
nging scroll, ink and colors on silk, 172.5 × 5 cm. Palace Museum, Peking. From Rogers l Lee, *Masterworks of Ming and Qing Painting n the Forbidden City*, no. 33.

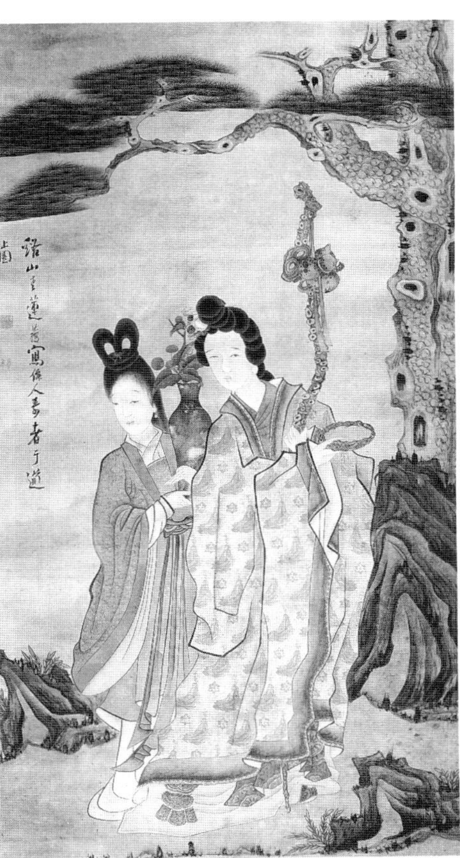

3.36 (center). Ch'en Hung-shou, "Immortals Presenting Symbols of Longevity."
Hanging scroll, ink and colors on silk, dimensions unknown. National Palace Museum, Taipei.

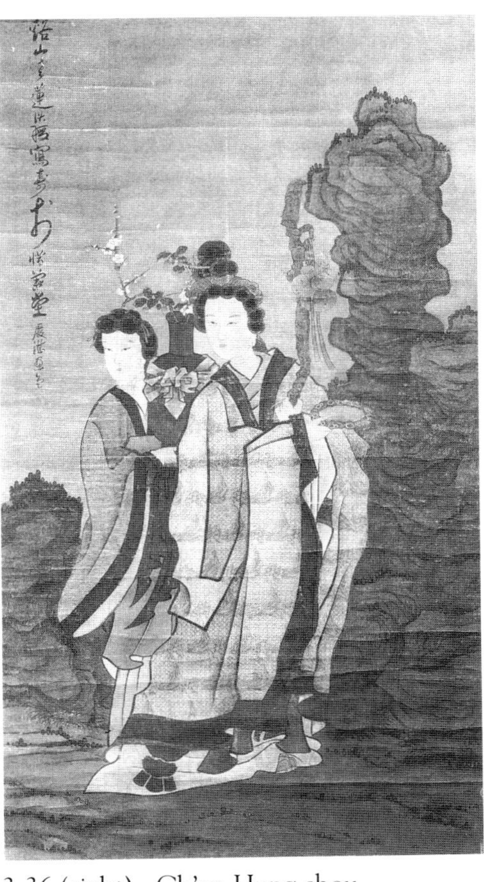

3.36 (right). Ch'en Hung-shou, "Female Immortals."
Collection of Yen-huang Art Museum. From *Yen-huang i-shu-kuan ts'ang-p'in chi* (Old Paintings and Calligraphy in the Yen-huang Art Museum), 1992, pl. 55.

Beijing (figure 3.36C)—the last with a note added to Chen's signature, again, stating that the coloring was done by Yen Chan. One can conjecture that these were workshop productions, done in multiples to be sold to people who needed pictures for presentation on someone's birthday, or perhaps for a wedding anniversary.[91] Formerly we would have worried about which version is authentic, assuming that only one was; now we incline to accept them, or some of them, as studio works, produced for the market, and to account in this way for their hardness and insensitivity.[92] They stand apart clearly from the one-of-a-kind, personalized paintings done by Ch'en Hung-shou himself, presumably for people with whom he had closer personal relations, or to whom he was more indebted.[93]

The studio mode of collaborative production was obviously suitable for certain kinds of paintings and not for others. In the "Portrait of Ho T'ien-chang" scroll (figure 3.37) Ch'en Hung-shou did only the figures, allowing his disciple Yen Chan to paint the setting of trees and rocks and a third painter, presumably a portrait specialist, to paint the face of the subject. Yen Chan also painted under his own name. Anne Burkus cites a record of a family of a prominent official with whom Ch'en Hung-shou was acquainted, when they needed a Buddhist icon, summoning Yen Chan to do it in the master's style.[94]

These are honest collaborations, acknowledged in the inscriptions, each artist performing his assigned task under the master's direction. Early landscapists, such as Kuan T'ung and Li Ch'eng,[95] are said to have enlisted figure specialists to insert the images of humans into their paintings; we read also of three artist friends active in Szechwan in the tenth century who would work together to produce religious figure compositions for temples.[96] A painting made under the order of the T'ang Emperor Hsüan-tsung titled "The Gold Bridge" and depicting the imperial procession returning to the capital from the sacrificial ceremony performed on Mt. T'ai was executed by three leading court artists: Ch'en Hung painted the emperor and his favorite steed Shining White; Wu Tao-tzu painted the landscape and the attendants and carriages; and Wei Wu-t'ien, who specialized in animals and birds, painted the various animals in the procession.[97]

Most common among collaborative works in the later periods was the informal portrait done jointly by a portrait specialist and a landscapist, in which the subject is portrayed in some characterizing setting. The earliest extant example for which the artists can be identified is a portrait of the poet Yang Chu-hsi, painted in 1363 by the leading portrait specialist of the age, Wang I, and Ni Tsan, who added the pine tree and rocks (figure 3.38). Numerous others are known from the Ming and Ch'ing. There seems to have been no rule about who painted first. A letter from the collector Kao Shih-ch'i to Wang Hui accompanying a portrait of his mother asks Wang to fill in a landscape around it;[98] another from the late Ming landscapist Mi Wan-chung to a portraitist named Yüan-chün asks that a portrait be added to a landscape that Mi himself had painted.[99] Extant paintings of this kind lead to

3.37. Ch'en Hung-shou, Yen Chan, and Li Wan-sheng, "Portrait of Ho T'ien-chang." Handscroll, ink and colors on silk, ht. 35 cm. Suchou Museum.

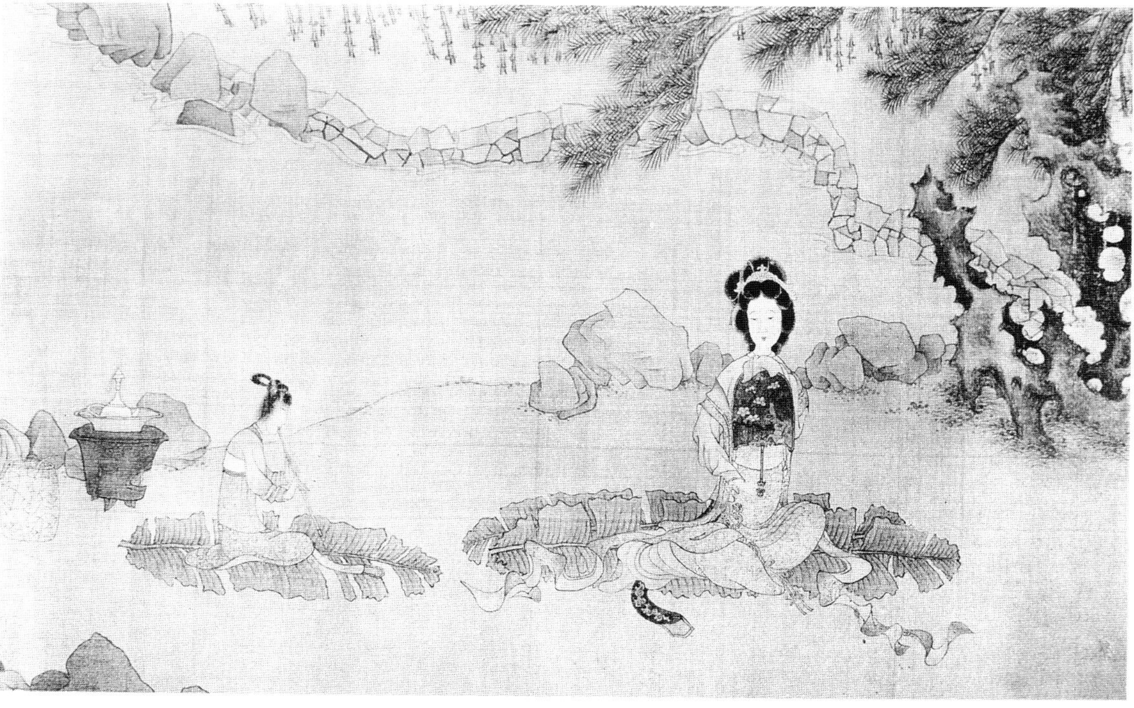

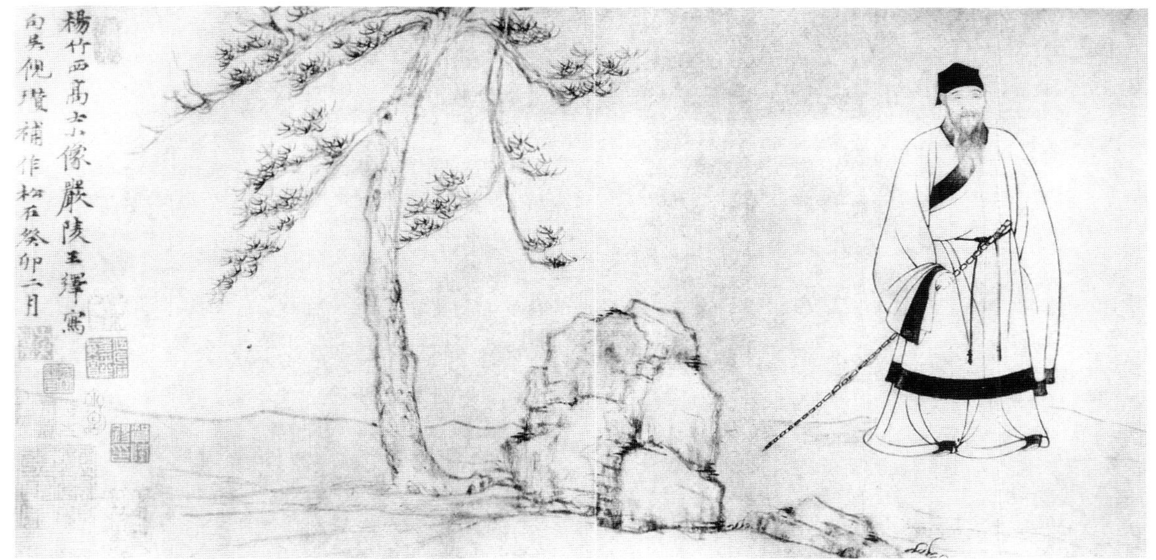

3.38. Wang I and Ni Tsan, "Portrait of Yang Chu-hsi Walking with a Staff."
Section of a handscroll, ink on paper, 27.7 × 88.8 cm. Palace Museum, Peking. From *Chung-kuo li-tai hui-hua* vol. 4 (Peking, 1983), plate 72.

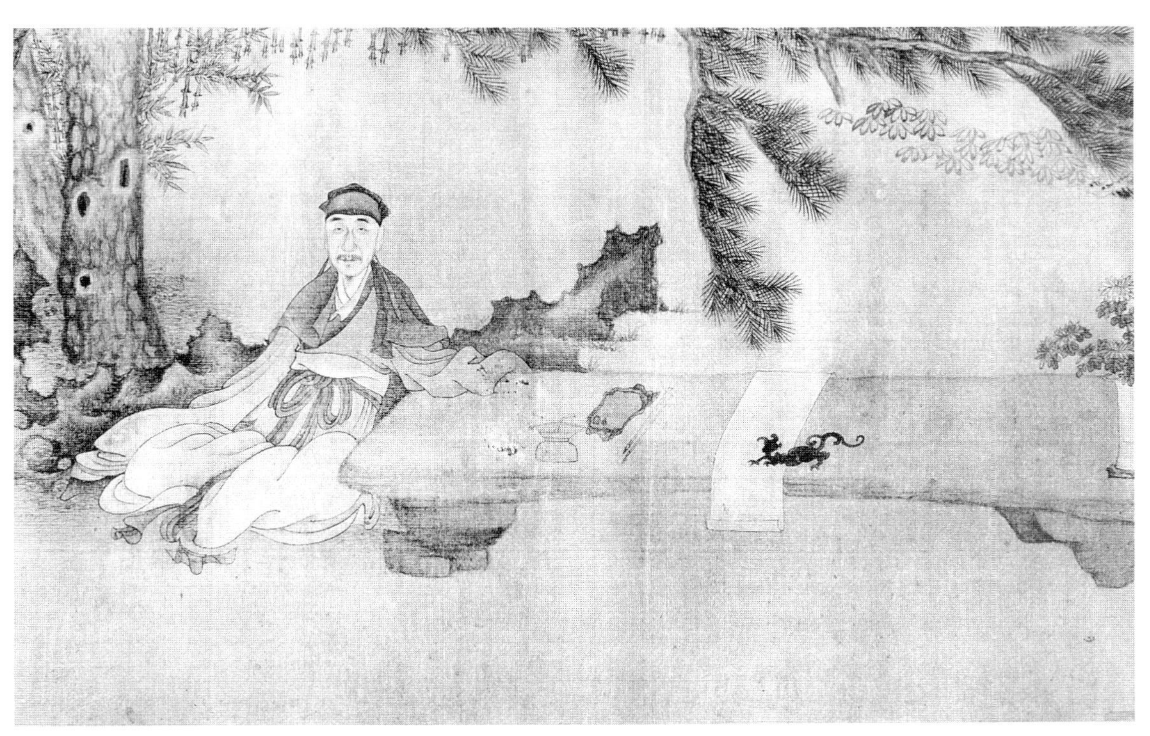

the same conclusion: in some it is obvious that the landscapist painted the setting first, leaving a space for the portraitist to insert the face or figure, while others appear to have been done in the opposite order.

With the recorded cases of artists who employed assistants to paint parts of their pictures without acknowledging their contributions, we move beyond legitimate collaborations into deliberate deceptions. A letter from a dealer to the late eighteenth-century painter Ch'en Man-sheng,[100] accompanying two fans painted by another artist, asks Ch'en to "supplement" them, or add something to them; one assumes some kind of chicanery.[101] Of another artist of the same period named Wang Chiao-ch'i it was said that his paintings to repay social obligations were done by several of his apprentices, with Wang only "embellishing them with a few brushstrokes."[102] A step beyond this and we are in the realm of ghostpainting, a practice to be considered in the last chapter.

FOUR

The Painter's Hand

In China, as in the West, the idea that a painting derives its value in large part from its style, especially from its facture and "touch," the marks of the artist's brush-in-hand that make it up, appears relatively late in the history of the art as part of a larger complex of changes in the way paintings are experienced and appraised. The fundamental change is from the view of a painting as a picture, a view focused on the subject and on the effectiveness of the work as representation, to the view of a painting as an object for aesthetic contemplation and as the creation of a particular master.

The change happens earlier in China than in the West, and is closely bound up there with the rise of the scholar-amateur movement, which had its beginnings in the late eleventh and early twelfth centuries but reached full maturity only in the fourteenth, when it also came to dominate theorizing about painting. The well-studied shift in writings about landscape, from praising it for its capacity as convincing representation that could make the viewer "feel as if he were in the very place" to reading it (in the eleventh-century Mi Fu's words) as "a creation of the mind" of the artist,[1] reflects this change. By the mid-Sung, Mi Fu's son Mi Yu-jen (1075–1151) could write of painting as "delineations of the

I want to dedicate this final chapter to the late Alexander Soper, because it addresses some of the same problems that interested him; because it draws frequently on his writings and translations; and simply out of affection and respect for his achievements.

mind," and his older contemporary Kuo Jo-hsü could see it as "imprints of the mind"; both link it in this capacity with calligraphy.[2] Chinese painting is thus brought to the state that Norman Bryson (placing it in opposition to Western painting) recognizes as permitting "a maximum of integrity and visibility to the constitutive strokes of the brush" and as "the work of the brush in 'real time' and as extension of the painter's own body."[3]

The insistence on seeing a painting as a structure of distinct marks made by a moving hand, and on reading this structure as a direct expression of the artist's inner self, the artist having in effect inscribed himself onto the picture surface, deflects attention from properly pictorial values, which (as outlined in the opening chapter) come to be regarded as philistine concerns. The early statements of this attitude are well known, from Su Shih's dismissal of "anyone who judges paintings on the basis of likeness" as childish, to Ni Tsan's lofty pronouncement that he doesn't really care whether or not his bamboo paintings look like bamboo, since all he wants to do is "express the feelings in his breast." The criterion of *hsing-ssu,* "form-likeness" or verisimilitude, which the Yüan-period critic T'ang Hou puts at the bottom of his list of qualities to look for in a painting,[4] was discredited, and thereafter could scarcely be introduced other than pejoratively in respectable Chinese writings on painting. The rhetoric of anti-representation proved so powerful, and was so successful in linking form-likeness to lower levels of cultivation and connoisseurship, that artists who chose to violate the expressive-brushwork aesthetic in pursuit of naturalistic effects were likely to be belittled by critics.

It had not been so in the early centuries, when painters had been praised for capturing in varying degrees the "bones," "flesh," and "soul" of their subjects, whether humans or horses, and sometimes for illusionistic renderings so lifelike as to fool the eye into mistaking the image for the real thing, although the higher rankings were always reserved for artists whose depictions conveyed in addition some special insights. Magic realism and magic were inseparable: a story about a painting of a fish that was hung on a river bank to attract otters[5] is followed directly by another about a painting of a dragon that brought heavy rain.[6] As late as the eleventh century there is an account of a painting of pheasants so lifelike that falcons would attack it,[7] and even into the Southern Sung period, illusionism kept its aura of magic. Teng Ch'un in the twelfth century writes of an artist named Tao Hung whose painting of a cat would keep away mice from any household in which it was hung, while hanging his painting of the God of Wealth would ensure prosperity for the household.[8]

Again as in the West, the suppression of the artist's hand was for the early periods one aspect of realism. The fine-line drawing characteristic of early painting served to bound the forms and contain the washes of color, and although it could be expressive in its quiet way, it was generally free of gestural eloquence and individualistic quirks. Breaks with the orthodoxy of fine-line drawing and color wash appear already in the T'ang, and the early mode gradually gives way, especially in landscape painting, to styles rendering tactile surface and volume as well as shape, often with color reduced to transparent washes or eliminated altogether, as ink monochrome gains in popularity.[9] But throughout the Sung, these new stylistic moves are generally made in pursuit of more visually convincing and penetrating representations of the subjects, a project to which personal expression through brushwork is irrelevant. Paintings of animals from the tenth century (figure 4.1) through the thirteenth present themselves as products of close observation and objective portrayal, an effect for which the suppression of the artist's hand is crucial. The same is true of typical Sung paintings of other subjects: flowers, birds, even figures. Works of this kind reveal the shallowness of the pat formulation in which Chinese paint-

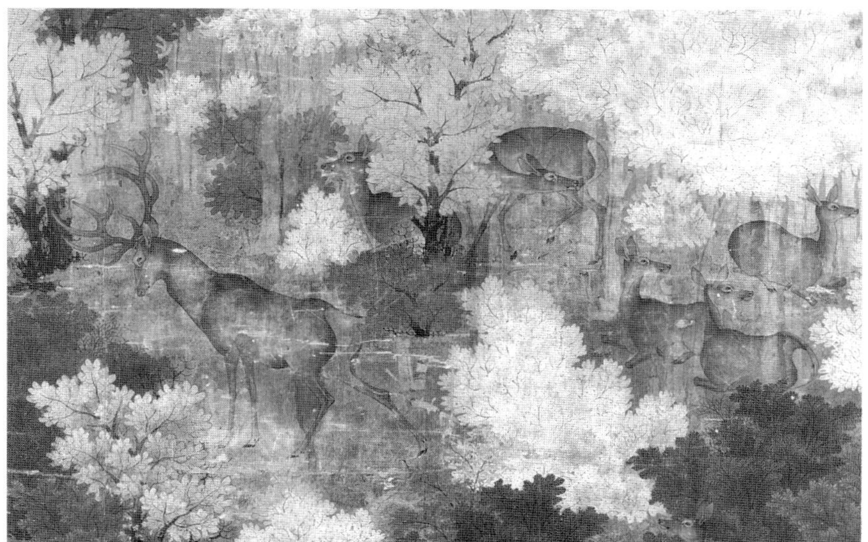

4.1. Anonymous, Liao dynasty? (10th–11th cent.), "Deer in an Autumn Forest." Detail from a hanging scroll, ink and colors on silk, 118.4 × 63.8 cm. National Palace Museum, Taipei, Republic of China.

ing is "unconcerned with outer appearances, pursuing only the inner essence" of the things it depicts.[10]

I have introduced before an anonymous picture of bamboo, old trees, and rocks in winter (figure 4.2), probably late tenth or early eleventh century in date, as a supreme exemplification of the ideal of concealing the painter's hand in order to concentrate the viewer's attention on the image, which appears to have come into being without the intervention of human art, like a creation of nature. And that is exactly how the works of great masters of this period, such as Li Ch'eng and Fan K'uan, are praised by their contemporaries: they create as nature does, without willfulness or any assertion of the self. By the thirteenth century these same artists had become, for Chao Hsi-ku (who was quoted earlier as a proponent of the new amateur-painting ideal), "scholar-officials who, when they were inspired, would leave behind a few brushstrokes."

Narrowing the Range of Subjects

The diversion of interest from the imagery of the painting to its making and its maker, at least on the elite levels of appreciation, accompanies a sharp reduction in the range of what was considered to be suitable subject matter for good painting. The cultivated artist, always apprehensive of being mistakenly classed with the artisan-painters who were willing to depict stimulating and entertaining subjects assigned by others, limited his repertory generally to themes that were harmonious and charged with auspicious meanings, and that could be understood as reflective of his own rich but stable inner life. Collectors tended to follow the same preference for the aesthetically pleasing, and for pictures that did not challenge the ideal order of the Confucian world.

Alexander Soper addressed this phenomenon in a book published in 1967, pointing out that while a tenth-century poet can write that "in Six Dynasties painting combats are frequent," there are almost no references to paintings of warfare in the standard accounts of T'ang, Five Dynasties, or Sung painting—much less, one can add, from later periods. (Japanese artists, free from such constraints, continued to produce great battle pictures, such as the thirteenth-century "Heiji Wars" scroll, figure 4.3.) After discussing the disappearance of this once-popular theme and suggesting that it was "suppressed under the influence of the Confucian ideal (with its tangle of moral and aesthetic implications)," Soper

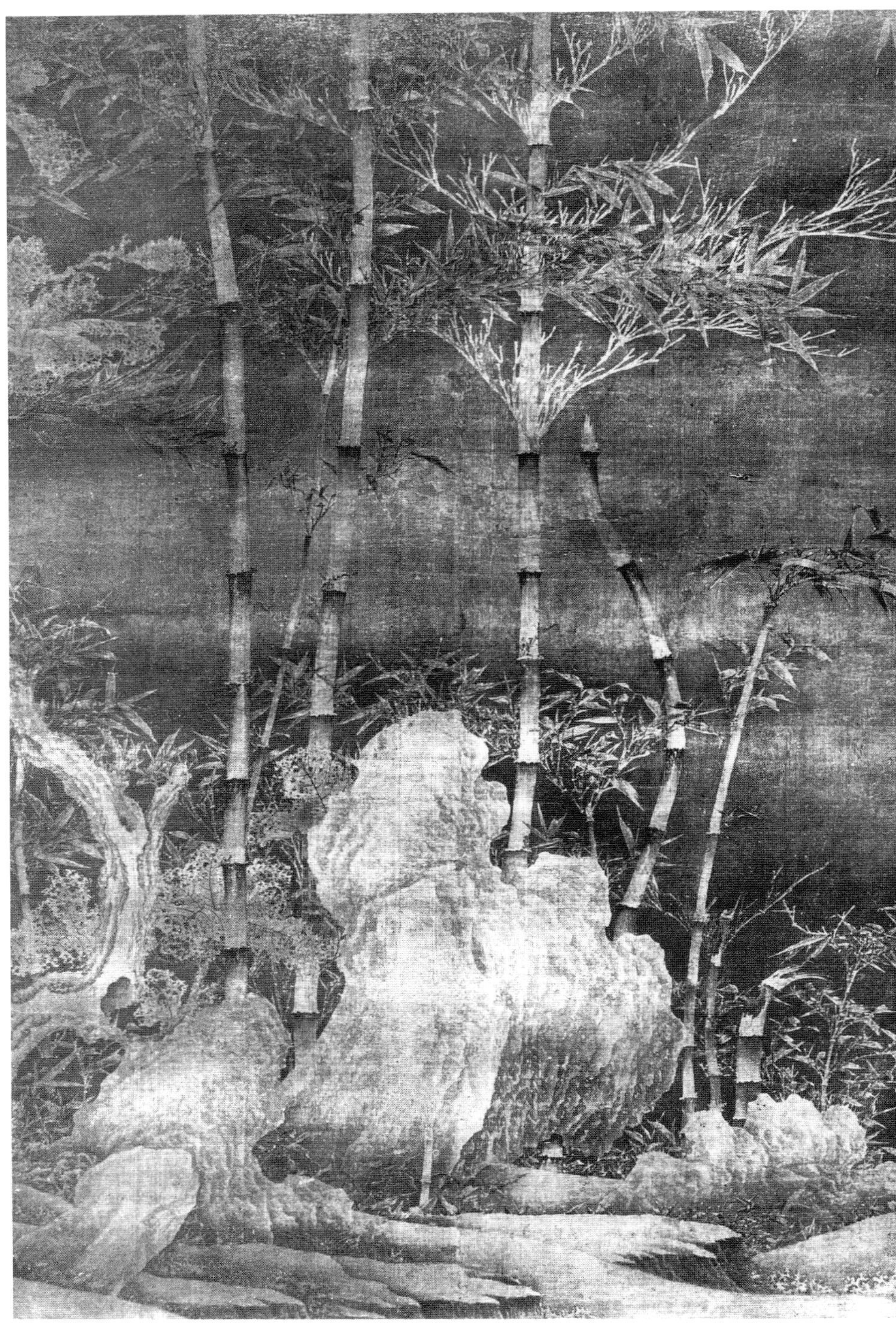

4.2. Anonymous, 10th century? (old attribution to Hsü Hsi), "Bamboo and Old Tree Growing by Rocks." Hanging scroll, ink on silk, 151.1 × 99.2 cm. Shanghai Museum.

quotes Mi Fu saying that "People today simply do not paint history pictures,"[11] and concludes: "The decline of such themes of actual or suggested violence I see as merely the most conspicuous aspect of a process that ended by depriving all figure painting in China of any serious hold on the emotions."[12]

Wu Tao-tzu in the eighth century had depicted the demon-queller Chung-k'uei gouging out the eye of a demon, and Huang Ch'üan in the tenth did another on the same theme, changing only a detail: his Chung-k'uei used his thumb, rather than the index finger, to do the gouging.[13] No later painter, to my knowledge, undertakes this arresting if gruesome subject. (A picture by Jen Po-nien, figure 4.4, approaches it.) The tenth-century master Chang Nan-pen specialized in portraying fire, which he used to enhance the power and terror of his Buddhist images.[14] Fire is scarcely to be seen in later Chinese painting.[15]

Among surviving Sung paintings we can still see a few—all anonymous—that depict the grotesque and the violent, such as a picture of village elders doing an exorcist dance (figure 4.5), or the earliest version of the "Clearing the Mountain of Demons" theme (figure 2.27), or one of blind men fighting, with a seller of nostrums added as a sardonic comment on gullibility (figure 4.6). A work done in 1074, known only in records, portrayed the misery of people in the capital suffering from a famine; it was meant to criticize the policies of the prime minister, Wang An-shih, as responsible for the disaster.[16]

The phenomenon to which Soper called attention can be seen even more broadly as a marked constriction in range of subject matter in Chinese painting from its early stages into its middle period in the Sung dynasty. This has been explained as a consequence of the great rise of landscape in the ninth and tenth centuries, and that is surely a major factor in it. It can also be argued, as I have elsewhere,[17] that paintings of the early periods typically convey far more visual information than later ones do. With what we can learn from an anonymous tenth-century work depicting a flour mill powered by a water wheel (figure 4.7), for instance, we could reconstruct the entire apparatus, as well as the social organization surrounding it. A fourteenth-century artist depicting the same subject (figure 4.8) reveals no understanding of the mechanism, and no interest in it. Underlying this change is the well-studied decline in China's engagement in technological innovation in this same period, and one can write,

4.3. Anonymous, Kamakura period (mid-13th cent.), "The Night Attack on the Sanjō Palace," from Heiji Monogatari scroll. Section of a handscroll, ink and colors on paper, ht. 41.3 cm. Museum of Fine Arts, Boston (Fenollosa-Weld Collection).

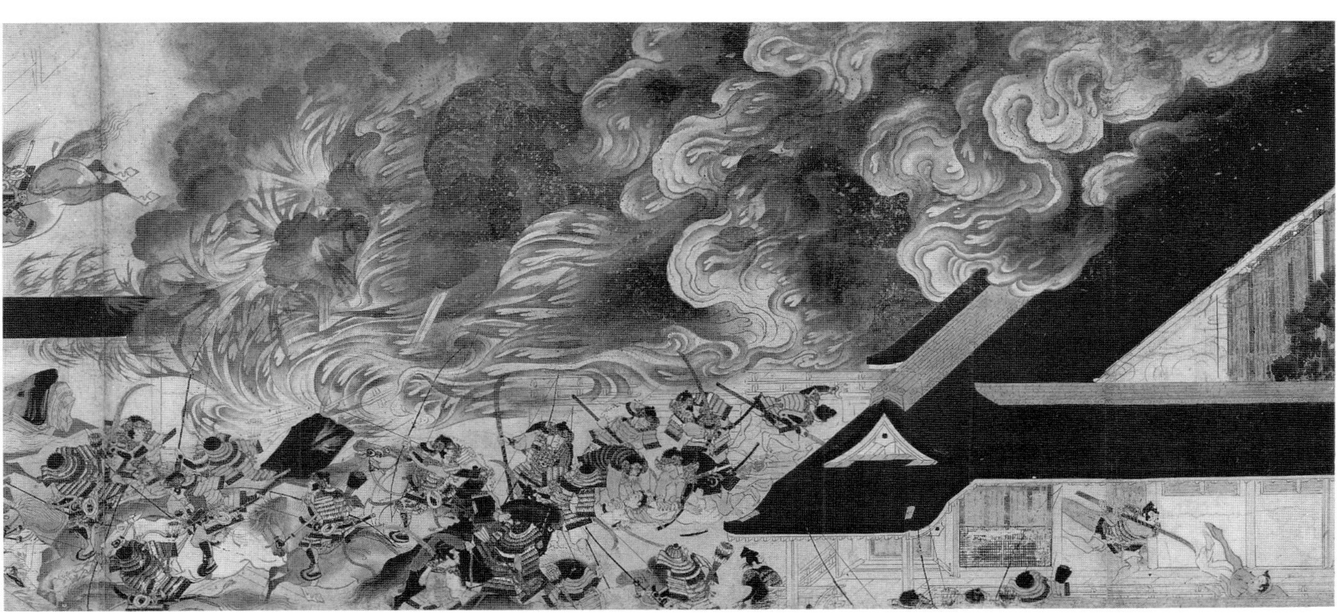

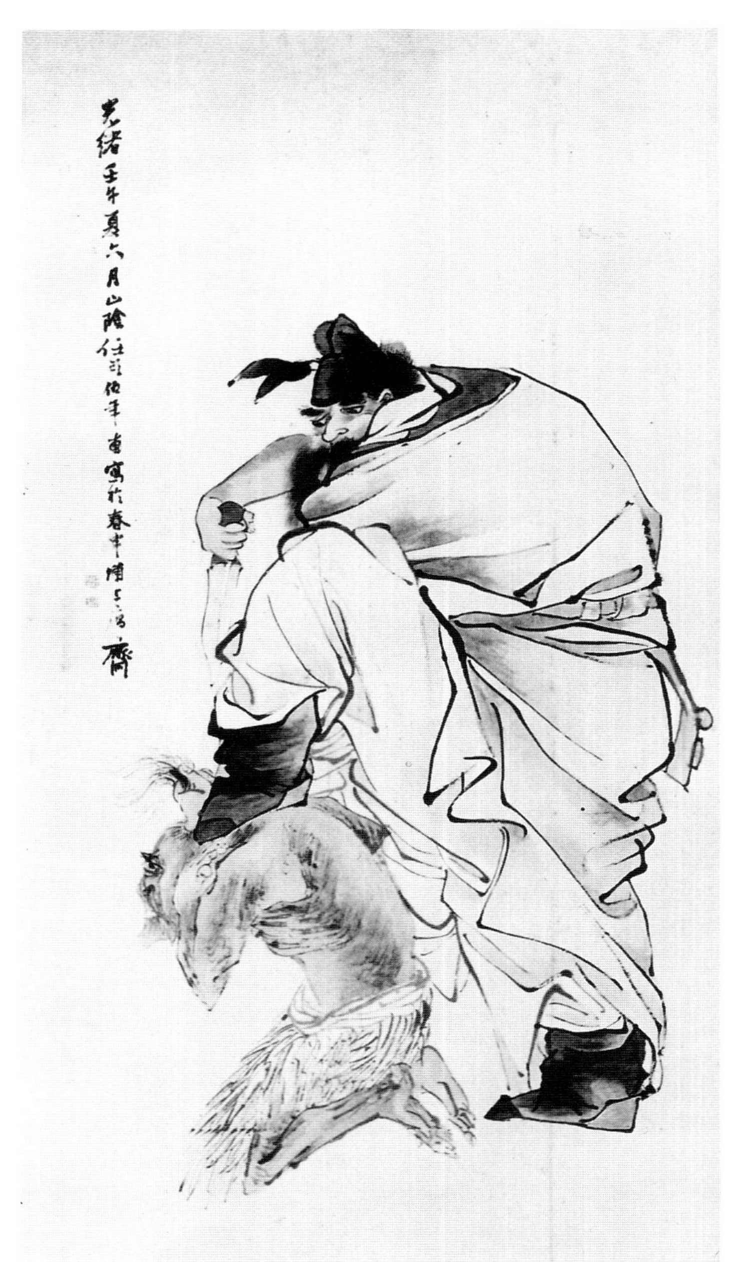

4.4. Jen I, "Chung K'uei Killing a Demon."
Dated 1782. Hanging scroll, ink and colors on paper. Collection of Yeh Ch'ien-yü. From *Chung-k'uei pai-t'u* (Canton, 1990), plate 34.

as I have, of a corresponding loss in the Chinese painter's involvement in the project of describing or exploring the physical world.[18] Soper is also right, however, in holding the Confucian ideal, with its strictures against strong emotional stimuli that disturb the placidity of the mind, responsible for some part of this thematic narrowing.[19] The unremitting emphasis on spiritual values and poetic resonances beyond the image in the writings of Sung scholars redefined the proper conditions for the creation and appreciation of paintings so as to rule out as plebeian the simple pleasure in visually engrossing and entertaining pictures that the Chinese, like any other people, had once enjoyed.[20]

Beginning with the Southern Sung period, the great age of idealized imagery, dishar-

4.5. Anonymous, Sung period (11th or 12th cent.), "Exorcism Dance."
Hanging scroll, ink and colors on silk, 67.5 × 59 cm. Palace Museum, Peking.

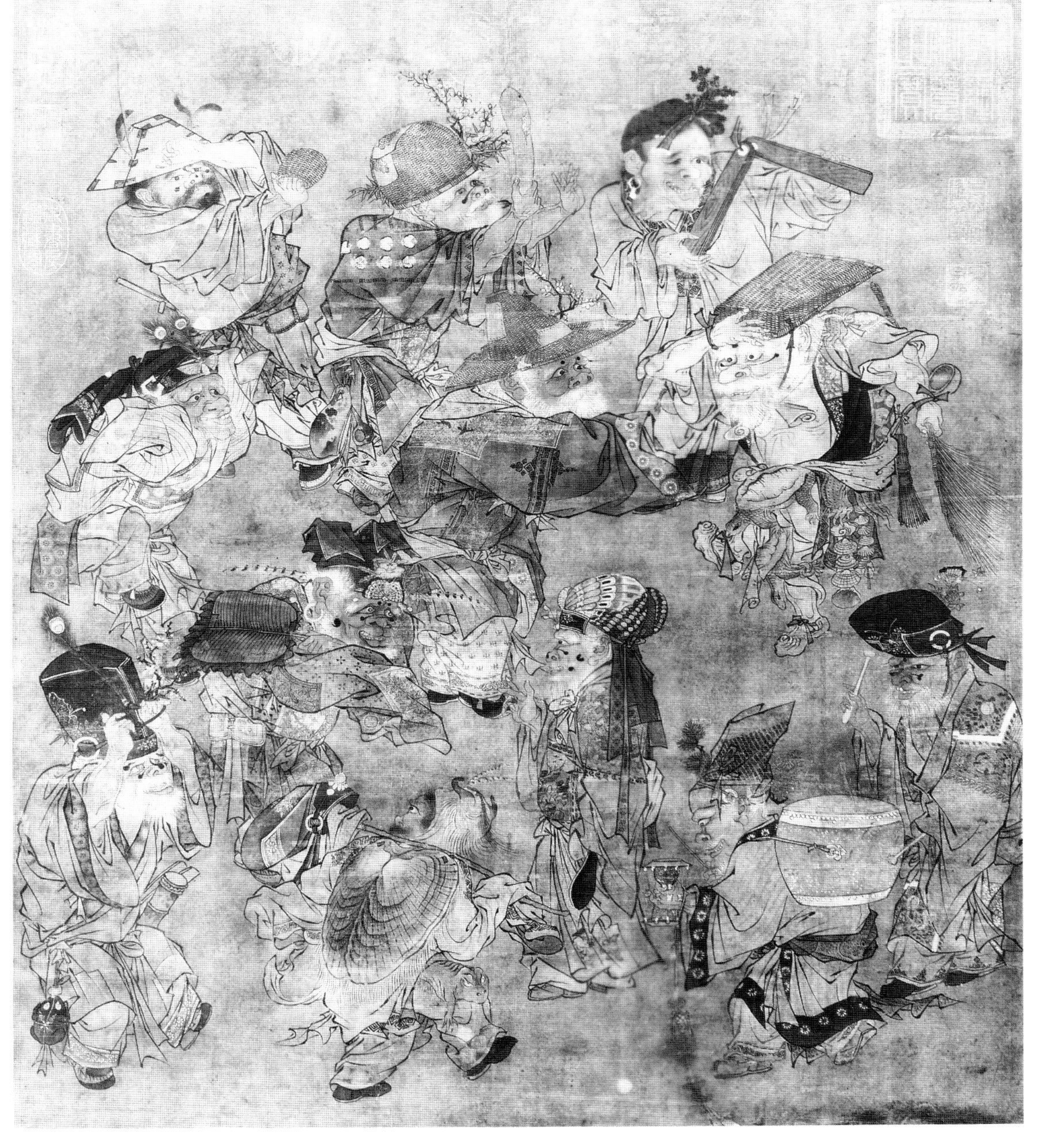

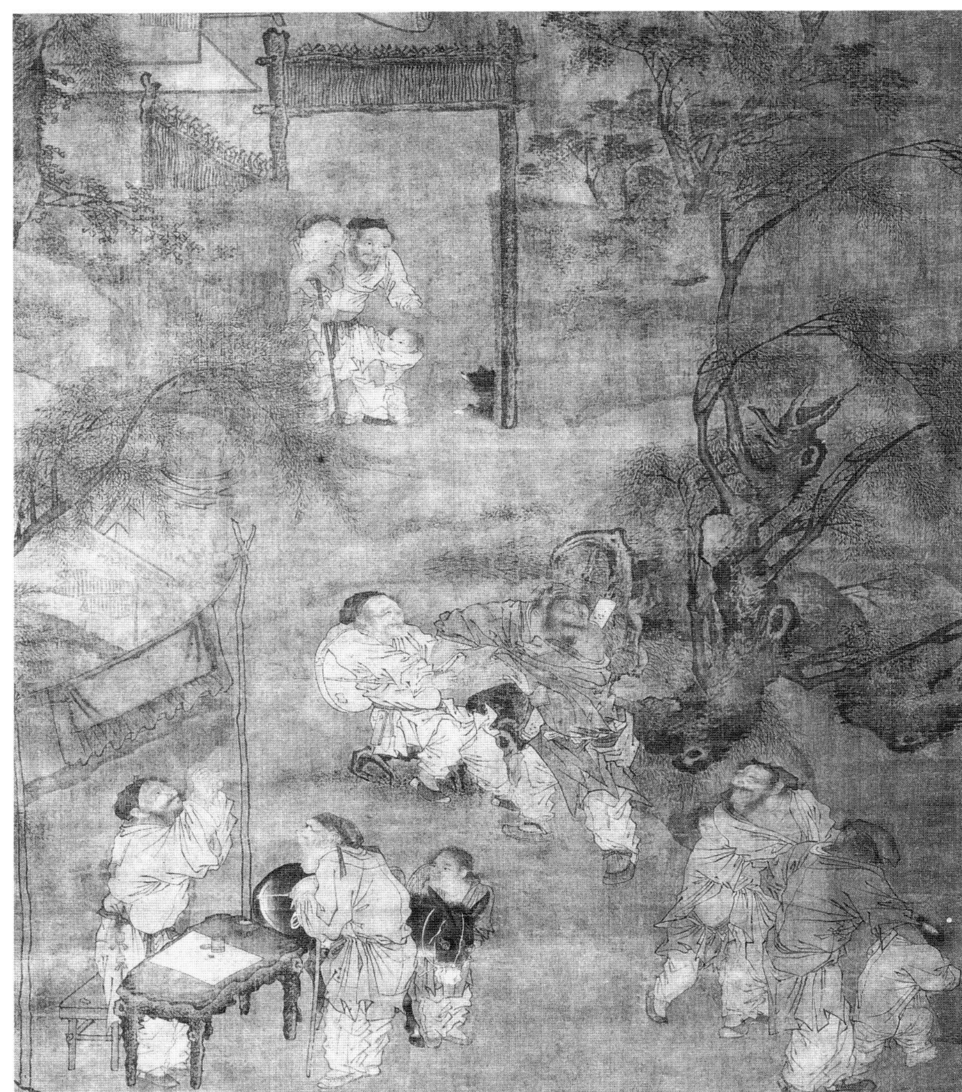

4.6. Anonymous, late Sung period (13th cent.?), "Blind Men Fighting." Hanging scroll, ink and colors on silk, 82 × 78.6 cm. Palace Museum, Peking.

monious subjects all but disappear from painting. The world presented by Southern Sung artists is largely exempted from harshness and accident. Yuan painting, while on the whole more earthy and less idealized, similarly eschews unpleasant subjects. One can of course find exceptions, such as portrayals of the Taoist adept Li T'ieh-kuai (figure 4.9), who returned from an out-of-body experience to find his physical frame destroyed and was forced to inhabit the infirm body of a beggar. But the exceptions are few, at least among surviving works. The same is true of the Ming, when Chou Ch'en's well-known series of "Beggars and Street Characters," painted in 1516 (figure 3.29), stands as almost a lone example of an artist's willingness to turn his gaze away from the comfortable gentlemen, lovely ladies, and picturesque peasants who inhabit Ming paintings to look hard at the underside of Suchou society. In this, as one might expect, he had no following that we know of, at least until the eighteenth century, when the boundaries of subject matter in Chinese painting suddenly expand again.

Magic realism, technical skills, the presentation of unusual and absorbing subjects, special insights into the beings and phenomena of

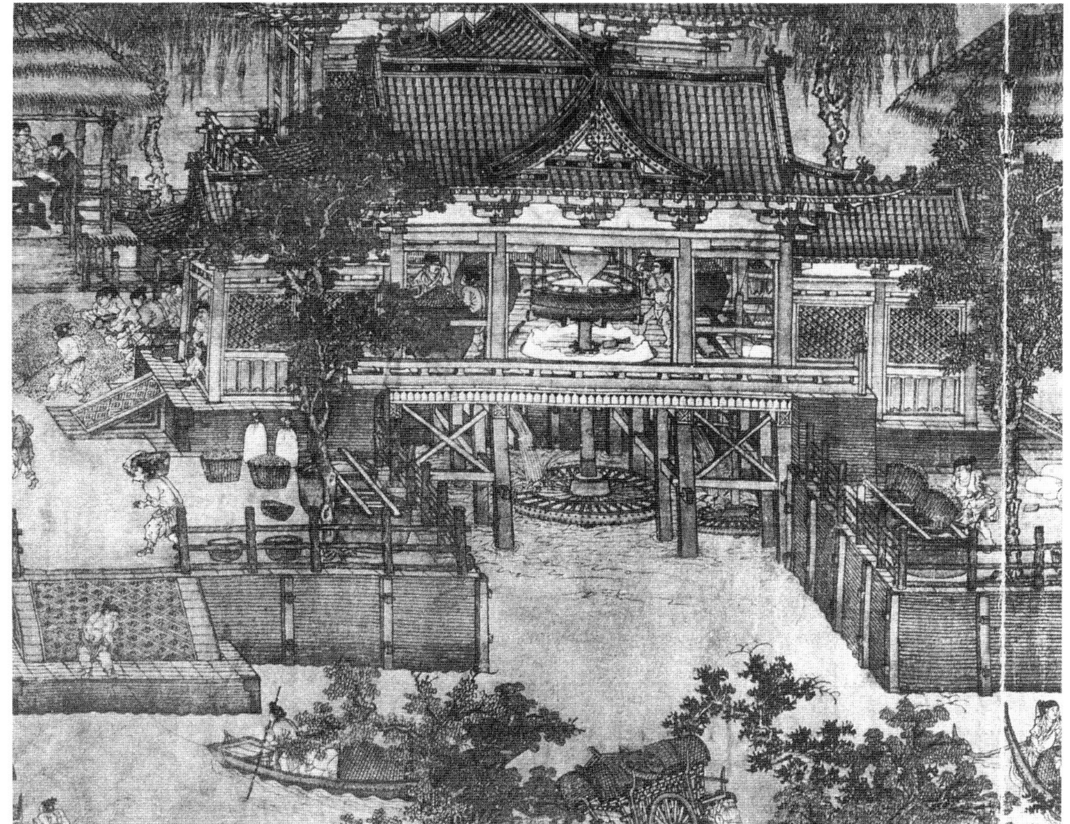

4.7. Anonymous, 10th–11th century (attributed to Wei Hsien), "Flour Mill Powered by Water Wheel." Detail from a handscroll, ink and colors on silk, 53.2 × 119.3 cm. Shanghai Museum.

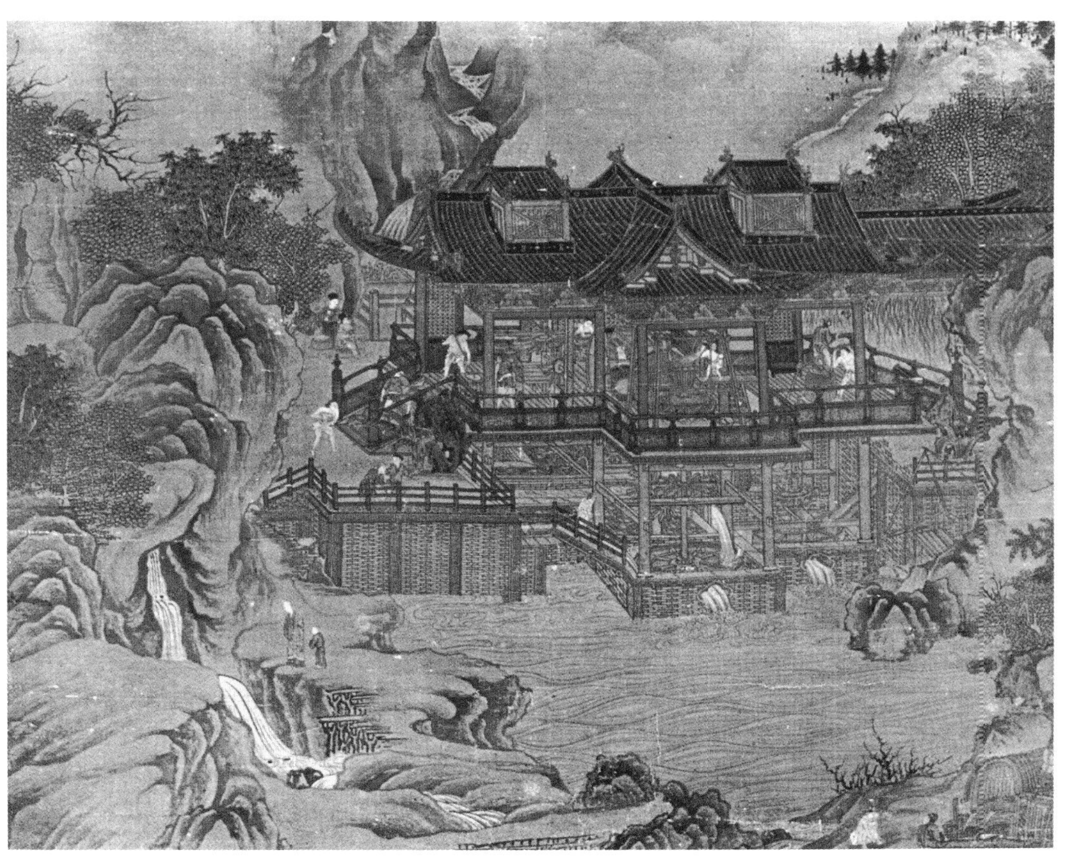

4.8. Anonymous, Yüan period, "Water Mill on a Mountain Stream." Detail from a hanging scroll, ink and colors on silk, 153.5 × 94.3 cm. Liaoning Museum. From *Liao-ning po-wu-kuan ts'ang hua* (Shanghai, 1986), plate 35.

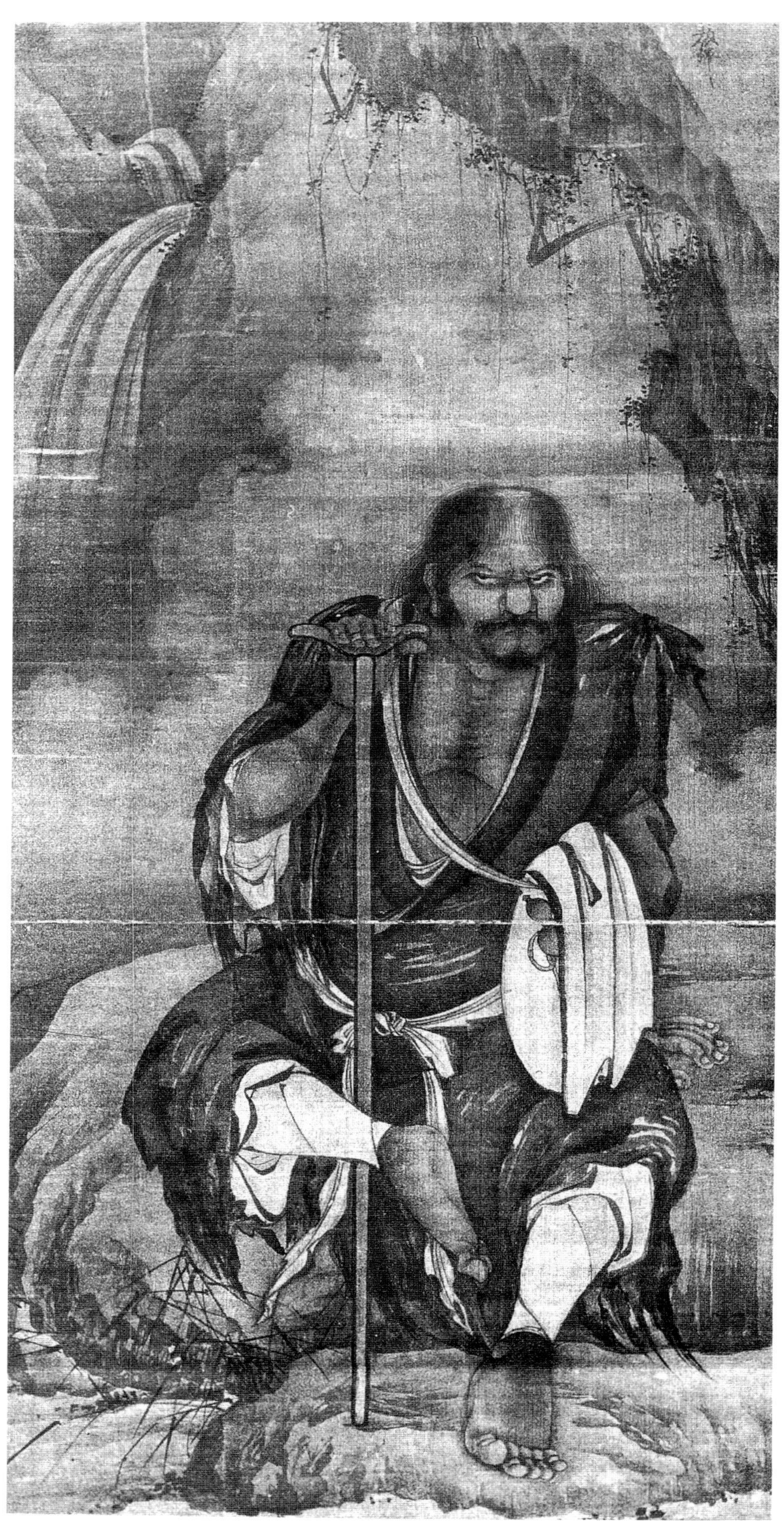

4.9. Yen Hui (early Yüan period), "The Taoist Magician Li T'ieh-kuai." Hanging scroll, ink on silk, 146.5 × 72.5 cm. Palace Museum, Peking.

the world, and the ability to convey these in visually convincing representations—all these early criteria for excellence in painting give way in the later centuries to criteria focused on brushwork and other elements of style, and on forms and motifs considered to be expressions of a cultivated mind—on qualities, that is, that were held to derive from the artist's status and character. The change was also, then, in ways of thinking about the artist, and different types of artists.

Types of Artists: Status and Style

It was not until the middle Sung period that painting was accepted, along with poetry, musical performance, and calligraphy, into the small group of polite arts that the gentleman might practice as leisure-time activities and modes of self-cultivation. But the idea that a good artist must be an exceptional person, and somewhat nonconformist, was much older. In a well-known story told by the fourth–third-century B.C. Taoist philosopher Chuang-tzu, a certain lord calls together all his scribes to paint pictures; one of them arrives late, unhurried, and sits half-naked with his robe loosened and his legs spread out. The lord says "He will do. He is a real painter."[21] With Chuang-tzu's story one can begin to discern the emergence of an ideal image or myth of the artist for China that parallels the growth defined for the European tradition by Ernst Kris and Otto Kurz in their 1934 book on the image of the artist.[22] Tracing this development in China, which could be the subject of another book, would lead to such paradigmatic masters as the fourth–fifth century Ku K'ai-chih, whose penetrating and idiosyncratic portrayals of his subjects were linked to his personal eccentricities; the divine Wu Tao-tzu in the eighth century, who was said by Chang Yen-yüan (a century after his time) to have painted only after he had drunk wine, and who "borrowed the creative powers of Heaven" to draw dynamic and full-bodied figures with dazzling swiftness; perhaps the eleventh-century Ts'ui Po, another virtuoso who worked without preparatory sketches and was "by nature careless and indulgent";[23] and the thirteenth-century Liang K'ai, called Liang Feng-tzu or "Crazy Liang," another heavy drinker who displayed his unorthodox temper by resigning from the imperial academy, leaving behind his golden belt (the highest award a court painter could receive), and by working sometimes in a swift, abbreviated manner.

The heirs to these, who exemplify the mercurial "Bohemian" temperament and mysterious talents of this artist-type, are Ming masters such as Wu Wei (figure 4.10), Shih Chung, T'ang Yin, and Hsü Wei, painters whose nonconformist stance in society correlates with distinctive traits of style in their paintings, traits that had come to signify the temperament ascribed to them. By this time, artists who belong to this type in their behavior, in the names they take for themselves (with words such as "transcendent," "wildly crazy," and "fool"), and in their styles, occupy a particular situation in Ming society, that of the "educated professional" artist—the educated man, that is, who somehow fails to pass the examinations for entry into the bureaucracy and attain an official position, the goal toward which higher education in China was normally directed, and who settles into the status of the professional painter, while continuing to distinguish himself and his paintings from those of the *hua shih* or *hua kung,* the so-called artisan-painter.[24]

Artists of this type, while they do not until the Ming succeed one another closely enough to make up a continuous lineage, do form a kind of sporadic tradition that represents one prevalent image of the artist in China. It is the image that corresponds most closely to the myth of the artist in Europe as defined by Kris and Kurz. Painters of this type, in both Europe and China, typically exhibit precocious talent for drawing at young ages; they paint with impressive swiftness, virtuosity, and seeming

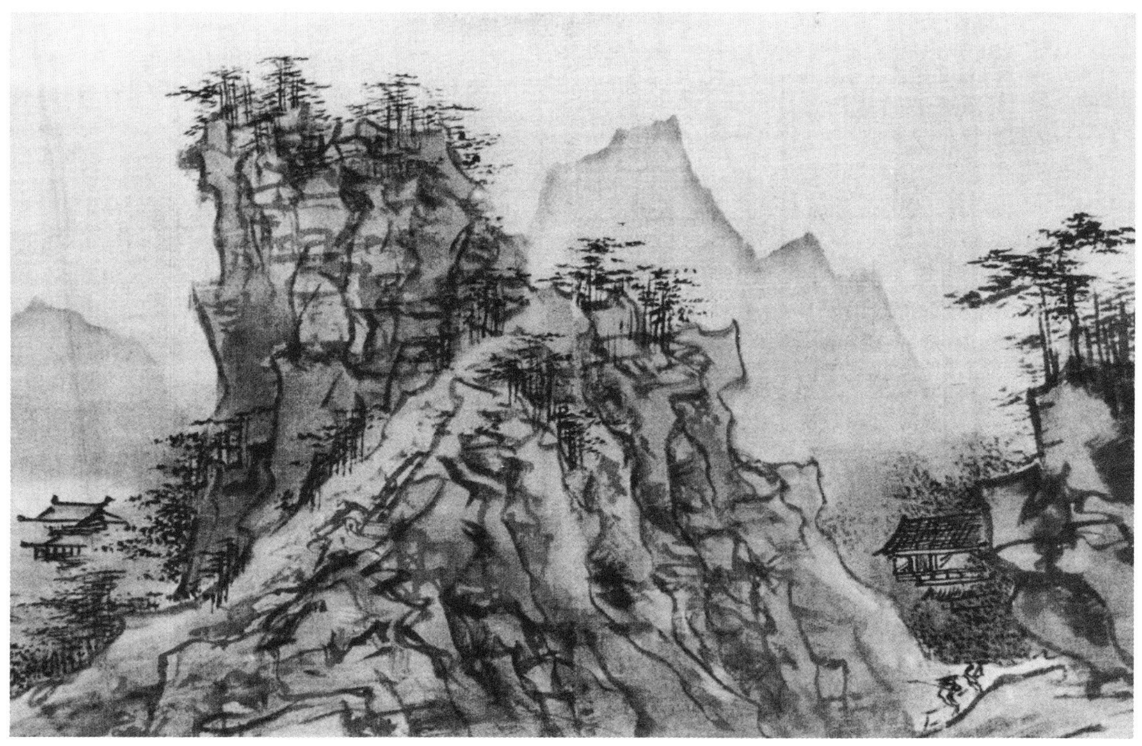

4.10. Wu Wei, "A Myriad Miles of the Yangtze River."
Dated 1505. Section of a handscroll, ink and light colors on silk, ht. 27.8 cm. Palace Museum, Peking. From *Chung-kuo mei-shu ch'üan-chi,* vol. 6, plate 127.

ease; they seem to be (as Kris and Kurz write) "driven by an irrepressible urge, in a mixture of fury and madness akin to intoxication" (in China it was frequently real intoxication, a fondness for drinking being a recurrent trait of these artists); they portray beautiful women (figure 4.11), who are associated in the popular imagination with the artist's free love-life; they consort with people of high rank as if on an equal footing.

The development of this type from the early periods, and its gradual separation from the *hua kung* or *hua shih,* the artisan painter, a separation signaled already in Chuang-tzu's anecdote, represents a distinct elevation in the status of the painter, at least in potential, and facilitates in turn the appearance and acceptance of a third type: that of the scholar-official-amateur painter. As already noted, this type is decisively established in the late Northern Sung period, but men of high position were already practicing the art of painting much earlier, and the tension between the artist's status and his artisanlike skills was already causing problems. The sixth-century scholar-official Yen Chih-t'ui, in his *Yen-shih chia-hsün,* a "remarkable manual of worldly wisdom" (Soper) composed for his sons, advises them on the dangers of practicing calligraphy or painting, citing cases of men of high rank who were proficient in these arts and were humiliated by being treated as craftsmen and "handymen" on call by their superiors, or who escaped this disgrace only through the privilege attendant on their elevated positions.[25] Yen's advice predates the better-known anecdote in which the seventh-century Yen Li-pen, after being subjected to that kind of indignity when he was ordered to portray a rare bird in the garden in the presence of the emperor and his courtiers, went home and advised his children against becoming painters.[26]

Yen Chih-t'ui prefaces his notes on scholar-officials and aristocrats who painted by observing that "From ancient times on down, many noted gentlemen have happened to be adepts [at painting]." This statement anticipates the fully developed literati painting ideal, but stops short of claiming that because they were "noted gentlemen," their paintings were somehow better than those of artists who occupied lower positions in the social order. A move toward that claim was made already in the ninth century by Chang Yen-yüan, who writes: "From ancient times those who have excelled in painting have all been men robed and capped and of noble descent, rare scholars and lofty-minded men who awakened the wonder of their own time and left behind a fragrance that shall last a thousand years. This is not a

4.11. T'ang Yin, "The Courtesan Li Tuan-tuan Presenting a Peony to the Poet Chang Ku."
Detail from a hanging scroll, ink and colors on paper, 122.5 × 57.2 cm. Nanking Museum. From *Nan-ching po-wu-yüan ts'ang-hua* (Shanghai, 1981), plate 20.

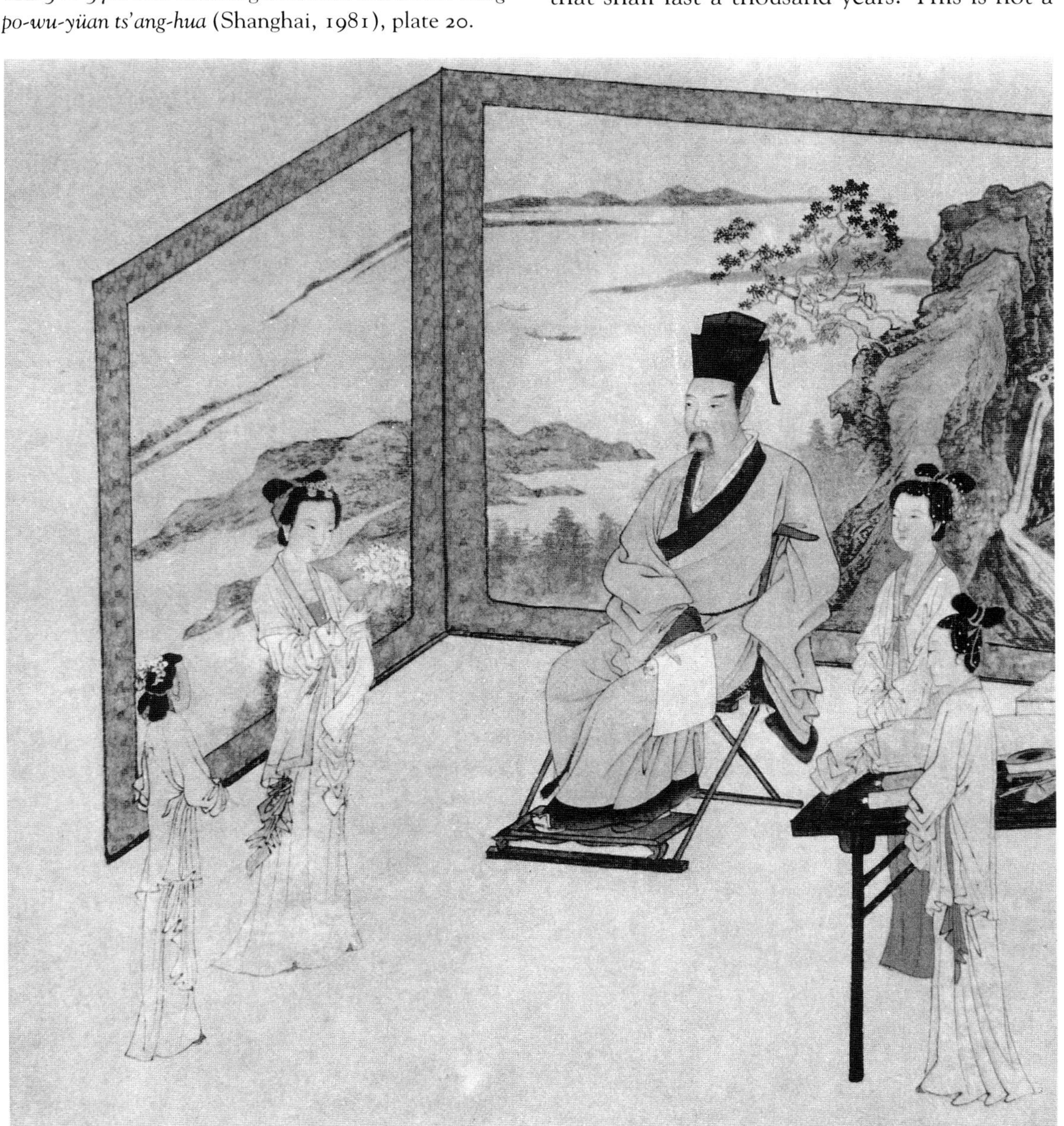

thing that humble rustics from village lanes could ever do."[27] At the same time, Chang's frank admission that his own works as an amateur painter were unsatisfying even to himself seems to acknowledge that personal cultivation in the artist need not lead to high quality in the painting: "In painting too my work does not come up to my idea [of what it should be], because I only do it to amuse myself."[28]

From the idea of the artist as an interesting and somehow unusual person to the idea that people of elevated social status would be the best artists might be seen as a natural move, since in Chinese thinking cultured and creative people were normally upper-class people. The next step was to claim that the gentleman's painting was not only better, but fundamentally different in kind. That claim is made in the eleventh century by Kuo Jo-hsü, who observes that in his view most of the outstanding paintings of the past were the work of "high officials, talented worthies, superior scholars, or recluses living in cliffs and caves," a statement echoing Chang Yen-yüan's, but then goes on to say that these gentlemen-artists had "lodged their elevated and refined feelings in their paintings."[29] Artists of this higher order were not representing, that is, so much as expressing. The new emphasis on painting as expressive form allowed it to be seen as an of extension of calligraphy, in which the idea of manifesting one's feelings and character in brushstrokes and visual forms was much older, and which had been practiced in that spirit by the literati from long before. It also, since the literati artist was endowed with poetic sensibilities that could be manifested in his paintings, opened the way for the endlessly reiterated equation of painting with poetry, in which paintings are taken to be "soundless poems" and poems "paintings with sound," a formulation too familiar, not to say hackneyed, to require more than a passing reference here.[30]

The qualities ascribed to artists of this scholar-amateur type differ sharply from the typical attributes of what was defined as the Bohemian or romantic type. No claims of precocious skills in representation are made for the scholar-amateur artists; they are stable in temperament, not mercurial; they are typically presented, not as nonconformists, but as epitomizing the established Confucian virtues; while they may in their real lives have been womanizers, they are never portrayed that way, since such behavior would violate the decorum expected of them. Holding the status in society that raised them above the other artist types required that they remain aloof from exactly the traits that defined the romantic image of the artist. Conversely, the classically educated man who failed to attain scholar-official status and turned to painting for his livelihood, as T'ang Yin and others did, could relinquish one set of characterizing attributes and embrace another. That he remained the same person as before is beside the point, since I am talking about social roles, about how these are reported by writers of conventionalized biographies, and about how these roles correlate with expectations made of the artist and with his actual practice of painting.

Types of Brushwork: Style and Status

That the subjects and styles used by painters tend to correlate with their social roles is a matter I have discussed elsewhere, and will not argue again at length here.[31] The social and expressive implications of brushwork types, however, deserve close analysis and extended study of a kind that has not been done.[32] Insisting on seeing the brushwork of each master as a simple expression of his individual temperament has impeded the recognition that class distinctions operated here also.

Certain types of brushwork signified corresponding qualities in the man who wielded the brush, qualities that were socially conditioned and defined. The refinement and reserve attributed to the literatus were typically manifested in brushstrokes that were sensitive and unassertive, and were read as traces of a hand endowed with, and disciplined by, those virtues. The brushstrokes, especially as used in landscape painting, were often of the type called "dry"; amateur-literatus painters are sometimes praised for "sparing their ink as if it were gold." No one would have said this of Tai Chin, or T'ang Yin, although both were quite capable of excellent dry-brush painting on occasion. Many of the scholar-amateurs in their landscapes used brushwork that was overlaid stroke on stroke, compounding dryer with wetter, darker with lighter, instead of drawing in discrete, decisive strokes. Such compound brushwork could be read as signifying an unhurried deliberation and the exercise of thought, ideally tempered by some quiet passages of spontaneity. (The literati sometimes also did quick "ink-plays," to be sure, the implications of which were somewhat different.) A slight wavering, suggesting hesitancy, was common in literati brushwork (figure 4.12), and was taken, not as indicative of infirmity, but as a sign of eschewing strong volition or positive purpose, and as an aspect of cultivated Confucian amateurism, located beyond technical skill, not short of it.

It is worth pointing out that while there is some overlapping with the code of signification for calligraphy, the mismatches are more striking; the issues and values attached to brushstroke types and the adoption of old modes in the two arts do not correspond, much as the literati (and their modern epigones) try endlessly to persuade us that they do. This can easily be demonstrated if we juxtapose details from the paintings of a succession of artists with their calligraphy, artists such as Chao Meng-fu (figure 4.13, cf. 4.12), or Huang Kung-wang, or Ni Tsan, or Ch'en Hung-shou.

4.12. Chao Meng-fu, "Village By the Water."
Dated 1302. Detail from a handscroll, ink on paper. Palace Museum, Peking.

4.13. Chao Meng-fu, Inscription from "Sheep and Goat."
Handscroll, ink on paper, ht. 25 cm. Freer Gallery of Art, Washington, D.C. (31.42.).

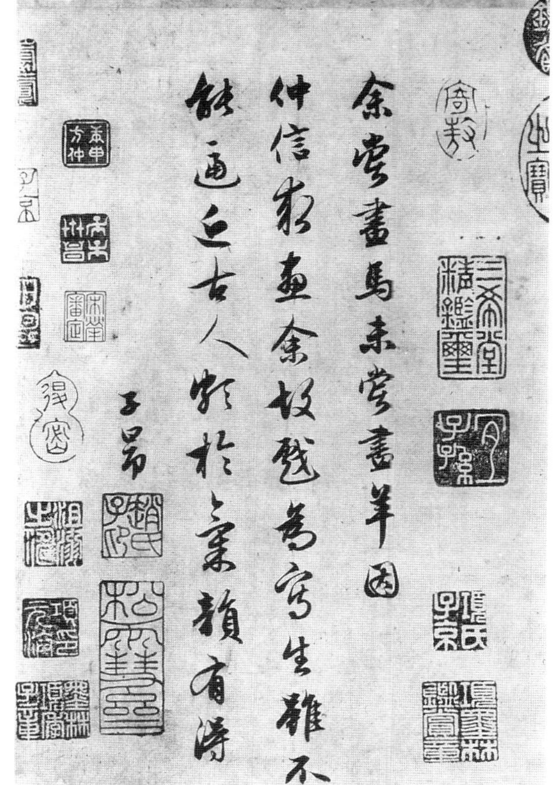

The obviousness of the dissimilarities recalls a device of Michael Baxandall, who in a memorable lecture put a slide of a painting on one side of the screen and a slide of a printed description of the same painting on the other, pointing out that they did not look alike. Even simple points, such as that pictures look fundamentally different from writing, sometimes need to be made.

All the literati traits of brushwork in painting and their significations stand in contrast to the more fluent and openly accomplished types of brushwork, which in the literati rhetoric were directed at impressing the viewer with the artist's technique and pleasing his eye, or at more open displays of temperament, and were typically employed by artists of the other types. So, at least, in the Ming dynasty; the associations of course changed with time, and would be differently defined if attention is turned to later periods.

Since the more reserved kinds of brushwork, and the plain, unexciting subjects for which they were characteristically used, signified the upper social and cultural levels, the patrician as opposed to the plebeian, the appreciation of these elevated the viewer's status by implying corresponding qualities and tastes in him. The same period in which the scholar-amateur ideal arose, the Northern Sung, saw also a sharp upsurge in collecting of works of art and antiquities, and a concentration on acquiring and appreciating authentic products from the hands of prestigious masters. As noted earlier, the new attitude tended to shift the emphasis away from the functions and meanings that paintings of certain subjects had originally carried, a shift that was thus another realization of the literati painting ideal, since the literatus insisted always on rising above mere functionalism, whether in his public life or in his artistic creations.[33] The artist of this type, as has been outlined, painted in principle for like-minded people who could savor the subtler aesthetic qualities of his work without being diverted by baser considerations of technical skill, decorative beauty, or entertaining and socially useful subjects. In practice, this meant painting pictures intended essentially for enthusiasts and collectors of painting (figures 4.14, 4.15); and the symbiotic relationship thus established between artist and recipient, based in principle on the exercise of high taste on each side, enhanced the status of both. From Chang Yen-yüan in the ninth century to Chao Hsi-ku in the thirteenth and T'ang Hou in the fourteenth, writers who were themselves collectors and connoisseurs worked to establish a disinterested kind of appreciation, above crass concerns with function and the market, concentrated on elusive values beyond representation, as the right basis for judging and acquiring paintings.

Inevitably, then, the passion for collecting paintings, especially works by well-established amateur masters in the styles that signified high levels of culture, spread through all those segments of society that possessed the leisure and means for this pursuit. And so one arrives at the often-noted situation in which the status of a family was said to depend on whether or not it possessed a work by Ni Tsan, or Hung-jen.[34] The seventeenth-century dealer Wu Ch'i-chen, who advised and supplied the merchant families of the Hui-chou or southern Anhui region as well as others, uses a similar formulation for antiques, claiming that "the difference between refinement and vulgarity" in a family "depended on whether or not they owned antiquities."[35] He tells us of a certain Mr. Wang, a rich official in Yangchou, who notices "that it is a fashion to enjoy collecting curios and antiques." Because Wang himself is ignorant of how to do it, he commissions Wu Ch'i-chen to collect for him, saying "I intend to build up a great collection. Without you I cannot outrun other people" and agreeing to pay any prices Wu asks. "His reputation in connoisseurship," Wu concludes, apparently without irony, "became known in both south and north."[36]

In this early stage, when the merchant fami-

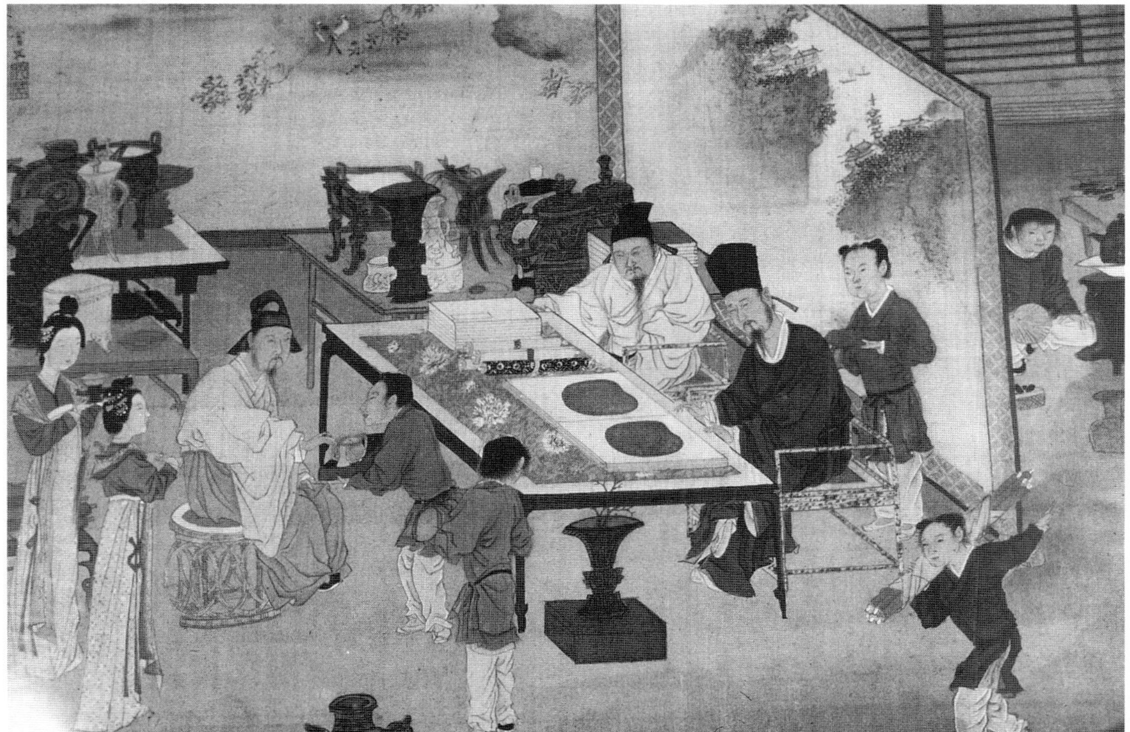

4.14. Ch'iu Ying, "Examining Antiquities." Detail from an album leaf, one of an album of ten leaves, ink and colors on silk, each 41.1 × 33.8 cm. Palace Museum, Peking. See *Chung-kuo mei-shu ch'üan-chi,* vol. 7, plate 70/2.

lies were still striving for a position of dignity in Chinese society to match their wealth—an effort in which the collecting of art and antiques was one part—and when some of them no doubt still lacked cultivation, it was possible for the literati to be snobbish toward them. One of the best of the Anhui merchant-collectors, Ch'eng Chi-po (d. 1626), owned the famous "Rivers and Mountains After Snow" handscroll ascribed to the eighth-century master Wang Wei, along with Chao Meng-fu's "Water Village" of 1302 and other notable works. Wu Ch'i-chen praised the collection after seeing it at the house of Ch'eng's son in 1637.[37] But his acuity did not save him from the scorn of the litterateur and official Ch'ien Ch'ien-i (1582–1664), who wrote in 1642 that after the death of the previous owner of the putative Wang Wei, "the scroll was purchased by a rich man from Hsin-an [Huichou, i.e., Ch'eng Chi-po]. Thus a fine work of mist and clouds fell into a heap of copper cash for more than thirty years; but I was able to rescue it."[38]

Shen Te-fu (1578–1642) was similarly outraged when he learned that a famous piece of T'ang-period calligraphy had been purchased for a high price by a rich Hui-chou merchant-collector: "It is just as bad as the daughter of Hsü Kao-yang being sold and married to the chief of the southern barbarians. It is even worse than the lady Wang Chao-chün being married to a western barbarian."[39] Shen Te-fu recognized three levels of taste in his time, with the "men of elegance" at the top, "art-loving gentry" in the middle, and "gullible merchants of Hsin-an" or Hui-chou at the bottom.[40]

That the relationship between the cultivated literati and the rich merchants was really one of mutual benefit, however, was recognized already at that time by the more percep-

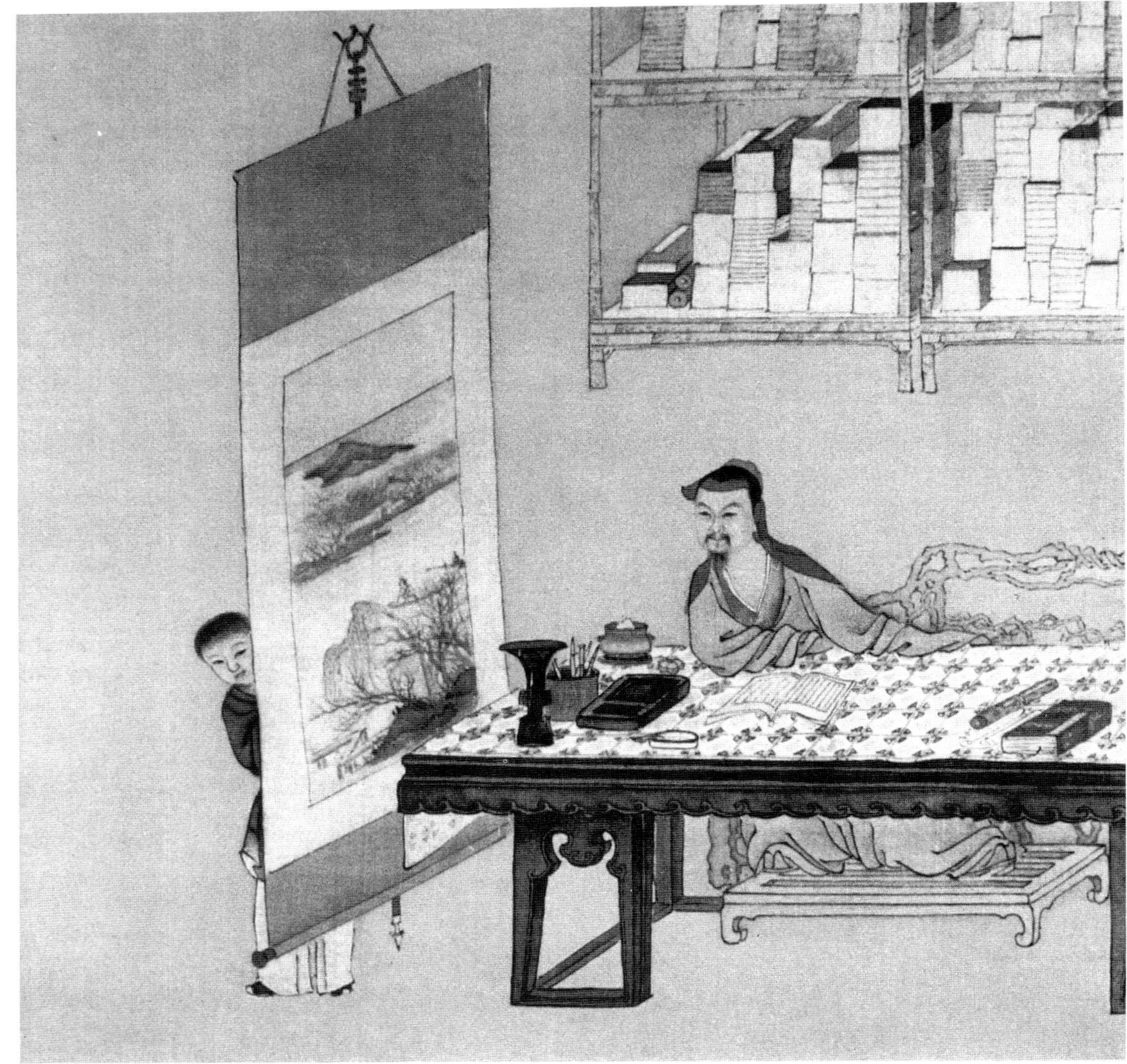

4.15. Yü Chih-ting, "Ch'iao Lai in His Study," from series of three portraits of Ch'iao Lai. Hanging scroll, ink and colors on silk, 37.4 × 29.3 cm. Nanking Museum. From *Ming Ch'ing jen-wu hsiao-hsiang hua-hsüan* (Shanghai, 1982), plate 32.

tive: a late Ming miscellany records an exchange between Chan Ching-feng and a certain Master Feng-chou in which Feng-chou remarks that "When the Hui-chou merchants see a Suchou literatus, they are like flies swarming on a piece of mutton," to which Chan Ching-feng replies, "When Suchou literati see a Hui-chou merchant, they are *also* like flies swarming on a piece of mutton." Feng-chou laughs without replying.[41] By the eighteenth century, especially in Yangchou, the situation had reversed itself, and the merchants, at least some of them, had established themselves well enough to consort with the literati as equals, or even, by turnabout, to adopt patronizing attitudes toward them.

The literati claim to exclusive possession of high taste, on which the success of Tung Ch'i-ch'ang and others as connoisseur-advisers depended, should not, of course, be accepted as simple truth. It would be unjust to attribute plebeian tastes to the merchant collectors as a group. Some of them belonged to old estab-

4.16. Wang Chih-jui (active mid-17th cent.), "Landscape."
Dated 1666. Hanging scroll, ink on paper, 77.6 × 42.4 cm. Anhui Provincial Museum, Hefei. From *Anhui ming-jen hua-hsüan* (Selection of Paintings by Noted Anhui Artists) (Shanghai, 1961).

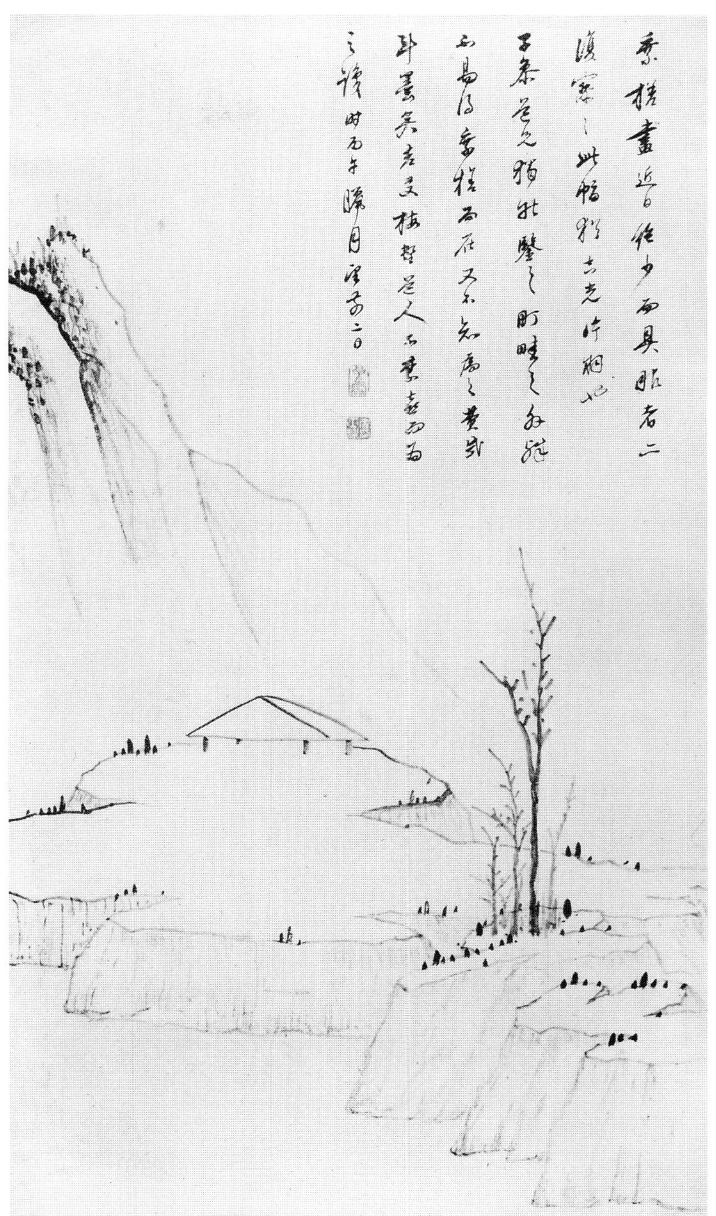

lished families and were indistinguishable from the literati; or, to put it another way, many of the literati in this period engaged in commerce. Moreover, elite values in art as elsewhere had a way of spreading quickly, and were not, in the end, so very difficult to acquire and exercise. In the Ming-Ch'ing rhetoric of connoisseurship it was still the academic, detailed, and decorative ways of painting that were held to be the popular ones that "pleased people's eyes," so that to scorn these and collect the subtler kinds was to separate oneself from the crowd and evince a higher taste. In fact, those who did so were by this time more likely to be *joining* the crowd: the critical discrediting of the conservative and academic manner of painting, and the spread of the literati attitudes among well-off patrons and collectors, had gone so far by the late Ming and early Ch'ing as to put excellent painters like Ch'en Hung-shou in difficult situations. It was works in the literati styles, whether spare and austere (figure 4.16) or rough and spontaneous looking, that seem to have been really popular and vigorously sought after. For collectors, to prefer Yüan painting to Sung was to lay claim to the aesthetic high ground, much as preferring Bach-and-before, Stravinsky-and-after was once, during my student days, the indicator of a truly cultivated ear among young music listeners.[42]

The Literati Painter and His Audience

Another great shift between the middle and late period of Chinese painting is in the relationship of the scholar-amateur painter to his audience. The literati-painting ideals I have been outlining pertain properly to the truly amateur artists but were carried over and made to apply to other kinds of painters as well. This set of ideals had been formulated in a period and under conditions in which education and culture normally accompanied social position and power, and were suited to the situation in which the cultivated painter, who in many cases came from an affluent family and held an official post, could afford to practice his art purely as an avocation and distribute his creations among his acquaintances without calculating recompense very closely. Those conditions begin to break down already in the Yüan, when educated men barred from public office were forced into other means of earning their livings, including the sale (or virtual sale) of the products of their "leisure-time" activities. In the Ming, service in the faction-ridden bureaucracy could be perilous and only marginally rewarding, so that leaving it by choice was common. But, as the case of Wen Cheng-ming demonstrates, even after one had resigned from service and moved into the position of *chü-shih* or retired scholar-official, one continued to enjoy the privilege and prestige of having served at all, and the demand for one's works was accordingly enhanced. One might, then, find oneself with scholar-official status but without the financial independence associated with that status, and under considerable pressure from people who wanted to acquire one's works.[43]

By the seventeenth and eighteenth centuries, the marked increase in merchant-class and middle-class patronage, by people who might not belong to the established gentry themselves but who wanted paintings by artists of some status and prestige, combined with the equally great increase in out-of-work literati willing to respond to this demand so long as certain conventions and proprieties were observed to create a new, more difficult relationship, one in which status based on birth and education was often higher on the artist's side, and status based on wealth and (sometimes) political power higher on the side of the recipient. Or, to put it more bluntly, educated and cultivated painters (along with calligraphers and poets and litterateurs) having to respond, more than they liked, to demands from less cultivated but rich and powerful clients, or seekers after their works. The phenomenon is part of a larger one, the commodification of literati culture in the later centuries in China.[44]

The artists' dislike of seeing their art commodified, their ways of avoiding at least the appearance of this, and their aversion to seeing their works fall into the hands of people who were not their social equals, formed underlying themes in the preceding chapters. Good painters could not all afford to be amateurs, but neither could they in good conscience subordinate their creative impulses openly to the conditions of the market or the preferences of clients whose tastes might be lower than theirs. Always in their minds were statements like Mi Fu's in the eleventh century that "Calligraphy and painting cannot be discussed in terms of prices; scholars cannot be bought with goods."[45] For those who held the scholar-amateur's belief in art as self expression, the marketing of their work was like selling a piece of their inner life. And yet, in good Chinese fashion, they found means of accommodating their practice to their needs, as we have seen, and found ways also of preserving their dignity. We may recall the early Ch'ing painter who agreed to do a birthday painting for a client, and allowed the client to specify the subject, but gave the client to understand that his level of culture made him "not at all like the common artisan-painters," ending, defiantly and more than a little poignantly, "I paint pictures for other people, but I really paint for myself, ha ha!" This is a single letter preserved by chance, but must represent an attitude that was widespread among cultivated Chinese artists who lived by their art.

Kung Hsien (figure 4.17), in an inscription on a major work given to a persistent official who promised him in return an allowance of rice and wine every month to the end of his life, assuaged the pangs of professionalism by, as Jerome Silbergeld puts it, "smirking at those who propped up their own status with the products of his brush." Kung Hsien writes:

> I recall that at the age of thirteen I was already able to paint. Now, fifty years after, I am exerting myself in the "inkstone field" [i.e., profiting from my painting]. I plough in the morning and harvest in the evening, barely making enough to support my-

self. You might call me crude, but gentlemen and officials do not consider me crude. In their tall carriages, drawn by four steeds, they come personally to my rustic door. Can it be because my dry brush and left-over ink are considered valuable among these men?[46]

A recorded letter from a certain Wu Tiensheng, although he was a calligrapher and not a painter, presents such an engaging picture of the artist struggling to hold his art as the outcome of pure inspiration elevated above the mire of functionalism, response to inducements, expectation of rewards, and the servility of writing a dedication, that it seems worth including here. Wu is replying to someone who asked for a piece of his calligraphy.

To use my calligraphy as a useful (functional) thing is something I don't want to do. To use it to trade for goods is something I hate to do. What I really want is to sit among the blue mountains and white clouds with good friends, a coat on my shoulders, or with famous flowers [courtesans] around a banquet table. Then my inspiration comes, I splash the ink and begin to write. Smoke and clouds fill the room, all my desires are fulfilled. When I do calligraphy for a beautiful woman's fan as she sings, or write on a famous woman's skirt, while the maid burns incense and the boy servant holds the inkstone: at that moment I can take the brush and write even for a whole day without being tired. But if I have to write to requite favors *(ying-ch'ou)* I quickly become tired. To be forced to do it, to fulfill endless requests, is really tiring. . . But this is not the most terrible thing, which is to write [a dedication to] someone of high position at the end of my inscription. This I could never do, shamelessly, in several decades. However, you are asking me to do this most hateful thing. If I write it for you, it will be unfair to myself; if I don't, it will be unfair to you. I don't want to do either. Why don't you just leave [the paper] on my table, and don't worry about the time [for me to finish it]. When I'm drunk and without shame, I can do it; my heart won't condemn my fingers. What do you think of that idea?[47]

By the mid-eighteenth century, when mercantile values and attitudes had come to be more broadly accepted, acknowledging the

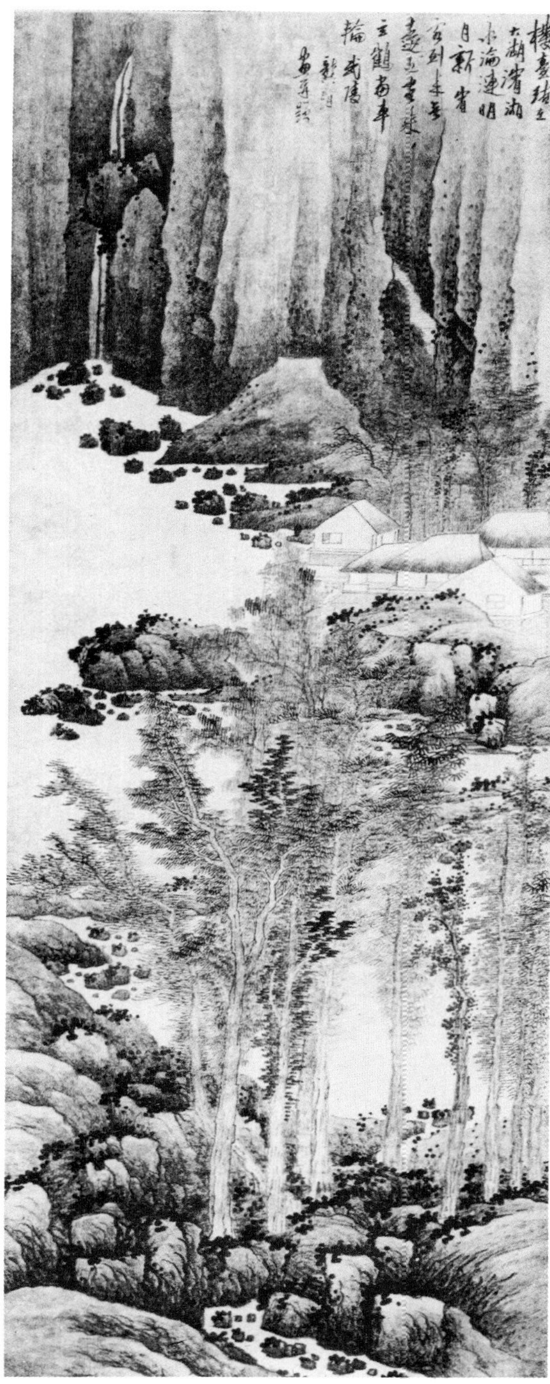

4.17. Kung Hsien, "Thatched Houses on a Lakeshore."
Hanging scroll, ink on paper, 218 × 82.8 cm. Chi-lin Provincial Museum. From *Chung-kuo mei-shu ch'üan-chi* 9, no. 111.

sale of one's paintings for a living was not uncommon, and artists who did so could even present their positions in a positive light, in open defiance of the centuries-long effort of literati writers to discredit the institution of painting as an honorable profession. Chin Nung, after listing "sages of ancient times" who engaged in even baser occupations such as husking rice or cleaning urinals, writes: "It is not that I intentionally put myself in such a low and disgraceful position and demean myself. Most importantly, it is decent for one to be independent. As long as one is self-supporting, whatever one's profession may be, it cannot be looked down upon as low and disgraceful."[48]

His friend Cheng Hsieh made the same argument, that open sale of paintings is more honorable than attaching oneself to a single patron and working at his bidding.[49] Cheng justified his position further by distinguishing within his paintings those produced out of mercenary motives from those inspired by friendship: he sold paintings of orchids to the rich in Yangchou to make a living, he writes, but painted more seriously when the recipient was a high-minded intellectual such as Chin Nung.[50] (Without questioning Cheng's sincerity, one may note that given the homogeneity of his output in subject and style and quality, it is not easy for us now to tell which were which.) Even with this easier acceptance of painting as an income-producing activity, artists continued to agonize.

A painter named Wang Tzu-jo in the nineteenth century printed a price-list for his works, and his friends helped out by informing people where they could be bought. Wang composed a poem to console himself: "I paint green mountains leisurely in exchange for money;/ Friends follow the ancient sages and come to my aid./ Pitying myself for being in this embarrassing position,/ I lose myself in painting green mountains."[51]

Painters in Europe also faced the problem of seeing their art commodified; the artist who refused commissions to preserve his independence is known there also. (Salvator Rosa is an example.) A seventeenth-century Italian dealer complains about the difficulty of commissioning pictures from living artists, saying it is much easier to buy old paintings.[52] An important difference is of course that much more of European painting was public in nature, done for churches, princely palaces, or great families, and commissioned by those institutions and their representatives, while Chinese patronage is so regularly small-scale, usually (except for court patronage) one-on-one, that the very applicability of the term "patronage" to it has been questioned.[53] The private character of most Chinese painting in the later centuries made it easier for the artist to argue that he was painting only for his own pleasure, or (as Chinese artists sometimes write in inscriptions) that he is misunderstood in his own time and will be truly appreciated only in the future, or at best that those among his contemporaries who are in tune with his paintings are very few (the dedicatee of course being one of them.)

Fabricating the Painter's Hand

Much of Chinese literati painting, then, in its plain subjects, unassertive styles, and often self-revelatory inscriptions, presents itself as the very antithesis of a public art: ideally, it is a privileged communication between the artist and some congenial contemporary. And so it was, in ideal cases. But the ideal was fragile; the acceptance of such paintings as indicating a degree of closeness with the artist in fact multiplied the demand for them, spreading it far beyond the circle of people who could legitimately claim that kind of closeness; and the demand was inevitably translated into market-like transactions. In the cases of highly regarded literati artists, these transactions were not uncommonly false at both ends: at one, the recipient was not really an intimate of the artist, but only someone willing to pay the price of seeming to be so; at the other, the products of the artist's hand that he received were frequently the products of someone else's. In simpler language, what he got was often a fake.

The problem, of course, was that the demand for the brush-traces of prominent artists of high status or reputation was likely to exceed by far their ability, or at least their willingness, to wield their brushes and meet the demand. But to suppose that the seekers went away empty-handed would be to underestimate once more the genius of the Chinese for finding accommodations. One that was popular in the later periods—and which had a negative effect, I have argued, on the overall level of quality in Chinese painting of recent centuries—was for the artist simply to increase his output by adopting rough-brush manners, simpler imagery, and more repetitive modes of production.[54] But another way to supply a demand that exceeded the artist's capacity was through the production of forgeries, a practice in which the Chinese again surpass all rivals in sophistication and ingenuity. Literati painting, with its disdain for technical finish and its reliance on highly personal, easily identifiable styles, was especially susceptible to imitation. Focusing attention on the hand of the painter, then, facilitated the fabrication of it.[55]

Ch'ien Hsüan in the early Yüan, for instance, an artist whose fastidious painting in fine, even line and flat washes of color was seen as a manifestation of the same purity of mind that motivated his loyalist withdrawal from public life upon the fall of the Sung, complains in an inscription on a recently discovered painting (figure 4.18) about the appearance of numerous forgeries of his work: he has decided to "put forth new ideas" and adopt a new pen name for signing his works "to make the forgers feel ashamed of themselves," and to distinguish his paintings from theirs—at least until they also began to use the new signature, which was probably no more than a week later. Shen Chou in the middle Ming, whose amiable broad-line drawing and ingenuous imagery were also relatively easy to imitate, inspired such a copious and excellent output of forgeries during his lifetime that, the story goes, when he tried in his late years to reacquire some of his own earlier works, he got forgeries among them.[56] His contemporary Chu Yün-ming tells us that if an original painting by Shen appeared in the morning, a copy could be seen by noon, and ten or more by the end of the day.[57]

4.18. Ch'ien Hsüan, "Lotuses."
Handscroll, ink and light colors on paper, 42 × 90.3 cm. Excavated from the tomb of Prince Chu T'an, early Ming.

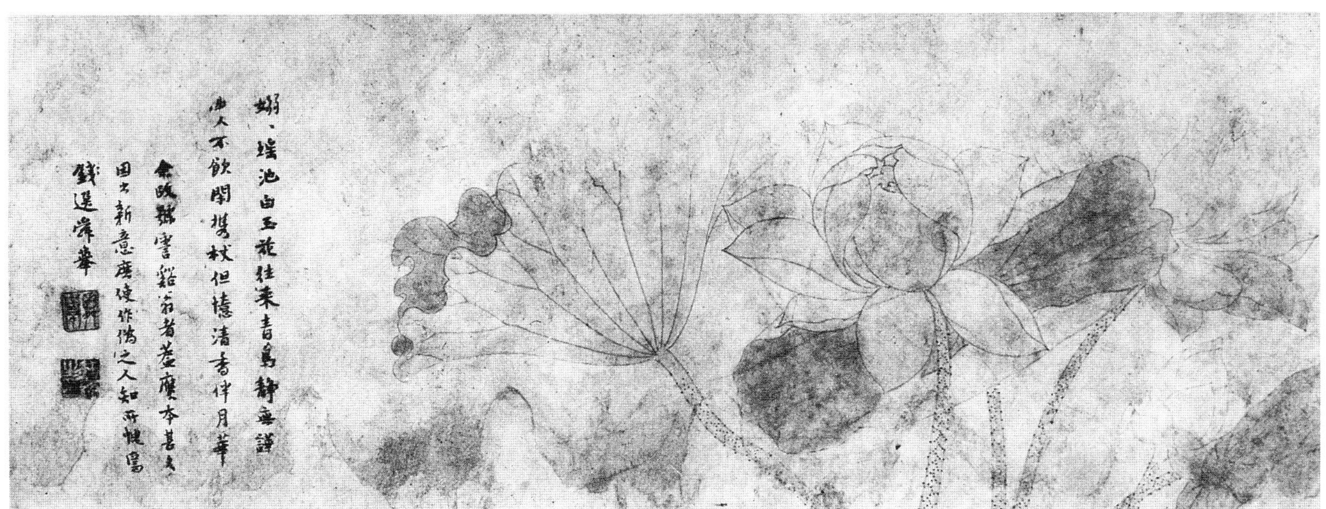

The early Ch'ing landscapist Wang Hui was in his early years so adept at imitating old styles that unscrupulous Suchou dealers, probably with the artist's connivance, would add signatures of early masters to his paintings and sell them under the false names.[58] Works by Wang with such "early" signatures can still be seen today in great collections (figure 4.19). Later, when Wang Hui was well established as a painter and was working mostly in a looser, more easily imitable style that was distinctively his own, he was in turn the target of forgers, some of them his own disciples. The same was true of the Anhui artist Hung-jen after his paintings had come to command high prices, according to Chou Liang-kung, who comments that the forgeries by Hung-jen's disciples were "mere skeletons" of his works.[59] It is true that none of the lesser Anhui masters can achieve the same effects of volume and substance within the limitations of the linear manner.

The numerous stories of prominent Chinese artists whose works were forged during their lifetimes are not surprising. We can observe the phenomenon in our own time, for instance, in the case of the late Chang Ta-ch'ien—another example, like Wang Hui's, of the great forger being himself forged.[60] What are more surprising are the number of accounts in which the artist himself connives in this deception, even participates in it. Both Shen Chou and his pupil Wen Cheng-ming are said to have put their signatures and seals on imitations of their works, to help some person who needed money, even when the person was the forger himself. Their justification was that the sellers were poor, the buyers rich.[61] This is a very different response from Ch'ien Hsüan's effort to foil the forgers by adopting a new name. Wen Cheng-ming appears to have been completely aware that his pupil Chu Lang, who is said to have sometimes "ghostpainted" works for Wen to sign, was also selling forgeries of Wen's paintings. In a well-known story, a servant sent by a Nanking collector bringing presents to exchange for one of Chu Lang's fakes comes by mistake to Wen Cheng-ming, who laughs, accepts the presents, and says "I'll paint him a genuine Wen Cheng-ming; he can pass it off as a fake Chu Lang."[62]

The examples introduced in chapter 3 of artists who employed family members and assistants to do the coloring or otherwise take part in the production of their paintings bring us to the borderline between legitimate artistic practice and deliberate deception. Most recipients of an artist's work probably would not have objected strongly to receiving a painting colored in part by someone other than the master himself, since coloring was generally regarded as superficial embellishment, and also, as it was usually applied in washes in later Chinese painting, revealed little or nothing of the artist's handwriting.[63] The recipients would surely have been more upset if they learned that some of the brush drawing was by an assistant, and most of all if they were told that the whole painting was executed by someone other than the artist whose hand they were paying for. A preserved letter from a patron named Chang Ying-chia to Wang Hui, accompanying gifts, asks him for a sixteen-leaf album of landscapes in old styles and a handscroll in the Huang Kung-wang manner, and requests specifically that these be painted by Wang himself, not by his assistants.[64] The implication is that Wang Hui was known to employ ghostpainters for some of "his" works.

Ghostpainters

The English term "ghostpainter" (coined by analogy with the better-known "ghostwriter," someone who pens a book for a celebrity who lacks the time or the literacy to do it himself or herself) is used to translate the Chinese *tai-pi*, literally "substitute brush." *Tai-pi* can be legitimate, as with professional letter-writers (one still sees signs with this word in Chinese streets), or illegitimate, someone who does calligraphy or painting for another to pass off

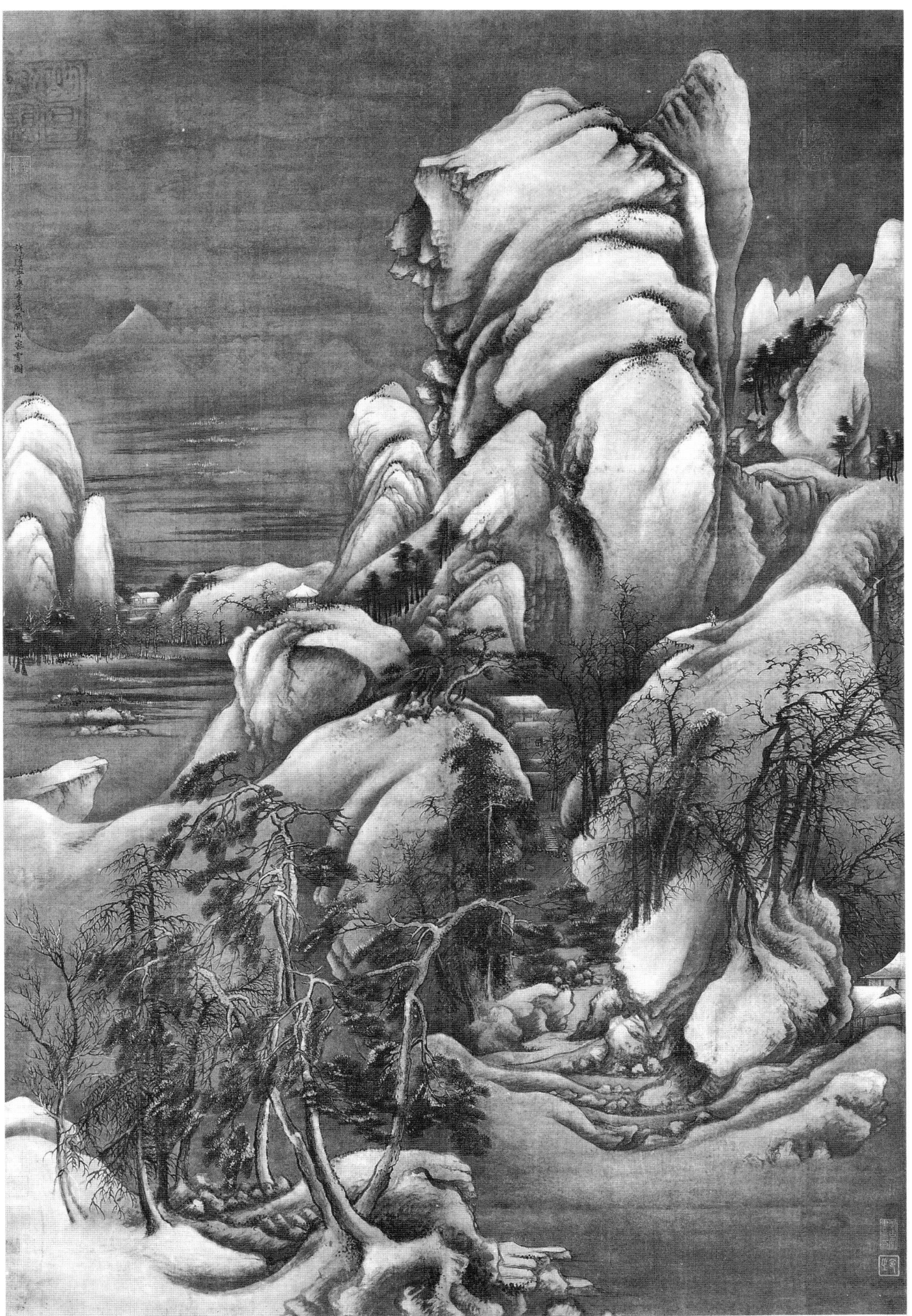

4.19. Wang Hui (false signature of Hsü Tao-ning, ca. 1000–1066), "Heavy Snow on a Mountain Pass." Hanging scroll, ink and colors on silk, 121.3 × 81.3 cm. National Palace Museum, Taipei.

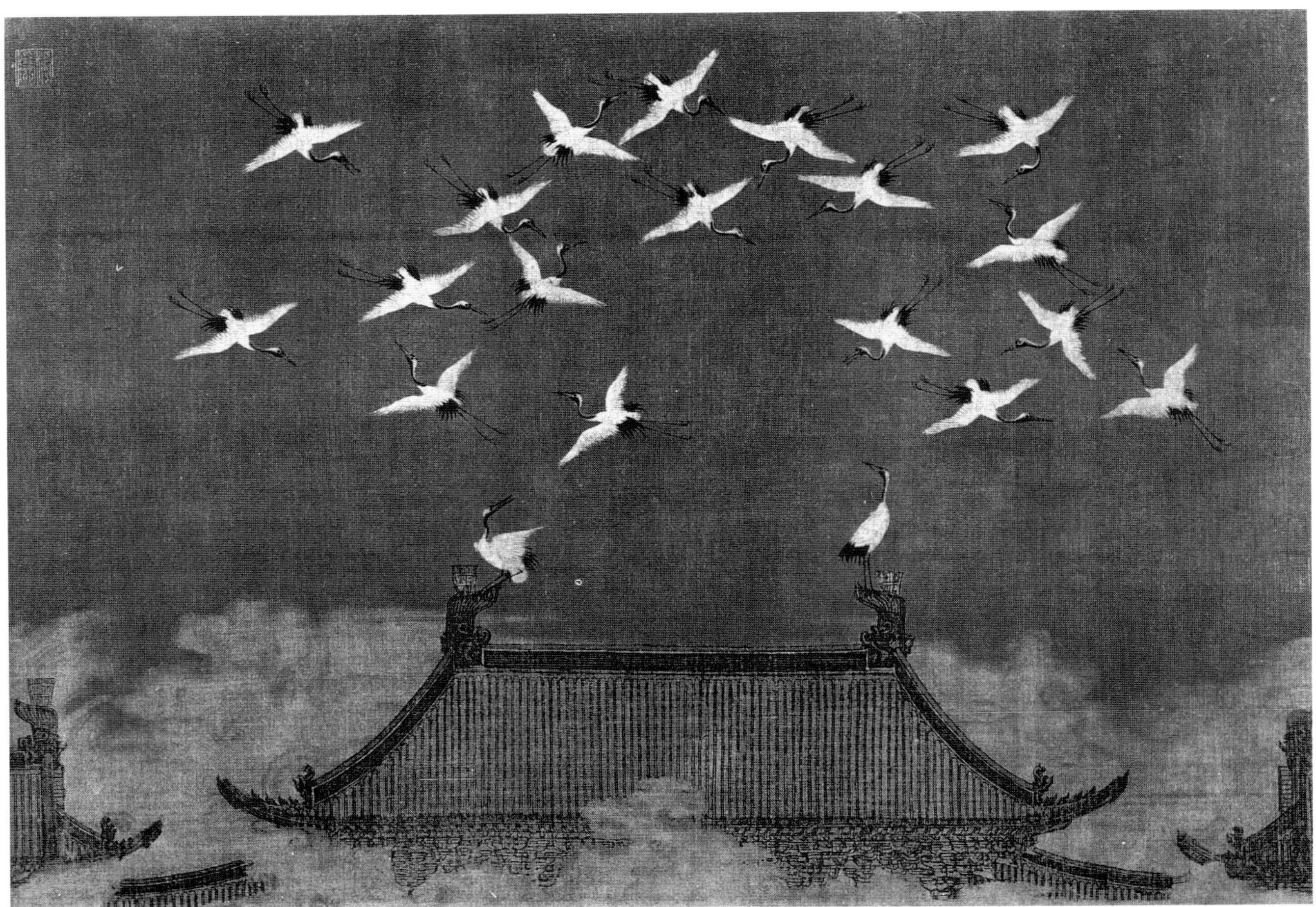

4.20. Emperor Hui-tsung. "Auspicious Cranes Over the Palace."
Dated 1112. Large album leaf mounted in a handscroll, ink and colors on silk, 51 × 138.2 cm. Liaoning Provincial Museum. From *I-yüan to-ying,* no. 3 (1978), plate 2.

as his own work, typically with the addition of that person's genuine signature and seals. There were two principal reasons for employing a *tai-pi* to do one's painting: because he had superior technical skills, or because his time was less valuable than one's own, so that one could gain more from the "ghosted" work, by sale or presentation, than one paid the *tai-pi* for painting it.

Instances of the first type, the employment of artists of greater technical skills than one's own, can be suspected or even assumed for certain extant and recorded Sung paintings, but are hard to document, since the fiction of the purported artist's authorship is usually preserved by those who write about the work. When one reads of the Emperor Hui-tsung painting "thousands" of album leaves of flowers, plants, and animals to be seen in his palace gardens, and "nearly a thousand" pictures of auspicious phenomena that occurred during his reign, or holding a great party at which bundles of his paintings and calligraphy were given to the assembled ministers and officials,[65] one can suspect that some part, perhaps most, of this copious output was done by court artists working under his direction. Among extant paintings signed as his works are some, such as a painting of auspicious cranes appearing over a palace rooftop (figure 4.20), or the several copies of pre-Sung works purportedly made by the emperor himself, that are executed in such a finished, time-consuming manner as to render them unlikely to be from the imperial hand.

The same suspicion can be directed at accounts of officials who were not otherwise known as painters, or at least not as technically accomplished ones, but who are credited with creating what must have been detailed, complex compositions. Examples include Cheng Hsia, who is recorded as having "painted" in 1074 the *Liu-min t'u* depicting people suffering from famine in K'ai-feng,[66] and the early Southern Sung official Lou Chu (1090–1162) who "painted" the original *Keng-chih t'u* or "Pictures of Ploughing and Weaving" for presentation to the Emperor Kao-tsung.[67] The writers of the accounts in which these men "painted" or "made" the pictures may have been completely aware that they were really done by anonymous artisan-painters working under the officials' direction, and were simply following a literary convention by which "made it" could be read as "had it made" or "directed its making." If this supposition is correct, one can assume that the officials provided guidance and expertise on the subjects, and perhaps even preliminary sketches, much as an abbot in Europe might give iconographic directions and other guidance to someone commissioned to make paintings or sculpture for a cathedral. A case that seems to exemplify this pattern is that of Ch'ao Yüeh-chih (1059–1129): himself an amateur painter of small landscapes with water birds, he "redesigned" Li Kung-lin's famous painting of the White Lotus Society because he was dissatisfied with it, entrusting the actual execution of the work to a court artist; and he may have "made," in a similar way, a set of pictures representing his own garden.[68]

These cases (which are, granted, somewhat hypothetical) differ from instances of ghostpainting in later times in that the desideratum is not the painter's hand as such, but a well-executed, persuasive pictorial presentation of some special subject, a project beyond the capacity of the official or the emperor himself. Artists in the later periods who employed ghostpainters, by contrast, are typically said to have done so when they were too busy to respond to requests for their works or had accepted too many commissions. A recorded inscription for a painting by Mi Yu-jen, written only thirty years after his death, claims that Mi was one who did this: "When the old man was not ill, his doors would be filled daily with grandees coming to ask for his paintings. Being unable to bear the bother and trouble, he often ordered his disciples to make imitations, upon which he signed the two characters 'Yüan-hui.'"[69] Tai Chin is said to have painted at least one of the pictures commissioned of the Imperial Academy master Hsieh Huan; officials who discovered the deception complained.[70] Wen Cheng-ming reportedly used both Chu Lang and Ch'ien Ku as ghostpainters; a letter is recorded in which someone sends paper to Ch'ien, asking him to paint a picture of tall pine trees and rocks, and then take it to Wen Cheng-ming to get his signature on it.[71]

The ghostpaintings reportedly done for T'ang Yin by his older contemporary Chou Ch'en represent still another situation.[72] T'ang had studied painting with Chou, but had become much more famous, both because of his more colorful personality and higher status as a failed scholar-official, and because he was, in the end, the greater painter. The two differed not so much in technical capacity as in the far greater demand for T'ang's paintings. It must have made sense, then, for T'ang to augment his output with works by his teacher Chou Ch'en, especially since the styles of the two, when they were working in their conservative, Sung-derived mode, were so similar. Chou's "Peach-blossom Spring" of 1533, for example (figure 4.21), if provided with a "T'ang Yin" signature, would probably fool most connoisseurs.

There are numerous reports of Ming and Ch'ing artists who used ghostpainters when

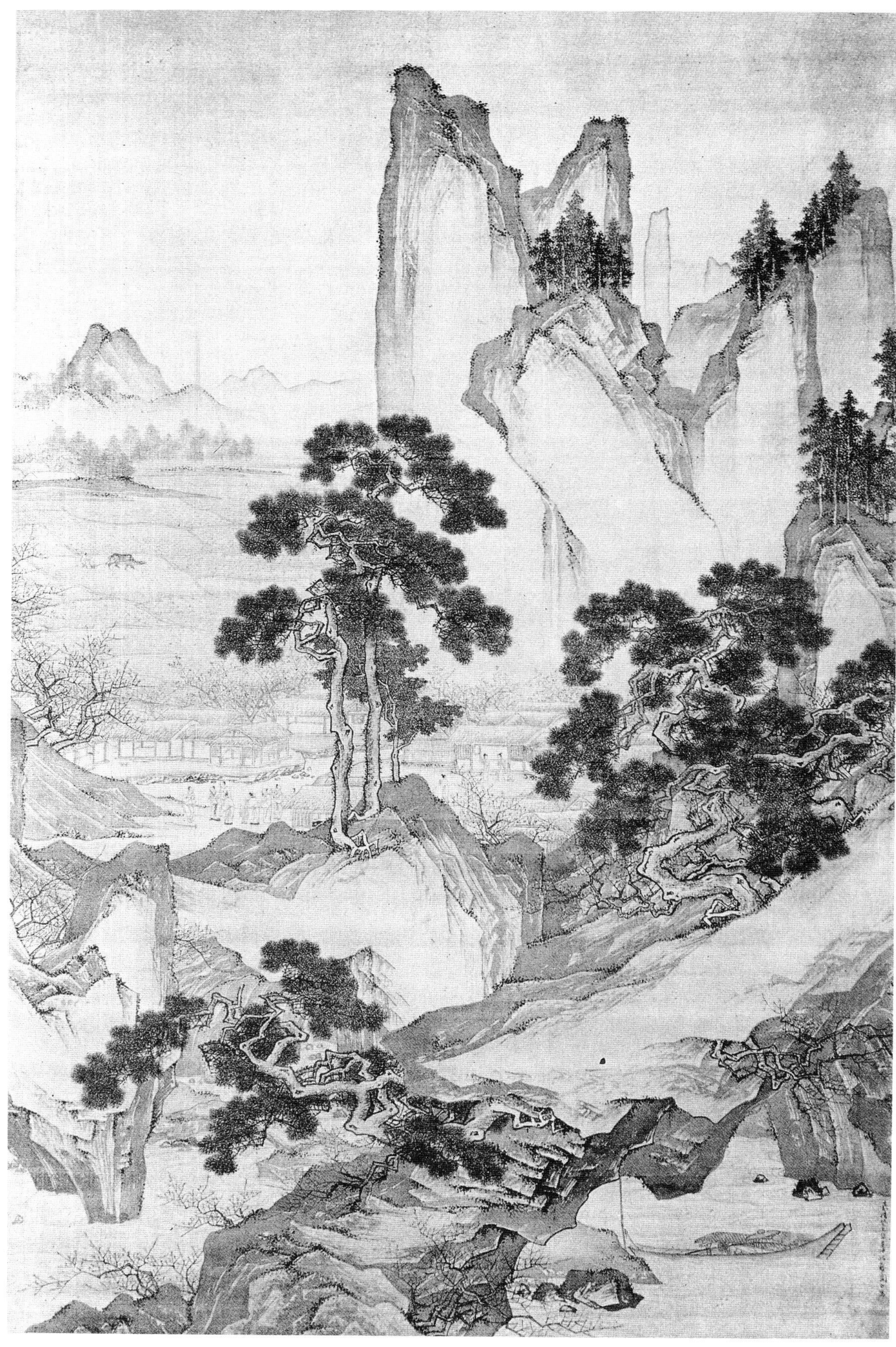

4.21. Chou Ch'en, "The Peach-Blossom Spring." Dated 1533. Hanging scroll, ink and colors on silk, 161.2 × 102.3 cm. Soochow Museum. From *Chung-kuo mei-shu ch'üan-chi* 7 (Shanghai, 1989), plate 42.

they were too busy or otherwise unable to meet the demand for their paintings. Ch'iu Ying is said to have had his students and his daughter do his paintings for him on occasion. It is even said that Shen Chou had his disciples copying his paintings, since the number of requests for them exceeded what his hand could produce.[73] The notorious late Ming minister Ma Shih-ying used the painter Shih Lin in this way;[74] Chiang T'ing-hsi, an early Ch'ing court official whose flower-and-bird pictures were much in demand, used his childhood friend Ma Yüan-yu;[75] Jen Po-nien used his daughter Jen Hsia;[76] Wu Ch'ang-shih used Wang I-t'ing and Chao Tzu-yün;[77] the Empress Dowager Tz'u-hsi used two women in her court.[78] The two most interesting and often-discussed cases, however, are those of Tung Ch'i-ch'ang and Chin Nung, and I will conclude with those.

Tung Ch'i-ch'ang and His Ghostpainters

It is evident that Tung Ch'i-ch'ang discriminated, within his production of paintings, between serious, one-of-a-kind works done for friends and people he esteemed, often on special occasions, and works produced without any recipient in mind, many of them relatively formulaic pictures in which he invested less time and thought (figure 4.22). Noted earlier was his practice of reinscribing paintings of the latter kind with a dedication when presenting them to people. Hsingyuan Tsao has also pointed out that Tung appears to have used a seal with his official title only (or mostly) on paintings intended for the general audience and clientele, for whom Tung's rank figured large among the reasons for wanting one of his works.[79]

Tung's disdain for these faceless admirers,

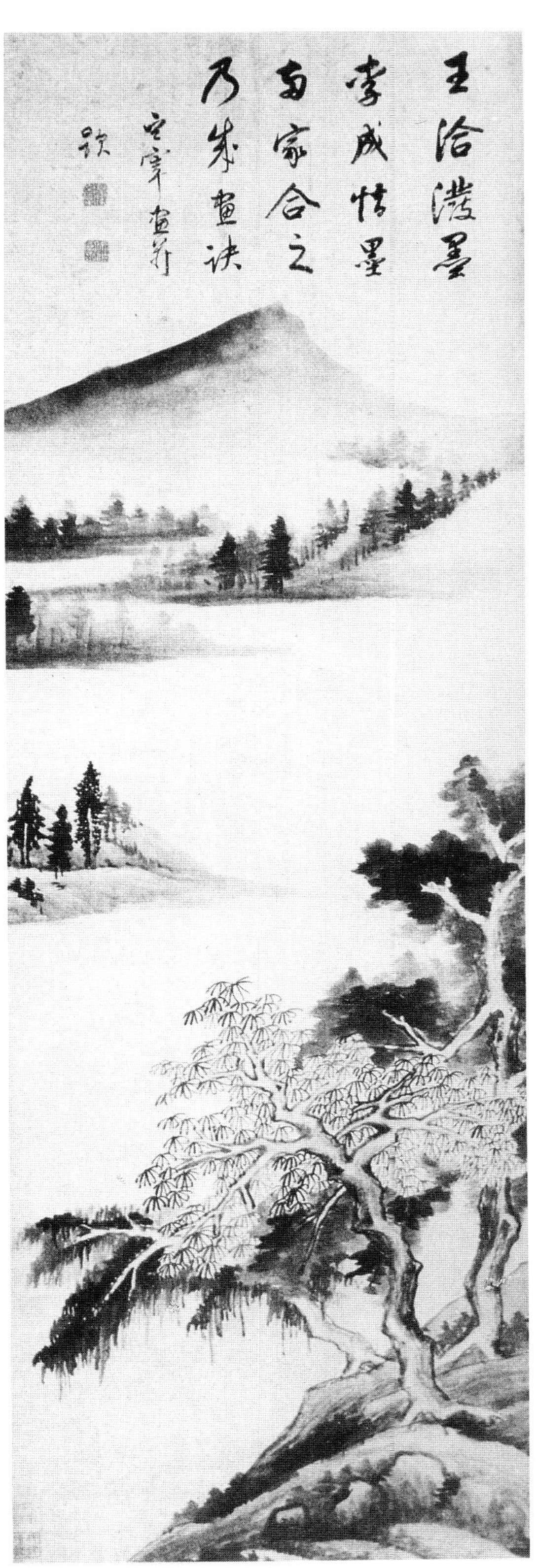

4.22. Tung Ch'i-ch'ang, "Landscape in the Manner of Wang Hsia and Li Ch'eng." Hanging scroll, ink on paper, 225.7 × 75.4 cm. Shanghai Museum.

expressed even while he benefited materially from supplying their requests, is evident in his writings and underlies his disinterest in the quality or even the authenticity of what they received. He writes:

> My painting has become so popular now that it "moistens a lot of my friends' emaciated intestines" [allows them, that is, to profit by doing forgeries of it]. There is a certain Mr. Wu [Wu I] who, using my name, travels around painting for people. Wherever I go, the gentry and literati show me their collections of my paintings. I would like to leave this authenticity problem for people in the future to solve, although I know very well that these paintings are fakes.[80]

His friend Ch'en Chi-ju, claiming that "less than one out of ten" of the works circulating under Tung's name was really from his hand, argues that this dissemination served to enhance his fame, writing that "those who borrow the Master's name for a living have spread the Master's fame by selling the forgeries at home and abroad. . . If in my lifetime I have seen anyone's fame grow a hundredfold, the Master is surely the one."[81]

Tung himself apparently had no worries that his reputation would suffer; since he himself was willing to paint generic Tung Ch'i-ch'angs of modest aesthetic merit, it did not trouble him that others painted them as well. Theirs might in fact be in some ways better than his.[82] Writing self-deprecatingly in an inscription on one of his lesser albums of landscapes, he remarks that "The people who make so many fakes of my paintings these days can take this as one of their [fake] Tungs."[83]

From being unconcerned about forgeries of one's own works (as Shen Chou and Wen Cheng-ming had reportedly been before) to employing ghostpainters oneself to make them is an easy step, and there is ample testimony by writers of Tung's time and shortly after that he took it. A recorded letter from his friend Ch'en Chi-ju to Shen Shih-ch'ung, a local landscapist of secondary rank, reads: "My old friend, I am sending you a piece of white paper together with a brush-fee of three-tenths of a tael of silver. May I trouble you to paint a large-size landscape? I need it by tomorrow. Don't sign it—I will get Tung Ch'i-ch'ang to put his name on it."[84]

Ch'ien Ch'ien-i, in his *Lieh-ch'ao shih-chi* (1649), wrote that Tung "treasured his own paintings the most; even when noble men and important people asked him sincerely for his paintings, he would let his ghostpainters do them for him"—so as to keep the genuine ones for himself, that is.[85] The early Ch'ing scholar Chu I-tsun wrote that "When Tung Wen-min [Ch'i-ch'ang] was tired of painting to repay obligations, he often asked Chao Tso and the monk K'o-hsüeh to paint for him, pictures that he would sign himself."[86] (Figure 4.23 is a section of a handscroll inscribed by Tung as having been painted by him for K'o-hsüeh, which may in fact have been ghostpainted by K'o-hsüeh for Tung.) The early Ch'ing scholar Ku Fu reports that after Chao Tso's death Tung employed two others, Chao Ch'iung and Yeh Yu-nien, to paint landscapes which he would inscribe, sign, and stamp with his seals.[87] And Chou Liang-kung, also in the early Ch'ing, wrote of Tung:

> When he completed paintings, his servants replaced them [with copies?] When people begged for his paintings, he usually had other artists do them for him. With forgeries, he would happily sign his name on them, not minding it at all. His household had a number of concubines, each of whom had silk ready to ask for his paintings. When he was tired of painting, they would sing and recite poems to persuade him to continue. Those who bought his genuine paintings often got them from his concubines.[88]

The gossipy tone of these writings, especially Chou Liang-kung's, should not induce one to dismiss them altogether. What is known about Tung's circumstances and his expressed tolerance for forgeries of his works makes it unlikely that they are entirely invented.

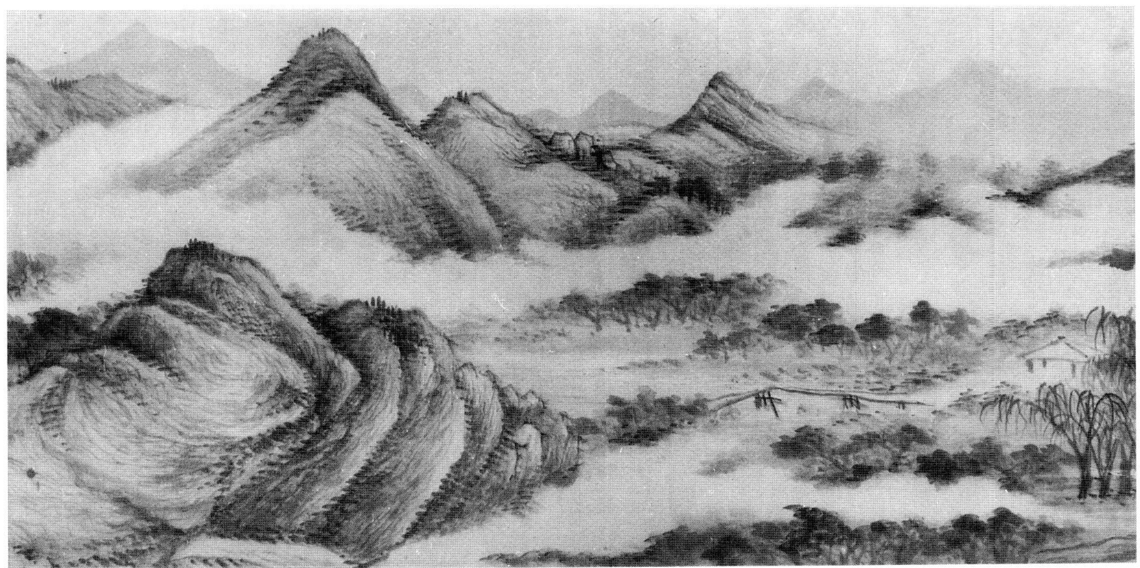

4.23. Tung Ch'i-ch'ang (ghostpainted?), "Landscape for K'o-hsüeh."
Dated 1626. Section of a handscroll, ink and colors on paper, ht. 31.8 cm. Shanghai Museum.

Chin Nung and His Ghostpainters

The evidence for Chin Nung (figure 4.24) in the eighteenth century having employed ghostpainters is even fuller: he himself acknowledges it in his writings, as do his close friends, and the names of several of the painters who worked for him are known.[89] In an inscription on a self-portrait presented to a student named Hsiang Yün, Chin Nung relates that Hsiang had learned from him the technique of painting blossoming plum branches, and had become so adept at doing them in Chin's manner, closely enough to fool even connoisseurs, that he sometimes ghostpainted them for Chin, in order, as Chin puts it, "to help me cope with the big demand for them everywhere."[90]

In Hsiang Yün's own account of the matter, Chin Nung is not so much too busy as simply too lazy. "The old man loved money, but would not lift his brush. Therefore, I compliantly painted nonstop. As long as I signed the old man's name in his peculiar lacquer-brush style after I had finished, people would express their admiration and great joy."[91] More sympathetically, one can note that Chin Nung was in poor health during these years, and that his eyesight may have been deteriorating. And he had, as noted earlier, rejected the system of individual patronage to place his works on the open market and preserve his independence.

Other artists employed by Chin Nung to fabricate his works include a certain Chu T'ing-ku, who is said to have received over ten letters of commission from him; another named Yang;[92] and Chin's pupil Lo P'ing, who went on to become an established painter himself, and who would "beg the master to inscribe" his imitations, after which "people fought to buy them."[93] A painting of Chung K'uei with Chin Nung's signature (figure 4.25) resembles Lo P'ing's figure paintings enough to raise the suspicion that it is by him. Even Chin Nung's good friend Cheng Hsieh seems to have been involved in the industry of producing Chin Nungs. He writes in a poem: "Kao Feng-han's left-handed works and Chin Nung's calligraphy [are much sought after]. Friends from near and far have asked me for them. Short and long letters [from them] are all gone; even forgeries by me are gone."[94]

Chin Nung turned to painting as a principal

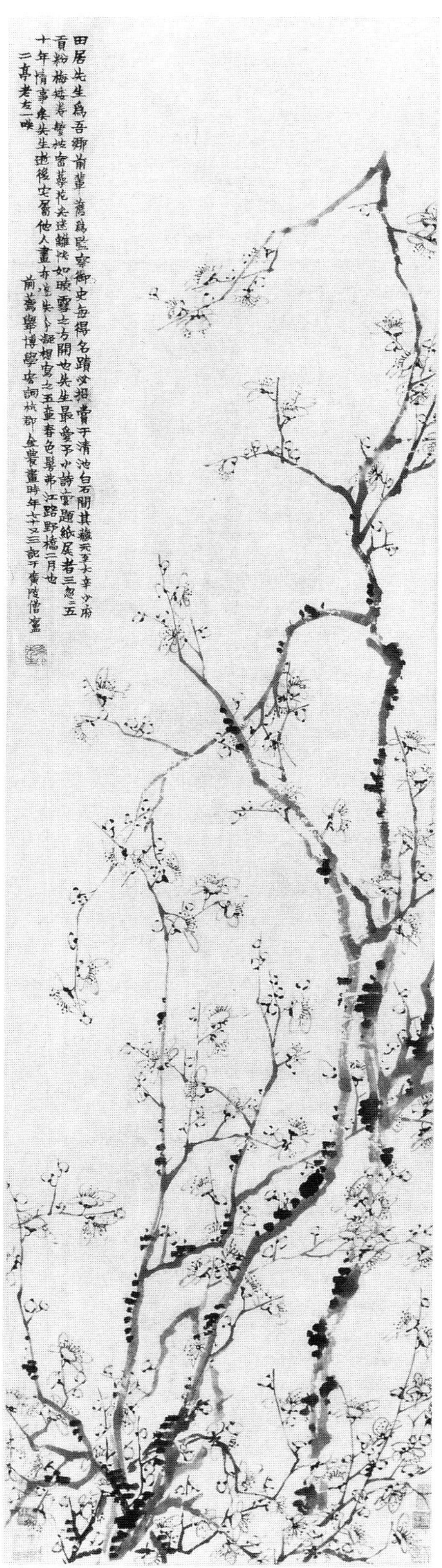

source of income only around 1748, when he was in his mid-sixties. Earlier, he had lived as an itinerant antique dealer, and by selling objects such as inkstones and paper lanterns. His assistants ground the stones and fabricated the lanterns; Chin would inscribe the inkstones for engraving and decorate the lanterns with his crotchety calligraphy and idiosyncratic paintings, elevating them by these additions from the status of craft objects to that of objects of art, and raising accordingly their value on the market.[95] He had become accustomed, then, to thinking of his touch and his taste as marketable commodities. He had become, in fact, as Svetlana Alpers writes of Rembrandt, "an entrepreneur of the self."[96]

The correspondence of certain of Rembrandt's practices and circumstances, as Alpers presents him, to those of Chin Nung is striking. (The two artists are in most other respects, such as medium and subjects and style, as far apart as two painters could be; I mean to suggest no more than that similar conditions in the economic and social history of art can stimulate similar responses in artists.) Rembrandt, she writes, "made himself a free individual, not beholden to patrons. But he was beholden instead to the market" (p. 88). In Holland of the seventeenth century, as in Yangchou of the eighteenth, artistic production was accommodating to a commercial culture, and paintings were made in larger numbers for sale at relatively low prices to ordinary, middle-class people, the ones called in Europe the bourgeoisie, who had benefited enough from the general prosperity to begin acquiring them (p. 94).

One effect of this situation was to induce artists to adopt modes of painting that demanded less of their time, including looser modes of brushwork. By stripping away such

4.24. Chin Nung (1687–1764), "Branches of Blossoming Plum."

Dated 1759. Hanging scroll, ink on paper. University Art Museum, University of California, Berkeley.

conventional criteria as painstaking finish, fine materials, the amount of time spent in producing the work, and realistic portrayal as the bases of value for his works, Rembrandt (and Chin Nung, and Tung Ch'i-ch'ang) took away from the client the prerogative of deciding whether or not the picture he received was acceptable (pp. 98–99); what the client got was not offered as a product that met established criteria, but as a Rembrandt (or a Chin Nung, or a Tung Ch'i-ch'ang), beyond conventional criticism. Rembrandt, Alpers writes, "made art of an unprecedented kind, which he commodified" (pp. 98–99, 110). And: "His works are commodities distinguished from others by being identified as his; and in making them, he in turn commodifies himself" (p. 118). It is no accident that these two are, for their respective traditions, the first artists to paint large numbers of self-portraits (figure 4.26).[97] Tung, self-centered as he was, did not; he was no figure painter.

Nor is it coincidence that both artists, while engaged in marketing the products of their hands, participate also in the fabrication of those products by others. Alpers opens her book, and ends it, in the context of the recent revelations that many of the world's great Rembrandts are the works of studio disciples and followers. "Why is it, then," she asks, "that this sense of property in self does not preclude that replication of self which we find in every area of Rembrandt's work? . . . Why does it not preclude his encouraging other artists to pass themselves off as himself?" (p. 119). And she ends by calling Rembrandt "an artist whose enterprise is not reducible to his autographic oeuvre" (p. 122).

To write this is not to answer the question completely, nor can I do so for Chin Nung or Tung Ch'i-ch'ang, except by pointing out once more that it is exactly when the master's touch becomes central to the value of the work, and is commodified, that replications of it are most likely to appear, as they will for any reproducible commodity that is heavily in demand; and

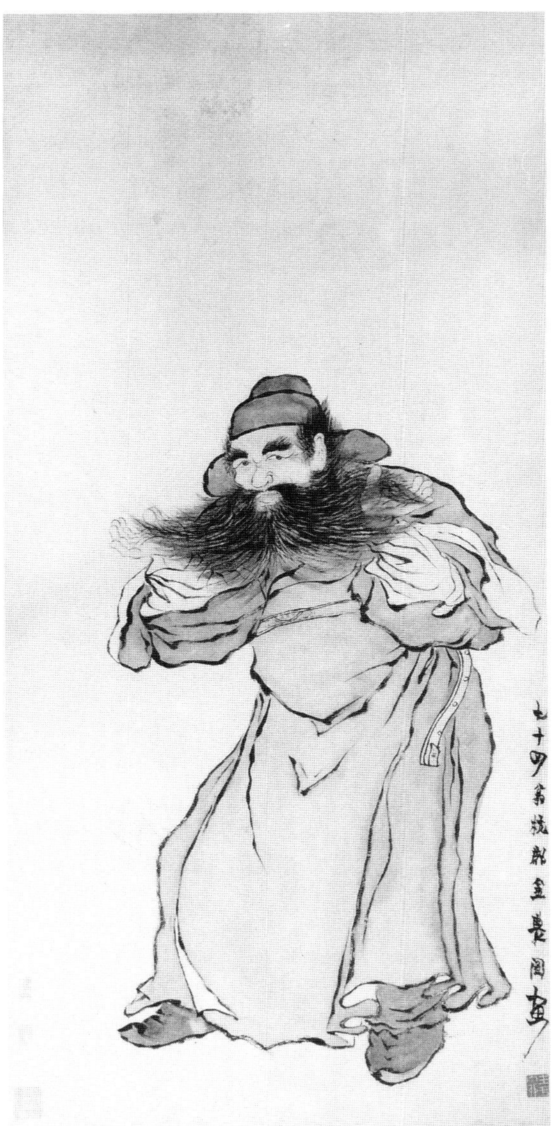

4.25. Chin Nung, "Chung K'uei."
Dated 1760. Hanging scroll, ink and colors on paper, 113.3 × 54.5 cm. Shanghai Museum.

by suggesting that once he has created the product and the demand for it, the artist may find it more attractive to share in the increased benefits of production by multiple hands than to attempt ineffectively to reserve those benefits to himself.

As a final twist, one may move out into the audience and recognize that those who sought and received Chin Nung's paintings, and prob-

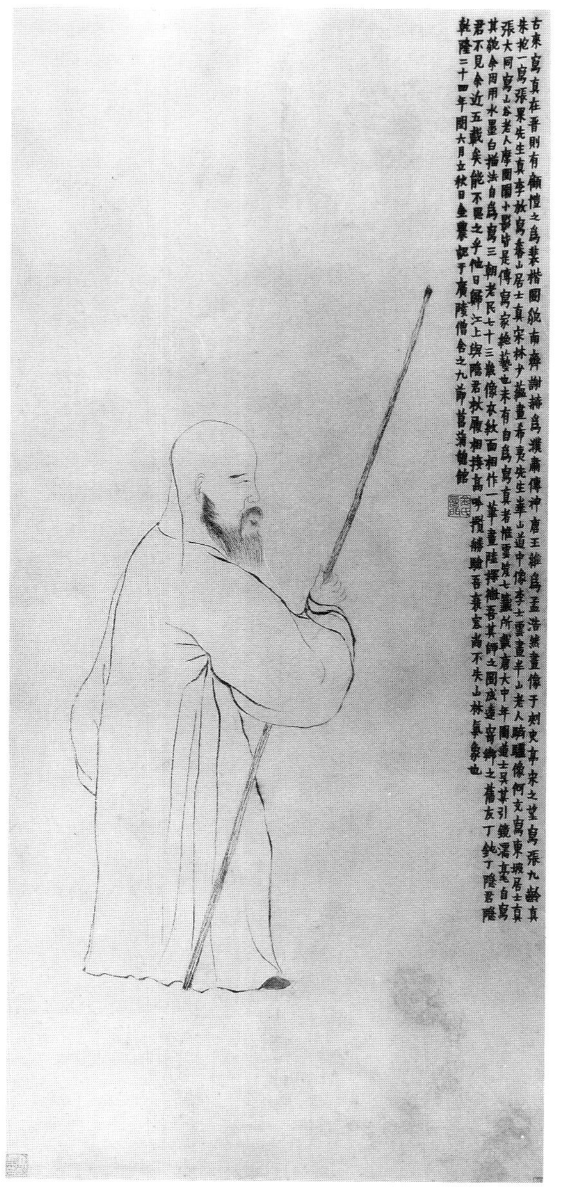

4.26. Chin Nung, "Self Portrait: Walking with a Staff."
Hanging scroll, ink on paper, 131.3 × 59.1 cm. Palace Museum, Peking.

ably Tung Ch'i-ch'ang's and Wang Hui's as well, must have been aware that their chances were good of getting a ghosted work. This can be assumed from various indications, such as the letter to Wang Hui quoted in which the writer asks that the album he is ordering be painted by Wang himself, or a letter from Chin Nung to a friend apologizing for not delivering the painting he had requested and offering as an excuse that his disciple and ghostpainter Lo P'ing (figure 4.27) had been very busy lately, and was away at the time. (Chin promises to pass on the request to Lo P'ing when he returns, and to "ask him to set aside his other engagements so that he can finish the work for you.")[98]

Again, one can only speculate on what permits this peculiar tolerance: did the client want only a painting that would signify his closeness with Chin Nung, or one he could use as a present to someone who would not know the difference?[99] Those of us who have moved extensively in the mysterious world of Chinese and Japanese dealers and collectors know very well the formulations by which a painting is spoken of as "80 percent genuine" or "50 percent genuine"; these designations initially seem strange to us, for whom authenticity is an all-or-nothing matter. They refer not so much to the odds that the work is from the master's hand as to its degree of semblance to an authentic work, or to the percentage of people who, when shown it, will accept it as from the hand of the master. Even good imitations were respectable and useful in China, for instance as symbolic presents to the emperor.[100]

In any case, a transaction in which a painting passes from the hands of an artist who signs it but did not paint it to a recipient who knows the artist did not paint it but is more or less satisfied with what he gets can be taken as the ultimate consequence of the phenomenon with which this long chapter began, the displacement of value from qualities of the image to the presumed traces of the painter's hand. And it moves us toward the modern age, in which big prices are paid at auction for works signed by Ch'i Pai-shih, or Fu Pao-shih, or Shih Lu, by rich buyers who know very well the risks they are running but are undeterred in their pursuit of the painter's hand, or a reasonable approximation of it.

Tung Ch'i-ch'ang was a great artist; Chin Nung was at least a very fine artist; so were they

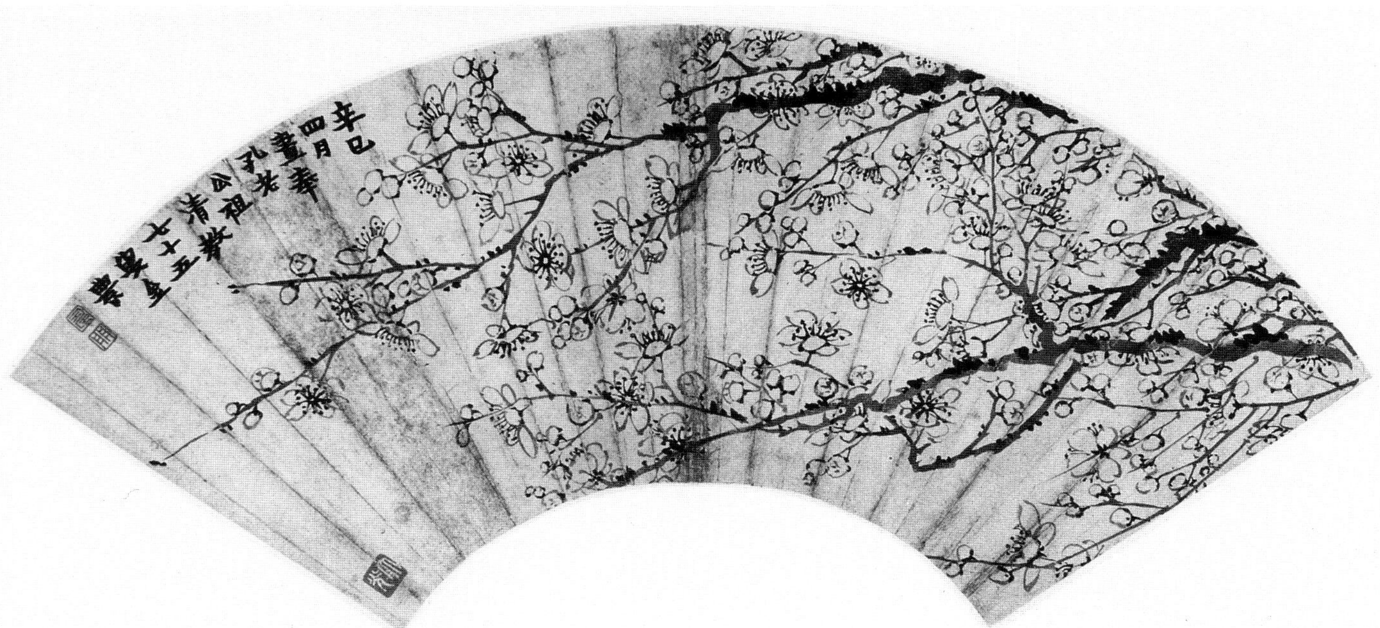

4.27 (top). Chin Nung, "Blossoming Plum." Dated 1761. Fan painting, ink on mica-powdered paper. Collection of Sun Ta-kuang, Hefei. From *Ssu-wei shu-wu chen-ts'ang shu-hua chi* (Hefei, 1989), plate 128.

4.27 (bottom). Lo P'ing, "Blossoming Plum." Dated 1762 (or 1792). Fan painting, ink on mica-powdered paper. Collection of Sun Ta-kuang, Hefei. From *Ssu-wei shu-wu chen-ts'ang shu-hua chi* (Hefei, 1989), plate 141.

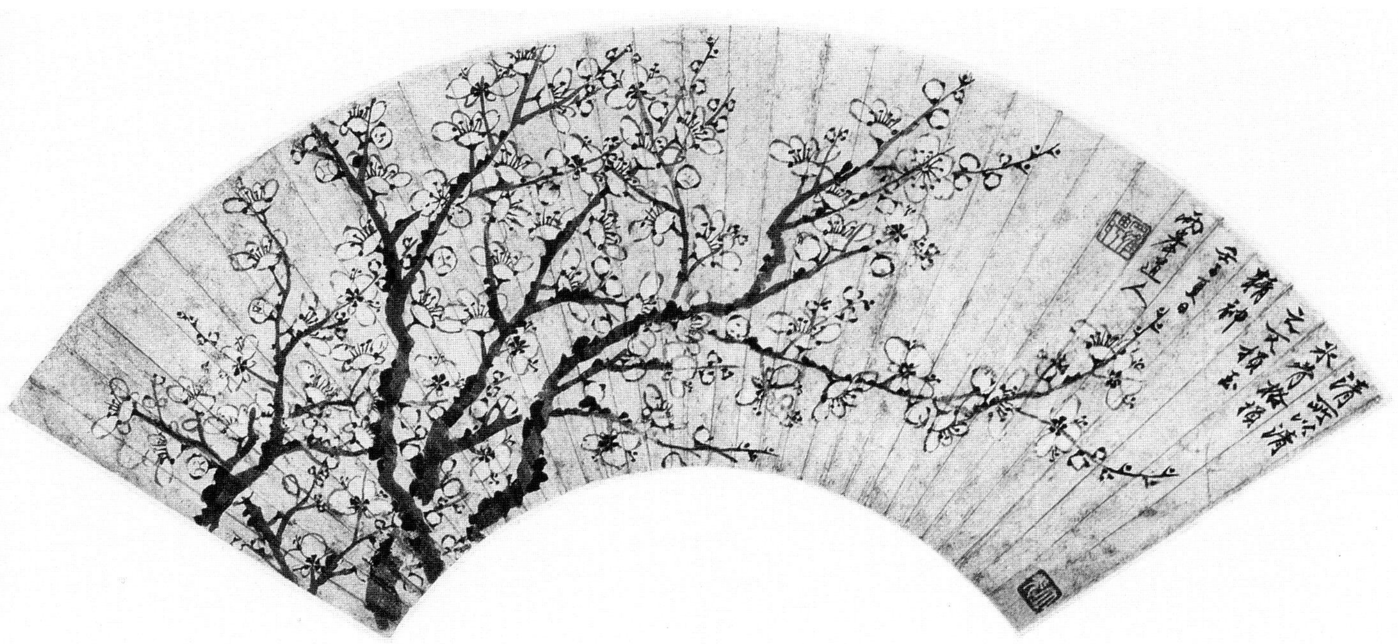

all, excellent artists. Nothing I have written is meant to suggest otherwise. If Lo P'ing in fact painted some of the best Chin Nungs, this is more to Lo's credit than Chin's discredit. Tung and Chin and the others went on painting high-level works even while they watched, and took part in, the replication of their stock-in-trade products. If an exhibition of the finest works of Tung Ch'i-ch'ang or Chin Nung, by our present-day judgment, turns out to contain a few pieces from the hands of others, it is no less representative of the highest achievements of Tung and Chin, who created the taste by which we judge. And if Chinese painters, stripped in this study (and in others that precede it and will follow and supplant it) of the false garments in which they have commonly been vested, prove to have earthy needs and ambitions as well as transcendental spiritual and aesthetic aspirations, they are not diminished by this, only made more human and, I believe, more lovable.

Notes

1. Adjusting Our Image of the Chinese Artist

1. This is, of course, a quick and highly oversimplified statement of the matter; for a more reasoned and nuanced one, see Jonathan Spence, "Western Perceptions of China from the Late Sixteenth Century to the Present," pp. 1–14.

2. A recent, surprisingly strong statement of this change by a Chinese writer is that of David Yen-ho Wu, who, dealing with the question of how Chinese perceptions of surrounding peoples affected their sense of cultural identity, writes: "most Chinese have believed that the Han people were the race of China, one that had absorbed people of all languages, customs, and racial and ethnic origins . . . Recent studies, however, have shown that the existence of a superior Chinese culture is, at best, a myth. The Chinese people and Chinese culture have been constantly amalgamating, restructuring, reinventing, and reinterpreting themselves." "The Construction of Chinese and Non-Chinese Identities," *Daedalus* (Spring 1991), issue titled *The Living Tree: The Changing Meaning of Being Chinese Today,* pp. 159–79.

3. Susanne Hoeber Rudolph, "Presidential Address: State Formation in Asia: Prologomenon to a Comparative Study," *Journal of Asian Studies* 46, no. 4 (November 1987): 736; the last sentence quoted by William T. Rowe, "Modern Chinese Social History," p. 261.

4. From the biographical entry on Cheng Min in Yao Weng-wang, comp., *An-hui hua-chia hui-pien* (Hefei, Anhui Provincial Museum, 1979), p. 315. T'ang Yen-sheng, a native of Anhui who took his *chu-sheng* degree in 1644, was a minor painter himself; see Yü Chien-hua, *Chung-kuo mei-shu-chia jen-ming tz'u-tien* (Shanghai: Shanghai Renmin Meishu Chubanshe, 1981), pp. 1088–89.

5. Huang Yung-ch'üan, "Cheng Min 'Pai-ching-chai jih-chi' ch'u-t'an," in *Mei-shu yen-chiu,* 1984, no. 3, pp. 39–40 and 49–50. The diary, which exists in manuscript, covers the years 1672–76.

6. See Joseph R. Levenson, "The Amateur Ideal in Ming and Early Ch'ing Society: Evidence from Painting," pp. 320–41. It is worth noting that this antispecialist feeling, the "amateur ideal," arises in the Sung period just when specialization is becoming stronger, with a great rise of population in the cities and the accompanying social changes. For this phenomenon, see Robert M. Hartwell, "Demographic, Political, and Social Transformations of China, 750–1550," pp. 365–442; also Jacques Gernet, *Daily Life in China on the Eve of the Mongol Invasion, 1250–1276.* Similarly, as will be discussed in chapter 4, anticommercial arguments in art come to the fore just when art is most in danger of commercialization. These cases and others suggest that Chinese idealized formulations are typically directed away from some actual and current situation, serving to claim for the writer and his audience some exemption from the reality, or to express unease or alarm about the reality.

7. Nathan Sivin, "Ailment and Cure in Traditional China: A Study of Classical and Popular Medicine before Modern Times, with Implications for the Present" (manuscript), p. 14. I am grateful to Sivin for permitting me to cite this essay. It should be noted that his argument is not (as my quotation might imply) that medicine as practiced by "amateurs" in China was somehow inadequate, but the reverse, that traditional Chinese medicine as practiced by these men was as likely to benefit the patient as modern Western "scientific" medicine.

8. Anne Burkus, "The Artefacts of Biography in Ch'en Hung-shou's Pao-lun-t'ang chi," pp. 13–17, 22–23. Burkus in her recent writings, however, such as her "Invitations to Paint: Chen Hongshou's Birthday Pictures and the Question of His Professional Status," offers strong qualifications to the portrayal of Ch'en as a professional master. On Chinese biographical writings generally, see Denis Twitchett, "Problems of Chinese Biography," in Arthur F. Wright and Denis Twitchett, ed., *Confucian Personalities* (Stanford: Stanford University Press, 1962), pp. 24–39; and also, for a discussion of the "formulaic character of Chinese biography" and how the impact of the individual was "seen in terms of the Confucian socio-moral network," Robert M. Marsh, *The Mandarins: The Circulation of Elites in China, 1600–1900,* pp. 88–92.

9. Kuo Jo-hsü, T'u-hua chien-wen chih, see Alexander Soper, *Kuo Jo-Hsü's Experiences in Painting (T'u-hua chien-wen chih)* (Washington, D.C.: American Council of Learned Societies, 1951), p. 95.

10. Wang Chih (1379–1462), *I-an wen-chi,* in *Ssu-k'u ch'uan-shu,* Taiwan reprint, 1971, ch. 37, p. 45. The translation is by Mary Ann Rogers, from an unpublished essay on Tai Chin.

11. James Cahill, *The Distant Mountains: Chinese Paintings of the Late Ming Dynasty, 1570–1644,* p. 222.

12. The point was made by Julia Andrews in "Popular Imagery in the Art of the Elite: The Case of Cui Zizhong."

13. The biography is by Shao Ch'ang-heng (1637–1704), printed in his *Ch'ing-men lu-kao*; an English rendering in Victoria Contag, *Chinese Masters of the 17th Century,* pp. 17–18.

14. See Wang Fangyu and Richard Barnhart, *Master of the Lotus Garden: The Life and Art of Bada Shanren,* pp. 280–85 for translations of these letters.

15. Jao Tsung-i, "Landscape Paintings by Chu Ta in the Chih-lo Lou Collection and Related Problems," pp. 507–15; English summary, pp. 516–17.

16. A parallel can be seen in the way Western art historians, especially the Germans, concentrated until recently so exclusively on matters of style and its interpretation as to encourage the observer to ignore the original function and meaning of the work. See Michael Podro,"The Disregard of Function," in *The Critical Historians of Art,* about how Hegel's pupil Schaase, writing in the 1830s, argued that the modern historian, by "prising free . . . the work of art from its functional and symbolic purpose," can discern relationships and sequences hidden from the artist's contemporaries, so that "the works can be seen exclusively in the context of each other" (p. 40). Few art historians today would find such positive value in divorcing the work from its original context, although the argument is still sometimes made that doing so permits one to concentrate on its purely aesthetic qualities.

17. On Anhui collectors, including merchant collectors, see Sandi Chin and Ginger Cheng-chi Hsü, "Anhui Merchant Culture and Patronage," pp. 19–24; Sewall Oertling II, "Patronage in Anhui During the Wan-li Period," pp. 165–75; and Jason Chi-sheng Kuo, "Hui-chou Merchants as Art Patrons in the Late Sixteenth and Early Seventeenth Centuries," pp. 177–88.

18. Joseph Alsop, *The Rare Art Traditions: The History of Art Collecting and Its Linked Phenomena Wherever These Have Appeared,* pp. 107–36.

19. Craig Clunas notes that two of the highest-priced paintings sold in the late Ming period "reached

these very high prices following the intervention in their favor of the arbiter Dong Qichang [Tung Ch'i-ch'ang]." Clunas, *Superfluous Things: Material Culture and Social Status in Early Modern China,* p. 125. See also where Clunas points out that when Tung Ch'i-ch'ang pawned the Huang Kung-wang "Fu-ch'un Mountains" scroll for 1,000 ounces of silver, "he had himself created a very large part of that value through the very fact of his ownership, manifested through colophons and seals" (p. 139).

20. For a strongly negative assessment of Tung Ch'i-ch'ang's connoisseurship, see Richard Barnhart, "Tung Ch'i-ch'ang's Connoisseurship of Sung Paintings and the Validity of His Historical Theories: A Preliminary Study," pp. 11/1–11/20. Without questioning either the data on which Barnhart based his judgments or the judgments themselves, one might wish he had acknowledged more the social and other pressures that must have prevented Tung, much of the time, from being entirely straightforward in revealing his real opinion of the work when he inscribed it in the presence of the hopeful owner, to whom he might well have been somehow indebted, or from whom he may have expected some material gain. The owner of the "Wintry Trees by a Lake," for instance, was the rich Nanking collector Hsü Hung-chi, whose hereditary title Wei-fu ("Prefect of Wei"), a variant of Wei-kuo Kung ("Duke of the State of Wei"), Tung includes in his inscription. Hsü is said to have acquired antique paintings from Tung when, after the 1616 riots that destroyed his estate, Tung badly needed money. One thinks of modern Chinese connoisseurs who, one is told, wrote authenticating inscriptions on paintings owned by friends when their real assessments of the works might be much lower.

21. Michele Marra, in *The Aesthetics of Discontent: Politics and Reclusion in Medieval Japanese Literature* (Honolulu: University of Hawaii Press, 1991), pp. 1–4, discusses a parallel phenomenon for literature, writing: "The development of modern aesthetics has thus brought about the tendency of de-contextualizing, de-pragmaticizing, and de-politicizing the literary text." Marra goes on to add: "The move toward the creation of a new rubric for literature was not limited to the Western world," and describes how Motoori Norinaga, in what was "an extremely conscious political act," fabricated "a nativist tradition" of Japanese literature free from the didacticism of the Chinese literary heritage, and devoted to expressing the Japanese aesthetic sensibility of *mono no aware.*

22. James Cahill, *The Compelling Image: Nature and Style in Seventeenth-Century Chinese Painting,* chs. 1, 3; Cahill, *Distant Mountains,* chs. 2, 6, 7. I also discuss in *Distant Mountains,* especially chs. 2 and 3, the cases of late Ming artists who, I argue, were diverted or converted from the practice of more personal, flexible styles into greater conformity with the dictates of Tung Ch'i-ch'ang's "Southern school."

23. Cahill, *Distant Mountains,* pp. 34, 66.

24. Ibid., pp. 264–66.

25. William T. Rowe, "Modern Chinese Social History," p. 243.

26. Huai-an County Museum, Jiangsu Province, and the Authentication Group of Chinese Ancient Paintings and Calligraphy, *Huai-an ming-mu ch'u-t'u shu-hua* (Calligraphy and Paintings Excavated from the Ming Tomb at Huai-an) (Beijing, 1988). There were two scrolls found in the tomb; the reference here is only to the second, the one containing the collection of paintings made by Cheng Chün. My article "Hsieh-i in the Che School? Some Thoughts on the Huai-an Tomb Paintings" will appear in the forthcoming festschrift volume for Professor Chu-tsing Li.

27. See Miyeko Murase, "Farewell Paintings of China: Chinese Gifts to Japanese Visitors," *Artibus Asiae* 32 (1970):211–36.

28. James Cahill, *Three Alternative Histories of Chinese Painting,* p. 109.

29. Ju-hyung Rhi, "The Subjects and Functions of Chinese Birthday Paintings"; Jerome Silbergeld, "Chinese Concepts of Old Age and Their Role in Chinese Painting, Painting Theory, and Criticism," pp. 103–14.

30. Scarlett Ju-yu Jang, "Ox-Herding as an Ideal Alternative to Officialdom," in "Issues of Public Service in the Themes of Chinese Court Painting," pp. 153–61; see also her "Ox-Herding Painting in the Sung Dynasty," pp. 54–93.

31. Ch'en Hung-shou, *Pao-lun-t'ang chi,* comp. by Ch'en Tzu, late seventeenth century, reprint 1888, ch. 3, "Ch'en Chien lao-jen mai-yao lu-chi" (A record of old Ch'en Chien selling medicine).

32. See Ellen Johnston Laing, "From Elite to Popular: Transformations of Subjects in Chinese Paintings." Laing's paper treats New Year's pictures of this kind and others.

33. See Ginger Cheng-chi Hsü, "Zheng Xie's Price List: Painting as a Source of Income in Yangzhou," pp. 261–71.

34. See Cahill, *Three Alternative Histories,* pp. 102–9.

35. Ginger Cheng-chi Hsü, "Patronage and the Economic Life of the Artist in Eighteenth-Century Yangchow Painting," pp. 191–92.

36. Marilyn Fu and Shen Fu, *Studies in Connoisseurship: Chinese Paintings from the Arthur M. Sackler Collection in New York and Princeton,* p. 57.

37. Cahill, *Three Alternative Histories,* ch. 2.

38. James Cahill, *Hills Beyond a River: Chinese Painting of the Yuan Dynasty, 1279–1368,* pp. 122–25.

39. Richard Vinograd, "Family Properties: Personal Context and Cultural Pattern in Wang Meng's Pien Mountains of 1366," pp. 1–29.

40. Farewell pictures are especially numerous among the works of mid-Ming Suchou artists. For the increase in popularity of farewell parties and paintings in Suchou at that time, see Marc F. Wilson and Kwan S. Wong, *Friends of Wen Cheng-ming: A View from the Crawford Collection,* pp. 33–34. I have also written briefly about these in my *Three Alternative Histories,* pp. 38–39.

41. See Fu Shen, "Wang To and His Circle: The Rise of Northern Connoisseur-Collectors." Wang To's inscription on the "Tung Yüan" painting was written for his younger brother Wang Yung.

42. James Cahill, *Parting at the Shore: Chinese Painting of the Early and Middle Ming Dynasty, 1368–1580,* p. 258*n.* 18.

43. Peihua Lee, "Cloudy Mountains: An Amateur Style Taken by Professional Artists," pp. 22–27, 64–72.

44. David Sensabaugh, "Guests at Jade Mountain: Aspects of Patronage in Fourteenth-Century K'un-shan," pp. 93–100; and "Life at Jade Mountain: Notes on the Life of the Man of Letters in Fourteenth-Century Wu Society," pp. 45–69. This important category of Yüan-period paintings is also discussed by Claudia Brown in "Some Aspects of Late Yüan Patronage in Suchou," pp. 101–7.

45. Elizabeth Brotherton, "Li Kung-lin and Long Handscroll Illustrations of T'ao Ch'ien's 'Returning Home,'" p. 221. The material on Ho Ch'eng's painting was presented earlier by Brotherton in a paper for the College Art Association annual meeting, San Francisco, February 1989, session entitled "Paintings and Their Colophons."

46. Examples are cited in Jang, "Ox-Herding Painting."

47. Anne de Coursey Clapp, "The Commemorative Paintings of T'ang Yin." Clapp also uses this term in *The Painting of T'ang Yin,* discussing them especially in ch. 3, "Portraits Bring Gold: The Program of Commemorative Painting," and ch. 4, "Portraits in a Landscape: Style in Commemorative Painting."

48. The regularity of the pattern was noted by Alice Hyland, in a paper titled "Parting by the River Bank by Wen Chia, ca. 1563."delivered at the College Art Association annual meeting, San Francisco, February 1989. As discussant for this session, I cited the parallel in the Brotherton paper (see note 48) and suggested that "a work consisting of a certain kind of painting plus a certain set of poems by known writers made up a kind of established collaborative product for which the demand was high, or the rewards somehow substantial (in gifts and favors)" and that we might regard it as "a literati equivalent of a studio workshop production among avowedly professional masters." Anne Clapp's "Commerative Paintings," delivered at a symposium several months later put this speculation on a firm basis.

49. Clapp, "Commemorative Paintings," p. 1; and Clapp, *The Painting of T'ang Yin,* p. 48.

50. Clapp, "Commemorative Paintings," p. 2.

51. Ibid., p. 3.

52. Clapp, *The Painting of T'ang Yin,* pp. 70–71 and figure 1.8.

53. E. H. Gombrich, "The Aims and Limits of Iconology," p. 5.

2. *The Painter's Livelihood*

1. My project should not be misunderstood as an attempt to recover some objective reality that makes up the "real past" of Chinese painting. What I will piece together here is, to be sure, only another construction, with its own agenda and biases. But it is, I would argue, a construction more humanized, more believable, and in better accord with what can be taken to be the more reliable sources of information than previous ones have tended to be.

2. Introduction to Norman Bryson, ed., *Calligram: Essays in New Art History from France,* p. xvi. He also warns against "narrowly economic" readings of the relationships between works of art and their social context, pointing out that "lines of capital . . . are not the only lines that link the painter to the rest of the social world, for there is another flow that traverses

the painter, and the patron class, and all those who participate in the codes of recognition: the flow of signs, of discourse, of discursive power" (pp. xxv–xxvi). I have tried to deal with problems of the signification of motifs and styles in other studies (in *Compelling Image* and *Three Alternative Histories*) and cannot do so here, except glancingly.

3. James C. Y. Watt, "The Literati Environment," p. 5.

4. For a translation, see Robert H. van Gulik, *Chinese Pictorial Art as Viewed by the Connoisseur,* pp. 4–6. Wen Chen-heng (1585–1645) was the great-grandson of Wen Cheng-ming; he served for a time in the imperial palace, and died when the Ming fell. The notes on hanging paintings are included in ch. 5 of his *Chang-wu chih.*

After these Bampton lectures were delivered and in large part revised for publication, I read with great interest and admiration the book by Craig Clunas, *Superfluous Things.* Wen Chen-heng's text, along with several others of the same kind from the late Ming, is the subject of his first chapter, "Books about things: The literature of Ming connoisseurship," pp. 8–39. I have added some references to his extremely enlightening discussions in endnotes, but have not rewritten to take full account of Clunas' new insights into the social class implications and other aspects of taste and connoisseurship in the Ming.

5. Studies of this far-reaching change in Chinese society are conveniently summarized by Evelyn S. Rawski in her "Economic and Social Foundations of Late Imperial China," pp. 3–33. She writes of the "gradual and long-term trend toward the triumph of the market economy" (p. 6) and of "rich merchants partaking of such traditionally elite activities as book collecting, patronage of the arts, and the creation of elaborate gardens and mansions" (p. 9).

6. Kwan S. Wong, "Hsiang Yüan-pien and Suchou Artists," pp. 155–58, gives evidence for Wen Cheng-ming's sons Wen P'eng and Wen Chia having served as advisers to the greatest collector of their time, Hsiang Yüan-pien. Nineteen letters from Wen P'eng to Hsiang are recorded, and forty-nine more are said to be in a collection in China. For Wen Chen-heng, his brother, and earlier members of the Wen clan, see Clunas, *Superfluous Things,* pp. 20–25.

7. van Gulik, *Chinese Pictorial Art,* p. 3.

8. Jean-Pierre Dubosc, "A Letter and Fan Painting by Ch'iu Ying," pp. 108–12.

9. The play, *I-chung yüan,* or as Hanan renders it, "Ideal Love Matches," is in Li Yü, *Li-weng shih-chung ch'ü* (late Ch'ing edition). It is summarized with excerpts in Patrick Hanan, *The Invention of Li Yü,* pp. 169–75.

10. James Soong, "A Visual Experience in Nineteenth-Century China: Jen Po-nien (1840–1895) and the Shanghai School of Painting," pp. 59–60.

11. Jerome Silbergeld, "Kung Hsien: A Professional Chinese Artist and His Patronage," pp. 400–410.

12. Chou Liang-kung, ed., *Ch'ih-tu hsin-ch'ao,* chüan 7, p. 171. Reprint of the Hai-shan-hsien-kuan ts'ung-shu edition. In Wang Yün-wu, ed., *Ts'ung-shu chi-ch'eng ch'u-pien* (Shanghai: Shang-wu yin-shu-kuan, 1936.)

13. Burkus, "Invitation . . . Birthday Pictures," pp. 15–20.

14. Ibid., p. 16.

15. Chia-chi Jason Wang, "The Communication Between the Scholar Painter and His Client." Paper for "Painter's Practice," seminar, University of California, Berkeley, December 1989, p. 25; adapted from his translation.

16. Sybille van der Sprenkel, "Urban Social Control," p. 621.

17. Chan Ching-feng, *Tung-t'u hsüan-lan pien* in *Mei-shu ts'ung-shu* (Taipei: I-wen yin-shu-kuan, 1960). vol. 21, ch. 4.

18. See Ambrose Yeo-chi King, "Kuan-hsi and Network Building: A Sociological Interpretation," pp. 63–84. "Under such circumstances [in which there is no established relationship between two parties] an intermediary (*chung chien jen*) is often used as a cultural mechanism in *kuan-hsi* building. Through the intermediary the individual is able to associate with the "stranger" on relational terms" (p. 74).

19. Richard Strassberg, *The World of K'ung Shang-jen: A Man of Letters in Early Ch'ing China,* pp. 172–73.

20. See Wang and Barnhart, *Master of the Lotus Garden . . . Bada Shanren,* pp. 62–63.

21. *Ku-kung shu-hua lu* (Catalog of paintings and calligraphy in the Palace Museum, Taipei) (Taipei, 1965), ch. 3, p. 418. The letter is contained in an album of Ming letters titled *Ming-jen han-mo.* For another translation, see Shan Guoqiang, "The Tendency Toward Mergence of the Two Great Traditions in Late Ming Painting," pp. 3–9.

22. For Hsiao Yün-ts'ung's album, see Cahill, ed., *Shadows of Mt. Huang,* p. 30 and catalog no. 5.

23. A painted album of this kind is in the Suchou Museum, done in 1626 for the prefect of the city when he was about to leave his post. It is made up of ten scenes of the region by Chang Hung and other local masters, ten pieces of calligraphy by Suchou literati, and a long prose inscription praising the man's administration. See *Chung-kuo li-tai shu-hua t'u-mu* 6:1–180. Assembling cases of this kind will gradually clarify the circumstances in which topographical paintings were typically produced in China.

24. See Kathlyn Liscomb, "Wang Fu's Contribution to the Formation of a New Painting Style in the Ming Dynasty," pp. 39–78.

25. From Wang Fu's biography in the *Ming shih,* the Ming dynastic history; translation from Steven D. Owyoung, "The Formation of the Family Collection of Huang Tz'u and Huang Lin," in Li et al., eds., *Artists and Patrons,* p. 114.

26. Letter in Shanghai Museum; presentation by Shan Guolin in our seminar, December 14, 1989.

27. I Tsung-k'uei, *Hsin shih-shuo,* ch'iao-i section of chüan 6, pp. 19A–B, 1918. Reprinted in *Ch'ing-tai li-shih tzu-liao ts'ung-k'an* (Shanghai: Shanghai ku-chi shu-tien, 1982).

28. Stella Lee, "Art Patronage of Shanghai in the Nineteenth Century," Li et al., eds., *Artists and Patrons,* p. 224–25. This is Yao Hsieh's own version of Jen Hsiung's "discovery"; in another version, Jen's talent is first recognized by another patron, Chou Hsien. Both claimed, that is, to have "discovered" Jen Hsiung. The information for both this and the following note is from Ch'en Ting-shan, *Ting-shan lun-hua ch'i-chung* (Seven Essays on Chinese Painting) (Taipei: Shih-chieh wen-wu ch'u-pan-she, 1969.), pp. 114–15.

29. Ibid., p. 115.

30. *Ming-Ch'ing hua-yüan ch'ih-tu.*

31. Two letters by Hua Yen in Tientsin Municipal Museum. Information provided by Cai Xingyi.

32. Pi Lung, ed., *Ch'ing-hui-ko tseng-t'ai chih-tu* (1984), hsia 11a and shang 19b–20a, quoted in Marion Sung-hua Lee, "Wang Hui's 'Summer Mountains, Misty Rain' (dated 1668): A Seventeenth-Century Invocation" (M.A. thesis, University of California, Berkeley, 1990), pp. 41–42 and 43–44.

33. *Ming-jen han-cha mo-chi,* vol. 10 (unpaginated in original but equivalent to), pp. 22A–B [or letter *12 of 13 letters by Hsi Kang]. Collected by Hu-t'ou ch'ih-hou (Pan-ch'iao/Taipei: I-wen yin-shu-kuan reprint edition, 1976.)

34. Ibid., vol. 10 (unpaginated in original but equivalent to) pp. 21A and 21B [or letters *10 and *11 of 13 letters by Hsi Kang].

35. Ibid. (unpaginated in original but equivalent to) pp. 17A and 17B [or letters #2 and #3 of 13 letters by Hsi Kang].

36. Hanan, *The Invention of Li Yü,* pp. 34–35, points out that while Li embraced the "expressivist" theory of literature of Yüan Hung-tao and others, according to which literature is the direct expression of the writer's personal nature, it would be a mistake to read Li Yü's writings in this way: "But its descriptive validity in Li Yü's case is very limited . . . the medium of his ideas is, of course, not the personal nature as such but the created self-persona, point of view, voice—for which the expressivist theory, in its naivete, provided no place." Hanan adds, citing James Liu, that the concept of *shen-yün,* the "tone" or "flavor" of one's writing, in the theory of the mid-seventeenth-century Wang Shih-chen, allows for the poet's persona, as distinct from his personal nature, to be projected in the poem. Chinese critics themselves could, of course, express suspicion about the authenticity of artists' "elevated" motives and personae; seventeenth-century writings contain quite a few statements of such mistrust—see, for instance, Cahill, *Three Alternative Histories,* pp. 94–98.

37. Cahill, *Distant Mountains,* p. 28.

38. James Cahill, "Types of Artist-Patron Transactions in Chinese Painting," in Li et al., eds., *Artists and Patrons,* pp. 13–14, from Chang Keng, comp., *Kuo-ch'ao hua-cheng-lu,* chüan 3 (hsia), p. 60. Reprint of Sao-yeh shan-fang (woodcut) edition (Ch'ing). In Yü An-lan, ed., *Hua-shih ts'ung-shu* (Shanghai: Shanghai jen-min mei-shu ch'u-pan-she, 1962), vol. 6. Hereafter cited as *HSTS.* Shan Guolin doubts that the price can really have been so high, but the rest of the story may be true.

39. Michael Sullivan, "Some Notes on the Social History of Art," *Proceedings of the International Congress on Sinology,* Section on History of Art (Taipei: Academia Sinica, 1980), pp. 99–170, gathers these conveniently for periods from the T'ang through the Sung. For the Sung period, see also Shiba Yoshinobu, trans. Mark Elvin, *Commerce and Society in Sung China* (Ann Arbor: University of Michigan Center for Chi-

nese Studies, 1970), pp. 156–63, on temple and other fairs. Clunas,"Things in Motion: Ming Luxury Objects as Commodities," *Superfluous Things* (ch. 5, pp. 116–40), gives information on Ming dealers and the market from a number of sources; see especially pp. 133–38.

40. Chan Ching-feng, *Tung-t'u hsüan-lan pien* in *Mei-shu ts'ung-shu,* vol. 21, part 5, no. 1, chüan 1, pp. 21–22; chüan 2, pp. 69–70.

41. Chin and Hsü, "Anhui Merchant Culture and Patronage," p. 22.

42. Translated by Wai-kam Ho in his essay "Late Ming Literati: Their Cultural and Social Ambience," in Li and Watt, eds., *The Chinese Scholar's Studio,* p. 31.

43. Sun Tien-ch'i, *Liu-li ch'ang hsiao chih* (Peking: Beijing ch'u-pan-she, 1962), pp. 250 and 256.

44. Soong, "Jen Po-nien," pp. 119–20; also information from Pan Yaochang, in seminar presentation.

45. See the article on nineteenth-century Shanghai painters' associations by Huang Ho in *Duoyun,* vol. 12. Lee, "Art Patronage of Shanghai," p. 227, writes about two early artists' clubs: the Hsiao-p'eng-lai Ko Ya-chi, founded by Chiang Pao-ling (1781–1841) in his later years; and the P'ing-hua She or Duckweed Flower Club, founded in 1862. See also "Rules of the Shanghai Calligraphy and Painting Study Society in the 1930s," *Shanghai t'ung-chih-kuan ch'i-k'an, 1933–34,* no. 2, ch. 3 (Hong Kong: Longmen, 1965), p. 857.

46. Chou Hui, *Chin-ling so-shih,* p. 60a. Facsimile reprint of Ming Wan-li edition (Peking: Wen-hsüeh ku-chi k'an-hang-she, 1955).

47. Strassberg, *K'ung Shang-jen,* p. 174.

48. Clapp, *The Paintings of T'ang Yin,* p. 45.

49. Ibid., p. 98.

50. Ch'eng Cheng-k'uei's series of "Imaginary Journeys" scrolls and the inscriptions on them are discussed in Yang Xin, *Ch'eng Cheng-k'uei.* See also Wai-kam Ho et al., *Eight Dynasties of Chinese Painting,* pp. 311–12.

51. The handscroll is in the Palace Museum, Beijing, and is partly reproduced and discussed in Yang Xin, *Ch'eng Cheng-k'uei.*

52. Ch'eng Cheng-k'uei, *Ch'ing-ch'i i-kao* (colophon dated 1809), chüan 24, p. 11b.

53. James Cahill, "Tung Ch'i-ch'ang's Painting Style: Its Sources and Transformations," pp. 55–79, especially pp. 62–63.

54. In a preface probably written by Tung in 1599, see Celia Riely, "Tung Ch'i-ch'ang's Life," pp. 387–457; this passage on p. 408. Riely's essay also discusses a number of Tung's paintings done as political gifts.

55. It was common also in Europe for artists to receive goods instead of cash for their works; sometimes, instead of simple barter, the transaction took the form of an exchange of presents. See Margot Wittkower and Rudolf Wittkower, *Born Under Saturn: The Character and Conduct of the Artist*; they sum up: "Barter was not only a method of payment entirely acceptable to the gentleman-artist . . . but, in the form of 'presents,' it became the customary reward for artistic genius. In other words, by the seventeenth century such partial payments in kind were a sign of special appreciation accorded by grateful or rival patrons to artists of distinction" (pp. 22–23).

56. Jang, "Issues of Public Service . . . Chinese Court Painting," p. 46, citing Liu Tao-ch'un, *Sheng-ch'ao ming-hua p'ing,* chüan 3, p. 5a; see also Lachman, *Evaluations of Sung Synasty Painters,* p. 33.

57. Kuo Jo-hsü, *T'u-hua chien-wen chih* (Peking: Jen-min mei-shu ch'u-pan-she, 1963), chüan 4, pp. 98–99; Soper, *Kuo Jo-hsü's Experiences,* p. 65.

58. Ellen Johnston Laing, "Ch'iu Ying's Three Patrons," pp. 51–52. Cited in Clunas, *Superfluous Things,* p. 121.

59. Shan, "Tendency Toward Mergence," p. 3/10, quoting a preserved letter from Wen Chia to Hsiang Yüan-pien.

60. William Ding Yee Wu, "Kung Hsien (ca. 1619–1689)," pp. 14–15 (plate 58 reproduces letter); also Jerome Silbergelb, "Kung Hsien: A Professional Chinese Artist and His Patronage," p. 404.

61. Hsü, "Patronage and the Economic Life of the Artist," p. 176.

62. Ibid., p. 196

63. See (unpaginated) Preface to Fu Hua and Ts'ai Keng, eds., *Hsü-ku hua-ts'e* (Beijing: Jen-min Mei-shu Ch'u-pan-she, 1986).

64. Hsü Ch'in, *Ming-hua lu* (colophon dated 1673, reprint Shanghai: Shang-wu yin-shu-kuan, 1936), chüan 4, p. 36; see Cahill, *Parting at the Shore,* p. 252.

65. Feng Chih-po, *Kuo-ch'ao hua-shih* (colophon dated 1831, Yun-chien wen-tsui t'ang ts'ang-pan), chüan 7, p. 8, quoting from the local history of Lu Wei's district, Lou-hsien chih.

66. Hongnam Kim, "Chou Liang-kung," 1:134.

67. Ibid., p. 24.

68. Ibid., p. 23.

69. The best published study of prices for paintings in China in the early Ch'ing period is Hongnam Kim, "Chou Liang-kung and His *Tu-hua-lu* Painters," pp. 189–207, especially the last section, "Wang Hui: Economic Aspects of Chinese Painting," pp. 197–201. See also Clunas, *Superfluous Things,* pp. 130–33 and appendix 2, pp. 178–81, "Selected prices for works of art and antique artefacts c. 1560–1620," which includes some prices for paintings along with those for objects of other kinds. Shan Guolin, head of the Painting and Calligraphy section at the Shanghai Museum, in an oral presentation to my "Painter's Practice" seminar, December 14, 1990, gave a very detailed discussion of painting prices in the Ming-Ch'ing period, using information principally from artists' letters and other documents in the collection of his museum. The publication of his research will greatly advance our understanding of this subject. Professor Cai Xingyi also presented orally valuable information on this problem in the seminar. These and other materials can serve as the basis for a separate, detailed study of the prices paid for paintings in the late period in China.

70. See Ginger Cheng-chi Hsü, "Zheng Xie's Price-List: Painting as a Source of Income in Yangzhou," pp. 261–71.

71. Chou Liang-kung, *Tu-hua lu* (Shanghai: Shang-wu yin-shu-kuan, 1936), chüan 3, p. 29; trans. in Hongnam Kim, "Chou Liang-Kung," 2:14.

72. Chou Liang-kung, *Tu-hua lu* (Shanghai: Shang-wu yin-shu-kuan, 1936), chüan 3, p. 35, trans. in Kim, "Chou Liang-Kung," 2:14.

73. See Cheng Wei, "Lun Shih-t'ao sheng-huo hsing-ching, ssu-hsiang ti-pien, chi i-shu ch'eng-chiu" (Shih-t'ao—His Life, Thinking and Artistic Achievements,) in *Wen-wu,* 1962, no. 12, pp. 43–52, p. 47. This letter was translated and discussed by Weikuen Tang in a seminar paper on Shih-t'ao's patronage; a translation of it by Jonathan Hay is quoted in Alfreda Murck, "Yuan Jiang: Image Maker," p. 231.

74. From a letter reproduced in *Min-shin no sho* (Nihon Shogei-in). Information from Shan Guoqiang.

75. In the Shanghai Museum; information received orally from Zhu Xuchu.

76. Information received orally from Professor Cai Xingyi.

77. Quoted in [Tuan] Wu-jan, "Ming i-min hua-chia Wan Nien-shao" (The Ming Loyalist Painter Wan Shou-ch'i), in *I-shu ts'ung-lu* (Hong Kong: Shang-wu yin-shu-kuan, 1966), no. 6:272. The listing of prices in inverted order, highest to lowest, and the extreme gap between these, are puzzling features of the list; they are presumably facetious, intended to deflect the onus of commercialism while communicating a real message, perhaps something like: "My asking price for a major work is three taels, but if your expectations aren't too high, I'll give you something for three cents."

78. From *jun-lieh kuang-kao* (price-list announcements) published in old issues of *Hu-she yüeh-k'an* and *I-lin yüeh-k'an*; information from Pan Yaochang.

79. Ginger Cheng-chi Hsü, "Zheng Xie's Price List"; James Cahill, "Hsieh-i As a Cause of Decline in Later Chinese Painting," in *Three Alternative Histories,* pp. 100–110; and Cahill, "On the Periodization of Later Chinese Painting: The Early to Middle Ch'ing (K'ang-hsi to Ch'ien-lung) Transition," pp. 52–67.

80. Information from Shan Guolin, oral presentation to my seminar, December 14, 1989; and from Kim, "Chou Liang-kung and His *Tu-hua-lu* Painters," pp. 198–99.

81. Louise Yuhas, "Wang Shih-chen as Patron," p. 142.

82. *Ku-kung li-tai fa-shu chüan-chi* (Taipei: National Palace Museum, 1965), collection 27.

83. Ch'en Hung-shou, *Pao-lun-t'ang chi* (compiled by Ch'en Tzu, late seventeenth century, reprint Ch'ü-ssu-chia-shu, 1888), ch. 4 "Hua shui-hsien huan ch'ang-kung ching-hsien-chih."

84. Li Ji-hua, *Wei-shui-hsüan jih-chi* (Wu-hsing liu-shih chia-yeh t'ang-k'an, 1923), chüan 1, p. 41a.

85. Letter from Lu Shih-tao to a certain Lung-chih, included in Kawai Senrō, ed., *Shina bokuseki taisei,* 12 vols. (Tokyo, 1937–38), ch. 7; see also Burkus, "Invitations . . . Birthday Pictures," p. 18 top.

86. Cheng I-mei, *Ch'ing-mo min-ch'u wen-t'an i-shih* (Shanghai: Hsüeh-lin ch'u-pan-she, 1987), pp. 77–88.

87. Letter from Yang Wen-ts'ung to a certain Wang Cheng, included in *Shina bokuseki taisei,* ch. 7.

88. *Hsüan-hui-t'ang shu-hua lu* (Hong Kong: Hsüan-hui-t'ang, 1972), vol. 1, letters *123–124. Letters sent to a certain Nan Ying by the early Ch'ing landscapist Hsü Fang.

89. Letter preserved in the Shanghai Museum from the calligrapher Chin Ts'ung (1449–1501), who

was apparently serving as go-between for Wen, to a certain Tsung-lu saying that the painting by Wen he had requested for his child was completed, and stating what Wen wanted in return. Information received orally from Shan Guolin.

90. T'ao Liang, *Hung-tou shu-kuan shu-hua-chi* in *Ming-jen shu-ts'e* (Wen-yueh p'an-shih, 1882), vol. 4, chüan 6, p. 24a.

91. Karl-Heinz Pohl, *Cheng Pan-ch'iao: Poet, Painter, and Calligrapher,* pp. 56–57. The anecdote concerns him as a calligrapher, but he presumably could have been persuaded to paint by the same inducement.

92. Ch'en Ting-shan, *Ch'un shen chiu-wen* (Taipei: Shih-chieh wen-wu ch'u-pan-she, 1975), pp. 20–21.

93. Richard Rudolph, "Kuo Pi and His Diary," p. 185. Also see Brown, "Some Aspects of Late Yüan Patronage in Suchou," p. 4.

94. *Bunjinga suihen* V, *Jo I Tô Kishô* (Hsü Wei and Tung Ch'i-ch'ang), p. 166, an inscription on the Hsü Wei handscroll in the Tokyo National Museum.

95. Tuan Ch'eng-shih, *Ssu-t'a chi* (T'ang) (Peking: Jen-min mei-shu ch'u-pan-she, 1964), chüan shang, p. 15–16. Soper, *Artibus Asiae* 31, no. 1, p. 28; Sullivan, "Some Notes on the Social History of Art," p. 163.

96. Shih San-yu, *Chin-ling yeh-shih* (Chiang-su: Jen-min ch'u-pan-she, 1985), p. 361.

97. *Ming-jen han-cha mo-chi* (Taipei: I-wen yin-shu-kuan, 1976), collection 24, unpaginated, but equivalent to p. 24b.

98. Chiang Pao-ling, *Mo-lin chin-hua* (Shanghai: Sao-yeh shan-fang, 1925), vol. 3, chüan 7, pp. 3a–b.

99. P'an Tseng-ying, *Hsiao-ou-po kuan hua-chu wu-chung* (Shanghai: Shanghai shu-tien, 1987). See Chiang Pao-ling, *Mo-lin chin-hua* (Shanghai: Sao-yeh shan-fang, 1925), chüan 8.

100. T'ao Chen-pai and Ting Nien-hsien, eds., *Ming-ch'ing ming hsien pai-chia shu-cha chen-chi* (Taipei: Tsung-ching suo chih shih-chieh shu-chü, 1954); see Shan, "Tendency Toward Mergence," p. 3/10.

101. Teng Chih-ch'eng, *Ku-tung so-chi* (Peking: Ho-chi yin-shua chü-yin, 1926); information from Cai Xingyi; I have not, however, been able to relocate the passage.

102. T'ao Yüan-tsao, *Yueh-hua chien-wen* (Hangchow: Chiang-su k'uang-ting ku-chi k'o-yin-she, 1990), chüan 2 (chung), p. 4b.

103. Ibid.

104. Ch'ing-liang tao-jen, *T'ing-yü-hsüan pi-chi* (1791, reprint Shanghai: Shang-wu yin-shu-kuan, 1900), chüan 1, p. 1. The veracity of this story is doubted by Shan Guolin, who argues that no painting by Huang Shen could be equal in value in his time to the price of a girl.

105. Cheng-chi Hsü, "Cheng Hsieh's Price List," p. 1.

106. Kuo Jo-hsü, *T'u-hua chien-wen-chih* (Peking: Jen-min mei-shu ch'u-pan-she, 1963), p. 116; Soper, *Kuo Jo-hsü's Experiences,* p. 75.

107. *Ku-kung shu-hua lu,* 4 vols. (Taipei: National Palace Museum, 1965), vol. 1, chüan 3, pp. 42–43.

108. Chou Hui, *Chin-ling so-shih,* p. 158b–159a. Facsimile reprint of Ming Wan-li edition (Peking: Wen-hsüeh ku-chi k'an-hang-she, 1955).

109. Cahill, *Parting at the Shore,* p. 87, see plate 39.

110. Yuhas, "Wang Shih-chen," pp. 142–43.

111. A story of this kind is told of the early Ming artist Wang Fu; see my "Types of Artist-Patron Transactions," p. 17 and note 25.

112. Mayching Kao, "The Painting of Ku Cheng-i and Mo Shih-lung," pp. 12/4–12/5.

113. Kuo Jo-hsü, *T'u-hua chien-wen chih* (Peking: Jen-min mei-shu ch'u-pan-she, 1963), chüan 5, p. 123, Soper, *Kuo Jo-hsü's Experiences,* p. 80.

114. Examples of paintings by Tung Ch'i-ch'ang done for fellow officials, to win their favor or repay them for help, are discussed by Riely in "Tung Ch'i-ch'ang (1555–1636) and the Interplay of Politics and Art," as well as in her essay "Tung Ch'i-ch'ang's Life."

115. Wang Chien, inscription recorded in Lu Hsin-yüan, *Jang-li-kuan kuo-yen lu* (1892, reprint 1975), vol. 10, chüan 37, pp. 24b–25a, "Wang Lien-chou fang Sung jen chü fu . . ."

116. Letter from Chao Chih-ch'ien to an unidentified recipient, included in Kawai Senrō, ed., *Shina bokuseki taisei,* ch. 7.

117. Collection of Chang Ting-ch'en, Hong Kong; published as *Shen Shih-t'ien Ling-yin Shan t'u-chuan* (Shanghai, Wen-ming, 1924).

118. Silbergeld, "Kung Hsien: A Professional Chinese Artist and His Patronage," p. 409.

119. Jang, "Issues of Public Service . . . Chinese Court Painting," pp. 34–35, citing *Sheng-ch'ao ming-hua p'ing.*

120. Liu Tao-ch'un, *Sheng-ch'ao ming-hua p'ing* (Taipei: Shang-wu yin-shu-kuan, 1974), chüan 1, pp. 4b–5a.

121. Jang, "Issues of Public Service . . . Chinese Court Painting," citing *Hsüan-ho hua-p'u,* ch. 12, p. 333.

122. Wang Shih-chen, quoted by Rogers et al., *Masters of Ming and Qing Painting,* p. 127; I have used Rogers' rendering. See also Mette Siggstedt, "Zhou Chen: The Life and Paintings of a Ming Professional Artist," pp. 37–38.

123. See Laing, "Ch'iu Ying's Three Patrons"; also Laing, "Sixteenth-Century Patterns of Art Patronage: Qiu Ying and the Xiang Family," pp. 1–7.

124. Clapp, *The Painting of T'ang Yin,* p. 40.

125. Ibid., p. 43.

126. The inscription on this painting is summarized by Hsü, "Patronage and the Economic Life of the Artist," 1:10. Even though the extant painting appears to be a copy or imitation, the inscription can be provisionally accepted as authentic, since it is recorded in that most reliable of catalogs, An Ch'i's *Mo-yüan hui-kuan* (preface 1742). Anne Clapp believes the painting to be a forgery based on that record.

127. Contag, *Chinese Masters of the Seventeenth Century,* p. 13; original text in Chiang Ch'un, "Wang Shih-min yü Wang Hui ti kuan-hsi" (The relationship between Wang Shih-min and Wang Hui), *I-lin ts'ung-lu* (Hong Kong: Shang-wu yin-shu-kuan, 1962), 2:311–12; Cahill, "Types of Artist-Patron Transactions," pp. 22–23.

128. Kim, "Chou Liang-Kung and His *Tu-Hua-Lu* Painters," pp. 72, 97, and 118.

129. Ibid., p. 118.

130. Chiang Pao-ling, *Mo-lin chin-hua* (Shanghai, 1925), vol. 2, chüan 5, pp. 1b.

131. Cheng I-mei, *Ch'ing-mo min-ch'u wen-t'an i-shih* (Shanghai: Hsüeh-lin ch'u-pan-she, 1987); page ref. not found.

132. Wang I-chih, "Wu Ch'ang-shih yü Suan-han Wei" (Wu Ch'ang-shih and the Military Official Suan Han), in *I-lin ts'ung-lu* (Hong Kong: Shang-wu yin-shu-kuan, 1962), 2:333–34.

133. Chang Ming-k'o, *Han-sung-ko t'an-i tsao-lu* (preface 1908; Shanghai: Wen-ming shu-chü, 1923), chüan 5.

134. Especially enlightening are Daphne Lange Rosenzweig, "Reassessment of Painters and Paintings at the Early Ch'ing Court," pp. 75–86; Howard Rogers, "Hu Ching's *Kuo-ch'ao yüan-hua lu* and the Ch'ing Imperial Collection of Paintings"; and Yang Boda, "The Development of the Ch'ien-lung Painting Academy," pp. 333–56. Yang draws on the Ch'ing Records and other hitherto-untapped sources to construct a remarkably detailed picture of the organization and operation of the Academy in this period.

135. Chang Ming-k'o, *Han-sung-ko t'an-i tsao-lu,* ch. 6. See also Marsha Weidner et al., ed., *Views from the Jade Terrace: Chinese Women Artists, 1300–1912,* p. 159.

136. Hsü Ko, *Ch'ing-pai lei-ch'ao hsüan* (Shanghai: Shang-wu yin-shu-kuan, 1917; reprint, Peking, 1984).

137. A first and very valuable attempt, on which the following paragraph is largely based, has been made by Ellen Johnston Laing in her "Women Painters in Traditional China," pp. 81–101, especially pp. 88–91, "Painting as an Economic Asset." See also my own notes on the courtesan-artists of the Ming-Ch'ing transition, ibid., pp. 106–8.

138. Chou Hui, *Chin-ling so-shih,* p. 132a. Facsimile reprint of Ming Wan-li edition (Peking: Wen-hsüeh ku-chi k'an-hang-she, 1955).

3. *The Painter's Studio*

1. For these, see especially: Fritz van Briessen, *The Way of the Brush: Painting Techniques of China and Japan;* van Gulik, *Chinese Pictorial Art;* and Jerome Silbergeld, *Chinese Painting Style: Media, Methods, and Principles of Form.*

2. Lloyd E. Eastman, *Family, Fields, and Ancestors: Constancy and Change in China's Social and Economic History, 1550–1949,* p. 34.

3. *Ch'ing-pi-ko ch'üan-chi,* ch. 10, 7a–b; translation by Wen Fong in *Images of the Mind,* p. 126. See also Brown, "Late Yüan Patronage in Suchou," p. 105.

4. Wittkower and Wittkower, *Born Under Saturn,* pp. 35–36. Other entertaining examples involving Raphael and Michelangelo are introduced and discussed in the pages that follow; these bear on the problem of the reluctant artist and of negotiations that break down, situations of a type that will be considered for China.

5. Anne de Coursey Clapp, "Wen Cheng-ming: The Ming Artist and Antiquity," p. 13.

6. Burkus, "Invitations to Paint . . . Birthday Pictures," p. 19.

7. Rogers et al., *Masterworks of Ming and Qing,* p. 137.

8. Letter by Wang Shih-mou, included in *Hsuan-*

hui-t'ang shu-hua lu (Hong Kong: Hsüan-hui-t'ang, 1972), vol. 1, letter 102.

9. Chu-tsing Li, "A Thousand Peaks and Myriad Ravines," Chinese Paintings in the Charles A. Drenowatz Collection," Ascona, *Artibus Asiae separatum* 30, 1974, plate 72.

10. Marion Sung-hua Lee, "Wang Hui's 'Summer Mountains, Misty Rain,'" p. 35.

11. Burkus, "Invitations to Paint . . . Birthday Pictures," p. 28. An unpublished study by my student Weikuen Tang, "A Study of the Patronage and Meaning of Yü Chih-ting's Portrait Paintings," similarly concludes, on the evidence available to him, that in most cases the sitter stipulated the setting in which he would be portrayed.

12. Cahill, *Distant Mountains,* p. 217, quoting from Chou Liang-kung's *Shu-ying tse-lu.*

13. Wai-kam Ho, "Nan-Ch'en Pei-Ts'ui: Ch'en of the South and Ts'ui of the North," *Bulletin of the Cleveland Museum of Art* 49, no. 1 (1962):2–11.

14. Clapp, *The Painting of T'ang Yin,* pp. 37–38. Clapp's discussion of this recorded work, like her whole chapter, is exemplary as a sensitive treatment of the complexities and subtler aspects of the artist-patron relationship that never loses sight of the crucial importance of their differences in social rank.

15. Liu Tao-ch'un, *Wu-tai ming-hua pu-i* (Taipei: Shang-wu yin-shu-kuan, 1974), preface 1059 (in *Wang-shih hua-yüan*), p. 7b.

16. Kim, "Chou Liang-Kung," 2: p. 192. (Chou Liang-kung on Su Lin.)

17. Translation from Wen Fong, "A Letter from Shih-t'ao to Pa-ta-shan-jen and the Problem of Shih-t'ao's Chronology," *Archives of the Chinese Art Society of America* 13 (1959), p. 32.

18. Chou Liang-kung, *Ts'ang-ch'ü chi,* p. 40, quoted by Ginger Cheng-chi Hsü, "Patronage and the Economic Life of the Artist," 1:8.

19. Michael Baxandall, *Patterns of Intention: On the Historical Explanation of Pictures,* pp. 30–36.

20. Teng Shih, comp., *T'an-i lu,* in *Mei-shu ts'ung-shu,* vol. 15, section 3:10, pp. 288–89.

21. Huang Hsiu-fu, *I-chou ming-hua lu* (second half tenth century, edited in 1005, in *Wang-shih hua-yüan*) Printed in Ching dynasty from blocks of the Wan-wei-shan-t'ang edition, Hangchow, early seventeenth century, chüan shang, p. 1a–b.

22. Charles Lachman, *Evaluations of Sung Dynasty Painters of Renown: Liu Tao-ch'un's "Sung-ch'ao ming-hua p'ing,"* pp. 56 (Li Ch'eng), p. 60 (Kao K'o-ming).

23. Lachman, *Evaluations of Sung Dynasty Painters,* p. 27.

24. Teng Ch'un, *Hua-chi* (completed 1167, Peking: Jen-min mei-shu ch'u-pan-she, 1963), chüan 5, p. 55.

25. Ibid., p. 69.

26. Chou Hui, *Chin-ling so-shih* (Peking: Wen-hsüeh ku-chi k'an-hsing-she, 1955), 1:106.

27. Kuo Jo-hsü, *T'u-hua chien-wen-chih* (Peking: Jen-min mei-shu ch'u-pan-she, 1963, 1983 printing), chüan 3, pp. 62–63; Soper, *Kuo Jo-hsü's Experience,* p. 44.

28. Chou Liang-kung, *Tu-hua lu,* trans. in Kim, *Lives of Painters,* 2:46–47.

29. Wang Fangyu, in Wang and Barnhart, *Master of the Lotus Garden,* p. 42.

30. Ibid., p. 58.

31. Yu Chiao, "Tu-hua hsien-p'ing," *Meng-han tsa-chu* (Ching-i-t'ang ts'ang-pan, 1828), vol. 4, chüan 7, pp. 10a–b.

32. Ibid., pp. 20a–21b.

33. See Rogers et al., *Masterworks of Ming and Qing,* p. 155.

34. For color reproductions of the eight leaves of the album, see Paul Moss, *The Literati Mode: Chinese Scholar Paintings, Calligraphy, and Desk Objects,* no. 22, pp. 80–89.

35. Kim, "Chou Liang-kung," 2:189–90. (Chou Liang-kung on Liu Chiu.)

36. Charles Lachman, *Evaluations of Sung Dynasty Painters of Renown,* p. 87.

37. Yu Chiao, "Tu-hua hsien-p'ing," *Meng-han tsa-chu* (Ching-i-t'ang ts'ang-pan, 1828), vol. 4, chüan 7, p. 3a.

38. Letter by Tsao Hao in *Hsüan-hui-t'ang shu-hua lu* (Hong Kong: Hsüan-hui-t'ang, 1972), vol. 1, letter 179. Chang T'ing-chi in T'ao Chen-pai and Ting Nien-hsien, eds., *Ming-ch'ing ming-hsien pai-chia shu-tsa chen-chi* (Taipei: Tsung-ching hsiao che shih-chieh shu-chü, 1954), pp. 331–35.

39. Chou Liang-kung, *Tu-hua lu* (Shanghai: Shang-wu yin-shu-kuan, 1936), chüan 4, p. 47; on Wang Kuo-ch'un, see Kim, "Chou Liang-kung," 2:191.

40. Burkus, "Invitations to Paint . . . Birthday Pictures," p. 18.

41. See James Cahill, "A Rejected Portrait by Lo

P'ing: Pictorial Footnote to Waley's Yüan Mei," *Asia Major* n.s. 7, no. 1/2, (1959), pp. 32–39; Richard Vinograd, *Boundaries of the Self: Chinese Portraits, 1600–1900* pp. 84–91.

42. Translated in my "Rejected Portrait," pp. 33–34; and by Vinograd, *Boundaries of the Self,* p. 86.

43. Lachman, *Evaluation of Sung Dynasty Painters of Renown,* p. 37.

44. Jang, "Issues of Public Service . . . Chinese Court Painting," p. 38–39.

45. Yang Boda, "The Development of the Ch'ien-lung Painting Academy," relates how both proper court artists (*hua-hua jen*) and painter-officials (whom he terms *Han-lin hua-chia*) had to submit both their preliminary drawings and the finished paintings to the emperor for his approval.

46. A series of *hua-kao* or preparatory sketches in album form by the late Ming master Sung Mou-chin is recorded as being in the Bureau of Cultural Relics of Beijing Municipality, but has not been published. See *Chung-kuo ku-tai shu-hua t'u-mu* (Beijing: Cultural Relics Publishing House, 1986–), vol. 1, ching 4–11, no reproduction.

47. Cahill, *Hills Beyond a River,* p. 87.

48. Translation from Wen Fong, *Beyond Representation: Early Chinese Painting and Calligraphy,* p. 481.

49. Cahill, *Hills Beyond a River,* p. 175; Wen Fong, *Images of the Mind,* p. 126.

50. Li Jih-hua, *Tz'u-t'ao-hsüan tsa-chui* (Shanghai: Yu-cheng shu-chü, 19—), chüan 1, p. 14b.

51. Chiang Shao-shu, *Wu-sheng-shih shih,* late Ming (*Hua-shih ts'ung-shu* edition), pp. 70–71, referring to paintings by the late Ming portraitist Tseng Ching; quoted in Cahill, *Distant Mountains,* p. 213.

52. Cahill, *Distant Mountains,* p. 216 and figures 118–20.

53. Biographical notes on the men portrayed are written on facing pages; it is unclear whether these are contemporary with the paintings.

54. Cahill, *Parting at the Shore,* p. 204.

55. For a surviving example of a pounce from Tun-huang, on which half the composition is drawn in ink and half only pricked along the outlines, see Arthur Waley, *A Catalogue of Paintings Recovered from Tun-huang by Sir Aurel Stein,* plate 94 and 892 and 969 (Ch.00159). See also Jao Tsung-i et al., *Peintures Monochromes de Dunhuang,* pp. 10–13, for a discussion of pounce copies and *fen-pen.*

56. Hsia Wen-yen, *T'u-hui pao-chien* (Shanghai: Shang-wu yin-shu-kuan, 1934), chüan 1, pp. 2–3, section headed "Fen-pen." Li Jih-hua writes of being shown a Sung-period *fen-pen* of the Keng-chih t'u or "Pictures of Ploughing and Weaving," and remarks that it might be from the hand of Ma Ho-chih. *Liu-yen-chai pi-chi,* information from Cai Xingyi; the passage not relocated.

57. The role of *fen-pen* and other methods of copying in early figure painting are discussed in Jao Tsung-i, *Dunhuang;* Hsü Pang-ta, "Ts'ung pi-hua fu-pen hsiao-yang shuo-tao liang-ch'üan Sung hua: Ch'ao-yüan hsien-li t'u" (Two Sung paintings of "Heavenly Rulers Coming to an Audience" as cartoons for wall paintings), *Wen-wu* 1956/2, pp. 57–61; Mary H. Fong, "Wu Daozi's Legacy in the Popular Door Gods (Menshen) Qin Shubao and Yuchi Gong," *Archives of Asian Art* 42 (1989): 6–24; Tseng Yuho Ecke, "A Reconsideration of 'Ch'uan-mo-i-hsieh,' the Sixth Principle of Hsieh Ho," pp. 313–38. A dissertation on this topic by Sarah Fraser, University of California, Berkeley, is underway.

58. Liu Tao-ch'un, *Sheng-ch'ao ming-hua p'ing,* Charles Lachman trans., p. 41.

59. See Tseng "A Reconsideration of 'Ch'uan-mo i-hsieh,'" pp. 313–23.

60. For the entire album, which is in the Nelson-Atkins Museum, Kansas City, see *Eight Dynasties of Chinese Painting,* no. 254.

61. Kojiro Tomita and Hsien-chi Tseng, *Portfolio of Chinese Paintings in the Museum (Yüan to Ch'ing Periods)* (Boston: Museum of Fine Arts, 1961), plates 69–71, album of "Twenty Sketches of Landscapes, Rocks, and Trees." A recent study of this album by David Teh-yu Wang "holds reservation" about the idea that the leaves are sketches from nature (as I would also) and rejects the suggestion that they are copies after older paintings, in the end leaving open the question of just how they should be understood. Wang writes, "Under no circumstances should *fenben* be interpreted as 'copy,' a general misinterpretation of this term." A more accurate statement would be that they *need not* be copies; in fact, a great many, perhaps most of them, *are* copies, and the fact that they can also serve as sources for new paintings does not change this. See David Teh-Yu Wang, "The Album Attributed to Dong Qichang in the Boston Museum of Fine Arts," part 2, *Oriental Art* n.s. 38 (Summer 1992), no. 2:76–87.

62. For a reproduction of this scroll, see Wai-kam

Ho, ed., *The Century of Tung Ch'i-ch'ang, 1555–1636,* vol. 1, plate 19, pp. 172–73; for Ch'en Chi-ju's inscription, see the entry for the painting in ibid., vol. 2, p. 29.

63. For other leaves, see Wen C. Fong, ed., *Images of the Mind,* p. 120 and figures 113–15.

64. William Ding Yee Wu, "Kung Hsien's Style and His Sketchbooks," pp. 72–87.

65. Richard Barnhart, "Survivals, Revivals, and the Classical Tradition of Chinese Figure Painting," pp. 143–210.

66. Translation by Wai-kam Ho, quoted in Cahill, *Parting at the Shore,* p. 191.

67. Cahill, *Compelling Image,* pp. 27–32; Cahill, "Some Aspects of Tenth-Century Painting as Seen in Three Recently Published Works," pp. 1–36.

68. The Li Kung-lin painting is completely reproduced in *I-yüan to-ying* 30 (September 1985), plates 1–5; a detail in Osvald Siren, *Chinese Painting: Leading Masters and Principles,* vol. 3, plate 193.

69. National Palace Museum, Taipei, *Ku-kung ming-hua san-pai chung* (Three Hundred Masterpieces of Chinese Painting in the Palace Museum) (Taichung, 1959), plate 50.

70. Michel Foucault, *The Order of Things: An Archaeology of the Human Sciences* (New York: Vintage Books, 1973), p. xv.

71. A. Kaiming Ch'iu, "The Chieh Tzu Yüan Hua Chuan (Mustard Seed Garden Painting Manual I): Early Editions in American Collections," pp. 55–69.

72. An essay by Dajuin Yao makes a convincing case for seeing the series of illustrations to the 1498 edition of the *Hsi-hsiang chi* as works exhibiting already the high quality and originality that have usually been credited only to pictorial printing from the late Ming and after. See Dajuin Yao, "The Pleasure of Reading Drama: Illustrations to the Hongzhi Edition of The Story of the Western Wing," pp. 437–68.

73. See Barnhart, "Survivals, Revivals . . . Chinese Figure Painting," p. 189 and figures 34–35.

74. For these, see Alice R. M. Hyland, *The Literati Vision: Sixteenth-Century Wu School Painting and Calligraphy.* Letters from Wen Cheng-ming's sons Wen Chia and Wen P'eng also reveal them acting, in effect, as agents for their father, corresponding with clients. Letter by Wen Chia in *Ming-jen ch'ih-tu,* in *Ku-kung li-tai fa-shu ch'üan-chi* (Taipei: National Palace Museum, 1976–79), 29:157–58.

75. Information from Cai Xingyi in seminar.

76. Hsü Pang-ta, *Ku-shu-hua chien-tmg kai-lun* (Peking: Wen-wu ch'u-pan-she, 1981), p. 68.

77. See Rowe, "Modern Chinese Social History," pp. 246, 251–53.

78. Hsü, "Patronage and the Economic Life of the Artist," p. 141, citing Wang Po-min, "Ssu-ming hua-kung han-li shih-lüeh," *Chung-kuo hua yen-chiu,* 1983, no. 4: 196–209.

79. Peter Golas, "Early Ch'ing Guilds," pp. 555–80; and Hsü, "Patronage and the Economic Life of the Artist," pp. 139–42.

80. Hsü, "Patronage and the Economic Life of the Artist," pp. 167–68.

81. Chaoying Fang, "Li Jih-hua" in Chaoying Fang and L. Carrington Goodrich, eds., *Dictionary of Ming Biography, 1668–1644,* pp. 826–30.

82. Cahill, *Distant Mountains,* p. 27; Ho, "Late Ming Literati," p. 30.

83. Translations adapted from Tsao Hsingyuan, "Dong Qichang and Li Rihua: Literati Ideals and Socioeconomic Realities," pp. 21–22, quoting from Li Jih-hua, *Liu-yen-chai san-pi,* in *Liu-yen-chai pi-chi* (Chung-yang shu-tien edition), vol. 5, chüan 1, pp. 21–24.

84. For the parallel problem in Europe see Wittkower and Wittkower, "Dilatoriness of Artists," *Born Under Saturn,* pp. 40–41, They write that "As a rule patrons tried to assure punctual delivery by stipulating a time-limit in the legally binding contract, and a penalty in case of failure to keep to the promised date." But, they note, "transgressions were the rule rather than the exception."

85. Translated by Chu-tsing Li, *The Chinese Scholar's Studio,* p. 46.

86. Stella Lee, "Art Patronage of Shanghai in the Nineteenth Century," p. 228.

87. For Wu Tao-tzu's paintings being colored by his pupils Ti Yen and Chang Tsai, see William Acker, trans., *Some T'ang and Pre-T'ang Texts on Chinese Painting,* 1:237; for Wang Wei, see ibid., p. 237.

88. Barnhart, "Survivals, Revivals . . . Chinese Figure Painting," p. 150, quoting the *Hua shih* of Mi Fu. Also see Jang, "Issues of Public Service . . . Chinese Court Painting," p. 12.

89. Soper, *Kuo Jo-hsü's Experience,* p. 97.

90. Information from the essay by his nephew Kao Ping; in Klaas Ruitenbeeck, "Gao Qipei and the Art of Finger Painting," 1:456–67."

91. Rogers et al., *Masterworks of Ming and Qing.*

Rogers writes that the principal figure may represent Ma-ku, and that paintings of Ma-ku were given to couples on their silver and golden wedding anniversaries (p. 153).

92. Anne Burkus writes: "Inscriptions that appear on the birthday pictures themselves indicate that he did not produce these works for an anonymous public, but rather that he made them for relatives and friends" ("Invitations to Paint . . . Birthday Pictures," p. 12). This is true as far as it goes; but it does not account for the many paintings without dedicatory inscriptions, especially those that appear from their styles and signatures to be works from his middle period, the 1630s, works that probably had a functional character, birthday or other, and were sometimes done with the help of studio assistants. I would argue that these are indeed done for "an anonymous public," or for people to whom he was less close. The paintings with dedicatory inscriptions, that is, make up a selected group, not necessarily representative of Ch'en Hung-shou's whole output.

93. Ibid., p. 13. Examples discussed by Burkus include the 1638 "Lady Hsüan-wen-chün" (figure 3.8) and another done in 1649 for a man who had helped the artist with gifts of food during the harrowing period of dynastic change.

94. Ibid., p. 11.

95. Kao Shih-ch'i, *Ch'ing-ho shu-hua fang,* ch'en section, p. 30A, claims that Kuan T'ung never liked painting human figures, but asked a certain Hu I to do them for him, and that this was the beginning of such collaborative painting.

96. Huang Hsiu-fu, *I-chou ming-hua-lu* (printed in the Ch'ing dynasty from blocks of Wan-wei-shan t'ang edition, Hangchow, early sseventeenth century), chüan 11, p. 4b.

97. Jang, "Issues of Public Service . . . Chinese Court Painting," p. 20, citing Kuo Jo-hsü, *T'u-hua chien-wen chih,* ch. 5; see Soper translation, p. 76.

98. Pi Lung, ed., *Ch'ing-hui-ko tseng-tai ch'ih-tu* (1784), shang 17b, quoted in Marion Sung-hua Lee, "Wang Hui's 'Summer Mountains,'" p. 38.

99. *Ming-tai ming-jen mo-pao* (published by Chien-chen-she, 1943), vol. 4, unpaginated.

100. His name is properly Ch'en Hung-shou, but I use his style-name here to avoid confusion with the late Ming figure master Ch'en Hung-shou, whose given name is written with different characters.

101. *Ming-jen han-tsa mo-chi* (Taipei: I-wen yin-shu-kuan, 1976), vol. 4, unpaginated.

102. Chiang Pao-ling, *Mo-lin chin-hua* (Shanghai, 1925), ch. 16. Passage not relocated.

4. The Painter's Hand

1. See Fu and Fu, *Studies of Connoisseurship,* p. 57.

2. See Cahill, "Confucian Elements in the Theory of Painting," p. 130.

3. Norman Bryson, *Vision and Painting: The Logic of the Gaze,* p. 89.

4. Cahill, *Hills Beyond a River,* p. 164.

5. Chang Yen-yüan, *Li-tai ming-hua-chi* (Peking: Hsin-hua yin-shua-ch'ang, 1963), p. 104, Acker, trans., *Some T'ang and Pre-T'ang Texts,* 2:18.

6. Ibid., 2:19, on Ts'ao Pu-hsing.

7. Charles Lachman, *Evaluations of Sung Dynasty Painters of Renown,* pp. 43, 80.

8. *Hua-chi,* ch. 5 (*Hua-shih ts'ung-shu* edition), p. 35.

9. On this phenomenon, see Alexander Soper, "Standards of Quality in Northern Sung Painting," pp. 12–13.

10. I share here the feelings of Alexander Soper, who writes of early critical comments on painters: "The writer time and time again falls back on some immemorial platitude, worn round and featureless by centuries of rolling back and forth. Only the god of Chinese literature knows how many thousands of times it has been said, of one painter or another, that he exhausted the subtleties (or got everything possible out of) his subject. It is under a stimulus akin to irritation, then, that I have been moved to try to find out what more definite statements can be made, from the texts, regarding Chinese standards of critical evaluation in painting" ("Standards of Quality," p. 8.).

11. The same passage is translated by Richard Barnhart as "Nowadays people no longer paint narratives" in "Survivals . . . Chinese Figure Painting," p. 157. The Chinese term *ku-shih* or "old matters" permits either rendering.

12. Alexander Soper, *Textual Evidence for the Secular Arts of China,* pp. 65–68. See also Soper, "Standards of Quality in Northern Sung Painting," p. 10, on artists who "lapsed from the grand manner" by painting a marketplace, or life in the countryside, or "a mock battle on the stage," and were placed by critics at the bottom of the scale, in the "competent" class. Soper comments, "It is clear that such attempts to widen the subject-matter of art aroused the same sort

of distrust among conservatives in Northern Sung that was later vented in Japan on Ukio-e, or in the England of Reynolds' time on Hogarth." On the narrowing of the range of subjects depicted by artists from the early periods into the Sung, see also Lothar Ledderose, "Subject Matter in Early Chinese Painting Criticism," pp. 69–81; and John Hay, "Along the River During Winter's First Snow," pp. 298–301, on the decline of narrative and genre painting in this period.

13. Kuo Jo-hsü in Soper, trans., *Textual Evidence for the Secular Arts of China,* p. 100.

14. Ibid., p. 25.

15. As always, one could come up with a few exceptions, especially in the late period, from the eighteenth century, when artists begin to depict subjects that had before been taboo. Well-known examples are Hua Yen's pictures of animals fleeing from a brushfire, *I-yüan to-ying* no. 41, fig. 74 (back cover), and Lo P'ing's album leaf of a rabbit running beneath a burning tree, see *Bunjinga suihen,* vol. 9, *Kin Nô* (Chin Nung), plate 100.

16. The painting, titled *Liu-min t'u,* or "Destitute People," was "by" an official named Cheng Hsia—which may mean only that he planned and commissioned the work—and is recorded in the *Sung shih,* the Sung official history. A brief note on this painting is in Ferguson, "The Vagrant People: A Picture of Woe," *The China Journal* (January 1929), pp. 17–18. A number of politically slanted studies of this painting have been published in China; see, for one, Ling-hu Piao, "Kuan yü Sung-tai 'hua-yüan,' 'hua-hsüeh' chi Cheng Hsia 'Liu-min t'u" (On the Sung Painting Academy, Painting Institute, and Cheng Hsia's "Displaced People" Painting), *Duoyun* (1984), 6:190–96.

17. Cahill, "Some Aspects of Tenth-Century Painting."

18. Ibid.

19. On Confucianism and the emotions, see Cahill "Confucian Elements in the Theory of Painting," pp. 132–34.

20. Another good statement of the Sung literati preference for the plain and unassertive is that of Barnhart, "Survivals . . . Chinese Figure Painting," pp. 153–54; he introduces parallels from the appreciation of calligraphy and poetry in this period.

21. Susan Bush and Hsiao-yen Shih, eds., *Early Chinese Texts on Painting,* p. 42.

22. English translation published as *Legend, Myth, and Magic in the Image of the Artist: A Historical Experiment* (New Haven: Yale University Press, 1979). For the rise in status of the artist in Europe, see also Wittkower and Wittkower, *Born Under Saturn,* pp. 31–38. They write (pp. 32–33) about how some artists begin to be accepted into society, achieve terms of intimacy with their patrons, and even qualify as belonging to the elite themselves, from the late fifteenth into the early sixteenth century.

23. Richard Barnhart includes Ts'ui Po in the lineage of Wu Tao-tzu as an artist of "impetuous virtuosity and untrammeled personality," in "Survivals . . . Chinese Figure Painting," pp. 152–53.

24. Cahill, *Parting at the Shore,* pp. 163–66; Cahill, "T'ang Yin and Wen Cheng-ming as Artist Types."

25. Soper, *Textual Evidence for the Secular Arts of China,* pp. 11–13.

26. The anecdote is told by Chang Yen-yüan; see Acker, *Some T'ang and Pre-T'ang Texts,* 2:214.

27. Ibid., 1:153.

28. Ibid., 2:213.

29. Cahill, "Confucian Elements in the Theory of Painting," p. 129; Soper, *Textual Evidence for the Secular Arts of China,* p. 15.

30. See, for a good discussion of this formulation, Hans H. Frankel, "Poetry and Painting: Chinese and Western Views of Their Convertibility," pp. 289–307. It is invoked and discussed in several of the papers in the symposium volume edited by Murck and Fong, *Words and Images.* A shift corresponding to the one in China occurs in European attitudes to painting some six centuries later. See Rensselaer W. Lee, *Ut Pictura Poesis: The Humanistic Theory of Painting*: "[between the early sixteenth and early eighteenth century] the clear insistence that painting is primarily an art whose function it is to represent to the eye the forms and beauty of the external world was in eclipse. It was in eclipse, that is, during the two centuries in which the doctrine of *ut pictura poesis* was in process of evolution, when the critics were all too eager to turn the poet into a painter of pictures and the painter into one who shared subject matter and expression and a set of rules for good invention with the poet."

31. See note 24 above.

32. Stephen Goldberg has written on the semiotics of calligraphy in his "Court Calligraphy of the Early T'ang Dynasty," pp. 189–237.

33. This phenomenon was first identified and seriously considered by Joseph R. Levenson in his seminal article "The Amateur Ideal in Ming and Early Ch'ing Society: Evidence from Painting," pp. 320–41.

34. Kuo, "Huichou Merchants as Art Patrons," p.

185, citing Chou Liang-kung, *Tu-hua lu, Hua-shih ts'ung-shu* ed. ch. 2, p. 24; also Julia Andrews and Haruki Yoshida, "Theoretical Foundations of the Anhui School," in Cahill, ed., *Shadows of Mt. Huang,* p. 34. For the importance of name recognition in Ming collecting, see Clunas, *Superfluous Things,* pp. 67–69.

35. See James Cahill, *Distant Mountains,* p. 136, for the whole quotation.

36. Wu Ch'i-chen, *Shu-hua chi* (2 vols.; Shanghai: Jen-min mei-shu ch'u-pan-she, 1963), ch. 5, pp. 590–91. A point that is marginal to my discussion here but important for late Ming collecting is that other ways of investing wealth such as land purchase and capital investment in industry were not so accessible in China of this period as they were in Europe, a situation that made the acquisition of art and antiques even more attractive. For this point, see Clunas, *Superfluous Things,* pp. 161–62.

37. Kuo, "Hui-chou Merchants," p. 181, citing Wu Ch'i-chen, *Shu-hua chi,* pp. 78–79.

38. Kuo, ibid., citing Wen Fong, "Rivers and Mountains."

39. Shen Te-fu, *Fei-fu-yü-lüeh* in *K'ao-p'an yü-shih chi ch'i-t'a san chung* (Shanghai: Shang-wu yin-shu-kuan, 1937), p. 5, cited by Fu Shen, "Wang To and His Circle," p. 9.

40. Clunas, *Superfluous Things,* p. 87,

41. Ku Ch'i-yüan, *Erh-hsü Chin-ling so-shih,* second sequel to *Chin-ling so-shih* (late Ming; reprint, Peking: Wen-hsüeh ku-chi k'an-hsing-she, 1955), pp. 50b–51a.

42. For an illuminating discussion of how taste is associated with social and economic class, and the distinction between "pure" taste for the austere and aesthetically distancing vs. popular taste for the sensual and entertaining, see Pierre Bourdieu, *Distinction: A Social Critique of the Judgement of Taste,* especially pp. 30–32, 267–317, and 486–91. Bourdieu's discussion of the high-taste disgust for everything in art that is facile, "easily decoded and culturally undemanding" (pp. 486–88) might be a description of the attitudes of Tung Ch'i-ch'ang and his like-minded literati associates.

43. People in this situation, along with those who were never able to engage in official careers at all, would appear to occupy roughly the same position within Chinese society as that class of people in France, such as teachers, etc., whom Bourdieu defines as "richest in cultural capital and (relatively) poorest in economic capital," and whose taste was typically for "the austerity of pure works, Bach or Braque, Brecht or Mondrian, the same ascetic disposition that is expressed in all their practices" (p. 269). In China this taste for the astringent among the literati had, of course, particular roots as well in the Confucian tradition of associating austerity in one's personal life with the virtues of self-cultivation, lack of political ambition, etc. The beginnings of that tradition in the pre-Han and Han periods have been explored in great depth by Martin Powers in various writings, most recently in his *Art and Political Expression in Early China.*

44. The problem is discussed in Benjamin Elman, *From Philosophy to Philology*—"Professionalization in Late Imperial China," pp. 96–100; and "Official and Semiofficial Patronage." pp. 100–112. See also Clunas, *Superfluous Things,* especially pp. 141–65.

45. Mi Fu, *Hua shih* (Chi-ku-ko edition, reprint, Taipei: Shang-wu yin-shu-kuan, 1973), 26a.

46. Silbergeld, "Kung Hsien . . . and His Patronage," p. 406.

47. Teng Shih, comp., *T'an-i lu,* in *Mei-shu ts'ung-shu,* vol. 15, collection 3:10, p. 293.

48. Hsü, "Patronage and the Economic Life of the Artist," p. 172. Also, Chin Nung, *Tung-hsin hsien-sheng hua-chu t'i-chi,* in *Mei-shu ts'ung-shu* 1:3, p. 68.

49. Hsü, "Zheng Xie's Price List," pp. 7–11.

50. Letter by Cheng Hsieh; information from Shan Guoqiang, not relocated.

51. Chiang Pao-lin, *Mo-lin chin-hua* (Shanghai, 1925), ch. 16.

52. Francis Haskell, *Patrons and Painters,* p. 22 (Salvator Rosa), 121–22. Cf. the passages on the difficulties of dealing with artists cited from Wittkower and Wittkower, *Born Under Saturn,* in chapters 2 and 3.

53. One-on-one patronage was, of course, also common in Europe in the later periods: see Haskell, *Patrons and Painters,* ch. 5.

54. Cahill, *Three Alternative Histories,* pp. 100–110, "Afterword: Hsieh-i as a Cause of Decline in Later Chinese Painting."

55. A recent study of the nineteenth-century French landscapist Corot, concentrated on "how Corot's later practice, reception, and market strategies participated in the shaping of a modern public for landscape painting in mid-nineteenth-century France," indicates that the same elements I am associating here

in the situation of late Chinese painting—looser brushwork, critical concentration on the painter's hand and individual style, a proliferation of replications, a broader purchasing public—went together as an interdependent cluster of circumstances in Europe as well.

A summary by Amy Curlander of her "The Later Career of Camille Corot: Landscape Painting and Its Public Contexts, 1850–1867" describes the work as discussing "the critics' attempts to distinguish and privilege a discriminating viewer's apprehension of the signs of artistry in landscape painting—defined as a landscapist's 'style'—over the signs of manual and technical production—which are defined as painterly facility. Critical estimations of Corot's so-called late manner as both a highly conventionalized practice and one that emphasizes the painter's touch occupied an important place in these discussions. While these aspects of Corot's late manner were often taken to exemplify artistic style in modern landscape, they appeared in negative assessments of Corot as evidence of Corot's 'atelier de reproduction,' or as effects of the overproduction and mass circulation of a given landscape formula." Center for Advanced Study in the Visual Arts, National Gallery, Washington, D.C., Center 11: Research Reports and Record of Activities (1991), p. 70.

56. Cahill, *Parting at the Shore,* p. 94, citing Wang Shih-chen's *I-yüan chih-yen.*

57. Cited by Shan, "Tendency Toward Mergence," p. 3/7.

58. Chou Liang-kung, *Tu-hua lu* (Shanghai: Shang-wu yin-shu-kuan, 1936), chüan 2, p. 20; on Wang Hui, see Kim, "Chou Liang-Kung," 2:90.

59. Kim, "Chou Liang-kung," 2:86, Chou Liang-kung on Hung-jen.

60. See Shen C. Y. Fu and Jan Stuart, *Challenging the Past*; also Shen C. Y. Fu, "Chang Dai-chien's 'The Three Worthies of Wu' and His Practice of Forging Ancient Art," pp. 56–72. My own paper, "Chang Ta-ch'ien's Forgeries of Old-Master Paintings," written for the symposium "Chang Dai-chien and His Art," Sackler Gallery, Washington, D.C., November 22, 1991, is unpublished.

61. Wen Fong, "The Problem of Forgeries in Chinese Painting," p. 100 *n.* 24; and Shan, "The Tendency Toward Mergence of the Two Great Traditions in Late Ming Painting," p. 151, quoting from Wang Ao: "when people brought him [Wen Cheng-ming] imitation pictures asking him to sign them so that they would become salable, he did not refuse to satisfy them."

62. Cahill, *Parting at the Shore,* p. 217. The source of the story is a late Ming miscellany, and it may well be apocryphal.

63. For a good discussion of the denigration of color in Chinese writings on painting, see Jerome Silbergeld and Amy McNair, "Translators' Introduction" to Yu Feian, *Chinese Painting Colors,* pp. ix—xiv.

64. Pi Lung, ed., *Ch'ing-hui-ko tseng-t'ai ch'ih-tu,* 1784, xia 24a–b, quoted in Lee, "Wang Hui's 'Summer Mountains, Misty Rain,'" pp. 35–36.

65. Siren, *Chinese Painting: Leading Masters and Principles,* pp. 75, 79–80. The information about Hui-tsung painting "nearly a thousand" pictures of auspicious phenomena is from Teng Ch'un, *Hua chi,* ch. 1, p. 3; quoted by Julia Murray in "Welcoming the Imperial Carriage and Its Colophon." See also Peter Sturman, "Cranes Above Kaifeng," pp. 33–68.

66. See note 16 above.

67. Cahill, *Three Alternative Histories of Chinese Painting,* pp. 18–22; Wai-kam Ho, entry on the version attributed to Liang K'ai in *Eight Dynasties of Chinese Painting,* pp. 78–80; Thomas Lawton, *Chinese Figure Painting,* pp. 54–57, on the version by the Yüan artist Ch'eng Ch'i in the Freer Gallery of Art. The true origin of the painting might well be like that of the original *Sou-shan t'u* which, as recounted earlier, was painted for Sun Ssu-hao by his artist-in-residence Kao I and intended for presentation to the emperor.

68. See Brotherton, "Li Kung-lin and the Long Handscroll Illustrations," pp. 101–2, citing Richard Barnhart's dissertation on Li Kung-lin.

69. Fong, "The Problem of Forgeries in Chinese Paintings," p. 101.

70. Hou-mei Sung, "From the Min-Che Tradition to the Che School," p. 7. Also see Jang, "Issues . . . in the Themes of Chinese Court Painting," p. 327, from Li K'ai-hsien, 1502–1568, *Chung-lu hua-p'in.* In Rogers et al., *Masterworks of Ming and Qing Painting,* p. 117, Rogers assumes that the "ghosting" was done for only a single painting, and relates that four officials who had commissioned Hsieh to do the work discovered Tai doing it for him, and were upset.

71. Shan, "Tendency Toward Mergence," p. 3/8. On Wen Cheng-ming using his sons and Chu Lang as ghostpainters, see also Chan Ching-feng, *Tung-t'u hsüan-lan pien* (*Mei-shu ts'ung-shu,* vol. 21, section

5:1), appendix, pp. 227–28. Chan claims to be able to detect the fakes by their inferior brushwork.

72. That Chou Ch'en ghostpainted for T'ang Yin is related by two sixteenth-century writers, Ho Liang-chün and Wang Shih-chen. The stories have been branded apocryphal by recent writers on T'ang Yin such as Chiang Chao-shen (see Cahill, *Parting at the Shore,* p. 193*n.*4); Doris Jung Chu Tai, "T'ang Yin, 1470–1524: The Man and His Art," pp. 161–64; and Siggstedt, "Zhou Chen," pp. 35–36. But the truth is that we are all inclined to choose what to believe and what to disbelieve, where to direct our skepticism and where our acceptance, according to our predispositions; since these sources are no more (or less) unreliable than most others we all depend on for our information about Chinese artists, such doubts seem motivated less by healthy skepticism than by an intention (which I believe to be misdirected) to exonerate the artist from what the writers take to be demeaning charges. Similarly, Pa-ta Shan-jen was never really mad; Cheng Hsieh's price-list was not really that at all; the "strange masters of Yangchou" were not really strange or eccentric, but simply literati like all the others; one artist was as "professional" as another; and so forth—the urge toward a grand homogenization in Chinese painting studies still seems to me (after some years of railing against it) one of the deplorable tendencies in the field.

Writers who disbelieve the accounts of their artists' producing forgeries, or employing ghostpainters, or otherwise engaging in chicanery, should have known (as I did) the late Chang Ta-ch'ien, who played these games for pleasure and profit, with great skill and panache. Fastidious scholars of the future may well subject Chang to the same genteel whitewashing, which would have amused him immensely.

73. Han Ang, comp., *T'u-hui pao-chien hsü-pien* (1519, *Hua-shih ts'ung-shu* edition, reprint Shanghai: Shang-wu yin-shu-kuan, 1934), pp. 123–24.

74. Kim, "Chou Liang-kung," 2:189. (Chou Liang-kung on Ma Shih-ying.)

75. Rosenzweig, Daphne Lange, "Reassessment of Painters . . . at the Early Ch'ing Court," p. 80.

76. Ch'en Ting-shan, *Ch'un-shen chiu-wen* (Taipei: Shih-chieh wen-wu ch'u-pan-she, 1975), p. 131.

77. Cheng I-mei, *Ch'ing-mo Min-ch'u wen-t'an i-shih* (Shanghai: Hsüeh-lin ch'u-pan-she, 1987), p. 75.

78. Hsü Ko, *Ch'ing-pai lei-ch'ao-hsüan* (Shanghai: Shang-wu yin-shu-kuan, 1917; reprint Peking, 1984). Also, Chiang Pao-lin, *Mo-lin chin-hua* (Shanghai, 1921), vols. 6, 7, and 12.

79. Hsingyuan Tsao, "Art as a Means of Self-Cultivation and Social Intercourse: On the Social Function of Dong Qichang's Art," pp. 61–71. My reading of the re-inscribed paintings is a hypothesis, but one strongly suggested by the paintings and their inscriptions.

80. Adapted from the translation by Hsingyuan Tsao, "Art as a Means of Self-Cultivation," p. 62, from Tung's *Jung-t'ai pieh-chi,* vol. 2. For another translation see Shan, "Tendency Toward Mergence," p. 3/7. According to the early Ch'ing writer Chu I-tsun, Wu I served as Tung's ghost-calligrapher while Tung was at the capital; see Chu's *Yün-shih-chai pi-t'an* (Shanghai: Shang-wu yin-shu-kuan, 1937), ch. 2, quoted in Fukumoto Masakazu, "Geirin hyakusei no shi" (The Master of a Hundred Generations in Art), in Hironobu Kohara, ed., *Tô Kishô no shoga* (Tung Ch'i-ch'ang's Calligraphy and Painting), . . p. 149. Nelson Wu, relying on an unidentified source, reports that Wu I's forgeries were sometimes so good that Tung himself could not distinguish them from his own work (Fang and Goodrich, eds., *Dictionary of Ming Biography,* pp. 1222–23).

81. Shan, "Tendency Toward Mergence," p. 3/7, citing Ch'en's preface to an essay celebrating Tung's sixtieth birthday.

82. One thinks here of the anecdote about the Japanese potter Hamada Shôji, who, when asked whether he was not disturbed that a nearby potter in Mashiko was forging his works, answered: No, it would only enhance his reputation, since in the future the other's best pots would be attributed to him, and his worst to the other.

83. Wu Sheng, *Ta-Kuan lu* (preface 1713), chuan 19, p. 27b.

84. Cahill, *Distant Mountains,* p. 82; the letter is discussed in Hsieh Chih-liu, "T'an Tung Ch'i-ch'ang chih tai-pi" (On the Ghost Painters of Tung Ch'i-ch'ang) *Duoyun,* no. 23 (April 1989), pp. 117–18. It appears in a book by Wu Hsiu (1765–1827), who claims to have discovered it. Since the original letter cannot now be seen, it is of course possible to question its authenticity, but the use of ghostpainters by Tung Ch'i-ch'ang is amply attested otherwise, and there is no reason to doubt it. For a brief discussion of this letter and other evidence for Tung Ch'i-ch'ang using

ghostpainters, see also Fong, "Problem of Forgeries," p. 101.

85. Ch'ien Ch'ien-i, *Lieh-ch'ao shih-chi* (reprint, Shanghai, 1957), p. 32, quoted by Hsingyuan Tsao, "Art as a Means . . . Dong Qichang's Art," p. 63.

86. Tsao, "Art as a Means . . . Dong Qichang's Art," quoting from Ch'i Kung, *Ch'i Kung ts'ung-kao* (Beijing, 1983), p. 151. See also Fukumoto Masakazu, "Geirin Hyakusei no shi," p. 149. The passage is in Chu I-tsun's *Yün-shih-chai pi-t'an,* ch. 2. Chu was related to Tung Ch'i-ch'ang: his mother was Tung's niece.

87. Shan, "Tendency Toward Mergence," p. 3/8.

88. Chou Liang-kung, *Tu-hua lu,* translation adapted from that of Kim, "Chou Liang-Kung," 2:18.

89. Wu Erh-lu, "Chin Nung ho t'a te tai-pi-hua (Chin Nung and His Ghost Painters)," *Wen-wu* (1988), no. 12, pp. 69–78.

90. Hsü, "Patronage and the Economic Life of the Artist," pp. 179–80, quoting from *Tung-hsin tsu-hsien-chen t'i-chi, Mei-shu ts'ung-shu,* 1:3, p. 113. Hsiang Yün's forgeries of Chin Nung's plum paintings are discussed by Marshall Wu, "Jin Nong: The Eccentric Painter with a Wintry Heart," pp. 282–84. Wu identifies one of Hsiang's "ghosted" works by the presence of his seals in addition to a "Chin Nung" signature.

91. Hsü, "Patronage and the Economic Life of the Artist," p. 179, from Ch'en Yen, *Shih-i-shih shih-hua hsü-pien,* vol. 10. Quoted in Ku Lin-wen, ed., *Yang-chou pa-chia shih-liao,* p. 52.

92. Hsü, "Patronage and the Economic Life of the Artist," pp. 178–79, from Ch'en Yen, *Shih-i-shih shih-hua hsü-pien,* p. 57.

93. Jason Wang, oral report in seminar, "Painters' Practice in China," University of California, Berkeley, Fall 1989, citing *Meng-han tsa-tsu.*

94. Hsü, "Patronage and the Economic Life of the Artist," p. 199*n.* 51.

95. Ginger Cheng-chi Hsü, "Scholar, Artist, and Art Dealer: Jin Nong in Yangzhou," p. 24.

96. Alpers, *Rembrandt's Enterprise,* p. 118. Hereafter cited in text.

97. For a study of Chin Nung's self-portraits, including the sole extant one reproduced here, see Richard Vinograd, *Boundaries of the Self: Chinese Portraits 1600–1900,* pp. 112–19. Other cases of scholar-amateur artists who painted their own portraits are discussed by Pei-yi Wu in *The Confucian's Progress: Autobiographical Writing in Traditional China* (Princeton: Princeton University Press, 1990), pp. 196–203.

98. Hsü, "Patronage and the Economic Life of the Artist," p. 182; see also her "Scholar, Artist . . . Jin Nong," pp. 25–26. The letter is the seventh in the series of seventeen preserved in the Tokyo National Museum.

99. This may have been the motivation of Ts'ao Hsi (d. 1684), father of the famous salt commissioner Ts'ao Yin (1658–1712), when he asked Ch'eng Cheng-k'uei's father, who was serving with him in the capital, to do forgeries of Tung Ch'i-ch'ang's calligraphy for him: he probably meant to use them as political gifts. Ch'eng's father refused indignantly. Information from Cai Xingyi.

100. It is well known that in the private catalog of the early Ch'ing collector Kao Shih-ch'i (1645–1704), *Chiang-ts'un shu-hua mu,* many of the cheapest paintings, imitations of the old masters, are put in the category "to be presented to the emperor." (See Hin-cheung Lovell, *An Annotated Bibliography of Chinese Painting Catalogues and Related Texts,* pp. 40–41.) Moreover, the presence of a great many such works in the Ch'ing imperial collection would be difficult to account for otherwise than by supposing that these were acquired as symbolic gifts, exempt from close examination.

Bibliography (Works in English)

Acker, William. trans. and annotator. *Some T'ang and Pre-T'ang Texts on Chinese Painting,* 2 vols. Leiden: E. J. Brill, Sinica Leidensia, 1954–74.

Alpers, Svetlana. *Rembrandt's Enterprise: The Studio and the Market.* Chicago: University of Chicago Press, 1988.

Alsop, Joseph. *The Rare Art Traditions: The History of Art Collecting and Its Linked Phenomena.* New York: Harper and Row, 1981.

Andrews, Julia. "Popular Imagery in the Art of the Elite: The Case of Cui Zizhong." Paper for College Art Association annual meeting, Chicago, February 14, 1992.

Barnhart, Richard. "Survivals, Revivals, and the Classical Tradition of Chinese Figure Painting," in *Proceedings of the International Symposium on Chinese Painting,* pp. 143–218. Taipei, 1972.

Barnhart, Richard. "Tung Ch'i-ch'ang's Connoisseurship of Sung Painting and the Validity of His Historical Theories: A Preliminary Study." In Wai-kam Ho, ed., *Proceedings of the Tung Ch'i-ch'ang International Symposium,* 11/1–11/20. Kansas City: Nelson-Atkins Museum of Art, 1991,

Baxandall, Michael. *Patterns of Intention: On the Historical Explanation of Pictures.* New Haven and London: Yale University Press, 1985.

Bourdieu, Pierre. *Distinction: A Social Critique of the Judgement of Taste.* Richard Nice, trans. London: Routledge and Kegan Paul, 1984.

Brotherton, Elizabeth Chipman. "Li Kung-lin and Long Handscroll Illustrations of T'ao Ch'ien's 'Returning Home.'" Ph.D. dissertation, Princeton University, 1992.

Brown, Claudia. "Some Aspects of Late Yüan Patronage in Suchou." In Chu-tsing Li et al., eds., *Artists and Patrons,* pp. 101–10.

Bryson, Norman. *Vision and Painting: The Logic of the Gaze.* New Haven and London: Yale University Press, 1983.

Bryson, Norman, ed. *Calligram: Essays in New Art History from France.* Cambridge and New York: Cambridge University Press, 1988.

Burkus, Anne. "The Artefacts of Biography in Ch'en Hung-shou's *Pao-lun-t'ang chi.*" Ph.D. dissertation, University of California, Berkeley, 1987.

Burkus, Anne. "Invitations to Paint: Chen Hongshou's Birthday Pictures and the Question of His Professional Status." Paper for symposium on "Ming and Ch'ing Painting." Cleveland Museum of Art, May 1989.

Bush, Susan and Christian Murck, eds. *Theories of the Arts in China,* Princeton: Princeton University Press, 1983.

Bush, Susan and Hsiao-yen Shih, eds. *Early Chinese Texts on Painting.* Cambridge: Harvard University Press, 1985.

Cahill, James. *The Compelling Image: Nature and Style in Seventeenth-Century Chinese Painting.* Cambridge: Harvard University Press, 1982.

Cahill, James. "Confucian Elements in the Theory of Painting." In Arthur F. Wright, ed., *The Confucian Persuasion.* pp. 115–40. Stanford: Stanford University Press, 1960,

Cahill, James. *The Distant Mountains: Chinese Paintings of the Late Ming Dynasty, 1570–1644.* New York: Weatherhill, 1982.

Cahill, James. *Hills Beyond a River: Chinese Painting of the Yuan Dynasty, 1279–1368.* New York: Weatherhill, 1976.

Cahill, James. "Hsieh-i in the Che School? Some Thoughts on the Huai-an Tomb Paintings," to appear in the forthcoming Festschrift volume for Professor Chu-tsing Li.

Cahill, James. *Parting at the Shore: Chinese Painting of the Early and Middle Ming Dynasty, 1368–1580.* New York: Weatherhill, 1978.

Cahill, James. "On the Periodization of Later Chinese Painting: The Early to Middle Ch'ing (K'ang-hsi to Ch'ien-lung) Transition." In *The Transition and Turning Point in Art History,* pp. 52–67. Ninth International Symposium, Society for International Exchange of Art-historical Studies, Kobe, 1991.

Cahill, James. "Some Aspects of Tenth-Century Painting as Seen in Three Recently Published Works." *Proceedings of the International Conference on Sinology: Section on History of Art.* Taipai: Academia Sinica, 1992.

Cahill, James. "T'ang Yin and Wen Zheng-ming as Artist Types: A Reconsideration." *Artibus Asiae* 53, nos. 1/2 (1993): 228–248.

Cahill, James. *Three Alternative Histories of Chinese Painting.* Lawrence: Spencer Museum of Art, University of Kansas, 1988.

Cahill, James. "Tung Ch'i-ch'ang's Painting Style: Its Sources and Its Transformations." In Wai-kam Ho, ed., *The Century of Tung Ch'i-ch'ang, 1555–1636,* 1:55–79. Kansas City: Nelson-Atkins Museum of Art, 1992.

Cahill, James. "Types of Artist-Patron Transactions in Chinese Painting." In Chu-tsing Li et al., eds., *Artists and Patrons,* pp. 7–20.

Cahill, James, ed. *Shadows of Mt. Huang: Chinese Painting and Printing of the Anhui School.* Berkeley: University Art Museum, 1981.

Ch'iu, A. Kaiming. "The Chieh Tzu Yüan Hua Chuan (Mustard Seed Garden Painting Manual I): Early Editions in American Collections." *Archives of the Chinese Art Society of America* 5 (1951), pp. 55–69.

Chin, Sandi and Cheng-chi (Ginger) Hsü. "Anhui Merchant Culture and Patronage." In James Cahill, ed., *Shadows of Mt. Huang,* pp. 19–24.

Chou, Ju-hsi and Claudia Brown, eds. *Chinese Painting Under the Qianlong Emperor.* 2 vols. In *Phoebus: A Journal of Art History* 6, nos. 1, 2 (Phoenix, 1988–89).

Clapp, Anne de Coursey. "The Commemorative Paintings of T'ang Yin." Paper for Symposium on "Ming and Ch'ing Painting," Cleveland Museum of Art, May 1989.

Clapp, Anne de Coursey. *The Painting of T'ang Yin.* Chicago: University of Chicago Press, 1991.

Clapp, Anne de Coursey. "Wen Cheng-ming: The Ming Artist and Antiquity." Ascona: *Artibus Asiae* (1975), Supplementum 34.

Cleveland Museum of Art, comp. *Eight Dynasties of Chinese Painting: The Collections of the Nelson Gallery—Atkins Museum, Kansas City and the Cleveland Museum of Art;* with essays by Wai-kam Ho et al., Cleveland Museum of Art, in cooperation with Indiana University Press, 1980.

Clunas, Craig. *Superfluous Things: Material Culture and Social Status in Early Modern China.* Urbana and Chicago: University of Illinois Press, 1991.

Contag, Victoria. *Chinese Masters of the 17th Century.* Michael Bullock, trans. Rutledge, Vt. and Tokyo: C. E. Tuttle, 1970.

Dubosc, Jean-Pierre. "A Letter and Fan Painting by Ch'iu Ying." *Archives of Asian Art* 28 (1974–75), pp. 108–12.

Eastman, Lloyd E. *Family, Fields, and Ancestors: Constancy and Change in China's Social and Economic History, 1550–1949.* New York and Oxford: Oxford University Press, 1988.

Elman, Benjamin. *From Philosophy to Philology: Intellectual and Social Aspects of Change in Late Imperial China.* Cambridge: Harvard University Press, 1984.

Fairbank, John K., ed. *Chinese Thought and Institutions.* Chicago: University of Chicago Press, 1957.

Fang, Chaoying and L. Carrington Goodrich, eds. *Dictionary of Ming Biography, 1364–1644.* 2 vols. New York: Columbia University Press, 1976.

Fong, Wen. *Beyond Representation: Early Chinese Painting and Calligraphy, 8th–14th Century.* New York and New Haven: Metropolitan Museum of Art and Yale University Press, 1992.

Fong, Wen. "The Problem of Forgeries in Chinese Painting," *Artibus Asiae* 25 (1962), pp. 95–119.

Fong, Wen. "Rivers and Mountains After Snow (Chiang-shan hsüeh-chi), Attributed to Wang Wei (A.D. 699–759)," *Archives of Asian Art* 30 (1976–77), pp. 6–33.

Fong, Wen, ed. *Images of the Mind: Selections from the Edward L. Elliott Family and John B. Elliott Collections of Chinese Calligraphy and Painting at the Art Museum, Princeton University.* Princeton: Princeton University Press, 1984.

Frankel, Hans H. "Poetry and Painting: Chinese and Western Views of Their Convertibility." *Comparative Literature* 9, no. 4 (Fall 1957), pp. 189–307.

Fu, Marilyn and Shen C. Y. Fu. *Studies in Connoisseurship: Chinese Paintings from the Arthur M. Sackler Collection in New York and Princeton.* Princeton: Princeton University Press, 1973.

Fu, Shen C. Y. "Chang Dai-chien's 'The Three Worthies' of Wu and His Practice of Forging Ancient Art." *Orientations* (September 1989), pp. 56–72.

Fu, Shen C. Y. "Wang To and His Circle: The Rise of Northern Connoisseur-Collectors." Paper for symposium, Cleveland Art Museum, 1979.

Fu, Shen C. Y. and Jan Stuart. *Challenging the Past: The Paintings of Chang Dai-chien.* Washington, D.C.: Smithsonian Institution, 1991.

Gernet, Jacques. *Daily Life in China on the Eve of the Mongol Invasion, 1250–1276.* Trans. H. W. Wright. Stanford: Stanford University Press, 1970.

Golas, Peter. "Early Ch'ing Guilds." In G. William Skinner, ed., *The City in Late Imperial China,* pp. 555–80. Stanford: Stanford University Press, 1977,

Goldberg, Stephen. "Court Calligraphy of the Early T'ang Dynasty." *Artibus Asiae* 49, nos. 3/4 (1989), pp. 189–237.

Gombrich, E. H. *Norm and Form: Studies in the Art of the Renaissance.* 2d ed. London and New York: Phaidon, 1971.

Gombrich, E. H. *Symbolic Images: Studies in the Art of the Renaissance.* London and New York: Phaidon, 1972.

Hanan, Patrick. *The Invention of Li Yü.* Cambridge: Harvard University Press, 1988.

Hartwell, Robert M. "Demographic, Political, and Social Transformation of China, 750–1550." *Harvard Journal of Asiatic Studies* 42, no. 2 (1982), pp. 365–442.

Haskell, Francis. *Patrons and Painters: A Study in the Relations Between Italian Art and Society in the Age of the Baroque.* Rev. ed. New Haven and London: Yale University Press, 1980.

Hay, John. "Along the River During Winter's First Snow." *Burlington Magazine* (May 1972), pp. 298–301.

Ho, Wai-kam. "Late Ming Literati: Their Cultural and Social Ambience." In Chu-tsing Li and James C. Y. Watt, eds., *The Chinese Scholar's Studio,* pp, 23–36.

Ho, Wai-kam et al. *Eight Dynasties of Chinese Painting: The Collections of the Nelson-Atkins Museum, Kansas City, and the Cleveland Museum of Art.* Cleveland Museum of Art in cooperation with Indiana University Press, 1980.

Ho, Wai-kam, ed. *The Century of Tung Ch'i-ch'ang, 1555–1636.* 2 vols. Kansas City and Seattle: Nelson-Atkins Museum of Art in cooperation with the University of Washington Press, 1992.

Ho, Wai-ching, ed. *Proceedings of the Tung Ch'i-ch'ang International Symposium.* Kansas City: Nelson-Atkins Museum of Art, 1992.

Hsü, Ginger Cheng-chi. "Patronage and the Economic Life of the Artist in Eighteenth-Century Yangchow Painting." 2 vols. Ph.D. dissertation, University of California, Berkeley, 1987.

Hsü, Ginger Cheng-chi. "Scholar, Artist, and Art

Dealer: Jin Nong in Yangzhou." In Vito Giacalone, ed., *The Eccentric Painters of Yangzhou.* New York: China House Gallery, 1990.

Hsü, Ginger Cheng-chi. "Zheng Xie's Price List: Painting as a Source of Income in Yangzhou," in *Chinese Painting Under the Qianlong Emperor,* part 2, *Phoebus* 6, no. 2, Tempe, Arizona, 1991, pp. 261–71.

Hyland, Alice R. M. *The Literati Vision: Sixteenth-Century Wu School Painting and Calligraphy.* Memphis: Brooks Museum of Art, 1984.

Jang, Scarlett Ju-yu. "Ox-Herding Painting in the Sung Dynasty." *Artibus Asiae* 52, no. 1/2 (1992), pp. 54–93.

Jang, Scarlett Ju-yu. "Issues of Public Service in the Themes of Chinese Court Painting," Ph.D. dissertation, University of California, Berkeley, 1989.

Jao Tsung-i. "Landscape Paintings by Chu Ta in the Chih-lo Lou Collection and Related Problems." *Journal of the Institute of Chinese Studies of the Chinese University of Hong Kong* 8, no. 2 (December 1976), pp. 507–15; English summary, pp. 516–17.

Jao Tsung-i et al., eds. *Peintures Monochromes de Dunhuang.* Paris: Ecole Francaise d'Extreme Orient, 1978.

Johnson, David, Andrew N. Nathan, and Evelyn S. Rawski, eds. *Popular Culture in Late Imperial Culture.* Berkeley: University of California Press, 1985.

Kao, Mayching. "The Painting of Ku Cheng-i and Mo Shih-lung." In Wai-ching Ho, ed., *Proceedings of the Tung Ch'i-ch'ang International Symposium,* pp. 12/1–12/36. Kansas City: Nelson-Atkins Museum of Art, 1992.

Kim, Hongnam. "Chou Liang-kung and His *Tu-hua-lu* Painters." In Chu-tsing Li et al., eds., *Artists and Patrons,* pp. 189–208.

Kim, Hongnam. "Chou Liang-kung and His *Tu-hua-lu* (Lives of Painters)." 3 vols. Ph.D dissertation, Yale University, 1985.

King, Ambrose Yeo-chi. "Kuan-hsi and Network Building: A Sociological Interpretation," *Daedalus* (Spring 1991), pp. 63–84.

Kohara, Hironobu, ed. *Tô Kishô no shoga* (Tung Ch'i-ch'ang's Paintings and Calligraphy). 2 vols. Tokyo: 1984.

Kris, Ernst and Otto Kurz. *Legend, Myth, and Magic in the Image of the Artist: A Historical Experiment.* New Haven: Yale University Press, 1979.

Kuo, Jason Chi-sheng. "Hui-chou Merchants as Art Patrons in the Late Sixteenth and Early Seventeenth Centuries." In Chu-tsing Li et al., eds., *Artists and Patrons,* pp. 177–88.

Lachman, Charles. *Evaluations of Sung Dynasty Painters of Renown: Liu Tao-ch'un's "Sung-ch'ao ming-hua p'ing."* Leiden: E. J. Brill, 1989.

Laing, Ellen Johnston. "Ch'iu Ying's Three Patrons." *Ming Studies* 8 (Spring 1979), pp. 49–56.

Laing, Ellen Johnston. "From Elite to Popular: Transformations of Subjects in Chinese Painting." Paper for College Art Association annual meeting, session on "Cinnabar and Buddha Blue: Beyond the Colors of Ink in Chinese Painting," Chicago, February 15, 1992.

Laing, Ellen Johnston. "Sixteenth-Century Patterns of Art Patronage: Qiu Ying and the Xiang Family." *Journal of the American Oriental Society* 111, no. 1 (January–March 1991), pp. 1–7.

Laing, Ellen Johnston. "Women Painters in Traditional China." In Marsha Weidner, ed., *Flowering in the Shadows: Women in the History of Chinese and Japanese Painting,* pp. 81–101. Honolulu: University of Hawaii Press, 1990.

Lawton, Thomas. *Chinese Figure Painting.* Washington, D.C.: Freer Gallery of Art, Smithsonian Institution, 1973.

Ledderose, Lothar. "Subject Matter in Early Chinese Painting Criticism." *Oriental Art,* n.s. 19, no. 1 (Spring 1973), 69–81.

Lee, Marion Sung-hua. "Wang Hui's 'Summer Mountains, Misty Rain' (dated 1668): A Seventeenth-Century Invocation." M.A. thesis, University of California, Berkeley, 1990.

Lee, Peihua. "Cloudy Mountains: An Amateur Style Taken by Professional Artists." M.A. thesis, University of California, Berkeley, 1990.

Lee, Rensselaer W. *Ut Pictura Poesis: The Humanistic Theory of Painting.* New York: Norton, 1967.

Lee, Stella. "Art Patronage of Shanghai in the Nineteenth Century." In Chu-tsing Li et al., eds., *Artists and Patrons,* pp. 223–31.

Levenson, Joseph R. "The Amateur Ideal in Ming and Early Ch'ing Society: Evidence from Painting." In John K. Fairbank, ed., *Chinese Thought and Institutions,* pp. 320–41.

Li, Chu-tsing and James C. Y. Watt, eds. *The Chinese Scholar's Studio: Artistic Life in the Late Ming Period.* New York and London: Thames and Hudson, published in association with the Asia Society Galleries, 1987.

Li, Chu-tsing et al., eds. *Artists and Patrons: Some Social and Economic Aspects of Chinese Painting.* A publication of the Kress Foundation Department of Art History, University of Kansas. Kansas City and Seattle: Nelson-Atkins Museum of Art in cooperation with the University of Washington Press, 1989.

Liscomb, Kathlyn. "Wang Fu's Contribution to the Formation of a New Painting Style in the Ming Dynasty." *Artibus Asiae* 49 (1987), pp. 39–78.

Liscomb, Kathlyn. "The Role of Leading Court Officials as Patrons of Painting in the Fifteenth Century." *Ming Studies* 27 (1989), pp. 34–62.

Lovell, Hin-cheung. *An Annotated Bibliography of Chinese Painting: Catalogues and Related Texts.* Michigan Papers in Chinese Studies, no. 16. Ann Arbor: Center for Chinese Studies, University of Michigan, 1973.

Marsh, Robert M. *The Mandarins: The Circulation of Elites in China, 1600–1900.* New York or Glencoe: Free Press of Glencoe, 1961.

Moss, Paul, *The Literati Mode: Chinese Scholar Paintings, Calligraphy, and Desk Objects.* London: Sydney L. Moss, 1986.

Murck, Alfreda. "Yuan Jiang: Image Maker." *Chinese Painting Under the Qianlong Emperor,* vol. 2. *Phoebus* 6, no. 2, pp. 228–59.

Murck, Alfreda and Wen C. Fong, eds. *Words and Images: Chinese Poetry, Calligraphy, and Painting.* New York: Metropolitan Museum of Art, 1991.

Murray, Julia. "Welcoming the Imperial Carriage and Its Colophon: A Monument Recovered." Paper for workshop on "Paintings and Their Colophons," College Art Association meeting, San Francisco, February 1989.

Oertling, Sewall, II. "Patronage in Anhui During the Wan-li Period." In Chu-tsing Li et al., eds., *Artists and Patrons,* pp. 165–76.

Owyoung, Steven D. "The Formation of the Family Collection of Huang Tz'u and Huang Lin." In Chu-tsing Li et al, eds., *Artists and Patrons,* pp. 111–26.

Podro, Michael. *The Critical Historians of Art.* New Haven and London: Yale University Press, 1982.

Pohl, Karl-Heinz. *Cheng Pan-ch'iao: Poet, Painter, and Calligrapher.* Nettetal: Steyler, 1990.

Powers, Martin J. *Art and Political Expression in Early China.* New Haven and London: Yale University Press, 1991.

Rawski, Evelyn S. "Economic and Social Foundations of Late Imperial Culture." In Johnson, Nathan, and Rawski, eds., *Popular Culture in Late Imperial Culture.* pp. 3–33.

Rhi, Ju-hyung. "The Subjects and Context of Chinese Birthday Paintings." M.A. thesis, University of California, Berkeley, 1986.

Riely, Celia Carrington. "Tung Ch'i-ch'ang (1555–1636) and the Interplay of Politics and Art." A Chinese translation appeared in *Duoyun* 23 (1989), no. 4, pp. 97–108.

Riely, Celia Carrington. "Tung Ch'i-ch'ang's Life." In Wai-kam Ho, ed., *The Century of Tung Ch'i-ch'ang,* 2:387–457.

Rogers, Howard. "Hu Ching's *Kuo-ch'ao yüan-hua lu* and the Ch'ing Imperial Collection of Paintings." Manuscript.

Rogers, Howard et al. John Stevenson, ed. Introduction by Sherman E. Lee. *Masterworks of Ming and Qing Painting from the Forbidden City.* Lansdale: International Arts Council, 1988.

Ropp, Paul S., ed. *Heritage of China: Contemporary Perspectives on Chinese Civilization.* Berkeley and Oxford: University of California Press, 1990.

Rosenzweig, Daphne Lange. "Reassessment of Painters and Paintings at the Early Ch'ing Court." In Chu-tsing Li et al., eds., *Artists and Patrons,* pp. 75–86.

Rowe, William T. "Modern Chinese Social History." In Paul S. Ropp, ed., *Heritage of China,* pp. 242–62.

Rudolph, Richard. "Kuo Pi and His Diary." *Ars Orientalis* 3 (1959), pp. 175–88.

Ruitenbeeck, Klaas. "Gao Qipei and the Art of Finger Painting." *Proceedings of the International Colloquium on Chinese Art History,* July 20–24, 1991. Part 1: *Painting and Callligraphy.* 2 vols. Taipei: National Palace Museum.

Sensabaugh, David. "Guests at Jade Mountain: Aspects of Patronage in Fourteenth-Century K'un-shan." In Chu-tsing Li et al., eds., *Artists and Patrons,* pp. 93–100.

Sensabaugh, David. "Life at Jade Mountain: Notes on the Life of the Man of Letters in Fourteenth-Century Wu Society." In *Suzuki Kei Sensei kanreki kinen Chûgoku kaiga-she ronshû* (Essays on Chinese Painting: Festschrift for Professor Suzuki Kei), pp. 45–69. Tokyo: 1981.

Shan, Guoqiang. "The Tendency Toward Mergence of the Two Great Traditions in Late Ming Painting." In Waiching Ho, ed., *Proceedings of the Tung Ch'i-ch'ang International Symposium,* pp. 3/1–3/28.

Siggstedt, Mette. "Zhou Chen: The Life and Paintings of a Ming Professional Artist." *Bulletin of the Museum of Far Eastern Antiquities*, no. 54 (1982), pp. 1–239.

Silbergeld, Jerome. "Chinese Concepts of Old Age and Their Role in Chinese Painting, Painting Theory, and Criticism." *Art Journal* 46, no. 2 (Summer 1987), pp. 103–14.

Silbergeld, Jerome. *Chinese Painting Style: Media, Methods, and Principles of Form.* Seattle: University of Washington Press, 1982.

Silbergeld, Jerome. "Kung Hsien: A Professional Chinese Artist and His Patronage." *Burlington Magazine*, no. 940 (July 1981), pp. 400–410.

Silbergeld, Jerome and Amy McNair. "Translators' Introduction" to Yu Feian, *Chinese Painting Colors: Studies of Their Preparation and Application in Traditional and Modern Times*, pp. ix–xiv. Seattle: University of Washington Press, 1988.

Siren, Osvald. *Chinese Painting: Leading Masters and Principles.* 7 vols. London and New York: Lund Humphries and Ronald Press, 1956–58.

Sivin, Nathan. "Ailment and Cure in Traditional China: A Study of Classical and Popular Medicine Before Modern Times, with Implications for the Present." Manuscript, courtesy of the author.

Skinner, William, ed. *The City in Late Imperial China.* Stanford: Stanford University Press, 1977.

Soong, James. "A Visual Experience in Nineteenth-Century China: Jen Po-nien (1840–1895) and the Shanghai School of Painting." Ph.D. dissertation, Stanford University, 1977.

Soper, Alexander. "Standards of Quality in Northern Sung Painting." *Archives of the Chinese Art Society of America* 11 (1957), pp. 8–15.

Soper, Alexander. *Textual Evidence for the Secular Arts of China in the Period from Liu Sung through Sui.* Ascona: *Artibus Asiae* Publishers, 1967.

Soper, Alexander, trans. *Kuo Jo-Hsü's Experiences in Painting (T'u-hua chien-wen chih): An Eleventh-Century History of Chinese Painting.* Washington, D.C.: American Council of Learned Societies, 1951.

Spence, Jonathan D. *The Death of Woman Wang.* 1978; reprint, New York: Penguin Books, 1979.

Spence, Jonathan D. "Western Perceptions of China from the Late Sixteenth Century to the Present." In Paul S. Ropp, ed., *Heritage of China*, pp. 1–14.

Strassberg, Richard. *The World of K'ung Shang-jen: A Man of Letters in Early Ch'ing China.* New York: Columbia University Press, 1983.

Sturman, Peter. "Cranes Above Kaifeng: The Auspicious Image at the Court of Huizong." *Ars Orientalis* 20 (1990), pp. 33–68.

Sullivan, Michael. "Some Notes on the Social History of Art." In *Proceedings of the International Conference on Sinology*, Section on History of Art, Taipei, Academia Sinica, 1982, pp. 159–70.

Sung, Hou-mei. "From the Min-Che Tradition to the Che School (Part 2). Precursors of the Che School: Hsieh Huan and Tai Chin." *Ku-kung hsüeh-shu chi-k'an* (National Palace Museum Quarterly) 7:1 (Autumn 1989), pp. 127–32; English text, pp. 1–15.

Suzuki Kei Sensei kanreki kinen Chûgoku kaiga-shi ronshû (Essays on Chinese Painting: Festschrift for Professor Suzuki Kei). Tokyo: 1981.

Tai, Doris Jung Chu. "T'ang Yin, 1470–1524: The Man and his Art." Ph.D. dissertation, University of Pittsburgh, 1979.

Tang, Weikuen. "A Study of the Patronage and Meaning of Yü Chih-ting's Portrait Paintings." Manuscript, qualifying paper, 1988.

Tsao, Hsingyuan. "Art as a Means of Self-Cultivation and Social Intercourse: On the Social Function of Dong Qichang's Art." M.A. thesis, University of California, Berkeley, 1991.

Tsao, Hsingyuan. "Dong Qichang and Li Rihua: Literati Ideals and Socioeconomic Realities," pp. 21–22. Paper for seminar on "The Painter's Practice in China," University of California, Berkeley, Fall 1989.

Tseng, Yu-ho Ecke. "A Reconsideration of 'Ch'uan-mo I-hsieh,' the Sixth Principle of Hsieh Ho." *Proceedings of the International Symposium on Chinese Painting*, pp. 313–333. Taipei, 1972.

van Briessen, Fritz. *The Way of the Brush: Painting Techniques of China and Japan.* 7th ed. Rutland, Vt.: C. E. Tuttle, 1974.

van der Sprenkel, Sybille. "Urban Social Control." In William Skinner, ed., *The City in Late Imperial China.*

van Gulik, Robert H. *Chinese Pictorial Art as Viewed by the Connoisseur.* Rome: Istituto Italiano per il Medio ed Estremo Oriente, 1958.

Vinograd, Richard. *Boundaries of the Self: Chinese Portraits, 1600–1900.* Cambridge: Cambridge University Press, 1992.

Vinograd, Richard. "Family Properties: Personal Context and Cultural Pattern in Wang Meng's Pien

Mountains of 1366." *Ars Orientalis* 8 (1982), pp. 1–29.

Wakeman, Frederic, Jr. *The Great Enterprise: The Manchu Reconstruction of Imperial Order in Seventeenth-Century China.* 2 vols. Berkeley: University of California Press, 1985.

Waley, Arthur. *A Catalogue of Paintings Recovered from Tun-huang by Sir Aurel Stein, K.C.I.E.* Preserved in the Subdepartment of Oriental Prints and Drawings in the British Museum, and in the Museum of Central Asian Antiques, Delhi, India. London: Trustees of the British Museum and the government of India, 1931.

Wang Fangyu and Richard Barnhart. *Master of the Lotus Garden: The Life and Art of Bada Shanren.* New Haven: Yale University Press, 1990.

Watt, James C. Y. "The Literati Environment" In Chu-tsing Li and James C. Y. Watt, eds., *The Chinese Scholar's Studio,* pp. 1–22.

Weidner, Marsha et al., eds. *Views from the Jade Terrace: Chinese Women Artists, 1300–1912.* Bloomington: Indiana University Press, 1988.

Wilson, Marc F. and Kwan S. Wong. *Friends of Wen Cheng-ming: A View from the Crawford Collection.* New York: China House Gallery, 1975.

Wittkower, Margot and Rudolf Wittkower. *Born Under Saturn: The Character and Conduct of the Artist.* London: Weidenfeld and Nicolson, 1963.

Wong, Kwan S. "Hsiang Yüan-pien and Suchou Artists." In Chu-tsing Li et al., eds., *Artists and Patrons,* pp. 155–58.

Wu, Marshall. "Jin Nong: The Eccentric Painter with a Wintry Heart." In Ju-hsi Chou and Claudia Brown, eds., *Chinese Painting Under the Qianlong Emperor,* pp. 272–94.

Wu, William Ding Yee. "Kung Hsien (ca. 1619–1689)." Ph.D. dissertation, Princeton University, 1979.

Wu, William Ding Yee. "Kung Hsien's Style and His Sketchbooks," *Oriental Art* n.s. 16, no. 1 (Spring 1970), pp. 72–80.

Yang Boda. "The Development of the Ch'ien-lung Painting Academy." In Alfreda Murck and Wen C. Fong, eds., *Words and Images,* pp. 333–56.

Yang Xin. *Ch'eng Cheng-k'uei.* Shanghai, 1982.. In Chung-kuo hua-chia ts'ung-shu series.

Yao, Dajuin. "The Pleasure of Reading Drama: Illustrations to the Hongzhi Edition of *The Story of the Western Wing.*" In Wang Shifu, *The Moon and the Zither: The Story of the Western Wing,* pp. 437–68. Ed. and trans. by Stephen H. West and Wilt L. Idema. Berkeley: University of California Press, 1991,

Yuhas, Louise. "Wang Shih-chen as Patron." In Chu-tsing Li et al., eds., *Artists and Patrons,* pp. 139–54.

Illustrations

Frontispiece: Tu Chin, "Ladies in a Garden." Section of a handscroll, ink and colors on silk.

Li Shih-ta, "The Elegant Gathering in the West Garden." Section of handscroll, ink and colors on paper.

1.1. Cheng Min, "Old Trees by a Bridge." Small hanging scroll, ink on paper. 3

1.2. Cheng Min, "Viewing a Waterfall." Leaf, ink on paper. 5

1.3. Chao Meng-fu, "Orchids, Bamboo, and Rocks." Small hanging scroll, ink on silk. 6

1.4. Wu Pin, "The Road to Shang-yin." Handscroll, ink and colors on paper. 8

1.5. Chu Ta (Pa-ta Shan-jen), "Flowers Growing on a Cliff." Panel from screen, ink on silk. 9

1.6. Attributed to Tung Yüan, "Wintry Grove and Layered Banks." Hanging scroll, ink and light colors on silk. 13

1.7. Wen Jih-kuan, "Grapes." Horizontal painting, ink on paper. 14

1.8. Ch'en Hung-shou, "A Tall Pine and Taoist Immortal (Self-Portrait in a Landscape)." Hanging scroll, ink and colors on silk. 15

1.9. Ma Shih. "Watching Geese on an Autumn River." Short handscroll, ink on paper. 16

1.10. Wang E, "Farewell to Sasaki Nagaharu." Handscroll, ink on paper. 17

1.11. Wu Wei, "Farewell at Lung-chiang." Handscroll, ink on paper. 17

1.12. Ni Tsan, "Bamboo, Rock, and Frosty Trees." Hanging scroll, ink on paper. 18

1.13. Ch'en Hung-shou. "Scenes from the Life of T'ao Yüan-ming." Section of handscroll, ink and light colors on silk. 19

1.14 (left). Shen Ch'üan, "Pines and Cranes." Hanging scroll, ink and colors on silk. 20
1.14 (right). Li Shan, "Cranes and Pines, for the Seventieth Birthday of Huang-weng." Hanging scroll, ink and colors on paper. 20
1.15 (left). Chou Chih-mien,"Paired Swallows and Mandarin Ducks." Hanging scroll, ink and colors on silk. 21
1.15 (right). Jen I, "Pairs of Birds with Pine Tree." Ink and colors on paper. 21
1.16. Cheng Hsieh, "Bamboo Growing by Rocks." Hanging scroll, ink on paper. 22
1.17. Chin Nung, "Branches of Blossoming Plum." Hanging scroll, ink and color on paper. 23
1.18. Wang Meng, "Dwelling in the Ch'ing-pien Mountains." Hanging scroll, ink on paper. 24
1.19. Wen Cheng-ming, "Farewell to Te-fou." Hanging scroll, ink on paper. 26
1.20. Anonymous (old attribution to Tung Yüan), "A Taoist Temple in the Mountains." Hanging scroll, ink and colors on silk. 28
1.21. Detail from the same painting. 29
1.22. Ho Ch'eng, "Illustrations to T'ao Yüan-ming's 'Homecoming' Ode." Handscroll, ink on paper. 30
1.23. T'ang Yin, "Auspicious Clouds Over Yeh-t'ing (Wilderness Pavilion)." Section of a handscroll, ink and colors on paper. 31
2.1. General View of the Main Hall of a Chinese House. Drawing by Tai Nien-tz'u. 34
2.2. Lan Ying and Ch'en Yü-yin, "A Gentleman Celebrating His Birthday." Screen consisting of twelve hanging scrolls, ink and colors on silk. 35
2.3. Ch'iu Ying, "Divine Realm at the Peach-Blossom Spring." Hanging scroll, ink and colors on silk. 36
2.4. Kung Hsien, "Summer Mountains After Rain." Hanging scroll, ink on silk. 38
2.5. Ch'ien Ku, "Pictorial Record of a Journey from T'ai-ts'ang to Yangchou." Leaf, ink and light colors on paper. 40
2.6. Fei Tan-hsü, "Portrait of General Ch'u-chiang by Moonlight." Hanging scroll, ink and colors on paper. 42
2.7. Jen Hsiung, "Lady in Garden." Leaf, ink and colors on paper. 43
2.8. Hua Yen, "Cranes in Pines." Hanging scroll, ink and colors on silk. 44
2.9. Hsi Kang, "Mist and Haze in Autumn Mountains." Hanging scroll, ink on paper. 45
2.10. Anonymous, "Painting and Antiques Store." Section of a *fen-pen* (draft sketch) handscroll, ink on paper. 46
2.11. Chou Hsün, "Dragon in Clouds." Hanging scroll, ink on silk. 47
2.12. "Painting and Antique Markets." Detail from a handscroll, ink and colors on silk. 48
2.13. Ch'eng Cheng-k'uei, "Imaginary Travels Among Streams and Mountains." Section of a handscroll, ink and light colors on paper. 49
2.14. Tung Ch'i-ch'ang, "Drawing Water in the Morning." Hanging scroll, ink and colors on silk. 51
2.15. Anonymous (old attribution to Chao Ch'ang), "Plants and Butterflies." Section of handscroll, ink and colors on paper. 52
2.16. Chin Nung, "Stalks of Bamboo." Hanging scroll, ink on paper. 53
2.17. Lu Wei, "Travelers on a High Plateau." Hanging scroll, ink and colors on silk. 55
2.18. Wei Chih-huang, "A Thousand Cliffs Contend in Splendor." Section of a handscroll, ink and colors on paper. 56
2.19. Chang Hsün, "Landscape." Hanging scroll. 57
2.20. Shih-t'ao, "Bamboo, Orchids, Plantain, Pine, and Other Plants by a River." Section of a 12-fold screen, ink on paper. 58
2.21. Wan Shou-ch'i, "Landscape." Leaf, ink on paper. 59
2.22. Ch'en Hung-shou, "Spring Breeze and Butterflies." Handscroll, ink and colors on silk. 60
2.23. Hsü Wei, "Crab, Fish, and Vegetables." Section of a handscroll, ink on paper. 61
2.24. Ch'en Hung-shou, "Beautiful Woman with Fan." Hanging scroll, ink and colors on paper. 62
2.25. Huang Shen, "Lady Carrying a Ch'in." Hanging scroll, ink on paper. 63
2.26. Ts'ui Tzu-chung, "The Artist and His Host Saying Farewell in a Garden." Detail from hanging scroll, ink and colors on silk. 66
2.27. Anonymous, "Clearing the Mountains." Section of a handscroll, ink and colors on silk. 68
2.28. After T'ang Yin, "Great River at Entrance to Gorge." Leaf, ink and colors on silk. 69
2.29. Chang Feng, "Landscape." Leaf, ink on paper. 70
3.1. Ni Tsan, "River Pavilion, Mountain Colors." Hanging scroll, ink on paper. 73
3.2. Wen Cheng-ming, "Stone Cliff and Rainbow." Hanging scroll, ink on paper. 75
3.3. Ch'ien Ku, "Waiting for a Guest in a Mountain

Dwelling." Hanging scroll, ink and colors on paper. 76
3.4. Hsieh Pin, "Portrait of a Man" (setting painted by Lan Ying and Chu Sheng). Hanging scroll, ink and colors on silk. 76
3.5. Ch'en Hung-shou, "Lady Hsüan-wen-chün Giving Instruction on the Classic." Hanging scroll, ink and colors on silk. 77
3.6. T'ang Yin, "Enjoying Chrysanthemums by the Eastern Fence." Hanging scroll, ink and colors on paper. 78
3.7. Yüan Chiang. "The East Garden." Section of a handscroll, ink and colors on silk. 79
3.8. Attributed to Shen Chou, "The East Garden." Leaf, ink and colors on paper. 80
3.9. Ch'en Hung-shou, "Three Pines." Hanging scroll, ink and colors on silk. 81
3.10. Hsü Wei, "Boy Flying Kite." Section of a handscroll, ink on paper. 82
3.11. Wang San-hsi, "Autumn Landscape." Hanging scroll, ink and light colors on paper. 83
3.12. Leng Mei, "Amorous Couple." Leaf, ink and colors on silk. 84
3.13. Min Chen, "Portrait of Pa Wei-tsu." Detail of a hanging scroll, ink and colors on paper. 85
3.14. Ch'en Hung-shou, "Lotus and Rock." Detail from a hanging scroll, ink on paper. 87
3.15. Lo P'ing, "Portrait of Yüan Mei." Hanging scroll, ink and colors on paper. 88
3.16. Lang Shih-ning (Giuseppe Castiglione, 1688–1766), "One Hundred Horses (*fen-pen*, or draft). Section of a handscroll, ink on paper. 89
3.17. Lang Shih-ning (Giuseppe Castiglione, 1688–1766), "One Hundred Horses." Section of a handscroll, ink and colors on silk. 89
3.18. Ch'ien Hui-an, "The Night Journey of Chung K'uei and His Sister." Fan painting, *fen-pen*, ink on paper. 90
3.19. Li Jih-hua, "Landscape in Huang Kung-wang Manner." Leaf, ink on paper. 91
3.20. Wu Hsing-tseng, "Portrait of Chi Huang." Detail from a hanging scroll, ink and colors on paper. 92
3.21. Anonymous, "Portrait of Ko Yin-liang" Leaf, ink and colors on paper. 93
3.22. Anonymous, preparatory sketches (*fen-pen*) for a Buddhist painting. Section of a scroll, ink on paper. 94
3.23. Attributed to Wu Ts'ung-yüan, "Celestial Rulers of Taoism in Procession." Section of handscroll, ink on silk. 95
3.24. Anonymous (old attribution to Wu Tao-tzu), "Taoist Deity in the Clouds." Leaf. 96
3.25. Ku Chien-lung, "Various Scenes." Leaf, ink on paper. 97
3.26. Attributed to Hu Kuei, "Tartar Horses on a Plain." Section of a handscroll, ink (and slight colors?) on silk. 98
3.27. Tung Ch'i-ch'ang, "Rocks." Leaf, ink on paper. 99
3.28. After Ni Tsan, "Trees." Leaf, ink on paper. 100
3.29. Chou Ch'en, "Beggars and Street Characters." Leaves mounted on handscroll, ink and colors on paper. 101
3.30. Huang Ch'üan, "Birds and Insects Drawn from Life." Short handscroll, ink and colors on silk. 101
3.31. Anonymous, "One Hundred Horses." Section of handscroll, ink and colors on silk. 102
3.32. Ch'en Hung-shou, Two leaves from *Shui-hu yeh-tzu* (Water Margin Playing Cards): Wu Yung, Hsiao Hsiang. 103
3.33. Wang Chia-chin, "Tai K'uei Receiving the Emissary." Hanging scroll and detail from same, ink on paper. 104–5
3.34. Li Jih-hua, "Landscape with Houses." Section of handscroll, ink on paper. 106
3.35. Kao Ch'i-p'ei, "Chung K'uei" (finger painting). Hanging scroll, ink and colors on paper. 108
3.36 (left). Ch'en Hung-shou and Yen Chan, "Female Immortals." Hanging scroll, ink and colors on silk. 109
3.36 (center). Ch'en Hung-shou, "Immortals Presenting Symbols of Longevity." Hanging scroll, ink and colors on silk. 109
3.36 (right). Ch'en Hung-shou, "Female Immortals." 109
3.37. Ch'en Hung-shou, Yen Chan, and Li Wan-sheng, "Portrait of Ho T'ien-chang." Handscroll, ink and colors on silk. 110
3.38. Wang I and Ni Tsan, "Portrait of Yang Chu-hsi Walking with a Staff." Section of a handscroll, ink on paper. 111
4.1. Anonymous, "Deer in an Autumn Forest." Detail from a hanging scroll, ink and colors on silk. 115
4.2. Anonymous (old attribution to Hsü Hsi), "Bamboo and Old Tree Growing by Rocks." Hanging scroll, ink on silk. 116
4.3. Anonymous, "The Night Attack on the Sanjō Palace," from Heiji Monogatari scroll. Section of a handscroll, ink and colors on paper. 117

4.4. Jen I, "Chung K'uei Killing a Demon." Hanging scroll, ink and colors on paper. 118

4.5. Anonymous, Sung period, "Exorcism Dance." Hanging scroll, ink and colors on silk. 119

4.6. Anonymous, "Blind Men Fighting." Hanging scroll, ink and colors on silk. 120

4.7. Anonymous (attributed to Wei Hsien), "Flour Mill Powered by Water Wheel." Detail from a handscroll, ink and colors on silk. 121

4.8. Anonymous, "Water Mill on a Mountain Stream." Detail from a hanging scroll, ink and colors on silk. 121

4.9. Yen Hui, "The Taoist Magician Li T'ieh-kuai." Hanging scroll, ink on silk. 122

4.10. Wu Wei, "A Myriad Miles of the Yangtze River." Section of a handscroll, ink and light colors on silk. 124

4.11. T'ang Yin, "The Courtesan Li Tuan-tuan Presenting a Peony to the Poet Chang Ku." Detail from a hanging scroll, ink and colors on paper. 125

4.12. Chao Meng-fu, "Village By the Water." Detail from a handscroll, ink on paper. 127

4.13. Chao Meng-fu, Inscription from "Sheep and Goat." Handscroll, ink on paper. 127

4.14. Ch'iu Ying, "Examining Antiquities." Detail from an album leaf, ink and colors on silk. 129

4.15. Yü Chih-ting, "Ch'iao Lai in His Study." Hanging scroll, ink and colors on silk. 130

4.16. Wang Chih-jui, "Landscape." Hanging scroll, ink on paper. 131

4.17. Kung Hsien, "Thatched Houses on a Lakeshore." Hanging scroll, ink on paper. 133

4.18. Ch'ien Hsüan, "Lotuses." Handscroll, ink and light colors on paper. 135

4.19. Wang Hui (false signature of Hsü Tao-ning), "Heavy Snow on a Mountain Pass." Hanging scroll, ink and colors on silk. 137

4.20. Emperor Hui-tsung. "Auspicious Cranes Over the Palace." Leaf mounted in a handscroll, ink and colors on silk. 138

4.21. Chou Ch'en, "The Peach-Blossom Spring." Hanging scroll, ink and colors on silk. 140

4.22. Tung Ch'i-ch'ang, "Landscape in the Manner of Wang Hsia and Li Ch'eng." Hanging scroll, ink on paper. 141

4.23. Tung Ch'i-ch'ang (ghostpainted?), "Landscape for K'o-hsüeh." Section of a handscroll, ink and colors on paper. 143

4.24. Chin Nung, "Branches of Blossoming Plum." Hanging scroll, ink on paper. 144

4.25. Chin Nung, "Chung K'uei." Hanging scroll, ink and colors on paper. 145

4.26. Chin Nung, "Self Portrait: Walking with a Staff." Hanging scroll, ink on paper. 146

4.27 (top). Chin Nung, "Blossoming Plum." Fan painting, ink on mica-powdered paper. 147

4.27 (bottom). Lo P'ing, "Blossoming Plum." Fan painting, ink on mica-powdered paper. 147

Index

Page numbers in italics indicate illustrations.

Academy, 16, 17, 26, 69, 88, 93, 139
Acker, William, 161n87
Agents, 29, 40, 45
Alpers, Svetlana, 11, 144, 167n96
Alsop, Joseph, 150n18
Amateur ideal, 150n6
Amateurism, 5, 9, 22
Amateur painters, *see* Scholar-amateur
An Lu-shan, 64
Andrews, Julia, 150n12, 164n34
Anhui School, 3, 102, 136, 150n17
Antiques, 59, 128
Apprentices, 102, 105
Artist-in-residence, 65, 67, 69
Assistants, 18, 102, 105, 107, 136; *see also* Apprentices
Audience, 131, 145
Authenticity, 142

Bamboo, 21, 23, 53, 115
Barnhart, Richard, 96, 150n14, 151n20, 161nn65, 73, 88, 162n11, 163nn20, 23, 165n68
Baxandall, Michael, 79, 128, 159n19
Beijing, 48, 67
Bellini, Giovanni, 72
Biography, 7, 32, 64
Birthday, 27, 34, 52, 75, 81, 109
Birthday paintings, 19, 23, 36, 150n8
Blind men, 117, *120*
Bourdieu, Pierre, 164nn42, 43
Brotherton, Elizabeth, 152n45, 165n68
Brown, Claudia, 152n44, 157n93
Brushwork, 6, 114, 123, 126, 113–48 *passim*; *see also* Hand of painter
Bryson, Norman, 33, 114, 152n2, 162n3
Buddhist paintings, 93, 105
Burkus, Anne, 7, 37, 74, 109,

Burkus, Anne (*continued*) 150*n*8, 153*n*13, 158*n*6, 159*nn*11, 40, 162*n*92
Bush, Susan, 163*n*21

Cai Xingyi, 154*n*31, 156*nn*69, 76, 157*n*101, 160*n*56, 161*n*75, 167*n*99
Calligraphy, 27, 54, 56, 83, 106, 114, 123, 126, 127, 133, 144
Cash payment, 36, 50, 53, 67, 83
Castiglione, Giuseppe (Lang Shih-ning), 88, 89
Cha Shih-piao, 49
Chan Ching-feng, 39, 46, 130, 153*n*17, 155*n*40, 165*n*71
Ch'an, 12
Chang Feng, 67, *70*
Chang Hsiu, 54
Chang Hsün, 54, *57*
Chang Hung, 154*n*23
Chang Keng, 154*n*38
Chang Nan-pen, 117
Chang Lu, 84
Chang Ssu-chiao, 43
Chang Ta-ch'ien, 136, 165*n*60, 166*n*72
Chang Tai, 86
Chang Tsai, 161*n*87
Chang T'ung, 64
Chang Yen-yüan, 123, 125, 128, 163*n*26
Chang-wu chih, 33
Chao Ch'ang, 50, 88, 107
Chao Chih-ch'ien, 65, 157*n*116
Chao Ch'iung, 142
Chao Hsien, 154*n*28
Chao Hsi-ku, 8, 115, 128
Chao Kan, 100
Chao Lin, 25
Chao Meng-fu, 6, *6*, 27, 64, 127, *127*, 129
Chao Tso, 142
Chao Tzu-yün, 141
Ch'ao Yüeh-chih, 139
Ch'ao-yin, 26
Chekiang, province, 90, 103
Ch'en Chi-ju, 37, 95, 142
Ch'en Hung, 110
Ch'en Hung-shou, 7, 15, *15*, 18, 20, 59, 60, 61, 62, 81, 82, 84, 86, 87, 102, 103, *103*, 107, 109, 127, 131, 151*n*31, 156*n*83
Ch'en Man-sheng, 112
Ch'en Ming-ju, 107
Ch'en Ting-shan, 154*n*28
Ch'en Tzu, 103
Ch'en Yu-yin, 34, *35*
Cheng Ch'ien, 64
Cheng Chün, 16
Cheng Hsia, 139, 163*n*16
Cheng Hsieh, 21, 22, 54, 56, 60, 64, 143,
Cheng Hsien, 134
Cheng Min, 3, *3*, 4, 5, 22
Cheng P'an-ch'iao, *see* Cheng Hsieh
Cheng Wei, 156*n*73
Ch'eng Cheng-k'uei, 40, 49, *49*, 65, 155*nn*50, 52
Ch'eng Ching-e, 40
Ch'eng Chi-po, 129
Che School, 84
Ch'i Kung, 167*n*86
Ch'i Pai-shih, 146
Chia-hsing, 105
Chiang Chao-shen, 166*n*72
Chiang Pao-ling, 155*n*45
Chiang T'ing-hsi, 141
Chieh-tzu-yüan hua-chuan, 100
Ch'ien Ch'ien-i, 129, 142
Ch'ien Hsüan, 135, *135*, 136
Ch'ien Hui-an, 88, 90
Ch'ien Ku, 40, *40*, 58, 74, *76*, 139
Ch'ien T'ung-ai, 29, *30*
Ch'ien-lung emperor, 67, 103
Children, 23
Chin, Sandi, 150*n*17, 155*n*41
Chin Nung, 23, 53, *53*, 58, 105, 134, 141, 143, *144*, 145, *146–47*, 148, 164*n*48
Chin Ts'ung, 156*n*89
Ch'in (zither), 30
Ching Hao, 77
Ch'ing-pien Mountains, 24, *25*
Ch'iu, A. Kaiming, 161*n*71
Ch'iu Shih, 103
Ch'iu Ying, 36, 50, 52, 59, 67, 72, 86, 91, 102, 141, 153*n*8
Cho Erh-kan, 39
Chou Ch'en, 67, 96, 98, *101*, 120, 139, *140*, 166*n*72
Chou Ch'i, 80
Chou Fang, 86
Chou Feng-lai, 52
Chou Hsün, 46, *47*
Chou Liang-kung, 18, 45, 54, 67, 74, 82, 86, 136, 142, 153*n*12, 156*nn*71, 72, 159*n*18, 165*nn*58, 59
Chü Chieh, 53
Chu I-tsun, 142
Chu Lang, 136, 139, 165*n*71
Chu Ta, (Pa-ta Shan-jen), 9, 18, 40, 52, 77, 82, 83
Chu T'ing-ku, 143
Chu Yüan-chang, 25
Chu Yün-ming, 135
Chü-shih (retired scholar-official), 132
Chuang-tzu, 123
Chung K'uei, 33, 90, *108*, 116, 143, *145*
Clapp, Anne de Coursey, 27, 49, 74, 77, 152*nn*47–52, 155*n*48, 158*nn*5, 124, 159*n*14
Clearing the Mountains, *see Sou-shan t'u*
Clubs for artists, 48
Clunas, Craig, 150*n*19, 153*nn*4, 6, 155*n*39, 156*n*69, 164*nn*34, 36, 40
Collaborations, 18, 27, 109, 110
Collecting, 11, 33, 128
Collectors, 45, 150*n*17
Colophons, 26, 27
Coloring, 19, 103, 107, 136
Commemorative paintings, 27
Commissions, 27, 35, 40, 48, 56, 107
Commodification, 132, 134, 145

Compound brushwork, 127
Concubines, 24, 61, 142
Connoisseur, 128, 130
Connoisseurship, 11, 12, 114
Contag, Victoria, 150*n*13
Copying, 67, 94, 95, 138
Corot, Camille, 164*n*55
Court painting, *see* Academy
Courtesans, 69, 70, 124, 132, 133; *see also* Prostitutes
Cranes, 19, 43, 138, *138*
Curlander, Amy, 165*n*55

Decontextualizing, 10, 12
Dowry, 64
Drafts, *see Fen-pen*; *Hua-kao*
Dry brushwork, 127, 131
Dubosc, Jean-Pierre, 153*n*8

Eastman, Lloyd E., 158*n*2
Elman, Benjamin, 164*n*44
Erotic art, 84
Exorcist dance, 117, *119*

Fairs, 48
Fakes, 135; *see also* Forgeries
Fan K'uan, 8, 98, 115
Fan-lin, 79
Fang, Chao-ying, 161*n*18
Fang Hsün, 67, 84
Fans, 49, 52, 106
Fan shops, 48
Farewell paintings, 17, 25, 151*n*27, 152*n*40
Fei Tan-hsü, 41, *42*
Fen-pen (draft sketch), 46, 84, 88, 90, 94, 96, *96*, *97*, 160*n*57
Feng Ch'iu-ho, 61
Fire, 117
Fishing, 23
Fong, Mary H., 160*n*57, 165*n*69
Food, 53, 60, 132
Forgeries, 18, 46, 135, 136, 145; *see also* Fakes; Ghostpainters
Foucault, Michel, 100, 161*n*70
Frankel, Hans H., 163*n*30
Fraser, Sarah, 160*n*57
Fu, Marilyn, 152*n*36
Fu, Shen, 152*nn*36, 41, 162*n*1, 164*n*39, 165*n*60
Fu Pao-shih, 146
Fu-pen, see Fen-pen
Fukumoto, Masakazu, 166*n*80, 167*n*86
Functionalism, 128, 133
Functional paintings, 17, 19, 35, 105
Funeral, 64

Garden, 77, 79, 139
Genre, 31
Gernet, Jacques, 150*n*6
Ghostpainter, 69, 105, 107, 136, 138, 139, 142, 143
Gifts and favors, 64; *see also Kuan-hsi*
Go-between, 36, 39, 41, 45, 53, 72, 83
Golas, Peter, 161*n*79
Goldberg, Stephen, 163*n*32
Gombrich, E. H., 31, 152*n*53
Grotto, 25
Guild, 105

Hamada, Shoji, 166*n*82
Han Kan, 98
Hanan, Patrick, 153*n*9, 154*n*36
Hand of the painter, 113, 134, 135, 144, 146
Handscroll, 26
Hangchou, 19,65
Hartwell, Robert M., 150*n*6
Haskell, Francis, 164*nn*52, 53
Hay, John, 163*n*12
Hay, Jonathan, 156*n*73
Heiji Wars scroll, 115
Ho, Wai-kam, 155*n*42, 159*n*13, 161*n*66, 165*n*67
Ho Ch'eng, 27, 29, 152*n*45
Ho Liang-chün, 166*n*72
Holidays, 33
Horses, 89, 99, *102*
Hospitality, 65
Hsi Kang, 43, *44*, *45*
Hsia Wen-yen, 18
Hsiang Sheng-mo, 107
Hsiang Yüan-pien, 52, 67, 153*n*6
Hsiang Yün, 143
Hsiao Yün-ts'ung, 41, 154*n*22
Hsieh, Chih-liu, 166*n*84
Hsieh Huan, 139
Hsieh Pin, 74, *76*
Hsieh-i mode, 16, 22
Hsieh-sheng, 99
Hsing-ssu (form-likeness), 114
Hsu, Ginger Cheng-chi, 22, 56, 150*n*17, 151*n*33, 152*n*35, 155*n*41 156*nn*70, 79, 157*n*105, 158*n*126, 159*n*18, 161*n*78, 164*n*48, 167*nn*90–92, 94, 95, 98
Hsü Fang, 156*n*88
Hsü Hsi, *116*
Hsü Hung-chi, 151*n*20
Hsü Kao-yang, 129
Hsü Pang-ta, 160*n*57, 161*n*76
Hsü Tao-ning, *137*
Hsü Wei, 60, 61, 82, *82*, 123
Hsü-ku, 53
Hsüan-tsung, T'ang emperor, 110
Hu Chen, 54
Hu I, 162*n*95
Hu Kuei, 95, 98
Hu Yü-k'un, 67
Hua shih (painting master), 72, 123, 124
Hua Yen, 43, 163*n*15
Hua Yün, 67
Hua-kao, 86, 88, 93; *see also Fen-pen*
Huaian, 16
Huang Ch'üan, 99, *101*, 116
Huang Chü-pao, 99
Huang Ho, 155*n*45
Huang Kung-wang, 43, 74, 88, 136, 151*n*19
Huang Lin, 154*n*25
Huang Shen, 61, 63, 105
Huang Yen-lü, 9, 18, 52
Huang Yung-ch'üan, 4, 149*n*5
Huang-ti, 20
Hui-chou, 46, 128
Hui-chou merchants, 11, 129, 130

Hui-tsung, emperor, 138, *138*
Hung-jen, 128, 136
Hyland, Alice R.M., 152*n*48, 161*n*74

I Chun-tso, 61
I Yüan-chi, 50, 67
Illusionism, 90, 114
Immortals, 25
Ink-plays, 127
Inscriptions, 26
Isabella of Spain, 72

Jang, Scarlett Ju-yu, 151*n*30, 152*n*46, 155*n*56, 157*n*119, 158*n*121, 161*n*88, 162*n*97, 165*n*70
Jao Tsung-i, 150*n*15
Japan, 17, 115
Jen Hsia, 107, 141
Jen Hsiung, 41, *43*
Jen I, 37, 54, 107, 117, *118*, 141, 153*n*10
Jen Po-nien, *see* Jen I
Ju-mien t'an, 74
Jun-li, jun-pi (moistening the brush), 4, 54, 61, 85

K'ai-feng, 139
Kan Feng-tzu, 82
Kao, Mayching, 157*n*112
Kao Ch'i-p'ei, 107, *108*
Kao Feng-han, 61, 143
Kao I, 67, 165*n*67
Kao K'o-kung, 25, 82
Kao Shih-ch'i, 110, 162*n*95, 167*n*100
Kao Wen-chin, 94
Kao-tsung, Sung emperor, 139
Keng-chih t'u, 139
Kim, Hongnam, 54, 155*n*66, 156*n*69, 158*n*128, 159*n*16, 165*n*59, 166*n*74, 167*n*88
King, Ambrose Yeo-chi, 153*n*18
Kite, 82
K'o-hsueh, 142
Kris, Ernst, 123
Ku Cheng-i, 64
Ku Chien-lung, 94, 97
Ku Ch'ing-p'u, 82
Ku Fu, 142
Ku K'ai-chih, 123
Ku Te-hui's Jade Mountain Retreat, 27
Ku-shih, 162*n*11
Ku-tung so-shih, 61
Kuan T'ung, 110
Kuan-hsi, 39, 50, 65, 74, 153*n*18
Kuan-yin, 59, 74, 82
Kung Hsien, 37, *38*, 52, 54, 65, 74, 77, 96, 132, *133*, 153*n*11
K'ung Shang-jen, 39, 49, 65, 153*n*19
Kuo, Jason Chi-sheng, 150*n*17, 164*nn*34, 37, 38
Kuo Chung-shu, 82
Kuo Hsi, 67
Kuo Jo-hsü, 7, 107, 114, 126, 150*n*9, 155*n*57, 163*n*13
Kuo Pi, 60
Kurtz, Otto, 123
Kwan, S. Wong, 153*n*6

Lachman, Charles, 159*nn*22, 23, 162*n*7
Lady Hsüan-wen-chün, 77
Laing, Ellen Johnston, 151*n*32, 155*n*58, 158*nn*123, 137
Lan Ying, 34, *35*
Landscape, 24
Lang Shih-ning, *see* Castiglione, Giuseppe
Lantern Market, 46
Lawton, Thomas, 165*n*67
Ledderose, Lothar, 163*n*12
Lee, Marion Sung-hua, 154*n*32, 159*n*10, 162*n*98
Lee, Peihua, 152*n*43
Lee, Rensselaer W., 163*n*30
Lee, Stella, 154*n*28, 161*n*86, 165*n*64
Leng Mei, 84, 103
Leonardo da Vinci, 72
Letters, 35, 37, 107, 132
Levenson, Joseph R., 150*n*6, 163*n*33
Lewis, Wyndham, 14
Li, Chu-tsing, 159*n*9
Li Ch'eng, 7, 82, 110, 115
Li Jih-hua, 90, *91*, 105, 107, 156*n*84, 160*n*50
Li Kung-lin, 99, 102, 139
Li Shih-ta, 14
Li T'ieh-kuai, 120, *122*
Li Yü, 37, 153*n*9
Liang K'ai, 123
Lieh-ch'ao shih-chi, 142
Lin Nu-erh, 70
Ling Kan-ch'u, 59
Ling-yin, mountain, 65
Liscomb, Kathlyn, 154*n*24
Li-tai ming-hua chi, 107
Literati artist, *see* Scholar-amateur
Liu, James, 154*n*36
Liu Chiu, 84
Liu Lü-ting, 65
Liu Tao-ch'un, 84, 155*n*56
Liu-li-ch'ang district, 48
Liu-min t'u, 139
Lo P'ing, 86, 88, 143, 146, *147*, 148, 163*n*15
Loehr, Max, 24
Longevity, 19, 23, 34
Lou Chu, 139
Lu Chih, 64
Lu Shih-tao, 156*n*85
Lu Wei, 53, 55, 107

Ma Ho-chih, 160*n*56
Ma Shih, 16, *16*
Ma Shih-ying, 141
Ma Yüan-yü, 141
Mandarin ducks, 20
Markets, 45, 46, *46*
Marra, Michele, 151*n*21
Marsh, Robert M., 150*n*8
McNair, Amy, 165*n*63
Medicine, 20, 30, 36, 59, 60
Merchants, 11, 18, 33, 61, 128; *see also* Hui-chou merchants
Mi Fu, 24, 82, 113, 116, 132, 164*n*45
Mi Wan-chung, 110
Mi Yu-jen, 113, 139

Min Chen, 84, 85
Moistening the brush, 4, 54, 61, 85
Monetary payments, 36, 50, 53, 67, 83
Mounters' shops, 48
Mu Sheng, 41
Mu-fu, 69
Murase, Miyeko, 151*n*27
Murray, Julia, 165*n*65
Music, 64, 123
Mustard Seed Garden Manual of Painting, 100

Nanking, 49, 67
Nanking Museum, 90
New Year's pictures, 20
Ni Tsan, 3, 18, 43, 65, 72, *73*, 88, 95, *100*, 110, *111*, 114, 127, 128
Norinaga, Motoori, 151*n*21

Occasional paintings, 19, 24, 35
Oertling II, Sewall, 150*n*17
Office, 132
Official service, 26, 27, 132
Officials, 64, 65, 139
Orchids, 21, 23
Orthodox School, 43, 67, 74
Ou-yang Hsiu, 59, 74
Owyoung, Steven D., 154*n*25

Pai-yueh, mountain, 40
Pan Yaochang, 155*n*44, 156*n*78
P'an Kung-shou, 41
Pao-kuo Ssu, 48
Paradise, 25
Pa-ta Shan-jen, *see* Chu Ta
Patronage, 22, 33, 67, 74, 103, 134, 150*n*17
Pawn shops, 86
Peach-Blossom Spring, 64, 139, *140*
Pei, General, 64
P'eng Nien, 40
Perugino, 72
Piao, Ling-hu, 163*n*16
Pines, 19, 43, 81
Playing cards, 41, *103*
Plowing and weaving, pictures of, 139
Plum, 21, 23, 143, *147*
Po Chü-i, 67
Podro, Michael, 150*n*16
Poetry, 64, 67, 123, 126
Pohl, Karl-Heinz, 157*n*91
Political gifts, 50, 65
Political meanings, 17, 26
Pornographic art, 84
Portrait, 74, 84, 86, 90, 109
Pounce, 91, 160*n*55
Powers, Martin, 164*n*43
Preface, essay, 27, 30
Prices, 46, 50, 54, 85, 106
Price lists, 22, 48, 54, 56, 58, 64, 134
Prints, 102
Professional, 35
Professional painters, 7, 14, 15, 54, 65, 77, 123
Prostitutes, 61

Quick and spontaneous art, 16

Rawski, Evelyn S., 153*n*5
Reclusion, 23, 26; *see also* Seclusion
Reily, Celia, 155*n*54, 157*n*114
Rembrandt, 11, 96, 144, 145
Retirement, 18, 20, 23, 27
Returning Home, 27
Rhi, Ju-hyung, 151*n*29
Rogers, Mary Ann, 150*n*10, 158*n*134, 162*n*91, 165*n*70
Rosa, Salvator, 134
Rosenzweig, Daphne Lange, 158*n*134, 166*n*75
Rowe, William T., 151*n*25
Rudolph, Richard, 157*n*93
Rudolph, Susanne Hoeber, 2, 149*n*3
Ruitenbeeck, Klaas, 161*n*90

Schaase, Karl, 150*n*16
Scholar-amateur, 7, 8, 16, 21, 74, 113, 123, 124, 126, 131
Scholars, The, 54
Seal carving, 56
Seclusion, 20, 25; *see also* Reclusion
Secretariat, 69
Self-expression, 16, 22, 27, 123, 126, 132
Self-portrait, 145, *146*
Sensabaugh, David, 27, 152*n*44
Servants, 37, *37*
Shan Guolin, 41, 59, 154*nn*26, 38, 156*nn*69, 80, 157*nn*89, 104
Shan Guoqiang, 153*n*21, 155*n*59, 156*n*74, 164*n*50, 165*n*71
Shanghai, 48
Shao Ch'ang-heng, 46, 150*n*13
Shen Chou, 64, 65, 79, *80*, 135, *136*
Shen Shih-ch'ung, 142
Shen Te-fu, 129
Shen-nung, 20
Shen-yün, 154*n*36
Shiba Yoshinobu, 154*n*39
Shih, Hsio-yen, 163*n*21
Shih Chung, 64, 123
Shih Lin, 141
Shih Lu, 146
Shih-t'ao, 39, 54, 69, 77
Shui-hu chuan, 102
Sickman, Laurence, 94
Siggstedt, Mette, 158*n*122, 166*n*72
Silbergeld, Jerome, 132, 151*n*29, 153*n*11, 155*n*60, 158*n*1, 164*n*46, 165*n*63
Siren, Osvald, 165*n*65
Sivin, Nathan, 5, 150*n*7
Sketchbooks, 95
Sketches from nature, 88, 98
Soong, James, 153*n*10, 155*n*44
Soper, Alexander, 115, 118, 124, 162*nn*9, 10, 12
Sou-shan t'u, 67, *68*, 117, 165*n*67
Spence, Jonathan, 2, 149*n*1
Status of artist, 35, 72, 123, 124, 126, 131, 132
Strassberg, Richard, 153*n*19, 155*n*47

Stuart, Jan, 165*n*60
Studio, 18, 45, 49, 53, 102, 103
Sturman, Peter, 165*n*65
Su Shih, 114
Subject, 115, 117, 139
Suchou, 27, 46, 72, 106, 120, 130, 136
Sullivan, Michael, 154*n*39
Sun Ssu-hao, 67, 165*n*67
Sun Tien-ch'i, 155*n*43
Sun Wei, 81
Sung, Hou-mei, 165*n*70
Sung Hsü, 14
Sung Mou-chin, 160*n*46
Szechwan, 110

T'ai, mountain, 110
Tai, Doris Jung Chu, 166*n*72
Tai Chin, 8, 127, 139
Tai K'uei, 102, *104–5*
Tai-pi, see Ghostpainter
T'ang Hou, 114, 128
T'ang I-fen, 41, 69
T'ang Yen-sheng, 4, 149*n*4
T'ang Yin, 27, 30, *30*, 49, 67, 77, *78*, 123, *125*, 126, 127
T'ang-ch'ao ming-hua lu, 94
T'ao Ch'ien, 18, 20, 27, 107
T'ao Yüan-ming, *see* T'ao Ch'ien
Ta-ti Ts'ao t'ang, 77
Ta-yu, 77
Tang, Weikuen, 156*n*73, 159*n*11
Tao Hung, 114
Taoist Temple in the Mountains, 25
Temple, 46, 61, 93, 110
Teng Ch'un, 114
Ti Yen, 161*n*87
Tsao, Hsingyuan, 141, 161*n*83, 166*nn*79, 80, 167*nn*85, 86
Ts'ao Hsi, 167*n*99
Ts'ao Pu-hsing, 162*n*6
Tseng Ching, 160*nn*51, 59
Tseng Kuo-fan, 69
Tseng Yuho Ecke, 160*n*57
Tsou Che, 84
Ts'ui Chüeh, 67
Ts'ui Po, 67, 123
Ts'ui Tzu-chung, 9, 65
Ts'ui Yüan, 65
Tuan-fang, 69
Tung Ch'i-ch'ang, 8, 11, 25, 50, *51*, 65, 95, 106, 130, 141, *141*, 145, 148, 151*n*19, 155*n*53
Tung Yüan, 12, *13*, 25, 28
Twitchett, Denis, 150*n*8
Tz'u-hsi, empress dowager, 69, 141

van der Sprenkel, Sybille, 153*n*16
van Gulik, Robert H., 153*nn*4, 7, 158*n*1
van Briessen, Fritz, 158*n*1
Vinograd, Richard, 24, 152*n*39, 160*n*41, 167*n*97

Wakeman, Frederic, 2
Wan Shou-ch'i, 54, 59, 156*n*77
Wang, Chia-chi Jason, 153*n*15, 167*n*93
Wang, David Teyu, 160*n*61
Wang An-shih, 117
Wang Ao, 77
Wang Chao-chün, 129
Wang Chi, 52
Wang Chia-chin, 102, *104–5*
Wang Chiao-ch'i, 112
Wang Chien, 65, 157*n*115
Wang Chih, 8, 150*n*10
Wang Chih-jui, *131*
Wang E, 17
Wang Fangyu, 83, 150*n*14, 159*n*29
Wang Fu, 41
Wang Hui, 43, 67, 74, 77, 110, 136, *137*, 146
Wang I, 110, *111*
Wang I-t'ing, 141
Wang Kuo-ch'un, 86
Wang Meng, 24
Wang Po-min, 161*n*78
Wang San-hsi, 83, *83*
Wang Shih-chen (Ming), 58, 64, 67, 74, 158*n*122, 166*n*72
Wang Shih-chen (Ch'ing), 154*n*36
Wang Shih-min, 67
Wang To, 25, 152*n*41
Wang Tzu-jo, 134
Wang Wei, 64, 107, 129
Wang Yü, 83
Wang Yüan-ch'i, 83
Warfare, 115
Water Margin, 102
Water Wheel, 117, *121*
Watt, James, 33. 153*n*3
Wax stencils, 94
Wedding pictures, 20, 109
Wei Chih-huang, 54
Wei Kuan-ch'a, 82
Wei Wu-t'ien, 110
Weidner, Marsha, 158*n*135
Wen Chen-heng, 33, 153*nn*4, 6
Wen Cheng-ming, 25, 34, 59, 60, 74, *75*, 102, 132, 136, 139
Wen Chia, 39, 52, 152*n*48, 153*n*6, 161*n*74
Wen Fong, 158*n*3, 159*n*17, 160*n*48, 165*n*61
Wen Jih-kuan, *14*
Wen P'eng, 153*n*6, 161*n*74
West Lake, 19
White Lotus Society, 139
Wilson, Marc F., 152*n*40
Wine, 60, 124
Wittkower, Rudolph and Margot, 72, 74, 155*n*55, 158*n*4, 161*n*84, 163*n*22, 164*n*52
Women painters, 69
Wong, Kwan S., 152*n*40
Woodblock printing, 100
Workshops, 103, 105
Wu, David Yen-ho, 149*n*2
Wu, Marshall, 167*n*90
Wu, Nelson, 166*n*80
Wu, William Ding Yee, 155*n*60, 161*n*64
Wu Ch'ang-shih, 54, 69, 141
Wu Ch'i-chen, 46, 128, 129
Wu Erh-lu, 167*n*89
Wu Hsing-tseng, *92*
Wu I, 142, 166*n*80

Wu K'uan, 29, 64
Wu Pei-yi, 167n97
Wu Pin, 8, *15*
Wu School, 27
Wu Tai-ch'iu, 60
Wu Tao-tzu, 61, 64, 93, 94, 96, 105, 107, 110, 116, 123
Wu Ta-ch'eng, 69
Wu Tien-sheng, 133
Wu Ts'ung-yüan, 82, 93
Wu Wei, 17, 61, 123
Wu-hsing, 25, 64

Yang Boda, 158n134, 160n45
Yang Chu-hsi, 110
Yang Wen-ts'ung, 156n87
Yang Xin, 155nn50, 51
Yangchou, 22, 23, 54, 58, 86, 128, 130, 134, 144
Yangchou School, 21
Yangchow, 86, 134
Yao, Dajuin, 161n72
Yao Hsieh, 41, 154n28
Yao Weng-wang, 149n4
Yeh-t'ing, 29
Yellow Crane Tower, 46
Yen Chan, 103, 107, 109
Yen Chih-t'ui, 124
Yen Hui, *122*
Yen Li-pen, 124
Yen Sung, 67
Yen Yu-nien, 142
Yen-shih chia-hsün, 124
Yoshida, Haruki, 164n34
Yü Chih-ting, *130*, 159n11
Yu Ch'iu, 103
Yü Garden, 48
Yüan Chiang, 79, *79*, 107
Yüan Hung-tao, 152n36
Yüan Mei, 86, *88*
Yuhas, Louise, 156n81, 157n110
Yün Shou-p'ing, 103, 107

Zen, 12
Zhu Xuchu, 156n75

Designer: Teresa Bonner
Text: Goudy Old Style
Compositor: The Composing Room of Michigan, Inc.
Printer: Edwards Brothers
Binder: Edwards Brothers